LIVING WITHOUT THE DEAD

· ·

LIVING WITHOUT THE DEAD

LOSS AND REDEMPTION IN A JUNGLE COSMOS

· ·

PIERS VITEBSKY

THE UNIVERSITY OF CHICAGO PRESS

Chicago and London

Piers Vitebsky is Emeritus Head of Anthropology and Russian Northern Studies at the Scott Polar Research Institute at the University of Cambridge, England. He is also professor at the University of Tromsø, the Arctic University of Norway, as well as honorary professor at the M. K. Ammosov North-Eastern Federal University in Yakutsk, Siberia, Russia. Further photos, films, and linguistic documentation can be found at http://www.piersvitebsky.org.

The University of Chicago Press, Chicago 60637
The University of Chicago Press, Ltd., London
© 2017 by Piers Vitebsky

Published 2017
Printed in the United States of America

26 25 24 23 22 21 20 19 18 17   1 2 3 4 5

ISBN-13: 978-0-226-85777-0 (cloth)
ISBN-13: 978-0-226-47562-2 (paper)
ISBN-13: 978-0-226-40787-6 (e-book)
DOI: 10.7208/chicago/9780226407876.001.0001

Library of Congress Cataloging-in-Publication Data

Names: Vitebsky, Piers, author.
Title: Living without the dead : loss and redemption in a jungle cosmos / Piers Vitebsky.
Description: Chicago : The University of Chicago Press, 2017. | Includes bibliographical references and index.
Identifiers: LCCN 2016058030 | ISBN 9780226857770 (cloth : alk. paper) | ISBN 9780226475622 (pbk. : alk. paper) | ISBN 9780226407876 (e-book)
Subjects: LCSH: Savara (Indic people)—Funeral customs and rites. | Spiritualism—India. | Shamanism—India.
Classification: LCC DS432.S37 V58 2017 | DDC 305.8959/5—dc23
LC record available at https://lccn.loc.gov/2016058030

♾ This paper meets the requirements of ANSI/NISO z39.48-1992 (Permanence of Paper).

To my Sora friends,

may their ancestors and descendants not lose each other
through religious conflict; to all the generations of my own family;
and to the inventors of portable voice recorders, who have made it
so much more possible to know other worlds

. . . so that what humans have done should not fade with time
(ὡς μήτε τὰ γενόμενα ἐξ ἀνθρώπων τῷ χρόνῳ ἐξίτηλα γένηται)
HERODOTUS,
Histories (meaning "Researches," the first surviving work
of anthropology, ca. 430 BC) 1.1

There are none now in Phoenicia, that lament the death
of Adonis; nor any in Libya, Creta, Thessalia, or elsewhere, that
ask counsaile or helpe from Jupiter. The great god Pan hath
broken his pipes.
SIR WALTER RALEIGH,
The History of the World (London, 1614),
bk. 1, chap. 6, para. viii, p. 96

All over the world we can sense . . . the Great God Pan breaking his pipes;
and it is now open to us, as it was scarcely open to Raleigh, to see this
process as the essence of human history . . . the brutal natural selection of
belief systems.
JOHN DUNN (1979: 59)

I don't care about debts or illness, I'd be sad to be a Christian.
LOKAMI,
Sora shamaness, 2005 (author's field notes 62.53)

CONTENTS

(A bibliographic essay entitled "The Sora 'Tribe'—Animist, Hindu, Christian" can be downloaded at http://www.press.uchicago.edu/sites/Vitebsky.)

DRAMATIS PERSONAE

Women's names generally end in -i, men's names in any other vowel. Names are usually stressed on this final vowel: Onontí, Pilantó, Limanú, and the author's own Sora name, Pirinó.

RAJINGTAL VILLAGE
Inama, the author's first Sora friend
Paranto, Inama's son, the author's "nephew"
Ononti, the great funeral shaman of their village; the author's first shaman
Gallanti, a healing shaman who graduates to become Ononti's hesitant
    successor as funeral shaman
Taranti, Gallanti's sister, a young shaman who later gives up her calling
Lokami, the author's "niece," a little girl who becomes the confident
    successor to Ononti and probably the last great funeral shaman
Asongroi (Fly-Shit), Lokami's father, a healing shaman
Soimani, a young woman and friend of the author
Oransu, an early Baptist convert with a robust attitude

LADDE VILLAGE
Dumburu, a shaman who lives on a remote clifftop, also feared as a great
    sorcerer
Sorni and Jamani, Dumburu's wives
Arambo, Dumburu's son, first met as a child, now a Baptist catechist

SOGAD VILLAGE
Monosi, early Baptist leader with a complex love life, later becomes a
    freethinking philosopher of comparative religion and the author's closest
    companion (it is unusual for a man's name to end in -i, or to be stressed
    on the first syllable: Mónosi)
Onai, Monosi's first wife
Sidoro, power-crazed headman
Rijanti (female) and her successor Uda (male), funeral shamans
Jamano, Uda's elder brother, and Ranatang, Jamano's son
Sagalo and Panderi, lovers dogged by tragedy, and their son baby Disamor

Sompani, who struggles to succeed Uda; named after Sompa, the first
   shamaness
Rondang, a shamaness of the healing tradition
Dangdang, male funeral singer and dancer, great raconteur of myths
Mengalu, the greatest funeral singer and dancer, dragged down by
   accusations of sorcery
Sundanto and Doddo, oboists for funeral dancing

MANENGUL VILLAGE
Doloso, a great but domineering male funeral shaman
Ambadi, first met as a child, daughter of Doloso who refuses to succeed him
Rajani, Doloso's actual successor, a woman with whom he shares his powers
   grudgingly
Likini, a beautiful girl who becomes Monosi's second wife while he is still
   married to Onai, thereby precipitating a crisis in his relation with the
   Baptist church

OTHER CHARACTERS
Sojono, a friendly man from Borei village
Pubic-Haired Sompa, the primal Sora shamaness, also known as Sompa of
   the Coiled Pubic Tresses (it is unusual for a woman's name to end in -a)
Kittungs, old Sora creator gods, male and female, including Kittung-Woman
   who gave birth to everything in the world, though they have done nothing
   much since
God, the one and only kittung of the Christians, who is still very active
Jisu, God's only begotten son (he has no begotten daughter)
Rama, Krishna, and Hanuman, kittungs of the mainstream Hindus
Jagannath (English: Juggernaut), a former kittung of the Sora, stolen by
   Oriya Brahmins in the Middle Ages
Mel Otis, Miss Munro, Dave and Ruby Hayward, Canadian Baptist
   missionaries
Damano, strict early Sora Baptist pastor who introduced the prohibition on
   alcohol
Enusai, Dulupet, and Pilipo (= Philip), Sora Baptist pastors; also Buyajo the
   deacon, all male
Father Joseph Moolan, a Catholic priest from Kerala who permits alcohol
Orjuno, chief priest of the alphabet worshippers
Pettua and Gorsang, brothers from Tımlo village who belong to the Bisma
   sect of neo-Hindus

Bala, a helpful Oriya bank manager

Jogi Ganta, a Pano police informer (*barik*), interpreter, and spectacularly inventive extortionist

Prakash, a good Pano

Policemen, block development officers, revenue officers, forest guards

Prime Minister Rajiv Gandhi, on the morning of his assassination

Sun-Woman, a blacksmith who molds fetuses into shape from molten metal

Thousands of ancestors

Members of the predatory Kond tribe, disguised as were-leopards

Ordinary jungle leopards (recognizable by the absence of gold earrings and nose-rings)

INTRODUCTION

This book is about a world I have been privileged to share for the last forty years. It is also about the process through which I have watched that world change into something utterly different.

The millions of travelers on India's crowded east-coast railway halfway between Kolkata and Chennai can have no inkling of the life of the aboriginal tribes in the blue, hazy mountains inland. The Sora of southern Odisha (Orissa) are one of the numerous "tribes" who inhabit the country's interior. Even among tribes, their culture is unique. In the 1970s they held what may well be the most elaborate form of communication between the living and the dead documented anywhere on earth. Almost every day in every village, living people engaged in conversations with the dead, who would speak, one after another, through the mouth of a shaman (*kuran*) in trance. Together, living and dead would chat, weep, or argue for hours at a time.

For the first few years, this was my mystery and my quest for understanding: How can people think they know what happens after death to those they love, and why does it matter so much? How could this society come up with this particular answer, and act it out so wholeheartedly? What levels of reality, belief, and make-believe did it involve? I presented my interpretation of that subtle and complex worldview in a book called *Dialogues with the Dead* (Vitebsky 1993).

Over the forty years since I first met them, the Sora themselves have changed drastically. Even while I was working out my interpretation and presenting it to the world, the Sora I had known as children were turning away from all this toward Baptist Christianity, and sometimes to fundamentalist Hinduism. These new faiths from outside leave little room for the old, local way of doing things. As young adults deny their parents the funeral they long for, with memorial stones and buffalo sacrifices, my older Sora friends have a new reason to fear dying: they know that their children will no longer converse with them beyond the Christian grave or the Hindu pyre.

I too have been forced to change the direction of my quest to meet this new mystery, to understand why the next generation of Sora have completely rejected that indigenous religion and the entire way of life that went with it. If the world of the shamans and their clients was as fulfilling as it so recently seemed, how have their children come to repudiate it so suddenly and so utterly? How can people abandon the beliefs that constituted their identity and seemed to match their innermost feelings? Fieldwork in social or cultural anthropology is also detective work: the dogged pursuit of implicit meanings, the fitting of one clue to another, and the thrill of making connections. This book is an anthropological detective story, but in two stages: first to understand the earlier religion, and then to work out its rejection. Each stage helps to explain the other, and those later years have illuminated the early years with a new hindsight.

The story of the Sora does not concern just a remote jungle tribe: it is also the story of all of us. One of the major processes of our species, which has racked many, perhaps all, societies over thousands of years, is the rise and fall of fervently held beliefs, as humans continually strive to understand how the world works and the reasons for their happiness or suffering—and to act on these. What does it mean to be a person? When is there a gulf between generations, and is this a problem or a solution? Why is memory fragile, and does memory matter? When and why do we want to change our forms of power, agency, participation, and constraint? History contains many accounts of rapid conversions from local beliefs to outside religions, from the Vikings of Iceland who supposedly became Christians in the year 1000 to the Mongol khans who switched their shamanist people around between Buddhism, Manichaeism, Taoism, Christianity, and Islam, sometimes just on the strength of a theological debate. The Sora lives explored here reveal the dislocation and pain that these simple stories mask.

Anthropologists are exceptionally privileged to witness and participate in some of the most diverse human experiences. We explore what it might feel like to be someone totally different, while still retaining the perspective to report back to our own world. This tension is part of our method. In scholarship, one cites previous documentation as evidence. But in a discipline so deeply rooted in fieldwork, the documents eventually run out and the trail ends in direct experience. We know what we know through human interaction, so there can be no anthropological account of a society that does not derive from an anthropologist's relations with local people.

But this involvement can exact a price. An entire society has abandoned a way of thinking, feeling, and relating to each other that I had felt was a great achievement of the human mind and spirit, and I have found it difficult to enter the new Christian world of young Sora as comfortably as I had entered their parents' animist world. For me the change feels like a great loss. How can the Sora themselves now feel it as a great liberation? And when new systems bring relief from old dilemmas, why do they also bring new, unanticipated torments?

This book and my previous book (1993), along with Elwin (1955), are probably the most thorough documentation this community will ever receive, not only for "science" but also for Sora themselves. Even where the narrative sometimes reads like a novel, all the characters are real people, and names given are mostly their real names. Real names or pseudonyms, I have kept them consistent with my previous publications for ease of comparison; the only change is that I have given Monosi his more usual name rather than his birth name Mogana ("born during a moon eclipse," used in Vitebsky 2012) because he is such an important public figure; I have also given the villages of Alinsing and Tongseng their real names of Sogad and Guddara. With only small editorial adjustments for the sake of clarity or to protect people's secrets, I have described events as they actually happened. The epilogue explores ways in which I am working with Sora to edit this material and make it available within their own community.

Sora phonology is subtle, and there are many dialects; among those who can write (including myself), spelling is inconsistent. I have kept things simple in order to help the reader to imagine the sounds of words and names. Apart from ñ (similar to the same letter in Spanish, pronounced like ny) and an undotted i (ɪ, a back vowel that resembles a similar sound in Turkish or Russian ы), I reserve diacritics and linguistic commentaries for specialist discussions elsewhere (for Sora language sources, see the online bibliographic essay). Sora is full of glottal stops, which I write ', and sometimes with a double consonant—for example, in the name of the shaman Gallanti, which is pronounced Ga'lanti (and probably derived from a hidden d, as Gadlanti).

Sora culture is very verbal. I have edited and paraphrased some longer speeches, but mostly I have translated speakers' words exactly. There is no indirect speech construction, so that people mimic each other, supposedly verbatim. Thus instead of "He said he would come," Sora constructs "He said 'I will come.'" In translating, I have kept such constructions to convey the flavor of Sora speech and also to suggest a connection to the way shamans give voice to the dead. More difficult was translating pairs of parallel words or phrases, which increase as a speaker becomes more vehement. Where the elements are single words, a comma would slow down the flow, and so I have written, for example, "leave abandon that house that home!" (page 117). Even where the phrases are longer, the headlong pace of the original is best conveyed by not putting a comma between each half of a pair of phrases, as in "If you blub if you snivel, your words come out weak your words come out garbled" (page 318). Sometimes it is easier on the eye to put commas between pairs of longer phrases—for instance, "The sisters I'd abandoned long ago, the grandmothers whose path I'd seen, they led me along, they didn't scold me" (page 318). Whatever the stylistic problems of translation, and even while translating closely, I have made Sora speakers sound coherent because they are indeed coherent. Where any Indians speak English I have kept their exact wording, as this may also help the reader to hear their intonation, except for a Sarda Sora called Bijoy, where I have paraphrased from a long conversation.

For Bible quotations I have used the New English Translation. Though the King James Version may be familiar to many readers, it now has an archaic, grandiose flavor. The Sora Bible, like any modern missionary translation (and like the King James Version back in 1611), uses contemporary language. Indeed, for older Sora it seems strange, not because it is archaic, but because it runs ahead of current language by coining words to express new Christian concepts that only later enter mainstream Sora speech. The numbered references are the same in any version, though this is not without discrepancies: for example, at Psalms 60:3 the King James Version has God making us drink a "wine of astonishment," but in the New English Translation he more prosaically makes us drink "intoxicating" wine, and under the Baptists' temperance agenda of the Sora Bible he makes us drunk with grape juice (see page 203).

When talking generally I use "she" for shamans, since the most important kind, the funeral shamans, are usually women, and "he" for patients or other laypeople. Occasionally I have used "shamaness" for emphasis. The word for gods of any religion is *kittung*; and while "spirit" might seem an easy option for translating *sonum*, it is actually not easy at all. This subtle and complex word is the key to everything, and will remain untranslated.

· ·

TO THE UNDERWORLD WITH
ONONTI THE SHAMANESS

· ·

Rajingtal, 1975–76

Ononti—my first shaman, small and shrewd, secretive but humorous. So archaic that she could not recognize a human face in a photograph. A woman who could not sustain her marriage with a living husband, but who found fulfillment in dreams and trances by marrying a being in the Underworld.

I can still visualize Ononti as I first saw her in 1975, performing a funeral to transform a dead man from a ghost (kulman) into a proper spirit, a sonum, by going into trance and bringing him back to talk through her mouth with his living mourners. This Ononti is still quite young, yet she already has the lean face and forward-thrusting jaw of many older Sora women whose soft rounded features of their youth have been sharpened by toil and undernourishment.

In contrast to the dark-skinned and heavily dressed Hindu castes of the plains, the Tribal Sora have slightly upturned eyes and reddish-brown skin that glows against the cream homespun cotton of the women's knee-length skirts and the loincloths of the small, wiry men. Both women and men wear nothing above the waist except necklaces, nose-rings and earrings, and for women, huge circular wooden earplugs. The silver and gold come from bazaars in the plains that pulsate with bright colors in cotton, nylon, and plastic, but here in the Tribal hills most artifacts are homemade and share the color of the wood, leaves, and mud from which they are crafted; even the tiger stripes and moon discs on Ononti's face are tattooed with a thorn and dyed with the indigo-blue juice of a jungle berry.

Ononti, the great funeral shaman of Rajingtal village, purses her lips outward as she gives commands: lay out the mat like this, bring the pot of palm-wine over here, put the leaf-cups of rice offerings over there. Her long black hair is swept back into a bun and held in place with large silver hairgrips. The midday sun sprinkles her brow with sweat, which trickles over the pile of beads in her necklaces and down her bare chest. How often have I seen her sit on the ground like this and stretch her spindly shins and rock-toughened

Figure 1.1 Ononti, the great funeral shaman of Rajingtal, 1975

feet straight out in front ready for trance, while the audience—mostly other women—squat on their haunches around her in a huddle waiting for their dead relatives to appear?

Closing her eyes and turning a knifepoint on the ground in time to her chant, Ononti starts to sing in parallel couplets, repeating each line but changing one word at a time to enrich the meaning. I cannot yet follow any of this, but am told that she is calling on the female shamans who have lived before her for help as her soul starts to clamber "like a monkey" down the precipices that lead to the Underworld.

argalgalsi yuyunji	*bolongsi goden*
argalgalsi yuyunji	*banardub goden*
amen ade yuyung la	*janida goden*
amen ade yuyung la	*tanongda goden*

arsin do la tongñam nam	*yuyung la amen*
kerun do la tongñam nam	*yuyung la amen . . .*

clasping hands, grandmothers,	along the one-hand narrow path
clasping feet, grandmothers,	along the two-cupped-hands narrow path
you, grandmother,	along the tightrope path
you, grandmother,	along the impossible-balancing path
your monkey four-footed gait,	grandmother
your simian four-footed gait,	grandmother . . .

Her husky voice is momentarily overwhelmed by dancers as they surge past, raising a brief cloud of grit and shortening the life of yet another cheap cassette recorder on which I am filling tape after tape with words I cannot understand. The dancers loom over us, drums pounding, oboes blasting, women flexing alternate knees while hardly lifting their feet off the ground, men hopping from foot to foot. Some adults and older children have a sleeping infant on their hip jigging up and down in a sling, its ringed, snotty nose pressed against their body. Little girls bounce up and down in twos and threes with arms linked behind their backs, homemade cigars tucked behind their ears and tassels of long hair flying from the crown of their shaved heads. The dancers twirl on one foot as they brandish battleaxes, or black umbrellas as a substitute. There is an occasional outburst of whistling, war cries, and the bray of a brass horn from B up to F-sharp and back again. A sudden change of direction makes the densely packed body of dancers seem like one creature as they spill over a dike, fanning out, stomping, and spinning into a dry out-of-season paddy field.

The drums never stop, but now they are drifting far away. Nearby, with soft thumps, a dozen buffalo are being bashed on the skull to send their souls down to the dead man in the Underworld. After a long invocation, Ononti's voice peters out, and her head flops down onto her breast. Her soul too has reached there, leaving her body available to convey the voices of the dead as they come up one by one. In this deep trance her limbs have gone rigid, and bystanders rush forward to unclench them. It takes several people to flex her knees with a jolt and lay her legs straight again along the ground, and to unclench her fingers and bend her elbows before returning her hands to rest, limp, along her outstretched thighs.

Ononti sits motionless, then with a sharp intake of breath her body twitches, and the first in a long line of sonums announces its name. The first is a special helper (*ilda*), her sonum husband from the Underworld; others are her shaman predecessors and teachers (*rauda*), but most are the dead relatives of the man for whom they are planting a stone today, adding to the patrilineage's cluster (*ganuar*) of memorial standing stones. Some ancestors (*idai*) just stay for a brief chat and a drink of wine (palm toddy, *alin*) and a puff on a cigar, which Ononti imbibes on their behalf. But the dead man himself spends twenty minutes talking to his relatives. Sometimes the women weep; sometimes they engage him in heated arguments that draw in men too; occasionally there is a whoop of laughter.

What kind of miracle-worker is this tiny woman with limpid brown eyes who orchestrates the feelings of a community by incarnating those who have been close to them and bringing them to engage in dialogue? What are the living and the dead saying to each other—about his last illness, about his inheritance, about love, grudges, domestic trivia, sex? What kind of theater is she staging for her clients as they embrace her body in their longing for a dead man who no longer has flesh of his own? What is she herself feeling as she "becomes" him? And what can it mean for everyone to believe in all this?

For my first few months in Soraland I crouched beside Ononti, helping to loosen her limbs and hanging on to any word I could grasp. I did not know enough about my hosts' family dynamics, or even about their language. I was sure that these conversations were vital for understanding everything, but I did not yet know how much of my life I would devote to decoding them. Later there would be many more shamans, both women and men, in different villages and with different quirks of secrecy and openness. However, Ononti would remain the most enigmatic of all, from our first meeting in 1975 right up to her death thirty years later, and the occasion six months after that when her pupil Lokami went into trance and brought Ononti back to speak with me once again. Now that most young Sora have joined evangelical Christian or fundamentalist Hindu movements, those crackly, distorted cassette tapes bring back a world that is lost forever.

. . . .

The Sora are one of many peoples in central India who are called "Tribal" (*adivasi*: in India the English word "Tribal," whether as adjective or noun, amounts almost to an ethnic label, and so I have spelled it with a capital T). India contains several hundred "Scheduled" tribes, totaling over 100 million people, around 8 percent of the country's population (see the online bibliographic essay). Among these tribes, the Sora seem to have been the early inhabitants of a large area of eastern and central India, probably predating the much more numerous speakers of Indo-European and Dravidian languages who now live around them to the north and south, respectively. The Sora lan-

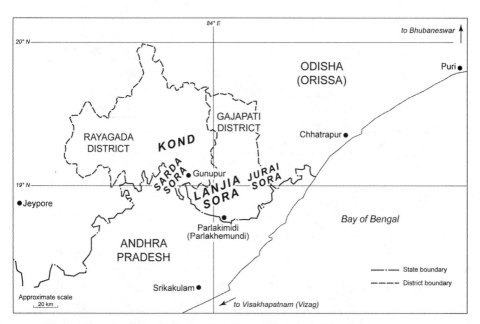

Map 1.1 Map of east-central India, showing main location of the Sora

guage belongs to the South Munda branch of the Austroasiatic family, a family that includes Cambodian and the languages of jungle peoples in Malaysia and Vietnam. The Roman historian Pliny located the "Suari" (i.e., Sora) along the eastern coast of India, and I have traced Sora village names far outside their present reduced range in the marginal region between the states of Odisha (until 2011 spelled Orissa) and Andhra Pradesh (with additional migrant communities in Assam). Today they number several hundred thousand, encompassing several subtribes and dialects, such as Sarda Sora and Jurai Sora. I have lived with the Lanjia Sora, the most remote and "Tribal" group, who are not enumerated separately but number perhaps 100,000 or more, in the most mountainous Sora heartland. This area is generally inaccessible to outsiders, and my periods of residence there over forty years, speaking Sora and living in Sora houses as a researcher in the 1970s and subsequently revisiting old friends, have been unique.

A people of the jungle with an ancient reputation for wildness, the Sora have lived for millennia in an ambiguous relationship with the Hindu world of rajas and temples. Both scholars and politicians argue about whether and how far the Sora and similar tribes are "really" Hindu. The Brahmin priests in the huge temple at Puri even claim that they stole their great Hindu god Jagannath

9

(Juggernaut), now seen as an avatar (incarnation) of Vishnu, from a primitive Sora cult in the jungle. I shall call the indigenous Tribal religion "animist," partly to distinguish it from other more classically Hindu movements in chapter 11 but also because this seems the best description of their understanding of the world. I use "animism" not as a primitivist category or as something residual when "world religions" are subtracted, but as a serious descriptive term for a cosmology in which features of the environment such as rocks and trees are considered to have a consciousness similar to that of humans. I shall later argue, however, that Sora are animists of a particularly humanistic kind. A discussion of these terms, along with references, will be found in the online bibliographic essay at press.uchicago.edu/sites/Vitebsky.

I was alerted to the Sora by a fascinating book by Elwin (1955), and in October 1974 I registered for a PhD in social anthropology at the School of Oriental and African Studies in London. In January 1975 I set out on a month's overland trek to Bhubaneswar, the state capital of Orissa, for a preliminary reconnaissance. I was hospitably received at the local university, but was told that the Sora were almost impossible to reach. An irresistible challenge! I bought a bicycle and pedaled for three days to Parlakimidi (now Parlakhemundi), a small town at the foot of the Sora hills that turned out to have bus connections after all, and then cycled a further twenty miles uphill to a Canadian Baptist mission hospital in a village called Serango (in Sora, Serung).

It was here, at "Bethany Bungalow," that I first learned to say *lemtam, sukka po, wan yirte?* (Hello, are you well, where are you going?). The missionary, Melville J. Otis, was a white man like myself, but bearded and with the glinting blue eyes of a religious ascetic. The New Testament had been translated into Sora by previous missionaries, and Mel was working on the book of Genesis at the start of the Old Testament. Non-Christian Sora had no writing, but the early missionaries had worked with a local Hindu scholar called Ramamurti to devise a script based on the Roman (Latin) alphabet with additional elements from the International Phonetic Alphabet. Mel's small team of Sora assistants included Monosi, who looked severe behind heavy black-rimmed glasses but would later become my closest friend and collaborator; and Monosi's mentor Damano, an elderly Baptist pastor who had lost an eye to a bear. Mel generously took me to services and weddings in surrounding villages, which all seemed to be Baptist. Relations between anthropologists and missionaries are traditionally prickly: we come to study a culture, they come to change it. I am not a Christian anyway, so I am surprised now to read in my notes: "God is in his mind every moment of the day and in everything he says and does, and it's a strengthening and joygiving state."

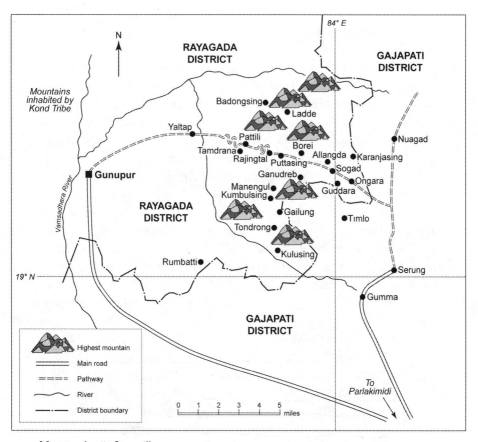

Map 1.2 Lanjia Sora villages

The path from Gunupur rises steeply just before Pattili and again before Rajingtal, where it opens out into a heartland of irrigated plateaus extending through to Sogad and leading on to steeply terraced valleys running up between the higher mountains. The map shows only villages mentioned in this book, but there are many others.

I was grateful for Mel's hospitality, but wary of the bungalow's seductive comforts, and keen to move on.

"Which area has the biggest shamans?" I asked him.

"I'm an ambassador of the King of Kings!" he parried. "Such things are not my business!"

I became more cunning, and waited. Turning the question around, I asked, "Where are you having the least success at converting?" He fell into the trap and named the area around Rajingtal and Sogad, where I have since spent much of my life.

I was told (correctly) that Sora would not work for money, so I hired a guide from the Pano, a Christianized "untouchable" caste who speak Oriya (or Odiya, the main language of Odisha) but also know Sora. With no language in common we climbed, teetering along the narrow retaining embankments above the stone walls of rice terraces that were banked up the valley in steps up to forty feet high as far as the groundwater would feed them; then up into the dry jungle with its slash-and-burn clearings of the shifting cultivation that the Forestry Service had spent a century trying to suppress throughout Tribal India; and down again into another system of rice terraces.

We met Sora weeding, cutting, and cooking along the way and passed through villages of single-story thatched houses, built of stone with their walls finished with red mud. People seemed quite reserved. I must have been a weird apparition anyway, but I did not fully understand their bitter resentment of the Pano, who live by trading and moneylending among the Sora. By evening we arrived in the Pano settlement of Puttasing, planted amid the Sora villages of my chosen region. We were over the watershed, both geographically and administratively: while Serung was an outpost of the administration in Parlakimidi, Puttasing was the end of a track coming up the other side from Gunupur. They were separated by mountains of over 3,000 feet, and we had come through a low pass between these. Puttasing had been established as a police station in 1866, when the British finally overran the area and hanged Sora resistance leaders or deported them to the Andaman Islands (Francis 1907: 258). For me, it has always retained a menacing legacy of violence as the base from which Pano and police clad in military khaki intimidate surrounding Sora villages, and it would be the source of many problems for me, as it was for the Sora.

But my first contact, who had been recommended to me by a previous French visitor, was a Pano. The Pano belonged to various Christian denominations, and Prakash was a Catholic lay preacher. I was lucky: he was a good-hearted man and widely liked. He spoke Sora and broken English, and led me each day to the nearest Sora village of Rajingtal. Sora villages are sited where the dry jungle slopes level out into irrigated paddy fields, giving access to both. Rajingtal was one of the largest villages, with 600 people, and fronted onto a large plateau of gently terraced fields.

Prakash was already a friend, and it would have been much harder to approach the Sora without him. But I soon saw that our association was also an obstacle. We visited his contacts, but were always received on their veranda, never invited inside. This was how they treated even a good Pano, since the Tribal Sora considered the Pano to be polluting. I needed to find a way to get closer.

Figure 1.2 Valley landscape, 1990s

Paddy fields are banked up above every valley behind stone retaining walls, as high as springs will allow. Beyond, some patches of jungle are still cleared annually for shifting cultivation, leaving only useful fruiting trees like wild mango. By the first decade of the twenty-first century these slopes will be widely planted with cashews (chapter 10).

The opportunity came through the men's drinking circles (*gasal*), which were scattered around the forest. These were the most open Sora grouping, loosely based on groups of lineage-brothers but also offering hospitality to any passerby. The gasals happened at dawn, midday, and dusk. I could never reach the morning session but started going to the others without Prakash, who did not drink. We sat on stones in a circle while each man poured his contribution of *alin*, the mildly alcoholic fermented sap that dripped from an incision in the crown of his fishtail-palm trees (*Caryota urens*), into a large pot that was gently warmed over a central fire. A hollow gourd attached to an extended bamboo tube circulated from drinker to drinker. Each man dipped the gourd into the pot to fill it and passed it to his neighbor, who held the peacock-quill spout two inches in front of him and aimed the stream of liquid elegantly and accurately into his mouth, before refilling it and passing it on. My first inept attempts at drinking blended easily with the general teasing and laughter. I began to learn Sora: *goba, ñama, panga,* "sit!" "hold!" "take!" (aha, there was the imperative ending). Much of my early vocabulary was about pouring alin and straining ants out of the froth on top, or interjections such as *nai! na! agguj!* (give it! take it! ouch!). *Issí!* meant "alas!" or "yuk!" while *u gai!* expressed surprise, indignation, or skepticism at someone's story.

I had come thousands of miles expressly to put myself at the mercy of strangers. But why should they trust me? The first person to take that leap was the open-faced Inama. I can still visualize the moment one evening when his eye caught mine. After our drink he took me back to the cavernous interior of his house where his children and two wives huddled in the glow of the fire at the far end. Wherever I have moved in Soraland for the forty years since then, this house has remained my safe haven. I felt confident as I flew home in March 1975 to report to the university that I had found the Sora, and to organize further funding.

I returned that November to begin my first long fieldwork, which would eventually last for seventeen months, until April 1977. By returning, I became a long-term presence rather than a freak occurrence. Each village contained several patrilineages (*birinda*), and one had to marry into a different lineage, whether in the same village or elsewhere. Inama and his equally warm and affectionate brothers Lakkia and Sumbara belonged to the large lineage of the headman, though theirs was not a very wealthy branch. The headmen, called *gomang* (also the adjective for "rich"), were appointed by the government, one to each village, along with a deputy (*dolbera*) and two further minor assistant posts. The position, along with a gold bangle of authority (silver for the dolbera), was inherited by his eldest son, though all members of his lineage were

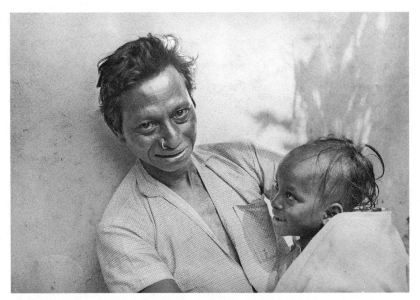

Figure 1.3 Inama, the author's first Sora friend, with his daughter, 1975

collectively called "the headmen" (*gomangenji*). Until the 1950s the headman had been the smallest link in a chain of feudal officeholders leading up to the raja of Jeypore nearly 200 miles to the west. The headmen's position between outsider and insider was ambiguous: they collected tax for the raja from the ordinary people (*roito*) of their villages. They often oppressed their roitos, but more gratifyingly, they also cheated the raja, and each year they feasted on a buffalo bought with the money they had withheld from him.

I continued to sleep in Puttasing, but was looking for ways to become more involved in Rajingtal. At the next stone-planting, which was for their grand-mother, the three brothers dressed me in a red sash with jingling brass bells and a red turban crowned with egret's feathers spliced down the spine to make them bounce, and made me dance with other men and women who carried the dead woman's possessions in tin trunks on their heads. I held a ceremo-nial brass axe aloft as we danced round their lineage's cluster of memorial standing stones. Bystanders hooted with laughter. The shaman Ononti was standing in front of the stones muttering invocations, but she gave me a sly smile. I felt very accepted.

A Brahmin teacher from town was watching this Festival of Tribal Folklore. "Why have you come?" he asked me.

"I've come to study their religion," I answered.

Figure 1.4 A reciprocal work party (*onsir*) in Kumbulsing, 1976
Houses are rethatched every year before the rains. Men and women work side by side, as in all tasks.

"You should study the Bhagavad Gita," he advised. "These people are not having religion." Among other aims, I hope this book will prove him wrong.

Another morning I slipped out of Puttasing at first light and past the Pano children's inescapable calls, in Sora, of *wan yirte Saibo* (Where are you going Sahib?) to join a work party harvesting sorghum. Such reciprocal parties (*onsir*) were composed mostly of lineage members and involved no cash, only the provision of alin and millet gruel for one's helpers. They made light work of any task, accomplishing a week's worth of digging, weeding, harvesting, or thatching in a few hours: we all do your task today, then mine tomorrow, and the next man's another day. Onsir work parties were a labor pattern of the poor, suited to the low-yield subsistence economy of shifting cultivation. They did not actually increase the total labor available, but focused it and made it more fun. Households, which were mostly nuclear families plus grandparents, kept a rough tally and got back more or less what they put in.

The headmen, and anyone who had more than the tiniest patch of irrigated paddy land, needed labor beyond their household's capacity to reciprocate. Paddy fields gave a yield above subsistence needs, and so the owner entered a more capitalistic economy in which he had to pay grain or cash for additional hired labor (*badi*), often to subsistence cultivators with no paddy land themselves, for planting, weeding, harvesting, and repairing the essential retaining walls. He might also take a second wife to gain her labor and that of her children. If he was lucky the first wife would welcome her (often she was her younger sister); if not he would build them separate houses. In Rajingtal, six men were polygynous, four of them in the headman lineage, where one had four wives and twelve children.

For our onsir, several young men and women set out at seven o'clock in single file, which is such an ingrained habit that Sora even walk like this along a wide, empty surfaced road in the plains. This was a culture without cushions or padding of any sort, even when sleeping on the hard earth floor. I thought I was used to going barefoot, but the physical hardship was a shock. For the first half hour we started along the worn but still sharp-stoned thread that wove along the center of a wider path—the "one-hand narrow path" of Ononti's song, and of lullabies: "May you walk in the smooth center and not on the sharp side pebbles." Then as the sun hit us, we started uphill, stepping nimbly from the top of one boulder to another.

While working, we moved upward shoulder to shoulder from the bottom of a steep hillside. We clambered over rough stones and jagged, thorny stumps left over from the previous season's burning, severing the ten-foot-high sorghum stems near the ground and tossing them headfirst behind us for a second team to harvest the grain.

Everyone worked hard, with short pauses for bantering and improvised songs: "Where is my *kundi* knife where is my *karatti* knife?" "I've cut my foot I've stubbed my toe." Girls and boys snatched each other's ornaments (*boten itsumtam?* "Who fancies you?"), and the gold necklace of a girl called Soimani somehow appeared round my neck. By noon I felt sick with the heat and was saved by the millet gruel and the alin (which made me drunk). By three all the grain-heads had been stacked, ready for threshing. The efficiency was astonishing.

I had been pressing Inama for somewhere to stay in his village, and after some initial embarrassment ("babies shitting all night") he had started inviting me to sleep in his house. At the evening gasal a few days later he suddenly announced that they had found me a spare house of my own. I was thrilled, but also alarmed. How would I run it, where would I find firewood, grain, pots, and water, how would I find a cook if no one would work for money?

That night when we came back from our gasal and had drunk our gruel we stood under the dappled light of the moon filtering through holes in the thatch. "We'll fix it before the rains," Inama promised. The Sora would not work for money, but it seemed they would do anything for friendship. Inama's brothers brought firewood and water, while his little boy Paranto lit the fire. "You'll be lonely on your own," explained Inama. "We'll give you some children." Paranto spread his ragged sheet on the cow-dung floor to sleep, and on the following nights other boys from various houses joined us too.

Ours was a typical Sora house, with an area for standing just inside the doorway above a massive wooden grain-pounding mortar set into the mud and cow-dung floor, while the rest of the house was divided horizontally by a grain-storage loft at chest height, under which one crouched and moved crab-like toward the hearth at the far end. It was one of a row with a common roof and high veranda, each house separated by a low wall, like a semicommunal longhouse. At only 19 degrees north, darkness fell around six o'clock all year round and lasted till six in the morning. Few people had flashlights that worked. There was a faint glow of firelight and murmured conversation from other houses nearby, and occasional remarks tossed by neighbors over our dividing wall, all so unlike the shrieking and quarreling of the Pano in Puttasing. By eight, except for an occasional baby's cry or the rustling of someone making up the fire, the village was completely silent.

I soon saw why. By two in the morning, women all around began to pound rice in their mortars with heavy pestles to remove the husks—tum-tum-tum-tum—and then toss it up and down in winnowing fans—swish, swish, swish. Wooden doors creaked open, and conversations started in the street outside. By three, Paranto had a pot of rice bubbling on our fire. By four, men were setting out across the hillsides to harvest the night's flow of alin. Cows clanged out to graze, and the faint predawn light revealed a Brueghel canvas of figures swathed in shawls and moving around purposefully. I had not realized that half the day took place before daybreak. Before six Inama arrived to take me drinking. "It's nearly midday," he exaggerated, handing me a *partad* twig as a toothbrush.

The weeds in the dry paddy fields held a heavy dew that chilled my bare feet, so that it was a relief to begin climbing up to our gasal on the sharp but drier stones. The hills resounded with bamboo flutes playing variants of the same five-note melody, crossing and recrossing each other up and down the scale. Each flute grew closer till a man burst into the stone circle with a pot dangling from his elbow on a rope of creeper bark, filled to the top with frothing, creamy liquid. One man lit the fire, squinting through the acrid first smoke, while others squatted, facing out from the circle to finish their toothbrushing, hawking, spitting out splinters, and scraping tongues, and yet others skimmed off insects with a leaf and tested the temperature, shouting, "Warm it up!" or "Take it off!" Alin palms were like artesian wells, pumping

Figure 1.5 Collecting palm-wine

Sundanto the oboist from Sogad (chapter 3) is cutting the growing infloresence to keep the sap dripping into a pot, where it will ferment naturally.

up underground liquid as if the earth's parched skin was sweating through pores. The vitamin-rich fluid was tapped far above ground at the tip, where the inflorescence was cut three times a day to prevent the palm from forming seeds (which would lead to its death) and keep the sugary sap dripping into a pot where it was fermented by airborne yeasts. Apart from watery rice or millet gruel, the Sora drank nothing else. They did not use animal milk, but alin was the breast-milk of a kittung, one of the mythic gods who made the world.

We often took alin back to the village to give to women, an act that could be either innocuous or flirtatious. My house was visited by girls who formed a clique around Ononti and who brought me well water in the morning in a stack of pots balanced on their heads. They mostly belonged to the headman lineage, living examples of an aristocratic tendency to keep daughters unmarried (though having affairs) and living with the lineage of their birth. They were lively, bold, and strong-minded. While men were tattooed with a thin badger stripe down the forehead flanked by two dots, women in addition had huge circles on their cheeks, sometimes with tiger stripes at the corners of their eyes. When I returned to England over a year later, the girls' faces there seemed literally blank. The Sora girls would invite me to help them thresh grain, or ask me to climb a tree (the only thing women were not supposed to do, apart from playing musical instruments) and stack up their firewood in the branches. They took me to rituals in other villages, afterward testing me to see what I had understood, and Soimani interrogated me about past girl-friends, pronouncing their names carefully and asking whether I still dreamed about them—a rare case of someone inquiring about my world. The gasal men teased me, and I consulted Inama. "Why don't you sleep with her," he advised, "but just a little (aji-aji)." But I had already heard about suicides of unhappy girls and knew I would be out of my depth. Besides, the Pano were always spying and seeking to provoke a scandal.

Everything hinged on language. A Telugu Brahmin teacher from Parlaki-midi called Ramamurti had written a Sora grammar and dictionaries (1931, 1933, 1938). I had not studied these before coming, so my start was slow. I later came to admire Ramamurti's grammar, but my eventual reward for not studying him was also great. Linguists gather data by eliciting phrases rather than by living with the people, and I was able to delve much more deeply into Sora idiom and poetics (Vitebsky 1978c). Ramamurti spoke Oriya and Telugu, and probably worked with bilingual informants from further downhill. I did not know either of these languages, and up here almost everyone was still monolingual and could explain complex points to me only in terms of simpler points that I had already grasped. Thus *ruben, nami, biyo,* (yesterday, today, tomorrow) were easy to understand from context, but it took me months of trial and error to distinguish from context alone between the slippery words for "recently" (*usung*, "just now," or *muyed*, "quite a bit earlier") and "later" (*namode*, "just a bit later," or *anggoi'ja*, "quite a lot later").

My children were endlessly lively and interested in everything, and told me much that the adults might have preferred to keep secret. At night by flashlight they helped me to distinguish between *atung* (pumpkin), *ateng* (very much), *ameng* (alive), *umeng* (quickly), *asang* (sour), *arang* (bitter), *alang* (straw), *alam* (thatch), and *angal* (firewood). They separated *uñul* (sweat) from *ud'ñul* (shadow), which I had confused because they both seemed to refer to the boundary of the body.

I developed a Rajingtal accent with the distinctive rising pitch of the men of the headman lineage, plus Inama's own personal exaggerated glottal stops. People often ended a sentence with *pede*, meaning "perhaps," so I did too. But it turned out that Pede was already my nickname, so they were actually addressing me, and when I copied them I was reinforcing the joke. This remained my name in Rajingtal, though other villages accepted my invention of Pirinó as a Sora version of Piers, which nobody could pronounce.

Sora has no indirect speech construction, so that gossip claims to reproduce people's exact words: " 'Why won't you come?' I said. 'Because you didn't give me the millet you owed me,' she said. 'Millet my shit! Didn't I give you two baskets full the other day?' I said . . ." People would repeat verbatim what I myself had supposedly said somewhere else, even down to the intonation and the grammatical mistakes. Indeed, *gam*, "say" or "speak," seemed to be the commonest syllable: *gamengamle*, "having said," *agamlai*, "we said," *gamtingji*, "they say to me": *gam-gam-gam* in every sentence. "How?" was *ian gamle*, literally "saying what?" rather than "doing what?" The answer "like this" was *enne gamle*, literally "saying this." Even the explanatory conjunction "because" was *gamlenden*, "if saying." Everybody and everything had to speak for themselves, and I came to see articulate speech as a defining sign of existence. As I grew to understand the importance of ritual dialogue, this would become a key insight. The dead, the sun, the earth—all made themselves known by speaking, and the shamans were their mouthpieces, not so much incarnating them as envoicing them.

Yet my increasing articulateness was still not enough to understand their speech or the incantations surrounding them. All illnesses and deaths were caused by sonums. Any shaman might do divinations to find out the cause of an illness, and I would be summoned day and night to watch them. Patients would come to find out which sonum had "stroked" (*sim*) them ("It hurts here, and here . . ."). They would bring a small basket of rice, and the shaman would pour it into a winnowing fan and brush her hand round and round in the rice, invoking her sonums to reveal the truth, until the motion sent her into trance. The shadowy interior of the house seemed to become one with the Underworld as she descended there by the flame of a small clay lamp to bring up ancestors to negotiate with the patient ("Why are you doing this to me?" "I'm angry with you because . . .").

The diagnosis that emerged in the divination would be followed up by an appropriate cure. Healing shamans, who were often male, had various repertoires of rituals for Sun-Sonum, Earth-Sonum, Leopard-Sonum, and many more. Some rituals were done in the house and others outside, and according to the attacking sonum would require the sacrifice of a chicken, pig, goat, or buffalo. The basic logic was one of substitution (*apanadu*). The sonum was summoned by an invocation, fed with the animal, and persuaded to release the patient. If all went well the sonum would stop eating the patient's soul and eat the animal's soul instead, while conveniently leaving its flesh for the living to share. Some sonums required trance and discussion, but not all shamans did trance, and some dealt with other sonums. I became very friendly with Asongroi ("Fly-Shit," named as a baby to make him unattractive to sonums), who specialized in Rattud-Sonum, which attacks travelers on the path and causes their sudden collapse. He would start his chant in the patient's house, then lead the sonum in a "banishing-rite" (*amdung-pɪr*) along a path out of the village to a site where he would chant again while others sacrificed a pig and sprinkled the blood onto the leaves and alin of his offerings.

Shamans were helped by sonums from the Underworld called ɪlda. Each shaman was married to one of these, and they had to cultivate this relationship. I became friendly with Gallanti, a young healing shaman who was training her teenage lineage-sister Taranti. On behalf of their clients as well as themselves, they offered a first taste of each ripening crop to their ɪldas and sprinkled it with blood spurting from the severed neck of a chicken or a goat. At the start of the hot season they also made offerings to Smallpox-Woman (*Ruga-boj*), a sonum who seemed to be the Hindu goddess Durga invading from the plains and bringing epidemic diseases. Smallpox scars resemble the eyes of a peacock's tail, and while in trance Taranti sang an extraordinarily beautiful song in the persona of a peacock. I did not understand much, but it was clear that the peacock was mapping its flight round every village in Soraland, and that it was being fed as a tribute (or bribe) to encourage it to go back to the plains until the following year.

I was curious about levels of dissociation, and sometimes tested shamans

Figure 1.6 Gallanti and Taranti dedicating the harvest

Gallanti (left) with her younger sister Taranti, making offerings to ancestors, 1976.

Figure 1.7 Talking with the dead at the *karja*
Kuttumi, the old shaman of Sogad (center), gives voice to the dead child Guma who committed suicide rather than go to school (page 83, at the karja*). The child's mother (left) fastens his necklace around her. On the right is Dosinto, during his failed attempt to become a shaman.*

by prompting them to repeat information that had emerged only while they were in trance, but they always avoided my trap. Their awareness of the outside world was ambiguous: once when Gallanti was in trance somone put her crying baby to her breast, and the male ancestor speaking through her protested, "Wait till a female sonum turns up!" Thirty years later I would be arguing with this same baby, by then a Baptist catechist, as he pressured his mother to give up her vocation.

Ononti did not do healing but belonged to a special, elite tradition of funeral shamans. Her rituals formed a sequence, from the inquest on the day after death to find out the cause to the stone-planting (*guar*) to a ceremony called lajab in which the dead strengthened the ripening rice to a big collective annual festival of the dead called karja. Funeral shamans performed for all lineages within their home village. I attended stone-plantings in nearby villages, each conducted by their own funeral shamans, almost always women, and all with an air of command like Ononti.

Everyone lived with a constant sense of fighting off death. I was shocked at how sick people could become and how quickly, but also amazed at how quickly they could recover and how robustly they continued working through what doctors would call dysentery, hepatitis, and malarial fevers, even as their bodies were continually drained by parasites from food contaminated by dust and flies. My inoculations against tuberculosis, smallpox, tetanus, and cholera, and my tablets against malaria and blackwater fever, gave me a complacent feeling of being indestructible when healthy, but I still suffered from sudden attacks of sickness that made me feel terribly mortal. People begged me for medicines, mostly for coughs, diarrhea, and fever. I disinfected and dressed hideous wounds from axes, knives, thorns, and rocks, but being untrained, I was reluctant to give out drugs (unlike the pharmacists in town who irresponsibly sold antibiotic tablets one at a time). The government compounder in Puttasing sold off his real medicine and charged patients for injections of useless distilled water, so I sometimes walked them across the mountains to the hospital in Serung or took them further to a big city. I felt compassion for my friends, yet there was also something almost ruthless about my quest, as each sickness also offered an interesting ritual—and something even more shameful, as I too became malnourished through sharing the diet of sloppy rice or millet gruel, with no oil and flavored at best with salt or chili. Like everyone else I craved animal protein, and each sacrifice promised each participant a sliver of pork fat, a piece of buffalo gristle, or a few splinters of chicken bone. I sometimes shared out onions, groundnuts, and small dried fish from the weekly market downhill, and once when I had bought six eggs for Inama's family they broke as I was walking back uphill, so I just sat on the ground and drank them all, raw.

It was not only recoveries that could be astonishingly rapid, but also deaths. A strong teenage boy called Gadino developed a high fever. His mother asked for medicine, while a shaman divined the cause and performed a cure with a buffalo sacrifice, as demanded by Duri-sım (Lumbago-Sonum), which causes joint pain. I wanted to see this new ritual, but the moment I saw the buffalo standing by, I had an uneasy premonition. The boy recovered—for a few days. Then he suddenly died. Men fired guns and hastened to cut down trees, while women wailed and washed his naked body in turmeric and dressed him in the finest loincloth. Two male pyre-lighters (siga) flung rice in four directions and tended the flames, while other men drummed the cremation beat, and the boy's mother squatted nearby, facing away from the pyre, cradling a baby in her arms, and howling a lament in verse couplets. I was to witness many more cremations, all too often for strong young adults like Gadino, as well as for tiny children like the one she was holding. It was a forceful reminder of the link between the fascination of my subject and the suffering of others.

After that day, Ononti seemed more forthcoming. That evening she asked me to bring her some alin from my drinking circle, as she had to fast and avoid grain before descending to the Underworld at the following morning's inquest. My spy Paranto said she now liked me because I had tried to save the boy.

The inquest and the later stone-planting were very rich, and I was beginning to follow a little more, though things did not always make sense. At night I would take my cassette recorder to Inama's house, but nobody could understand that I wanted help in picking out individual words. People had seen radios but not a machine with their own voices, and it was soon in demand for entertainment. There seemed to be no taboo on repeating Ononti's chants or the dialogues between living and dead, and it was interesting to hear people's laughter and comments, though these were beyond me, and I had no second machine to capture them. Batteries were heavy and scarce, and it was frustrating that everyone else was enjoying the words without being able to explain them to me. Once Ononti herself walked past, a huge basket of grain balanced on her head and a leaf-cigar tucked behind her ear. I felt a moment of tension, as if we had been caught red-handed. She paused, then turned back to us with a big grin. Thereafter: "Make it play (*abgugua*)!" "But the battery's running low." "No, make it play!"

Our relationship developed like a delicate courtship. "You should marry her, it would be a perfect match (*tamte*)," teased one of my drinking companions, "she'll shamanize and you'll write it down!" (*anin kurante, amen idolte*). He laughed when I replied that she had sex only with sonums.

There was so much more I needed to know, asking, pestering, not understanding: who are your helper sonums, how did you acquire them, what does it mean that you marry one of them? Whereas ordinary sonums were ordinary dead Sora, a shaman's helpers were a mixture of former shamans and ildas. The latter were Hindus from the high Kshatriya castes: bureaucrats, soldiers, armed policemen, even rajas, known in Sora ritual chants for their sharp, Aryan noses and round, pampered buttocks (*kupal-sam*)—the very same kinds of people who oppressed the Sora in ordinary life. It was these beings rather than ancestors who populated the wall-paintings daubed in white rice-flour paste onto a red mud wall inside the house of every shaman. For many important rituals, the shaman would sit on the floor facing her painting to enter trance. The paintings were a map of the Underworld, but with a particular message. They generally depicted a huge bo tree or fig tree (*tabar, rijoi*) which leads to the Underworld, its branches busy with monkeys, peacocks, pythons, and leopards. But they also showed multistory buildings with officials on

Figure 1.8 A shaman and his wall-painting

Doloso, the main funeral shaman of Manengul village (chapter 6), in 1998. Inside the frame are rows of warriors and armed policemen, with bureaucrats on chairs at the top and high officials riding horses and elephants at the bottom. The peepul trees outside the frame are crawling with monkeys.

elephants and bicycles, guarded by rows of soldiers or armed policemen. At the same time as being underground, these ilda sonums' residences were also contained in particular mountaintops. These sonums could speak Oriya and knew how to write, compelling the Sora dead to negotiate in dialogue with the living by "arresting" them and entering their names in the logbooks of Underworld police stations. It was her marriage in the Underworld that gave a shaman the power to enter trance, and the painting was like a landing or portal for the ilda, who was always the first sonum to speak. Suspended in front of the painting were gifts to this sonum husband: pots of uncooked rice that were changed every new moon, first fruits of each ripening crop, and the royal status symbols of fine cloths and umbrellas. The entire picture was heavily framed by an elaborate border, as if to capture and encapsulate this whole universe of power.

As with many female shamans, Ononti's marriage above ground had failed. Living husbands found it difficult to share their wives with another who was present not only when their wife went into trance but also when she was dreaming on the floor beside them. Ononti's two children in this world had died, but she had other sonum children in the Underworld. When she went into trance she would descend to meet her sonum husband, and he would come up and sing through her mouth in a special ilda tune. He would then act as a guide, bringing up other sonums to talk to her clients.

Ononti tranced side by side with another shaman called Maianti, and she was also training Datuni, an almond-eyed little girl with close-cropped hair, a huge cigar behind her ear, and a shrewd, appraising gaze. Little girls often seemed self-assured and enigmatic, unlike the boys, who seemed more child-like (and rarely smoked).

Datuni watched Ononti intensely and sometimes held her hand during rituals. She slept next to Soimani and in the morning would give her elaborate accounts of her dream trips to meet potential husbands in the Underworld. The fact that shamans were married to ildas and had children in the Underworld meant that I had to trace two kinship networks, one above ground and one below. What was the connection? Ononti had learned from a previous shaman called Doipani, and it was a moment of great discovery when I found out that Ononti's sonum husband was Doipani's sonum son. Doipani had learned from Kemai, who learned from Indiri. So did each shaman marry her teacher's sonum child? Yes! Living Sora had a typical North Indian kinship system, in which the offspring of the brother-sister relationship were cross-cousins (male *marongger*, female *maronsel*) who called each other brother and sister and could not marry for three generations. But shamans went against

Figure 1.9 Ononti surveying offerings before the karja festival
*Rajingtal, February 1976. Each bereaved house gives baskets of grain, a brass ring, a
pot of distilled alcohol (aba), and a buffalo. Squatting beside Ononti is her pupil and
intended successor Datuni.*

this by marrying their father's sister's son in the Underworld. So there was a
North Indian system operating above ground and a South Indian (Dravidian)
system in the Underworld.

By January, the rice had been harvested from the irrigated fields, and millets and sorghum from the dry hill-slopes. This was the best-fed moment
of the year, as everyone prepared for miñamgaj, the "month of blood." Any
stone-plantings left undone through poverty were now completed ready for
the karja, the village-wide annual festival of the dead around the February–
March full moon, when the whole landscape would throb with processions of
drummers and dancers.

Stone-plantings and karjas meant buffalo. For each person who died, their
heirs had to sacrifice one for the stone-planting and one more for each of
the next three annual lajab and karja festivals, making a minimum of seven.
These "buffalo of grief" (dukabong) were old, stringy cast-offs, but they still
cost 1–200 rupees each, which in 1976 was an enormous sum (while a good
buffalo for plowing cost 500). In addition, people would buy buffalo for the
funerals of other lineage members "out of compassion" (abasuyim bate). A
man's property was normally shared equally among his sons, and if he died

29

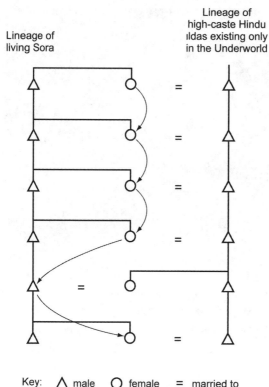

Lineage of
living Sora

Lineage of
high-caste Hindu
ıldas existing only
in the Underworld

Diagram 1.1 Succession between funeral shamans *The ıldas' relationship with living shamans is like an impulse always in quest of a successor. Shamans marry an ılda child of their predecessor, who is generally a father's sister of the lineage. Shamans also marry and have children among the living at the same time. Funeral shamans are usually women, but the schematic diagram shows the switch to the occasional man, like Doloso (chapter 6).*

Key: △ male   ○ female   = married to

without heirs it would revert to his closest lineage-brothers, so compassion shaded into the establishment of a potential right to inherit. Men took buffalo to the funerals of their cross-cousins too, and if the chain of inheritance within the lineage was weak—genealogically, emotionally, or politically—they might use this buffalo to stake a claim to their cousins' property (Vitebsky 1993: 68–73). When a married woman died, her own brothers would also bring a buffalo to the funeral staged by her husband's people. In any of these situations, the man's cross-cousins or the woman's brothers would also come in a solemn procession to collect some of the dead person's soul and ashes (fig. 4.2, p. 118), and take these back to their own site to incorporate them for a while into their own lineage's ancestor cult, with a duplicate stone-planting and even more buffalo offerings.

Sourcing buffalo in the plains was a niche occupation of the Pano. During the month of blood their lean, ebony-skinned figures would appear all over the hills with their black umbrella sunshades and colored lungis (sarongs), driving scrawny buffalo with a stick: "Ho-o ho-o ho-o!" Buffalo served as a special tool of economic oppression. Their cost was huge, but it was not paid at the time, being added to a debt that was skillfully managed so that the principal could never be paid off. Tribal land could not be legally sold to non-Tribals, but it could be sublegally mortgaged, and gangs of Pano would turn up at the Sora's threshing floor to carry off much of the harvest. Whatever grain the trader coerced out of his client counted as no more than compound interest, at hundreds of percent a year. In one lifetime a household would buy many buffalo for many funerals, and the incomprehensibly quantified cumulative debt would be passed down over future generations of Sora and Pano alike, locking them forever in an ugly economic embrace.

It was said that buffalo could not be bred in the hills. True or not, this ecological fatalism rationalized a sharp economic differentiation into specific roles of production and consumption. Several sites around the edge of the Sora hills hosted a weekly market that was a microcosm of occupational castes and economic classes, each with distinctive markers of physiognomy, costume, and body language. Our nearest market was on Wednesdays at Yaltap (Jaltar), on the way down to Gunupur. The walk took three hours from Rajingtal and much longer from remoter villages, with goods and a pot of alin on one's shoulder (for a man) or head (for a woman). Sora would buy salt, cloth, and pots, or iron for axes, arrowheads, and plow tips from the blacksmith caste, or chili, onions, and bananas from the loud women of the Relli caste. In exchange they sold tamarind for curries, creeper bark for rope, and enormous quantities of rice and millet.

Young people enjoyed going to market to see and be seen, and to make their own, often flirtatious, contacts. This was also where I would make contact with Sora from other villages, such as the handsome Ranatang from Guddara with a muscular torso and seven delicate gold necklaces glistening against his skin, at whose father's funeral I would one day sacrifice a buffalo myself. I found the market fascinating but also distasteful, since it clearly exposed the wretchedness of the Sora's situation. Groups of Pano armed with cudgels would sometimes accost them on the way and force them to part with their loads for much less than they would have received a few miles further downhill. Those who reached the market faced price rings of dealers from town who calculated by weight, which the Sora could not measure, rather than by the volume of their containers. Baskets were snatched and thrown briefly on the scales, and some money thrust into the seller's hand with a refusal to discuss further. Sometimes instead of cash they were given worthless IOUs, which they could not read anyway. Though Sora could count physical objects, or different-shaped coins and colored banknotes, they had difficulty counting nonmaterial things (so it was almost impossible to say "in six days' time"). The Oriya and Telugu languages count in tens, but Sora counts in twelves and twenties, and they could not do multiplication. I would astonish them at a feast as they struggled to count, say, seven rows of thirty-seven leaf-cups of rice by immediately saying "259" (two-hundreds two-twenties twelve seven, *bagu-soa ba-kudi miggal gulji*).

I first realized this inability to count when a youth asked, "Should I call you elder brother (*kaku*) or younger brother (*ubbang*?). How old are you?"

"I'm twenty-five," I said. "How old are you?"

"I'm a hundred."

"How do you know?"

"I've been alive a long time," he reasoned.

Enraged by the gross exploitation of the Sora, I made a study of their political economy and wrote it up as a report at the request of Bhupinder Singh, the Orissa government's commissioner for Tribal welfare (Vitebsky 1978a, 1978b). Reliable figures could not exist, but the direction and intensity of flow were unmistakable. Government programs aimed at "Tribal development" were still feeble in the 1970s, and far more wealth was leaving the area than coming in. At the end of market day a caravan of bullock carts would creak down to town with fat, unshaven Komati traders lounging on mounds of bulging grain sacks. The markets were an open hole through which the plant wealth of the hills and the lifeblood of the Sora drained away into the mouths and pockets of the plains. The deforestation and erosion that the forestry officials blamed on shifting cultivation were caused not by the Sora's own modest consumption needs, but by the demands of others that forced them into ecologically ruinous overproduction. Every Pano meal, wristwatch, radio, or fancy shirt, the bribe to a clerk in town for registering the legal ownership of a paddy field, or the massive "fines" extorted by the forest guards themselves—there was no other possible source for any of these except the sweat and digging tools of Sora agriculture. Since much of the fruit of their labor had already been taken in advance by moneylenders, there was nothing to do but to borrow some more. Then one's family would die from poverty, and one would have to borrow yet again for their funeral buffalo. Young men, and sometimes women, would go to work for a while in the Assam tea gardens (Kar 1981; Jha 1996) just to pump some cash into their family home in order to pay more bribes.

Sora had an old reputation for wildness, but in their relation with the wider world I saw mostly timidity. Ononti invited me to accompany her to Gunupur for three days while she ordered earrings and necklaces from the goldsmith caste. We were joined by Inama's brother Sumbara and another woman, and stayed with Sarda Sora acquaintances. My friends were clearly uncomfortable in this world of garish color, blaring music, and pushing crowds. Ononti was nervous of the armed police holding target practice nearby with rifles, even though (or perhaps because) these were the human counterpart of her own ilda-sonums, and represented the very power that she appropriated in her own trances. We took a group photo in a studio. Though Ononti was a commanding figure on her home ground, in the photo she looks distressingly diminished.

When we returned, Inama said to me, "I dreamed you went to town wearing just your loincloth and everybody laughed at you. I woke crying because they humiliated you." This was just how he dressed, and I had seen him being scolded for it by visiting officials in long trousers and ironed shirts. Inama and his brothers often expressed affection. They would put too much gruel in my bowl, and then finish what I left, saying, "It's all right, we're the same seed the same race (abo'nin a jabmol abo'nin a ja'ti)." Once when Sumbara and I were lying naked in a stream, he asked, "Do you really like me?" (jadi po itsumting?), which I think also meant "Isn't it amazing?" And indeed these people's intimacy was extraordinary, since we had come from such different worlds and been formed so differently.

The culmination of the ritual year was the karja, the annual return of the dead, which took place over three days and nights around the February–March full moon. Every house that had lost someone over the past three years gave that person a buffalo, along with complicated offerings of new pots, new cloths, brass finger-rings, and various baskets of husked rice, unhusked rice, and pigeon-pea (Cajanus cajanus). I was advised to give a cloth and a goat to the sonum of the old lady whose house I had inherited (I never found out why not a buffalo like everyone else). Rice from every house was ritually pounded into flour, then mixed with water to make a milk-like fluid, and everything was laid out, chanted over, and splashed with alin and "milk" again and again. Some people danced with wild peacocks stuffed and mounted on poles. Everyone wore their best homespun skirts or loincloths (with men sometimes changing sexes in a transvestite pantomime), and the drumming lasted almost without pause all day and all night. (Notebook: "Reload tapes—test flash—bandage gashed heel—clean lens—fix torch [flashlight]—label tapes—find microphone stick.")

Here if not in town, Ononti was supreme. She commanded; she danced and whirled while brandishing a sword above her head; she sat alongside Maianti as the two of them entered trance together. Hour after hour they brought up a succession of dead ancestors to laugh, weep, and argue with their living mourners, while "ancestor-women" (*idai-boj*) tended a lamp that was never allowed to go out, as it lit their way in the Underworld, and two groups of "ancestor-men" sang formalized debates between each dead person and their living mourners. The mood shifted between somber, wild, and hilarious, as ancestor-women and ancestor-men mimed a succession of grotesque and enigmatic scenes. On the first night, Ononti and Maianti sat on a cremation-ground, and it was very moving to watch a crowd conjuring up their dead by the light of the full moon. Another time, Ononti danced aiming a bow and arrow at the barricaded door of a bereaved house, before forcing the door open. Later, the funeral pyre–lighters danced a bamboo pole into the house, its alternating side branches cut short to form a ladder, and set it up so that it protruded through the thatch of the roof, while the shamans sat at the base, which was inserted into the mortar.

I could not understand the words, which anyway were inaudible through the drumming. I asked questions of bystanders, and was given fragmentary answers. At the end of the third night thirty buffalo (and my goat) were slaughtered. Then Ononti and Maianti dipped a sword in water and drew it along the body and the arms of each ancestor-woman, ancestor-man, and musician, and even along the length of each musical instrument, and ended by drawing this water along themselves. They had all been in close contact with the dead, and this anointing was to bring them back to the world of the living. Three years later, in the village of Sogad, I would perform as an ancestor-man and would undergo this rite myself.

For days afterward, children made miniature peacocks from squashed *aba* buds (*Madhuca indica*) and chicken feathers and danced them on sticks, or sat on the ground and pretended to trance. I caught some of the karja dancing and the midnight trances in other villages that were celebrating on different days, and it was fascinating how much the tone of each village varied. Soimani and her girlfriends had introduced me to nearby low-lying villages like Borei and Sogad, and I could return there alone. But I could not find my way to the remote mountain villages through the maze of jungle paths. I would often glimpse someone to call to across a hillside for directions: "Oi, which is the way?" (*Oi, wan santebe?*) "Over theeere!" (*Kudiii!*); but even so I had already spent hours lost in the midday heat or fearing nightfall (*togelting*, "it benights me") in the short twelve-hour days. There were also leopards and bears, to say nothing of Rattud-Sonums, prowling the paths: I had sometimes been very sick after a day's exertion in the sun.

So when a young Rajingtal man invited me to join a group going to the high mountain village of Gailung at night, I was delighted. He would introduce me to his friends!

Ononti was appalled. "Don't you know he's going to abduct a woman?" she said. "They're savages up there, they'll throw stones at you—and tear up your notebook!"

I could face stone throwing and paper tearing, but I had to be constantly on my guard against any incident that might lead to trouble with the authorities. By living with the Sora and learning their language I posed a direct threat to the Pano traders of Puttasing, and especially to their elite, the bariks. Bariks were assigned one to each village and acted as interpreters between the Sora and government officials. The Sora could not speak Oriya, and Oriya people— apart from the Pano—could not speak Sora. Each side had little idea what was being said to the other, supposedly in their own words. The bariks had a complete linguistic monopoly, since there was nothing an official could find out from the Sora or convey to them without the message passing through this bottleneck. The bariks were also in a position to be the most ruthless trad- ers and moneylenders. The barik of Rajingtal was Jogi Ganta, an elderly man with close-cropped white hair whose courteous manner concealed a brilliantly manipulative mind. Whereas most had only one or two Sora villages, Jogi's portfolio contained twelve villages, including Sogad, the richest prize of all.

Government attempts at development were still piecemeal, uninformed, and easily subverted. The State Bank of India's task was to find poor people and give them low-interest loans to lift them out of poverty. I made friends with bank officers, including a young Oriya called Bala who remains involved with my work to this day. Four years earlier, the field officer of the Gunupur branch had penetrated up to Rajingtal and persuaded two Sora to take loans for digging wells, at a mere 12.5 percent annual interest. By 1976 the repay- ments were so far in arrears that the manager asked me to investigate. It turned out that the entire business had been conducted in Oriya, through the mediation of Jogi Ganta. The Sora had not understood that the wells were to irrigate an additional rice crop in the dry season and that the loans were to be repaid from this increased productivity. They had naively hired Jogi's own Pano "laborers," who had absorbed all the money while digging a useless small hole. The loan was beyond recovery, while the Sora were scared off from the bank and driven back to Jogi's high-interest loans.

Jogi falsely obtained the title-deeds to people's paddy fields before they were issued by the revenue officer (tahsildar), burned them, and created false affidavits to say he had bought the fields himself; his son became postmaster and used razor blades to scrape out the deposits in savers' passbooks. But Jogi's greatest triumph was the great grain-bank fraud of 1958–65. The government built a large warehouse in the Pano village of Puttasing and deposited several tons of rice to be loaned out at 25 percent annual interest in kind. In the lean season both Sora and Pano borrowed grain; after the next harvest the Sora repaid and the Pano did not. By the end, the grain bank stood empty and delapidated, while Jogi and two advocates in Gunupur had profited spectacularly, some Sora headman collaborators had received a modest payoff, and government agencies down in town were deterred from trying to perform further good works in the hills.

I was hearing about the bariks' tricks in the words and language of their victims, and also sometimes hobnobbing with officials. The bariks' strategy was to start rumors and provocations that were shrewdly targeted to make these officials anxious about a free-range foreigner: I was a Christian missionary in disguise, I was a Naxalite terrorist broadcasting secret messages from my wristwatch, I was a sex maniac surrounded by half-naked women . . . These rumors had a very specific pattern: they circulated each time I went out of the area for any reason, so that they could take root before I came back. They were designed to get rid of me and wasted a lot of my time, but they also enriched my understanding of local political processes, and brought me into interesting and sometimes supportive interaction with officers in the police, intelligence, and other departments.

In April, as compensation for missing Gailung, Ononti took me to two more wholesome villages on the same path, called Manengul and Kumbulsing. We passed women gathering fleshy aba flowers (*Mahua indica*) to distill for the rainy season, and stayed with her friends, where I was introduced possessively as "our sahib" (*saibo len*). Having seen the path and made friends there, I later went back on my own, and then pushed further along the ridge to "savage" Gailung and tiny Tondrong, fewer than 100 humans at the absolute end of the trail, where the mountain fell away 3,000 feet to the plains below.

Even in the blazing April sun, these villages were cooler, even breezy. They were only a couple of miles apart, yet they were separated by difficult cliffs and dense vegetation, and each had its own character. Manengul was a clean, elegant world of gold ornaments and fine homespun skirts and loincloths, all overseen by a stern male funeral shaman called Doloso. Ononti's friend there was the deputy headman, whose daughter Rajani was Doloso's assistant shaman. Gailung was scruffy and cheerful: maybe they were brigands, but I was embraced and protected by a friendly headman. Kumbulsing was relaxed and untidy, and I made friends with a healing shaman called Gopindo who taught me to do shamans' wall-paintings myself. His nickname was Gege (meaning "Oops!"), because this was what he once exclaimed when he was curing a patient with pinching pains in her stomach. He was meant to extract a freshwater crab from her body to symbolize the removal of her illness, and kept one ready in hiding. But the crab popped out too soon, to much laughter.

These villages had many shamans. Some rituals were familiar from Rajingtal, though in simple impoverished Tondrong they were helpfully stripped down to basics; others were new, and they enlarged my horizons. Beyond the aristocratic Manengul each village seemed poorer than the previous one, with less water and level land for paddy fields, and the headman and barik progressively less significant. These villages were less socially stratified than Rajingtal, which suggested that the headman system fed on irrigated land and outside contact. In Tondrong the headman's family had recently been wiped out by Smallpox-Woman, who had also left her pockmarks on many other faces, and there was no barik at all.

I had been in Soraland only a few weeks, but I was becoming frustrated by Ononti's obscure language and her inability to explain anything. She allowed me to refill her sonum-pots at new moon with fresh grain, and when she was ill with fever she allowed me to make her tea. She was not hiding anything, but simply could not explain anything, perhaps at all, but certainly not to me. I had somehow imagined I might become apprenticed to a shaman, but this was not going to happen with her. Wherever I was I kept hearing of rituals I was missing somewhere else. Instead of refocusing my questions, I thought of relocating; maybe with another village, another shaman, things would be clearer.

I now knew hundreds of people by name, and was known by thousands. I could live on Sora food and could walk alone anywhere across the Sora mountains barefoot, with no clothes except a loincloth, no luggage except notebook, fountain pen and ink, razor and medicines, tape recorder and batteries, and no plan for the night.

Since everyone wanted to feed me, and no one would accept money, I worried about how to repay them. Everyone, rich or poor, was in debt to someone further up the food chain. But simply handing out money would create impossible situations, and if I sometimes did this, it had to be framed as a contribution to the costs of a particular illness or ritual. I did my share in work parties, and brought provisions from the market and good knives from the city. I took people to hospitals, interpreting and arguing (and paying) for their treatment. I gave new cloths or umbrellas to shamans when their sonums demanded them. Perhaps my most useful moment was when I was sent to negotiate with a forestry officer who was causing panic by enforcing a ban on shifting cultivation. This would have driven thousands into starvation, and I successfully persuaded him to leave the area alone.

There was one tantalizing village I felt I could not approach on my own. Ladde was high up on a forbidding, densely forested mountain. Few people went there. Ladde had a terrifying reputation for sorcery and violence: they roasted someone in the fire, they cut off someone's penis, two men cut each other's heads off (simultaneously?) . . . But it was the home of a great shaman called Dumburu, and I somehow got the idea that he would tell me what I needed to know.

"Don't go, they're sorcerers and axe murderers up there!" Ononti warned me.

One guide was too frightened to turn up on the agreed day, but Asongroi later agreed to take me to Ladde, as he had relatives there.

"If you must go, don't take any tapes of my singing," Ononti begged. "Dumburu will put sorcery on me!" She meant it. Dumburu was a great sorcerer too.

It was seven miles on the map, twice that on the path, hot, and hard work. The arrival was strange: climax or anticlimax? The village was scrappy, the houses unkempt. The people did look rough, and did not seem interested in engaging us as Asongroi led me through the village and up a cliff to a "baby-hut" (*o'onsing*) in the forest higher up. There was Dumburu himself. He had a strong face with a prominent jaw, and was self-possessed and confident. I could not tell if he was dangerous, but was glad to have Asongroi to introduce me. I asked Dumburu if I could stay with him. He seemed to be saying yes, but without the warm inviting enthusiasm I was used to in Rajingtal. If I came here I would have to get used to a very different Sora style.

We walked back to Asongroi's house in Rajingtal. By the light of the full moon he sang long, fascinating songs, and also told me the meanings of dreams. I already knew that the red threads in a skirt or loincloth foretold bloodshed, but he knew many more. Rain symbolizes tears because someone will die; much water means a good flow of alin, but if a woman dreams of being naked and ashamed, her family's alin trees will dry up; if you step in excrement, someone is sleeping with your partner.

That night I stayed in Asongroi's house. His little girl Lokami, who called me uncle (*dadi*, "father's younger brother"), was ill with a fever, and during the night I had a dream myself. A snake came into the house, picked up an egg in its distended jaws, and carried it off, head uplifted in a snaky posture.

Figure 1.10 Lokami as a child, 1976
She will later become Ononti's successor and the last funeral shaman of Rajingtal. Facing the camera is her father, Asongroi.

The family were still asleep on the floor next to me, but I chased the snake and forced it to put the egg down unharmed. In the morning the dream still felt very vivid, and I told Asongroi.

"That's so lucky," he said. "That was a child-swallowing sonum. You saved her life."

The next day, Lokami had recovered. I had no idea then that she would become Ononti's successor and one of last great Sora shamans. It would be nearly thirty years before she shared her own thoughts with me about the meaning of that dream.

2

. . . .

LEOPARD POWER AND POLICE POWER,
THE JUNGLE AND THE STATE

. . . .

From Rajingtal to Ladde, April 1976–February 1977

It was April, and the weather would only get hotter and hotter until the monsoon started in June. Most alin palms had dried up, despite the stimulus of watery crabs and fish sacrificed at their base. When the kittung creators made everything, they conveniently arranged for alin to flow in the dry season from September to March and for warming distilled aba to be available in the rains. But this hot period in between was a failure of their fluid ecology. I longed for the familiar sweet gulp, but there was nothing to drink but millet gruel made extra sour with cooling jungle leaves. Gasal groups amalgamated, thinned out, then disappeared altogether. Drinking spots became secret, and the usual friendly inquiry "Where are you going?" was met not with "For a drink—come along!" but with the off-putting lie "To empty my bowels (kampungban)."

Hillsides glowed all night from the burning of the slashed forest, which would release plant nutrients in the ashes when the rains came, while shamans beheaded chickens or goats and spurted the blood into the rice, millets, and pulses that were waiting to be sown. Always blood! Vegetation fed animals, but blood fed the seeds in return: this was also the logic of the human sacrifices (meriah) that the neighboring Kond tribe did in the nineteenth century, planting human blood and flesh in their fields on such a vast scale that the British mounted huge military expeditions to suppress the practice (Campbell 1864; Boal 1982; Padel 1995).

By May food was becoming scarce. There would be no new grain till the quick-ripening buroi (foxtail millet, Panicum/Setaria) in August. Poor families who had nothing but shifting cultivation were escalating their high-interest loans from headmen and Pano, though even the headmen's own rice lofts were nearly empty. Skinny Inama and Sumbara had already taken new loans immediately after the last rice harvest in January, to service previous loans. Even the well-formed bodies of their lineage-brothers Lakkia, Goianto, and Jani were losing muscle, and women's rounded bellies and shriveled breasts stood out from their emaciated ribs. It was as if I had acquired X-ray vision, as every movement revealed the metabolism within, from fleeting moods of hunger, exhaustion, or sensuality to life histories of childbearing, suckling, hernias, and tumors.

There was much sickness and death. Poverty forced many families to leave their dead as unfinished ghosts (*kulman*) until after the next harvest, and I learned the hard way that it was impolite to ask when they would do the stone-planting. On a damage-limitation mission after a Pano provocation I cycled down the bumpy track to Gunupur to meet officials whose thermometer showed 110° Fahrenheit (43° Celsius) in the shade.

Late at night on 15 May there was a distant rushing noise like a waterfall, approaching at high speed. Wave after wave of trees started heaving in the dark, closer and closer, with an almost visible whooshing noise. Yet where I stood, not a straw moved. I felt alarm: were we in the eye of a cyclone that would leave hundreds dead, earning us a brief mention among other disasters on an inside page of the *Indian Express*? Suddenly a wall of wind, rain, and lightning hit us, and the temperature dropped twenty degrees in an instant. There was no reaction from the silent houses around, and I realized this was just my first monsoon. This year it had come early.

At first light I met Lakkia wearing only a G-string and a tiny pubic cloth and with a digging stick (*kudala*) on his shoulder. It was time to sow the hillsides. The most handsome of many good-looking Sora men, he turned his head sideways with his familiar grin. "Don't come, it'll be sweaty!" (*yirdongai, uñul-dam!*) But I did go. At seven o'clock it was still cool, but then the temperature soared to the previous level or more, with added humidity. We were joined by Ononti, who was now very thin, and three other women and a boy. As with the sorghum harvesting, we started at the bottom of a slope and advanced on an even front, uprooting shallow weeds and hacking off the new top growth that had resprouted (*tam-bob*) on shrub and tree stumps since the burning a month before. One person sowed above us, and we then used our digging sticks to claw the ground downward over the seeds, sending rocks careering between our feet and crashing down the mountainside.

This was Neolithic agriculture, and it was only in living memory that wooden digging sticks, like plows, had acquired iron tips from the market. My participation would become legendary, but within a generation this form of shifting cultivation would end forever. We worked unceasingly amid the smell of hot vegetation, our muddy feet slipping on the abrasive mica rocks. For three hours I did not straighten my back. During a short rest we took a swig of rice-water, but already Ononti was sowing and hoeing again. When the boy killed a chipmunk, she paused to sing a mock-lament. As we ate the nutty orange flesh of wild butid tubers, she teased, "Write it down, photograph it!" After another hour's solid work I suddenly felt the sun doing me harm, and had to stop. My diet had long been poor. I had to take a break, or I would fall very ill.

I went to the South Indian hill station of Ootacamund, cool as an English summer, where I worked through my notes and recordings, mingled with the local Toda tribe and the town's cosmopolitan eccentrics, and became a judge at the flower show. Two months later, healthy and refreshed, I returned. I loved Rajingtal but knew I had to go to Ladde and live with Dumburu.

I approached the Sora hills by a new route from the west, crossing a racing river in spate, paddling through rice fields at blood heat, and then climbing along the ridge through Tondrong, Gailung, and Kumbulsing. Suddenly a woman's voice hailed me from a hillside: "E Pedeeeé!" With that name it could only be someone from Rajingtal. There stood Ononti with a tatty black cloth round her waist, and a big welcoming smile. She was picking leaves and mushrooms with two women from Soising, a village I had never visited.

The thatched housetops of Soising just peeped above a sea of green maize. The strappy leaves glistened in the afternoon sunlight, and in front of the deep shadows the air was thick with dragonflies. A moving puff of smoke indicated the progress of a woman with a cigar in her mouth and a pot of gruel balanced on her head. In a previous mood I would have rushed to find out names and genealogies, but now I was content to stay silent and enjoy an intimate scene of a kind that no longer exists today, now that rice is husked in electric mills. Just inside the house Ononti and her hostess stood facing each other across the mortar, pounding grain with massive wooden pestles, which bounced up again in a synchronized alternating rhythm, tum-TUM-tum-TUM. They talked and laughed in a low murmur as each one caught her rebounding pestle in alternating hands, bodies leaning in, bottoms out, and alternating feet sweeping loose grain back into the mortar between each thump. Ononti seemed radiant. Every movement of her body and every expression that flitted across her face were utterly beautiful. Her companion was younger but with a similarly strong face. The rain started pouring outside and cascaded off the thatch in a curtain across the open doorway. The cold light coming in met the glow of the fire inside to pick out each pore in the velvety skin of their backs. In thinking forward to Dumburu I felt like an unfaithful lover, but beneath my blissful surrender to this fragile moment was the anxiety of research not done—a job for which even the specification was unclear.

A few days later, I retraced the path that Asongroi had shown me from Rajingtal to Ladde, the rocky surface now awash with runoff water and acrid with the post-rainfall smell of burgeoning vegetation. (Notebook: "Take to Ladde: batteries, sandals, elastic band, ink bottle, envelopes, knife, umbrella, herbarium paper . . .") The midday village was empty, but I found the onward path up to Dumburu's aerie.

On walks up to Ladde I would stay with a friendly young man from Borei called Sojono, and was offered aba and gruel in several more "baby-huts" (*o'onsing*), tiny shelters where families lived in isolation for a few weeks during the rains, chasing monkeys and deer from their ripening millets. At other seasons these would stand empty as families retreated after the harvest to the more leopard-proof huddle of the village. Dumburu was unusual in making his o'onsing into his year-round home. The house faced a flat slab of rock where clothes and crops were laid out to dry. Next to us was a huge wild mango tree, which was smothered with an immense *laia* creeper (*Bauhinia* sp.) with woody stems rambling hundreds of feet like writhing pythons. The view was stupendous, through descending screens of mountains to the river Vamsadhara, which flowed through Gunupur, and up into the Kond range beyond. Down the other side of the mountain, one could just hear a rushing rain-filled river in a distant valley. Between showers, heavy clouds collapsed into the clefts between hills. Above us towered further cliffs, leading to a final plateau of forest. Everything was intensely green.

Dumburu was one of the most self-sufficient people I have ever met, and proud, with none of the deference I sometimes felt from other Sora. His senior wife Sorni had come to him by love marriage (*dari*), and his junior wife Jamani, in a common Sora pattern, was her younger sister. There was another, unrelated wife down in the village from an earlier marriage, but we never saw her. Sorni had two young sons, Arambo and Ronggia. When I arrived she was pounding the first of the new season's buroi under inadequate shelter in the teeming rain, and she hardly looked up. This was not indifference but a Ladde style in which I could be left alone in silence for hours. People were not unfriendly, but without the questioning: Where are you going, where have you been, have you done this, have you done that . . . ?

There were dug wells down in the village, but on our clifftop we drank rainwater from hollows in the rock. Dumburu was often away somewhere in the whiteness of the clouds, and we rarely went down into the village. His wives took turns to stand outside the hut and drive away animals with slingshots and cries of "Aaaagh! Tutututututututut!" Dumburu had designed an ingenious trap where a monkey entered a cage, tugged at a head of grain, and triggered a door that slammed shut. There were hot, steamy monsoon interludes, but often it was cold. At night we all slept on the floor of the baby-hut listening to torrents

Figure 2.1 Dumburu the fearless shaman, Ladde 1976

The spear is for protection against leopards and bears.

of rain beating on the broad-leaved trees all round, and getting up from time to time to push long sticks further into the fire.

Everything in Ladde was cruder and more basic than elsewhere, and the people were scruffier and wilder-looking. The men wore only tattered shorts, never loincloths, which by comparison would have seemed elegant, and the women wore tattered blouses. An air of poverty was accentuated by the half-overgrown holes in noses and ears with no gold or silver rings to fill them. Yet several men wore wristwatches. A work party of twenty young men came to harvest our buroi millet, and while Dumburu held baby Ronggia on his hip and looked on with a lordly air, they fiddled with a radio, discussed clothes and prices, and spoke partly in Hindi. It turned out they had all worked in Assam for lengthy periods, not so much to pay off extortionists, as down in Rajingtal, but simply for subsistence. This huge mountain had almost no level ground for paddy fields, and few springs to irrigate them. Unlike the lush valley-floor villages, here there were no rich pickings. The headman was insignificant, and the barik was a Hindu Paik who made more money by staying in Puttasing as postmaster. The 300 people of Ladde were the most remote Sora of all, yet paradoxically their familiarity with the outside world was more unmediated.

Ladde felt defined by jungle rather than by agriculture. The forest was a generation less degraded than elsewhere, and even today Ladde mountain stands out on a satellite image. It was probably the only village where people still ground wild mango stones and the pith inside palm trunks as emergency food. Dumburu was an experimental gardener who grew varieties of onions, chili, lentils, taro, and sweet potato I had not seen elsewhere, and was always pleased when I brought him new seeds or cuttings from elsewhere. But there was no escaping buroi. At first it had been a welcome change from the monotony of other grains ("delicious," note on 25 August) but I soon grew to loathe its gritty yellow texture ("yuk," 12 September). Pumpkins were also in season, and they too soon became oppressive.

Dumburu thought and spoke constantly about plants and animals. The creeper *palbun* is stomach medicine, the fleshy *kiri'loi* gives milk for wounds, *potoi'sa* fruit put in a stream kills fish, *ruteng* sticks rubbed together make fire, the root of a terrestrial orchid mixed in with seed before sowing keeps wild pigs away from the crop, this root cures snakebite, that root is a contraceptive . . . Similarly, the jungle animals from shamans' wall-paintings, which had largely disappeared everywhere else, still roamed here: porcupines, peacocks, monkeys, pythons, deer, wild goats, and monitor lizards (all edible). But even in Ladde, there were almost no bears or leopards left. I carried snake antivenom injections plus adrenalin, and expected to use them here (though in fact I never did). Dumburu used animal parts in medicine, and would grind a dried monkey's hand in a drink to reduce swelling caused by Earth-Sonum. "Can you get me some elephant bone?" he once asked me. "I can't get any round here."

Soon after I arrived, there was a wild boar hunt. The beaters included women and children. As we fanned out, I was led to my position by a small boy on all fours through a thicket of *regei'* shrubs with springy branches lined with curved, barbed thorns. My body was lacerated, and my feet filled with spines as the child chirruped, *yirai po yirai po, yirai yirai!* (Are you there are you there, come on come on!). The Sora had very little body hair, and considered it ugly and frightening. When a hair sprouted on their face the men would pinch it out between two coins. That little boy was fascinated by my hairy European legs and would stroke them in amazement, saying, "Like a bear!"

Dumburu laughed a lot as he played with his children. Ronggia was a baby, but Arambo was about five, and Dumburu said with pride that he would become a shaman. He was named after a relative whom Dumburu clearly adored, and who had been killed in a drunken quarrel: "He was such a lovely man, and they hacked him up with an axe!" The dead Arambo was always the first to speak in Dumburu's trances. Little Arambo was a strange child, almost constantly in tears, and I wondered whether he had difficulty living under the shadow of his namesake. Sometimes he would whimper rather than speak, or howl with a desperate choke to his voice. He would wake crying in the morning, and I wondered what other world he had visited, and whether he was scared by what he had seen or, on the contrary, regretted leaving it. At first I found his crying irritating, but later I spent many days carrying him on my shoulder around the mountain, and he started telling me about the sonums that he saw everywhere: "There's one over there, can't you see it?" We sat and shared jungle berries on various rocks while he pointed out medicinal plants and told me stories, once asking, "Is there death in your country?"

We had never established on what terms I was to stay with this family, or for how long. Dumburu was unhurried, but I was in a hurry, even though I was not sure what I was hurrying about. I was trying to use him for information, but he was also trying to use me. For what? He did not want money, though he made free with my shirts and knives. At some times he seemed indifferent to my presence; at others he was eager to take me to the jungle, where I was his only companion, to show me interesting places or plants. He wanted me to see every detail of his rituals, but often stalled my questions about them with "Just so" (*ed'tigoi* or *ude'nang*). In desperation I would ask leading questions. This was a very bad research method, as his answer to anything was usually

Figure 2.2 The author carrying Dumburu's son Arambo, 1976

yes. Sometimes I felt he was preventing me from making other contacts down in the village, and keeping me to show clients as a trophy.

Dumburu was reputed to be a dangerous sorcerer. I was not frightened of him, but I knew I was living with someone who was feared by others in the village and beyond. For a long time he promised to make me a special amulet, I thought as part of a process of teaching me. One day he produced three aromatic roots and some hairs from a bear. He singed some more bear's fur and little chips of leopard bone on a potsherd of hot embers, held the amulet in the smoke, and wafted it over me, then tied it round my upper arm and gave me some more smoke. Everything was quick and businesslike, with no chanting.

"Does this mean you're going to teach me?" I asked, naively. He just grinned, and turned to a patient who was suffering from Earth-Sonum. For her, he singed four kinds of root, ground them with chips of monkey bone into a potion, poured some of the liquid onto her big toes, and gave her the rest to drink.

"How long should I wear the amulet?" I asked.

"In three years I'll give you another one. Don't worry, I'm here (*batong-dongam, ñen daku*)!" This was Dumburu's signature message, which gave him the most far-flung clientele of any shaman. He might tease or be evasive, but in the end he was all-competent. His ironic remarks were delivered from a position of imperturbability—except for one day when he opened the door of our hut after only a few hours' absence to discover a huge termite hill under construction in the middle of the floor. *Asoooong!!* (Shiiiit!!) he exclaimed, followed by a big grin. Being all-competent, he knew how to light a fire on top of the termites so that they went away.

Almost every morning before dawn, someone would climb the cliff to our hut for a divination, and Sarda Sora patients with their unfamiliar dialect would come all the way from Gunupur, bringing a tiny basket of husked rice and often consuming more in cooked rice as guests. Dumburu's practice was unusually cosmopolitan from his time in Assam, and his props included jars of various substances and a stethoscope.

Suspended from the ceiling inside our hut were several round clay pots, with big leaves tied across their mouths and splashes of rice-flour water and blood across the underside. These were residues from Dumburu's specialty of rituals for women and babies afflicted by Sun-Sonum (Uyung-sım). This sonum was a complex concept. While Earth-Sonum (Labo-sım) illnesses clustered around an imagery of containment and wholeness, giving symptoms of swelling and blockage, Sun-Sonum illnesses were linked to symptoms of scorching and melting, such as open sores. The Sun was also the residence for the victims of accidents, murder, or suicide, which involved a violation of the boundary of the body so that their victims' souls would rise up to the Sun "like smoke." In addition, suicides also involved suspension on a rope from a height, symbolizing their journey across open space to the sky. These ideas were enhanced by a notion of suddenness and shock; but that of bodily dissolution was also linked to the imagery of metalworking, since this was how bodies were made, but also how they could be melted (so you should never insult a member of the Gansi brass-working caste, as they can kill you just by thinking about you while casting molten metal). Sun-Sonum had various subpersonalities, in particular Sun-Woman (Uyung-boj), who molded babies from molten metal in the womb, and her non-Sora-speaking blacksmith slave Dumb-Sun (Mommo-yung), who hammered them into shape. Sun-Woman also had a python called Moon-Eclipse-Sonum (Mo-gaj-sim), who caused eclipses by swallowing the moon and then vomiting it out again. This was a very dangerous moment, since by a parallel process the expulsion of the moon might cause the miscarriage of a fetus. Pregnant women did not look at the moon, and took special care to hide during an eclipse.

A mother came to our hut with a baby who was not feeding well. Maybe the python was suckling her nipple and putting its tail into the baby's mouth as a dummy? She held the baby throughout the ritual, and in their role as patient they seemed like one undifferentiated unit.

Dumburu stuck rice grains on the forehead of each of them, and began to chant. He sprinkled rice-flour water all around, and especially on the round underside of an upturned clay pot. This white fluid represented milk. Infants suckled for around three years, and since the Sora did not use wet nurses or the milk of other species, a mother's milk-flow was a matter of life and death.

Dumburu sat on his haunches and sprinkled some aba on the pot, while the mother tended a boiling pot of rice. Various baskets and leaves were added, containing husked rice, unhusked rice, buroi millet, aba spirit, and brass finger-rings. Dumburu added some bristles from a small pig and poured a belt of rice-water around all the offerings. Sorni passed a small jug of aba spirit round, and we all took a swig.

The pig was brought shrieking, and Dumburu held it under his left arm while feeding it from a leaf in his right hand. It licked some rice grains and aba liquid to confirm its willingness to die, and then another man dashed its head on the ground before piercing its throat and draining it of blood. Dumburu caught some blood in a leaf, then transferred some drops to the other leaves of grain, and splashed some blood over the upturned pot.

49

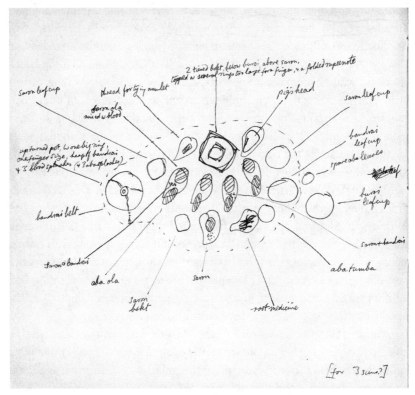

Figure 2.3 Dumburu's Sun-Sonum healing for mother and baby

The pot splashed with blood and rice-flour water is on the left (author's field notes 13.54).

While the pig was being singed and its hairs scraped off, Dumburu began his divination. This took the special form of "winnowing the bones" (*gum-jang*). The mother sat holding her baby on the mess of blood and "milk" on the upturned pot, while Dumburu tossed some rice up and down in a winnowing fan. Winnowing rice so that certain grains stood out was a regular form of divination and symbolized the revelation of something hidden. Usually the shaman would use it as an initial pointer but then go into trance for ancestor-sonums to discuss the case in more detail; but with this aspect of the Sun there was no need for trance. Ten little splinters of pig-bone emerged in the rice, and Dumburu showed them to me, explaining, "These came out of the baby."

He rolled some cotton threads into a string and incorporated several fibrous and fleshy roots into an amulet that he tied around the baby's neck. He then produced a Victorian coin and some iron nails. He laid the coin on the woman's head and the tip of a nail on the center of the coin, and started hammering in the nail. It suddenly disappeared, and he did the same with another nail, and another.

"She's got a hole in her head," he explained. "It's the python's open mouth and it keeps swallowing up her babies. The nails have gone through the coin and into her skull, and they'll fill the hole."

"When will you remove them?" I asked.

Everyone laughed. "We don't," Dumburu replied. Chanting again, he placed some raw rice and two rings inside the pot and tied some large leaves over the mouth with bark string. This pot would join the others in the roof of his hut.

I saw the disappearing nail act several times, and Dumburu was still doing it twenty years later. It was extraordinary to live with a gynecologist and see the process performed in our home. I calculated that half of all babies died within a few months of birth, and those that lived were festooned with Sun amulets. Most mornings a woman would turn up at dawn with an endangered infant in her arms or a void in her womb, to receive a diagnosis and sometimes a blood-splashed pot ritual. Once when my tape recorder fell apart I shook out the loose screws and said, "Look—Sun-bones (*Uyung-jangen*)!" Dumburu laughed heartily.

I visited Rajingtal, but was feeling ill; I thought it was because of a boil on my cheek ("Did a Ladde girl kiss you?"). I came back to Dumburu's exhausted and nauseous, and with bright orange urine.

"The sonums from Rajingtal have stroked you. I've seen them in a dream," he said. "It's their Rattud-Sonum." Of course I had passed their "police station" (*tana*) on the path. He passed a flame over my head and sat down, legs outstretched, to swish some rice grains in a winnowing fan. For the first time, I was a shaman's patient myself. Even in my drowsiness I appreciated how privileged I was to be the focus of a trance, but I was too ill to notice much. On the tape, after many preliminary sonums, there is one who says with an exaggerated Rajingtal accent, "We met you, deeeh! I said, 'he looks like a Sooora.' "

"Who are you?" demanded the women.

"Who am I? I'm Malagaaai."

"Let him get better, let him go!" urged Jamani. Now I understood why others spoke on a patient's behalf.

"On the paaath by the tamarind treee," continued Malagai, "that's where I met you: 'Now who is this maaan (*boten kan a mandraaan*)?' "

"I said 'Let him go, Uncle!' " Jamani repeated.

Afterward she explained, "They're saying 'Why did you leave us and go to Ladde?' " What could be clearer? The ancestors of the headman lineage where

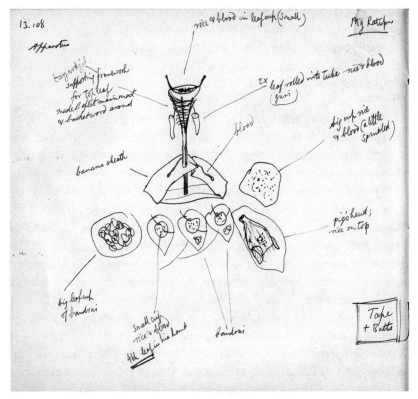

Figure 2.4 Dumburu's Rattud-Sonum healing for the author
I left the people of Rajingtal to live with Dumburu, and have been made ill by their offended ancestors (author's field notes 13.108).

I had lived with Inama, the father of Ononti my shaman, Malagai the father of Soimani, the girl who had flirted with me: sickness was not just a bodily condition, but an expression of the difficulty of disengaging from intimate relationships. The attacking sonums also included the father of my friend Asongroi, whom I had recorded during several of his Rattud cures. Now I was experiencing the same performance from the other side. I gave Dumburu twenty rupees to buy a pig from the village, and he disappeared down into the clouds while I stayed behind to vomit some more.

He brought the pig and started setting up the ritual. I knew the banishing-rite for Rattud: start in the house with a long chant and a leaf-cup of rice circling over my head, make the pig eat and drink from my hand, lead the pig and the sonum out along the path, set up the shrine with a little structure of banana leaves and three *sargia* leaves of rice and blood, eat everything on the spot, and don't take anything back. The sonums took the pig's soul and left the meat for us, and I did manage to eat a little piece.

That was on 16 September 1976. In the afternoon Dumburu offered a chicken to Leopard-Sonum. Who was the patient, what were the symptoms, why this, why that? It was hard to care, and I was sick all night. An old shamaness down in the village, with whom I had once danced, sent me a present of a pot of aba spirit that I could not drink, and I agreed when Dumburu's ildas told him in a dream that I should give them an expensive umbrella. Before dawn, another mother and child came for a divination . . . My notes straggle on for three more days, but it took half an hour between deciding to raise some boiled water to my lips and sipping it, and half a day to cross the hut to fetch a pen. Somehow, I managed to get out and walk twenty miles down to Gunupur, then take a bus 150 miles to Vizag (Visakhapatnam) and stagger into the hospital, where a Catholic nurse from Kerala confirmed, "You have hepatitis."

I had received a Sora diagnosis, but when I was seriously ill I had failed the test of relying on Sora treatment. I spent a month lying on a hospital bed drinking only starchy rice-water and taking Ayurvedic pills, and another two months walking increasingly steadily along the beach. I did not know what Dumburu had told people, and could not think of anyone who could read a letter.

Exactly three months later, at nightfall on 16 December, I slipped into Rajingtal and flitted unseen into Inama's house. In the firelight, by the bubbling of a pot, I sat quietly beside his wives as his little girl ran into my arms and lay there chattering, her hair bristly with a child's haircut. Finally Inama returned from his gasal, with the Sora gasp of surprise: "Ai!" There was perhaps no precedent for the scenes of embracing someone from another world, and as I stroked his smooth, polished back in turn I thought how my presence in his life was as extraordinary as his presence in mine. Inama's brother Sumbara came and held me and kissed me for half an hour, saying over and over again, "Issí!" (Alas!). Love was expressed through reminiscences of things done together, with hoots of laughter: you remember we went on a work party . . . you got drunk in the midday heat . . . remember how you bandaged Monsiro's hand? I had never felt so loved by a group of people, and wished I could stay with them forever. Dumburu's diagnosis was very perceptive.

After the well-fed Telugu townspeople and protein-rich fishing castes on the beach in Vizag, everyone looked sicker and thinner and tinier than I remembered them. "I was looking at that photo of all of us," Inama said, "and asking, 'When will he come?' Some people said, 'He's been bewitched by

Dumburu,' and others said, 'He's been axed to death far away in a quarrel over a woman.' But I knew you weren't dead. Once in a dream I saw you coming up the path and got up in the night to meet you. I looked, but there was no one there."

That night I shared a sleeping bag with Sumbara and his little boy. In the morning women passed to and from the well with their familiar Rajingtal faces and two or three large pots stacked on their heads, all smiles with the usual "When did you come?" I had dreamed that I was divining by tossing rice in a winnowing fan. They laughed, but it was a reminder that I had to return to Dumburu.

It had been two months since the last trickle of rain, and on the way up to Ladde people were working on little threshing floors. On some, the grains were still on the stalk, and were being trampled round and round by cows or buffalo. On others, the separated grain was laid out in long rows, while men and women walked up and down whisking plumes of dusty chaff off the surface with winnowing fans. There was no more distilled aba to drink, but plenty of alin.

The view from Dumburu's aerie was utterly transformed. The vivid green landscape had turned to dry deciduous forest. Dormant paddy fields slid down slopes in steps like glaciers of stubble, emphasizing the confines of their valleys. Between the trees on the unirrigated slopes around them, severed sorghum stalks undulated over the contours of the land like cascades of water swooshing down the hillside. By moonlight they gleamed silver.

Dumburu's youngest wife Jamani was very pregnant. She kept away from the moon, but was still chopping firewood. Dumburu had removed his sonum-pots from inside the baby-hut, as childbirth would be polluting for his high-caste ildas. One evening he needed to hunt some monkeys that were destroying his crops high up above our hut, and took my only functioning flashlight. I was left to sleep alone with Jamani and an old midwife.

In the middle of the night I woke to hear moans of "U gai, u gai, what shall I do?" and the faintest cry. The baby must have emerged. Jamani was in distress, and the midwife seemed helpless. The moon had set, and the embers of our fire had died right down. There were no matches, and it was completely dark. I groped my way to the foot of the cliff and called "E Dumburu!" again and again. There was no response.

I had seen Sora walking at night, holding a faint glowing brand against the ground, where it lit a pebble an inch in front but no more. I would have to do the same. I had climbed up this cliff path so many times in daylight, but now I had to remember it in sequence, matching this tiny red ember with the feel of the ground under my bare feet. I set out, trying to visualize those casual, unobservant earlier climbs. Here was the lumpy rock . . . the fern with wiry stems and arrowhead leaves . . . the sudden small bend . . . ah, the speckled fleshy arum plant, now in seed . . . the smooth rock . . . Somehow I reached the top, though I would have been unable to find my way down again until daylight. I called over and over: "E Dumburuuuú!"

There was intense silence, apart from the blood rushing in my own head. The outline of the mountain was intensely solid against a fluid starry sky. I waited, then called again. At length a distant wavering yellow light appeared, moving very slowly. Dumburu was walking, not running, but he was coming. He still held on to my flashlight as we descended to find the baby lying on the floor of the hut, with Jamani squatting over the half-expelled afterbirth. What was the use of the midwife? Dumburu fumigated Jamani's body with *sargia* resin and gave her some more to swallow, then teased out the placenta. I soaked my penknife in disinfectant, but he cut the umbilical cord on an old potsherd anyway, before burying everything under the floor where it had fallen. ("Topics to discuss with Dumburu, 25 December 1976: dreams and amulets; blood, semen and conception; why menstruating women continue cooking and working; enlarge my earring holes . . .")

After the birth, Dumburu put his ılda sonums' pots back in the hut. One month later, it was time to shave the baby's head, "for Sun-Sonum." There were two chickens, one each for Gadi-uyung (the Sun who molds) and Mommo-yung (Dumb-Sun, the one who hammers). The baby would be given her ancestor's name, Saibori, apparently at the insistence of the old namesake who would thereby "resprout" (*tam-bob*), just like vegetation that had been cut down to the ground. I did not yet know the significance of this name. The baby would also be blessed with old Saibori's nickname, Pu'tij (Swollen Vagina).

A man called Dunggu came to do the shaving. As well as various baskets of grain, pots of alin, and leaves, Dunggu's equipment included scissors and a cutthroat razor. Dunggu was a good informant. Where Dumburu tended to say, "Yes" or "Just so," Dunggu elaborated while Dumburu nodded agreement and added interesting details that I could never elicit from him alone. Dunggu's father too had been murdered. Was there any man in Ladde who did not die by leopard or axe?

Inside the hut Dumburu chanted as he poured alin into leaves. Dunggu went to where Jamani and the baby were sitting outside, waved a leaf over the baby's head, wet her hair, and shaved her. He plastered the cuttings with cow dung into a corner high up on the interior wall. This safe location would prevent anyone from reaching her hair and using it to harm her with sorcery.

Figure 2.5 Shaving baby Saibori for Sun-Sonum

Meanwhile, Dumburu fed both chickens with rice grains and alin, beheaded them, and sprinkled their blood onto leaves, while women looked after the boiling pots. As usual, there were separate chants over the blood for the "raw ritual" (*amengpır*) and later over the meat for the "cooked ritual" (*asinpır*).

We ate a small family meal on the rock slab outside the hut. These were the best moments, when Dumburu was relaxed and I was not trying to pump him for information. Sometimes he would spontaneously offer me an excursion to find a rare herb against conception or snakebite or eclipses, or to drink from a spring that flowed cool by day and warm by night.

"Let's go to Badongsing tomorrow," he said one day. "My sister's husband is ill, he wants me to sacrifice a goat to his father." He introduced me to this new village, where he described me in the third person as an exhibit and re-enacted some of our conversations. People seemed relieved to see him and reassured by his confident patter as he palpated the patient, blew into his ears, and stuck rice grains and goat's hairs onto his forehead and chest. He may have been feared as a sorcerer, but he was also respected as a healer.

While the goat was being cooked, Dumburu went into trance and divined. Many ancestors spoke, and I was much better able to understand them than previously. The main attacker said, "I met him on the path and asked for some alin, but he pretended he didn't have any." Another ancestor said, "Me too,

Figure 2.6 Mealtime with Dumburu's family
*Sorni is serving rice, Arambo and baby Ronggia are on the left. The winnowing fan in the
center is the same kind that shamans use for divination.*

you begrudged me alin in your soul (*puradan*)!" Living interlocutors said,
"Make him well again!" and various ancestors agreed to do so. Another relative jumped in and asked the ancestors for help. Two of his children had been
killed by the sorcery of a close relative, and now a third was threatened.

Later I asked Dumburu why. "Just so" (*ude'nang*), he started, but then he
told the story. The two men had shared the same inheritance, but the other one
did sorcery because he resented the way it was split. The patient had become
more prosperous, and the sorcerer resented the gold necklaces worn by the
child who was now sick. He had taken the child's discarded toothbrush stick
and leaf-cup, he had buried them in a secret pot, he had made a pact with
sorcery sonums . . .

And who was the dead man called Jigor who turned up in the trance to
complain that he had been murdered?

"They killed him because they suspected him of sorcery," Dumburu answered, and then added, "He was good, his soul was cool, he wasn't wicked."

So were sorcery accusations just an expression of bad feeling? Did anyone
really do it?

I had seen Dumburu remove sorcery from clients who came to the hut. He
would chant as he pulled little leaf-parcels of foul-smelling filth from their

stomach or chest, hold the bundles up for inspection, and toss them into the fire for permanent destruction. But perhaps a person who can undo sorcery is also a person who can do it? When I promised medicine to one man in the village, he was too frightened to come up to our hut to collect it, and when I fell ill and disappeared to Vizag, many people believed Dumburu had killed me. Behind the conventional joking ("Are you sleeping with Dumburu's wives? Are they tasty?"), what did people think he was teaching me now?

One day, during a casual conversation, Dumburu gave me a confession the like of which I have never heard before or since. "I learned sorcery from Kantino of Regidising," he said, "and after me it will go to little Arambo. I've got three sorcery sonums, one from Kantino, one from his father, and one of my own. They're small red dwarves. I see them in dreams and trances, and then I'm scared."

I was astonished by this sudden openness. "Why did you accept them?" I asked.

"I was too frightened to refuse," he answered. "We drink some medicine, then send those sonums off to do the errand. We add medicines and burn a victim's hair and toothbrushing stick in the fire, and then they will burn likewise."

I had heard that sorcery sonums can turn on their owner if he does not keep them fed with human victims.

"Yes, if they're hungry," he confirmed. Then, as if anticipating the question I could not ask, he added, "But I've never killed anyone. But I would if I was angry."

How far was he being truthful? He was angry, very angry, about the slaughter of old Arambo. That was a defining moment of his life, and he had often recounted how Arambo and his brother Sarneng had gone to a stone-planting party, the classic setting of a drunken homicide. "They were beautiful, young, and energetic like you and me . . . people were jealous of them. They hacked Arambo up with an axe, and stabbed Sarneng. They left knives in Sarneng's stomach, I took them out." It was this Arambo who then forced Dumburu to become a shaman. "After he was killed," Dumburu explained, "he came to me in a dream: 'Become a shaman,' he said. I was frightened, I said 'No,' but he made me ill so I had to do it."

However, others told me that Arambo and Sarneng had been the sons of notorious sorcerer parents, and had been killed preemptively to prevent them from inheriting this skill. It turned out their mother (a unique case of a female sorcerer) was the previous Saibori! So not only was Dumburu's son named after the murdered Arambo, but his newborn daughter had also received the name of a notorious sorceress.

"Old Saibori will guide baby Saibori when she becomes a shaman," Dumburu predicted. Perhaps, like my friend little Arambo, she was destined to become a sorcerer as well as a shaman? I was starting to see how every child's name brought with it a prehistory from the previous namesake. Old Arambo, young Arambo, Old Saibori, baby Saibori, like Dumburu himself—all were constrained and partly defined by the continuing reverberations of other people's relationships and actions.

. . . .

By now it was the end of December. A year before I had been settling into Rajingtal and developing my relationship with Ononti. The past Christmas Day, in 1975, I had been watching the winnowing of the rice and cradling Inama's youngest child in my arms as he sweated in a malarial fever. Now I had spent three months in hospital myself, and was struggling to find my place in Dumburu's very different environment.

At harvesttime, a portion of every seed or fruit had to be offered to a range of sonums. There was dancing around the village every night, while each household fed their own ancestors, and shamans fed their ıldas. Dumburu made a shrine out of a stone and peacock feathers, and tranced for an hour. As well as domestic rice, wild rice, and pulses, he offered bananas, late-fruiting pumpkins, and a goat, and added a chicken in my name. Now that we had given them to the sonums first, we were free to eat these crops ourselves.

Ladde was almost the only village that still performed a ritual at this season for another kind of entity. Kittungs were a class of male and female beings (sometimes conceptualized as one single kittung) who created the world, and an answer to a question about a custom was often "kittung set it up that way." There were myths, sometimes comical or obscene, about how kittungs had invented houses or plowing or daylight. Kittungs inhabited various mountains and large rocks, and there was one in the huge cliff above our hut. They were different from most sonums, in that they had never been ordinary people and did not cause illness. They were the closest things the Sora had to "gods."

Dumburu had seen British overseers on the Assam tea estates, and had his own view of kittungs: "Ancestors are Sora, and ıldas are brown-skinned police and officials and clerks who write by hand," he declared, "but kittungs are white, and they use typewriters." So the world was created by European typists!

Ladde had its own kittung, and in the center of the village there was a huge structure over a small stone shrine looked after by a special attendant, called a *buya*. Some other villages had a "buya" lineage, but everywhere except Ladde the hereditary buya priest's function was obsolete. I suspect that this shrine represented a core identity of the village as an inhabited place. Throughout the year it stood neglected inside a stone fence. Now it was opened up, and every house contributed a leaf full of rice and a bunch of pigeon-pea pods, while some added bananas and cigars. The buya and his assistants never tranced, but they sang a long chant that included the names of many ancestors, followed by another chant to ward off the sorcery of a long list of villages. An unusually enormous pig was sacrificed, and its head and tail added to the offerings. The buyas finished after dark by the light of the embers of their fire, and closed up the little shrine and the enclosure till the following year.

I now had two tape recorders, but even with new microphones and batteries, both machines failed, and I heard people saying, "Issí, he's upset (*sintate*)." Indeed, it did feel like a terrible loss, and I never had another opportunity to record any ritual associated with kittungs. However, the word *kittung* was to enjoy a revival, as it had been adopted by the Christians for their own god. There was already a Baptist church in Ladde, and the Christians treated Christmas as a harvest festival. I went that Sunday and saw some thirty adults and a few children listening to two church officials in white dhotis who addressed them from behind a table. The speakers questioned the congregation about the sermon, and got them to stand up and read, very hesitantly, from the Sora New Testament, which had just become available.

Who were these young Christians? A few had the pockmarked faces of smallpox survivors, so perhaps they had a special reason to be disillusioned with sonums. Behind one of the saris I thought I spotted Dumburu's own daughter by his first marriage. These were ordinary Ladde people, yet their clothing, manner, and facial expression seemed unaccountably different. They had changed into something else, yet this change was not simply on the surface. Something seemed to have changed inside them too.

This was different from old myths about shape-shifting, in which the inner person remained the same while their outer appearance changed as characters put on or pulled off a detachable skin. Those changes were temporary and reversible (unless a character's discarded skin was burned in a fire, which was the point of some of those stories). There was still one common form of shape-shifting: the temporary transformation of a human into a leopard (or tiger: the word kɪna means both, though those in wall-paintings were spotted not striped). A person might dream of being a leopard, and wander abroad in that physical form. It seemed everyone had met a were-leopard or knew someone who had. They had a different growl from ordinary leopards, and were much more dangerous. Many were-leopards retained telltale signs of their human identity, and many came from the Kond tribe. One man beckoned me into his baby-hut, and pulled out a tiny bundle containing a set of gold nose-rings and earrings. "I don't show these to everyone," he said, "just to you. They were worn by a leopard I killed." The rings were of a Kond style not worn by Sora. If a were-leopard was killed, the human dreamer would claw convulsively and die in his sleep. Perhaps a sleeping Kond far away had died at that moment. From Dumburu's clifftop one could see into their territory thirty miles away, and when I later visited Kond villages their tattooed faces were indeed busy with stripes and circles. It was tempting to interpret the Sora fear of were-leopards as a legacy of the Kond's former kidnappings for human sacrifices.

By the 1970s much of the jungle throughout Soraland had been stripped to grow surplus crops to pay bribes and fines; there were few leopards left. However, there were many recent leopard victims in genealogies. Deaths by Leopard-Sonum were highly contagious. The victim was not cremated in the lineage's usual place, but given a "jungle funeral" (*kandring guar*) in isolation far outside the village. His personal possessions were not inherited but burned, and even his fields were sold off to sever the link and prevent the repetition of his death in others.

I found out the extent of the leopard problem from an unexpected source. My own shape-shifting consisted of being sometimes on the run from officials and sometimes welcomed by them as a guest or colleague. One police subinspector in Puttasing invited me to a very good lunch of omelette and mutton, and during his siesta he let me browse through old records. I found a file from the 1930s on "unnatural death" cases. This term would make no sense in Sora, since there was no concept of the "natural," but it covered much the same shocking and contagious events as those attributed to the sonums of Sun and Leopard. There were murders, suicides, and accidents, as well as an occasional snakebite case. But by far the most numerous were what my host called "tigerbite cases," probably referring to leopards. In 1940 there were three man-eaters in the area, and the one in Rajingtal alone had killed eleven people. The Sora population must have been small in those days, making the number of those killed very high:

1935	12
1936	8
1937	9
1938	28
1939	?
1940	29

The records were also a treasury of FIRs (First Information Reports), and the time lag was just enough to link up with the family histories I was constructing backward from the present. The forms of "crime" in the 1930s seemed familiar: illegal distilling and unlicensed guns among the Sora, and "irregularities in weights and measures" by Komati merchants at the Yaltap market. The "principal sources of crime" were the Puttasing to Yaltap road, as well as the village of Sogad, where two men from different lineages had been fighting with false accusations and planted evidence to take over the position of headman.

In 1940 an English police inspector named Percy Gill wrote that this "unhealthy area" had not been toured by a superior officer for forty years, and that the stockade erected in the 1860s to prevent the Sora from rescuing prisoners was in disrepair. The bariks were "unsatisfactory," leaving officers "helpless." There was another category of people called police "informers," who were not Pano bariks but Sora headmen (so this must have been part of their supposed role?). Because of the way male names were often repeated (A son of B son of A), I could tell that these were the grandfathers of people I knew. One of them was a "very dangerous man" who withheld information in a murder case, while another was a "drunken and pigheaded fellow and in no way helpful to the police." Why indeed should a headman help the police, rather than just using them as a weapon against his personal enemies? In desperation at the mess, Gill staged a march of eighty men with 200 "coolies" to "show the flag." It was not recorded whether this made the bariks and headmen any more satisfactory or helpful. I needed much more time, and should have asked if I could take away the papers, for the next time I came that subinspector had been transferred, and his successor had burned everything.

The police were mostly of Paik and other Oriya Kshatriya castes, with mustaches and vermilion marks on their forehead from their morning worship of Hindu gods. The police station emanated intimidation and depression, all the grimmer for its magnetic effect on informers, peons, and other hangers-on. Its shadow fell more lightly on Ladde than on Rajingtal, since the constables in baggy khaki shorts and red-crested helmets rarely toiled up the mountain (though, just before I moved there, they had fined the village 600 rupees for distilling aba).

Fines and bribes were a gratuitous illegal "tax," imposed by government employees sent against their will to a "punishment posting" in this remote area "with no cinema." This was a highly structured exploitation. A school-master or medical compounder would make enough in two years to get married back in civilization. Among the police, the scale was larger, and one subinspector told me quite candidly the rates of bribes he demanded and how much he was obliged to pass upward in order to be left with 2,000 rupees a month for himself. These sums were staggering, since I calculated the legiti-mate annual land tax from a large village like Rajingtal to be only 500 rupees (for which the revenue officer charged 500–1,000 percent of what was writ-ten on the receipt), while the concession for charging five paise (cents) per head-load of produce entering the Yaltap market was sold to a Telugu Komati merchant for 1,200 rupees a year. Those higher up on short-term postings had to extort faster and harder than the lowly long-term constables, while the bariks monitored the wealth of every household in "their" village and advised when it was ready for milking. The grossest extortions of all were the roving foresters' random fines for cutting wood, since they had no local guidance on how much or how little their victims could afford.

Unnatural death cases topped the police Richter scale, for they brought the opportunity of a murder charge, with bribes of thousands. Some of those "leopards" in the 1930s may have been covering up for real murders by con-veniently removing the need to produce a body, but by the deforested 1970s there were few leopards left to carry the blame. Sometimes there were obvious murders, as when I was shown a dead woman sitting upright on the floor of a house with an unconvincing rope leading from her neck to the rafters. But another time in a genuine accident while I was still living in Rajingtal, a man was crushed by a rolling tree trunk. He was a landless outsider without kin, and had been doing shifting cultivation with a small lineage of impoverished young men. The dead man's state as a victim of Sun-Sonum was highly conta-gious, though in a different way from Leopard-Sonum, since it was his spilled, uncontained blood that was wandering around seeking further victims. The smell was already appalling. Ononti worried that I was becoming too involved with a dangerous sonum, but since nobody would take the initiative in cre-mating him, I myself rounded up a work party of Inama, Asongroi, and other friends from various lineages. Then in a somber banishing-rite, a pig was dragged along the ground out of the village to make a furrow for the bad blood to flow away. Every inhabitant washed from head to foot in the pig's blood mixed with special herbs, and also drank some. The dead man's possessions were destroyed, and even his salt-grinding stone smashed.

Pano spies were everywhere, so a police visit was unavoidable, and the young men asked for my support in facing them. However, the situation turned into a confrontation I had not expected. Inama stayed by my side, but some of the leading men of the headman lineage, my "brothers," turned up and in a loud shouting match accused the youths of murder. I joined in on the youths' side and used my English to work on the inspector, who finally agreed it was an accident and left. I later found out that he had taken 1,500 rupees behind my back with the barik's involvement, a sum equivalent to a dozen funeral buffalo. I was annoyed at being outmaneuvered by the policeman, but also shocked at the behavior of my friends. Apart from Inama, my relations with the other headmen became cool for a while. I had sided with strangers against my own brothers, and had not understood that the essence of morality was loyalty. I had to adjust my simplistic view of "Sora = good Outsider = bad," as I gradually discovered that some of the poor people around the village were my brothers' bonded laborers (kambari), who had lost their freedom for loans that were sometimes pathetically small. The youths falsely accused of this death had been forced to borrow the 1,500 rupees from the headmen and would now be trapped for generations. Loans as entrapment: no wonder Jogi's dupes had not understood the empowering potential of those loans from the State Bank.

The headmen of wealthy rice-villages like Rajingtal and Sogad had a small spark of the kingly imagery of the raja from whom their authority was ultimately derived. But it was the move to Ladde that made me appreciate the elemental force of the jungle. Despite the remittances from Assam, Ladde seemed closer to what Sora life must have been like before those politically sanctioned chieftainships were consolidated, when quarrels were pursued by axe rather than by police paperwork. I was observing two domains of power, which between them formed the ground of Sora existence: leopard power and police power, the jungle and the state. Leopards and armed policemen both featured prominently in shamans' wall-paintings. Each domain was dangerous and hard to negotiate with, but there was an important difference. The jungle was the domain of resources and production, whereas at this period before the development programs of the 1980s, the state gave almost nothing but only took. Police and other officials could be made amenable by turning them into ilda sonums. The sonums of the dead were as complex as social life itself; but they were kept under control by those same ildas, whose role was simpler, and more pointed. The ildas were caricatures of the state, and usefully adapted the ordinary police's main property of bullying and arresting by handcuffing those other sonums to bring them to dialogue.

At the time I was not interested in analyzing the political economy, just horrified at the exploitation while remaining determined to pursue ritual. It was only much later that I came to see these as two sides of the same coin. At that time my quest to understand Sora ritual seemed constantly frustrated. Dumburu's moments of friendliness were inconsistent. His sorcery admission was extraordinary, but I did not know what to do with these occasional moments of candor in the midst of our claustrophobic existence on the clifftop. Ononti too had been unable to explain things, but with Dumburu I sometimes felt that he was mocking me. He never called me "brother," as most other men did, but *gadi*, a rarely used word for an unrelated "friend," and he avoided physical contact except for a jab in the ribs during a joke. It all felt so different from the passionate embraces and shared sleeping bags of Inama's family. It had been foolish to hope that he would teach me explicitly, but his way of withholding information felt like a power game. I was not just a trophy, but also a prisoner.

January was the postharvest season for catching up on stone-plantings, before the big karja at the February–March full moon. Ladde was the only village that did not do the karja, and there were no stone-plantings due either. In despairing moments I felt I was back where I had been a year ago, but with my health severely weakened. It was time to move on. I could not go back to Ononti in Rajingtal, as that would be a return to an earlier form of frustration. I was invited to stone-plantings in other villages, and visited my contacts in Manengul and "Oops!" the wall-painter in Kumbulsing. Dumburu became used to my long absences. I left some supplies in Ladde, and he welcomed me and organized dances when I came to stay with him again, but I never returned there to live.

I was walking through the wide expanse of paddy fields below the large village of Sogad when I came across a huddle of women around a place where the Sogad stream ran through a deep cleft between the fields. In the moist shady undergrowth an old shamaness called Sinaki was sitting in front of an array of *laia* leaves, baskets of rice, and pots of alin. Beside her was an upturned pot with a model snake molded from rice-flour, and the long snake-like tail of a buffalo that was being butchered in the level fields overhead. This cure was for Ajora-sım, "Stream-Sonum," who was also connected with the Sun. Sinaki was smearing watery herbs and rhizomes onto a mother and baby to cool them, and singing a very long myth about a Sora girl who married a python. The girl's brothers were jealous, and challenged the python to carry out a series of human actions that are impossible with a snake's body, in order to prove that he was an unsuitable match for their sister. When she remained loyal to her husband, they treacherously chopped him up "into slices," *bartung-ertung*, and he went up to the Sun, where he became the python that is there to this day. Now the ancestors of every newly married woman resent when she starts to bear children for another lineage, and they attack her firstborn baby. To appease them she must perform this cure, but not in her husband's lineage where she now lives: she must go back and do it among the lineage of her birth, even if this is in a different village.

Sinaki specialized in this ritual, and this cool, python-welcoming stream was her regular spot. As she reached the comical episode where the brothers challenge the python to descend from a palm with a pot of alin crooked over his nonexistent elbow, she looked up at me and started giggling: *E Pirino, mangdating!* (E Pirino, you're making me laugh!) The men cutting up the buffalo plied me with alin and said, "Come and live with us in Sogad!"

3

WHAT THE LIVING AND THE DEAD
HAVE TO SAY TO EACH OTHER

Sogad, February–April 1977

On the morning of 14 February 1977, I watched several Sogad men with varied and beautiful faces squatting over the mortar inside the entrance of a house, singing a long list of ancestors' names in a slow, rhythmic monotone that I would later come to study down to the last syllable. They were facing the special materials for a child's naming ritual (adñimon): a heap of unhusked rice, five laia leaves with splashes of alin, a clump of riadi grass, an iron plow tip, and branches of kumbali thorn. Under the shady thatch of the surrounding houses women were stitching leaves into cups with bamboo splinters, with a murmur of conversation and laughter.

Three years earlier a newborn baby girl had fallen ill. This was diagnosed as the work of her ancestor Indiri, who wanted to resprout by passing on her name. A brass finger-ring had been tied to the baby's wrist and a buffalo promised to Indiri if she helped the baby to survive till she was weaned. Today, some three years later, the ring would be removed, the buffalo sacrificed, and the toddler confirmed as the next Indiri. In a darkened corner of the house sat Rijanti, the ancient funeral shaman of Sogad, chewing her cud and awaiting her moment. She was frail and completely blind, but her power was revealed when she stretched out her legs across the mortar and began her invocation in a faint, quavery voice. Young men straightened offerings, and women drew closer, ready to talk to the succession of ancestors who would speak through Rijanti's mouth to discuss the baby and demand a swig of alin. They chivied each ancestor ("Hurry up, it's nearly evening!"), until old Indiri herself arrived. She stayed for half an hour while a magnificent brass axe was put in the shaman's hand, fine homespun skirts were piled on her outstretched legs, and the child was given to her to inspect. By now I could follow the less difficult conversations:

"Mind you look after her," the child's mother urged the old Indiri.

"Of course, she's my namesake!" replied the ancestor. "And they say she looks like me." (Iten do, añimmar ñen. Do mungka ñen padle gamteji.)

"Then why did she get ill again recently?"

"That's not my fault, that was another lot, I didn't see them coming . . ."

The house became rowdy as relatives piled in, and a gourd full of alin circulated from hand to hand, constantly refilled from a bottomless pot. Outside, the buffalo was danced round the village, then tethered outside the house while the child's mother washed its head, forelegs, spine, and udders with turmeric water. Little Indiri was placed on the buffalo's back to emphasize an identification between them, then helped to walk up the plow tip and into the house. At the far end a large fire flickered over the red mud walls, with women squatting as they moved under the low rafters to fetch supplies, and men bending in the glow to prepare materials. In Dumburu's lonely clifftop hut I had been starved of such sensuous animal crowding. This was like the old days in Rajingtal, but with a greatly increased grasp of the language. People addressed remarks to me the same way they talked to each other. I even stopped taking notes as I basked in a new, fuller feeling of participation and acceptance.

The slow, careful chant always began with the long drawn-out syllable "No-o-o . . ." It was repeated when the buffalo's blood was sprinkled into leaf-cups for the "raw ritual" (ameng-pɪr), and again with the offering of meat for the "cooked ritual" (asin-pɪr), and several other times. These singers were the ancestor-men of Sogad, and they would become my breakthrough, my colleagues, and some of the most important friends of my life. Most of them have now died, but even without the help of a tape recorder, every one of those voices is still with me today, and their many moments of humor: Dangdang, the great mythologist, with an aquiline profile like a Roman emperor on a coin; Pasano, who was liked despite having an involuntary sorcery power that he could not control; Mejeru, lanky, with a cauliflower nose, a tease and a joker in his tattered loincloth, too poor to wear any gold at all; the affectionate and equally impoverished Aro; and Mengalu, the greatest performer of them all, with upturned Southeast Asian eyes, a mischievous impish expression, and an animated, indignant voice. Ancestor-men impersonated the ancestors of their own lineage; there were also ancestor-women, who performed for the dead of the lineage into which they were born and so were usually unmarried girls or widows who had returned home from elsewhere. Men dressed up as women tried to pull off each other's skirts, and I was goaded into a turmeric-splashing fight with Mengalu. "Everyone likes talking to you," he told me. "They say, 'He's a good man.'" What more could I want? But Mengalu was a complicated person who attracted sorcery accusations, and my loyalty would later be severely tested.

Figure 3.1 Portrait of Mengalu

This ritual was not about illness or death, and apart from the careful No-o-o chant, the mood was light and joyful. At night the ancestor-men formed two groups, singing long speeches at each other, with pauses for jokes that were sometimes obscene ("Has he got an erection, *padingte po*?" "Did you sleep with my mother, *yang ñen tule po*?") and sometimes satirized the accents and mannerisms of other villages, including Rajingtal. I recognized the motif of break-

Figure 3.2
Turmeric fight at
a baby's naming,
Sogad 1977

ing through the barricaded door of the house that I had seen in Ononti's *karja*,
but now I could see that this represented the return of old Indiri to the realm
of the living as she gave her name to the new child. So rituals that banished
(*amdung*) *sonums* out of the house were balanced by rituals that inducted them
back in (*amgan*). Meanwhile the branches of *kumbali* thorn were placed around
the boundary of the house to keep out other, undesirable *sonums* who were
not invited.

 The climax of the night came when the ancestor-men danced the abduction
of a bride. I can still see a magical image of Mengalu, axe on shoulder and
tiny oil lamp in hand, being led by two other ancestor-men, all swaying to the
beat and treading carefully between the seated crowd who packed the floor.
Mengalu scanned long and hard from side to side, looking for a woman. To
squeals of laughter he picked on a girl, hauled her to her feet, and ran off
with her.

 Two young men called Sundanto and Doddo, the main oboists in the orchestra, adopted me between bouts of playing. Sundanto became one of my
best explainers, but even so I did not understand when he said that this was a
new marriage of the dead woman in the Underworld.

 There was another naming three nights later for a little boy in the house
of Pasano, himself one of the ancestor-men. As the orchestra stuck up the
abduction beat Aro suddenly grabbed my hand, pulled me to my feet, and gave
me the lamp. With a thrill I realized it was my turn. Both of us bent double
under the loft; we loomed over the squatting women. I did my best to imitate
Mengalu and finally picked a girl, who giggled as we ran off to whoops of
laughter all round. I was sure that we were acting out the future marriage of
the new baby, but again Sundanto insisted that I had been impersonating his
deceased namesake. I could not make sense of this, so put it out of my mind
in the face of a bigger, very exciting realization. The old shaman Rijanti was

central, as Ononti had been in Rajingtal, but ancestor-men seemed far more prominent here. This was not just because Rijanti was frail, as in fact were several of the other shamans in Sogad. The elaboration of their performance seemed institutionalized. Here at last was a male role that might have room for me.

If the small hilltop village of Ladde was ritually minimalist, Sogad with its population of 800 was gloriously maximalist, even more than Rajingtal: more specialists, more cures, more songs, more myths, more pantomimes, more blood. Ononti's unworldly reticence and Dumburu's dark evasiveness both seemed far away. True, it was in Sogad that I had a dream of following an ılda sonum who stood in the doorway one night with a lamp and beckoned me, till I woke and found I had sleepwalked into a field under the cold moonlight. But mostly I realized that my early fantasies of apprenticing myself to a shaman were foolish. Other opportunities were appearing. In Sogad, the Sora cosmos suddenly became more complex, but it was this baroque efflorescence of ritual that would ultimately reveal the patterns and meanings that had been eluding me. Every day, and many nights, I would be summoned to witness a ritual, and was dazzled by more than a hundred kinds of sonum. There were the same events as in Rajingtal, such as the rituals for Duri-sım (Lumbago-Sonum) and Rattud-Sonum, both of them banishing-rites held on a path leading out of the village. But there were also strange esoteric sonums, such as Su-yung-tar (Painful-Sun-Vein), A-budbud-sım (Maggot-Sonum), A-lud-sing-boj (Dark-House-Woman), Badbad-kanti-boj (Woman Bricked Up in a Wall), Kındal-kan (Basket-Weaver's Epilepsy), Langgi-boj-sım (Lovely-Woman-Sonum, who seduces young men), and Kansid-ıl (a sonum that turns you into a Kond). I was the only person who stayed with Mejeru all night as he led Strangled-Peacock-in-a-Noose Cough (Udeng-mar-ku) out of a patient's house and into a field, where he killed a black cock and squatted in the moonlight singing a repetitive myth that lasted until dawn and exhausted my tape recorder.

As in Ladde, there were numerous rituals for infertile women or their fragile babies. The repertoire was even wider and included chants and amulets against Moon-Eclipse-Sonum (Mo-gaj-sım), Premature-Bud-Drop-Sonum (Ural-ba-sım), Adenung-ki (Shove-Out, i.e., miscarriage), and Sindinar-jo (Date-Fruit-Smear).

In Rajingtal I had already worked out the distinction between shamans who did funerals and those who did healing, and this distinction held up well in Sogad. The word for funeral shamans, s-an-atung, meant that they would satung (faint to the point of death) when they tranced. These, the most serious kind of shaman, were usually women, and their tradition was founded by a primal shaman called Kurutij Sompa (Pubic-Haired Sompa or Hairy-Vagina Sompa). In Sogad, the main sanatung shaman was old Rijanti, but there were also Sindai and another blind old woman called Kuttumi, as well as Uda, a middle-aged man in the hamlet of Guddara, an offshoot of Sogad across the paddy fields. I knew that sanatung shamans performed the funeral sequence of inquest, stone-planting, and karja, but it was not until I saw Rijanti performing the naming of a child that I made the obvious connection that the naming of a new namesake was also the final stage in the funeral of the previous namesake. The series of rites was not just a sequence but also a cycle, and this was the beginning of my realization that the entire cosmology was governed by a cyclical principle of repetition.

The naming and the stone-planting were landmarks, grand rites of passage at the beginning and end of each person's life. But most daily ritual activity concerned the period in between birth and death, as a person was assailed by a series of illnesses. This was the domain of the other kind of shaman, each with their own repertoire of skills, who performed cures, with or without trance. Thus Mejeru was a nontrancing shaman as well as an ancestor-man, and could deal with Strangled-Peacock-in-a-Noose Cough because it required the recitation of a myth, rather than dialogue.

Every ritual moved from the summoning of sonums to their arrival to their exhortation (and a negotiation if there was trance) to their feeding with raw blood and then cooked meat to their dismissal. Whatever took place between their arrival and dismissal was an attempt at manipulating them to change their disposition, and a result was supposed to follow shortly after. Yet while some parts of the process were automatic, negotiation introduced a much deeper dimension. I did not yet realize how thoroughly the dialogues between living and dead lay at the heart of Sora religion. Instead I became obsessed with making sense of all the categories of sonum, and tried classifying them according to various criteria:

The animal sacrificed (buffalo, goat, pig, chicken, rarely cow).
Their signature tunes, which were all melodic and rhythmic
    rearrangements of the same five-note scale, like Wagnerian leitmotifs.
The semiotics of their offerings (seven laia leaves for funerals, two
    banana leaves for Rattud, five for sorcery—but sometimes two, or was
    it four, and why did the species vary?).
The presence or absence of trance (surely this must be a fundamental
    distinction?).

The purpose of the ritual: Nonfuneral shamans had their own repertoires of divinations to find the cause of illness, cures to put it right, and blocking rituals to prevent the spread of particularly contagious sonums after a death by accident, suicide, epilepsy, or leopard. There were preventive rituals to forestall an attack or ward off sorcery, and seasonal rituals to offer the first fruits of a crop to a shaman's ıldas or her client's ancestors.

The location: There seemed to be a fundamental distinction between sonums that were kept inside the house and those that were led out along a path and dismissed beyond the village. Even this seemed to be about different occasions rather than different sonums, since the same ancestors might be fed by the hearth at one moment and driven out at another.

Each of my classifications matched some criteria but not others. My friends gave me details about leaves and tunes, and recited verses containing specific imagery. Yet my classifications did not make sense to them. I needed to look harder at how all those sonums actually related to people and their situations.

Looking back, I see that I was asking some of the right questions, but looking for answers in the wrong places. I was still thinking in terms of the English word *spirit*, rather than staying with the word *sonum* and seeing how it behaved. I was preoccupied with working out the songs and colorful symbolism of entities like Sun-Sonum, rather than with the words actually spoken in dialogues, which I wrongly considered less interesting. I had correctly grasped the distinction between funeral shamans and healing shamans, and also the important distinction between rituals to lead sonums into the house and to lead them out beyond the village. But I concluded from this that funeral shamans dealt with ancestors, while healing shamans dealt with sonums of the jungle. It would be a long time before I realized that the landscape was a map, not of domestic human space versus wild sonum space, but of a quite different distinction that was not between kinds of sonums, but between *ways of relating* to them.

I arrived at this notion of relating only gradually, after many false turns. However many divinations and cures I attended, it was often hard to understand why a particular illness was thought to have attacked a particular person. Some connections were obvious (someone close to you was killed by a certain illness, and now they attack you with the same symptoms), but others seemed far-fetched. How were they arrived at, and how did they come to feel convincing?

As part of compiling genealogies, I inquired about causes of death, and was surprised to discover that behind all the circumstantial details, those causes actually came down to a very small number of overarching categories. Moreover, these categories were not simply causes, but also groups of dead people. They were located in sites across the landscape that contained people who had previously died from similar symptoms, and who now resided there. Using these sites as an attack base, the residents might transmit their symptoms to a living person and draw that person in to join them. Thus there were numerous Rattud sites on paths across the landscape, and anyone walking past one of these sites might be seized by the Rattud-people residing there and come home with a rapid onset of illness. This had happened to me in Ladde, when I walked past a site of a Rattud-Sonum inhabited by members of my old village of Rajingtal. People killed by leopards resided in one of the various rocks called Leopard-House, from which they sent actual leopards to attack new victims; people who died through accident, murder, or suicide resided in the Sun, from where they might precipitate another similar event; those with skin lesions or convulsions went to sites of Leprosy-Sonum or Epilepsy-Sonum, respectively, and those with coughs, rashes, or epidemic diseases to Smallpox-Woman. There were also Earth-Sonums, which were located in cool, watery places such as springs. Where Sun-Sonum involved uncontainment, the messy rupturing of boundaries, and the loneliness of its victims, Earth-Sonums asserted cleanness, wholeness, and the integrity of boundaries. It was forbidden to urinate or defecate by an Earth-Sonum site, and this kind of sonum was responsible for illnesses and deaths with symptoms of swelling and blockage, such as constipation and death in childbirth; Sundanto too knew that he was at risk, since it could also take oboists because of their puffed cheeks. This symbolism extended from the body to the group: an Earth-Sonum site also served as a gathering point to bring together lineage ancestors who cultivated land near the spring.

These sonums represented a total Sora catalogue of human mortality, in which medical "illnesses" featured equally with other kinds of fatal event. It seemed there could be no other ways of dying. They were located around the landscape, so one could not avoid coming into contact with them. They seemed different from ancestor-sonums, who are known, named persons, so I called them Experience sonums, after the particular experience of death that they represented and perpetuated. Now I began to understand those other attacking sonums with highly specific names. Though some remained forever obscure, I could see, for example, that Ural-ba-sım (Premature-Bud-Drop-Sonum) and Adenung-ki (Shove-Out) were idioms through which Sun-

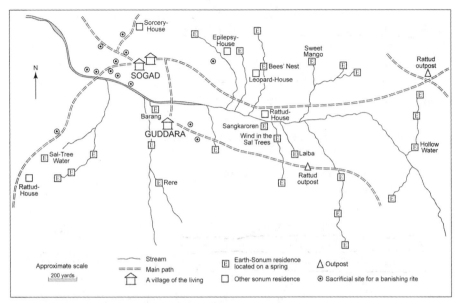

Map 3.1 Main sonum sites around Sogad and Guddara

Residences contain people who have died with matching symptoms. Rattud outposts attack travelers on paths. Banishing-rites direct the attacking sonums out of the village back toward their residence.

Sonum caused miscarriages, while Strangled-Peacock-in-a-Noose Cough, like Ranggi-sım (Wind-Sonum) and Siñol-sım (Rash-Sonum) was one of Smallpox-Woman's modes of attack. These were narrowly defined, split-off aspects of the more generic Experience sonum—sub-Experiences so to speak. I could even see some continuities in the symbolism of leaves, tunes, and other props. Most attacks were warded off with a cure, but if an attack led to death, the victim would end up residing respectively in the Sun or with Smallpox-Woman.

What about susceptibility? Most of the time one walked past these places and nothing happened, so why was one sometimes attacked? When I listed all the speakers in a trance, I realized that an Experience sonum like Rattud or Leopard did not speak in its own right, but only through its members, who were people one knew. Every divination was also a dialogue, which reached a diagnosis by constructing a story together. If the cure involved a further dialogue, the story was developed further. There were no illnesses or deaths without dead persons to cause them, but the attacking persons needed a connection and a motive. So the patient in Dumburu's cure who begrudged a drink of alin to his ancestors (pages 56–57) was made ill because those ancestors had a claim on him that he failed to honor. Another man suffered from a gurgling stomach with itching and clawing sensations, which was diagnosed as Rumbling-Tummy-Sonum (Kurkur-pung-sım). His father had been killed by a leopard and was now a member of the local Leopard-Sonum, and Rumbling-Tummy-Sonum was one of Leopard-Sonum's sub-Experiences. Through symptoms of a growling tummy the father was demanding a pig sacrifice from his son. In itself this sub-Experience is not fatal, but if not dealt with it could escalate into a physical leopard attack.

So ultimately the entire sequence of symptom, pain, divination, negotiation, and cure was an exploration and adjustment of relationships, feelings, and claims. Somehow both ancestors and Experience sonums were involved. The Experiences explained the symptoms, but the motivation for episodes of sickness was provided by attachment between persons, and these attachments could even become a sickness unto death. I do not know which came first, this realization or my increased attention to what was actually said in dialogue, but I began to see that an ancestor might equally express anger with the patient ("You didn't do this or that right") or love ("I miss you and want you to come and join me"). Also, it was not always clear who was feeling this attachment more intensely, the sonum or the patient. The living experienced it as sickness while the dead explained it as motive, often in the form of a reminder or claim: "Don't forget me!" The response might be indignant or evasive, but the claim could not be denied. Ancestors generally attacked their own lineage, and were not entitled to attack their in-laws ("Why should we feed you, you're not one of ours—aren't you ashamed?"). So while a ritual (pırpır) of what we might call healing did aim to cure a patient, it was equally a ritual of acknowledgment.

In any system of healing, patients must tolerate a certain rate of failure. People occasionally talked of incompetent or fraudulent shamans, and there was one enterprising male shaman who had seduced a pretty widow by saying in her husband's persona, "I want to sleep with you again, but now the only way I can do so is through this shaman's body" (a funny story to repeat at drinking circles). But more often it was the sonums who deceived in order to get a free feed they were not entitled to, or else patients said simply that it had not worked—this time. I came to see that moments of illness and their subsequent acts of acknowledgment were not separate cases, like files to be closed, but rather episodes in your ongoing existence, so that your medical history was also an active record of your social relationships.

My own violently fluctuating health was included in this reasoning, as when the Rattud-Sonum from Rajingtal claimed responsibility for my hepatitis in Ladde. Despite the pig I gave them, those Rattud-people might always resent my move away, so this would always remain a plausible diagnosis; and indeed the event did make me think more about Ononti and Soimani, my closest women friends in Rajingtal whose dead fathers had taken the lead in making me ill. In Sogad, I fell ill with fever and a rash after chasing a wild peacock for miles in the midday heat in the territory of a distant village. The peacock context easily linked the rash to Smallpox-Woman, and it turned out she had seen me running across the mountains and had sexually assaulted me. The way I understood this was that the cause had to be a sonum, but I could not easily be made ill by the ancestors of a village where I had no relationships. Smallpox-Woman was an alien sonum whose attacks were not always based on kinship, so it all fitted. Similarly, I was believed to be immune to sorcery and was sometimes asked for my secret medicine (which did not exist). Unlike my friends, I credited my apparent immunity to the fact that I was not involved in disputes over property or women, since those were exactly the domains where sorcery was exercised.

Sorcery, too, had to work within this total causal framework. On that night of laughter and acceptance when I was dancing the abduction of a girl, we also heard an ominous death-beat from a nearby veranda, so our joyful buffalo was not danced in that direction. A little boy called Mando, the child of Mengalu's sister, had died. There was already a disturbing rumor that the death had been precipitated by Mengalu's sorcery.

As was normal the body had been cremated immediately, and I went to the inquest the following morning. Rijanti was sitting on the mortar inside the doorway, sightless and toothless but still in absolute control. The women, packed into the small house, maintained a grim silence while she spent more than an hour working her way through numerous possible causes, with the child's teenage sister howling a lament on the veranda outside. Latecomers stepped gingerly over the rice grains, which Rijanti had flung from a knife tip into the open doorway as sonum-bait. With Ononti I had merely watched an inquest; now I could understand it. As Rijanti named each possible culprit she sandwiched two grains of rice between a pair of bael-tree leaves (*kulpada; Aegle marmelos*) and jerked them up and down in the flame of her lamp. This was a preliminary test before the trance. Snuffling and coughing, her blind eyes watering, she intoned some magical syllables in a special voice, "Peacock-Feather-Bundle-Sonum (Galbed-sim) *jado ate sedu?*" followed by a song about that sonum's attributes. Leopard-Sonum (Kına-sım) *jado ate sedu?* Earth-Sonum? Epilepsy-Sonum? Smallpox-Sonum? Rattud-Sonum? The woman who was bricked up in a wall? She moved on from Experience sonums to individual ancestors: this one, that one . . . ?

The lamp and the leaves did not react to any of Rijanti's questions. We were all pouring sweat, not just from heat but from tension.

"Ask about sorcery," the women kept muttering. Rijanti started naming notorious sorcerers in Sogad.

"Jibono's sorcery *jado ate sedu?*" Nothing happened. "Kondo's sorcery *jado ate sedu?*" Again nothing. "Mengalu's sorcery *jado ate sedu?*" The lamp suddenly flared up, and Rijanti peeled the two leaves apart. The two grains of rice had separated and stuck to different leaves.

This was a very strong pointer, and the grim women seemed vindicated. Further details would be revealed in the trance. Rijanti stretched out her legs, began her invocation, and quickly slipped away to the Underworld. Various ancestors turned up, but through the babbling that greeted them ("We sacrificed a goat for you, why did you do this to our child?"), they all denied responsibility ("It wasn't me, I don't know, why don't you ask so-and-so . . ."). Gradually they started to focus on the boy's older brother Sagalo, who had meanwhile somehow appeared in a corner of the house: "He slept with her . . . they had sex . . ." After a further hour of dialogue it emerged that Sagalo had seduced the girlfriend of Mengalu's son. In revenge, Mengalu had tried to kill him with sorcery: "bad magic . . . angry . . . he trussed up a black chicken and buried it . . . the randy dog . . . they did it several times . . ." However, Sagalo's soul was too strong, and the sorcery had ricocheted off him and killed his delicate little brother instead. I was sitting with Aro, and when little Mando himself appeared and whispered "Mother?" we too were in tears, like the women who showed the dead child his tiny shorts and shirt (the dead crave material attachment). They fed him through Rijanti's mouth with water, not alin, as he was still hot from the pyre. His sister redoubled her shrieking, while his brother Sagalo sat silent and rigid with remorse.

Mengalu was paying a terrible price for an act of greed some years earlier. He shared the same grandfather with the Monosi I had met in the mission bungalow. Mengalu's branch had many more male descendants, so their shares in that grandfather's land were getting smaller than the shares in Monosi's branch. Inheritance disputes were the commonest motive for sorcery, and they involved close brothers who should enjoy the most intimate cooperation. If Monosi's branch died out, then their property would revert to Mengalu. He gathered their discarded toothbrushing sticks, excrement, and soil from their footprints, and buried them in a pot along with the remains of a tortured black chicken trussed up in thread. Monosi somehow found out

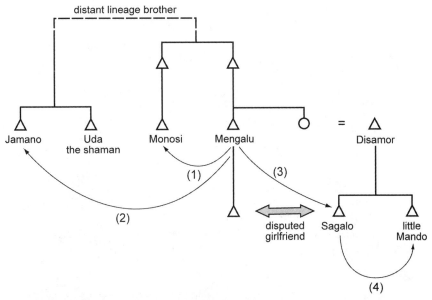

Diagram 3.1 Some sorcery accusations against Mengalu

(1) Quarrel over inherited land, Monosi exposes the sorcery and survives, will later be reconciled (page 147). (2) Quarrel over land, sorcery contributes to Jamano's death (pages 105, 107). (3) Quarrel between Mengalu's son and Sagalo over girlfriend. (4) Sagalo's soul is too strong, so sorcery bounces off and kills his little brother Mando.

about it and forced Mengalu to dig up the pot in a very public display. Since then, Mengalu has been a favorite suspect in one death after another. I never spoke about this to Mengalu, but he knew that I knew, and I think he was grateful that I remained his friend.

Of all your situations of unhealth, one will prove fatal. You will then be locked into a specific form of death, and become its agent against others. This Experience sonum will become a defining feature of your identity, more so than any other episode of claim and acknowledgment in your entire life. The inquest is thus an opportunity, perhaps a requirement, for a thorough review of your most important or controversial relationships. Two years later I witnessed another sadness in Sagalo's life. He was a landless youth and had made a love marriage (dari) with a girl called Panderi, very much against the wishes of her prosperous lineage. By May 1979 they had a one-year-old baby whom they had promised to name after Sagalo's deceased father, Disamor.

One afternoon Panderi returned home carrying the baby and feeling unwell. She died that same night. After the pyre had subsided the next morning, in the

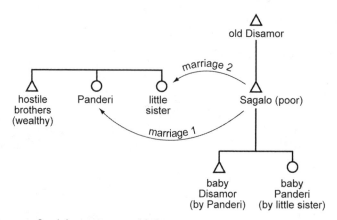

Diagram 3.2 Sagalo's marriages and babies
The dead Panderi encouraged Sagalo's second marriage and gave her name to the new baby, as an expression of love.

same house as before, I watched Rijanti go through the same procedure with pairs of rice grains inside pairs of bael leaves. "Our daughter-in-law, our child, our sister," she intoned between the names of Sagalo's male lineage ancestors, "was it the Sun, was it the Moon *jado ate sedu*, was it the Wind, was it . . . ?" This time there was no talk of sorcery, but a deeper probing of ancestors.

To Sagalo's people his wife's sudden collapse after a long journey was an obvious sign of Rattud-Sonum. Against this interpretation her brothers' family sent their womenfolk to eavesdrop on the veranda outside, and they were muttering about possible domestic quarrels; how could she have died so suddenly unless her husband had beaten her? And most unreasonably, since this was a cultural necessity: what did he have to hide that he had cremated her immediately? This inquest, too, was heartrending, as Panderi explained that she had been killed by a Rattud-Sonum associated with her brothers' lineage. The real target of the attack was her baby boy, who was now curled up asleep in a sling on the hip of a woman nearby. Panderi had been so devoted to her husband and child that she bent over the baby to shield him, and so the Rattud-Sonum's onslaught killed her instead (more on page 117).

The child's existence defied Panderi's brothers by confirming the validity of her marriage. Here was a situation of social conflict laid bare: what was everyone going to do about it? The brothers had already raided Sagalo's house and snatched back her personal belongings—a cruel gesture implying that the baby would not survive to inherit them. They also took home some of her ashes and her soul, but this would not be simply the usual duplicate stone-planting. They hoped that their rival inquest through a shaman from their own village would yield a conflicting verdict. However, sonums do not always say what we want them to say, and even in the setting of her brothers' house, the dead woman confirmed her story. To her brothers' fury, she also advised her younger sister to marry Sagalo in her stead (a common pattern for a second wife) and bring up the baby. All of this must have been a comfort to Sagalo. But meanwhile his baby son seemed unlikely to survive long enough anyway, since the Sora had no tradition of wet-nursing. I took no notes at that frantic time and do not remember how it happened, but somehow we got baby Disamor to a Catholic nuns' orphanage on the coast. He did survive on town milk, and Panderi's sister did indeed marry Sagalo.

This case shows that dialogues with the dead are simultaneously religion, psychotherapy, and law. In all these domains, even with rival rituals, dialogue must eventually lead to a consensus—for the moment. But then lineages will evolve, property will be divided, combined, and inherited afresh, and new conflicts will arise to be discussed with a new generation of sonums. Specifically, Panderi's sister came to Sagalo's house and renewed the cross-cousin link that her brothers had hoped to cancel; so if her brothers later died without a male heir, Sagalo's descendants could make a plausible claim on their fields, against more distant members of her brothers' own lineage. This conflict, too, if it ever happened, would be aired and resolved through the mouths of funeral shamans.

By February 1977, the harvest had been threshed and stored, the money-lenders had taken their monstrous share, and there was a rush to complete any unfinished stone-plantings for those who had died over the previous months. During this "month of blood," people were preparing for the karja, and I shared their excitement for my own reasons. The karja was the copestone of the entire funeral system. The previous year in Rajingtal I had seen Ononti and Maianti trancing in the darkened house and had stayed blearily awake through the three days and nights of dancing, and this year I had already caught sight of dancers in other villages, but I still had little idea of the whole. Now in Sogad I would work out what it all meant by studying the structure of the ritual from start to finish.

On Sunday evening, 27 February 1977, Mengalu led a row of ancestor-men in that year's "main house" (*muda-sing*) as they chanted over the mortar in the firelight, facing eighteen baskets of unhusked rice, each topped with a brass finger-ring. These were from the eighteen houses that had lost someone over the past three years. Mengalu was waving a tiny pot of last year's specially saved aba spirit up and down in time to the chant, and splashing it over a row

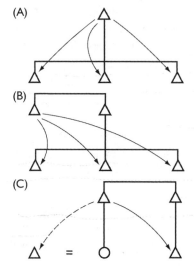

(A)

(B)

(C)

Diagram 3.3 Inheritance of a man's property, especially land
(A) Normally shared equally between his sons. (B) Where he has no sons, shared by the nearest males in his lineage. (C) His daughter's husband's people (marongger cousins) also participate in his funeral. If he dies without sons, they may use this participation to make a claim against his nearest patrilineal male relatives.

of eighteen leaf-plates sprinkled with rice grains. This house would stand for all the bereaved houses, and most of the activity would take place here. This was the same slow, careful, and very long monotone beginning with a long drawn-out "No-o-o . . ." that I had heard at stone-plantings and in the baby's naming two weeks earlier. The karja was for all the dead of the village combined, but each group of ancestor-men was chanting the names of their own lineage separately.

This was the rope-tying (jilud), a promise to those ancestors of what was to follow a few days later. Mengalu tied all the rings onto a string of sunsuni bark, then knotted the string eighteen times. Large pots of alin were poured, divided, shared, mixed, and drunk, to animated discussions of who would contribute what. The festival season demanded every drop that the landscape could pump up to the summit of the palm trunks. It was getting hotter, and some palms were already drying out from the sorcery of jealous men whose own trees had stopped yielding. The next day Aro took me to heal a tree high on a clifftop above Sogad. This tree was a victim not of sorcery, but of a different attack. The sap had been turned sour by a sonum called Leaf-Harvesting-Woman (Wab-ba-bojen), who climbs alin palms to steal the juice. Aro sacrificed fish and crabs from a stream and sang the myth of how she had once fallen from a tree while gathering edible leaves. As he banged the trunk with a stone to stimulate the flow of fluid, we heard the hills all around resounding with similar knocking.

I joined several ancestor-men at a drinking site, where Sundanto demonstrated melodies for me on his oboe: the Leopard tune, the hard-driven Sun tune for a suicide, the sad cremation tune when no one dances. The eighteen houses partly overlapped, as they were commemorating sixteen dead people. As the gourd of alin circulated, I began to collect the names of those giving buffalo, and their stories:

LOWER VILLAGE LINEAGE

Donuro, for his dead father Ilesu. This was the main house for this year's karja. Ilesu had been killed by the sorcery of a man called Jogoto who envied his wealth and conspired with Ilesu's ancestors in an Earth-Sonum to kill him.

Jumesia, for his son Eru, who was killed in a landslide while working as a laborer on the Chinese frontier. Like all accident victims, he was taken by Sun-Sonum.

Ganjillan, for his adolescent daughter Sabeni, who was taken with acute diarrhea by Ranggisim (Wind-Sonum), an aspect of Smallpox-Woman.

Puturu, for his elderly aunt (mother's sister, *awang*), who was taken by Earth-Sonum.

Sundayu, for his father Gunia, who was killed by the sorcery of the same Jogoto because he coveted his wife.

Pinaga, commemorating the same Gunia, who was his uncle (*dadi*, "father's younger brother"), offering a buffalo so that he could inherit some of his land.

Dandino, for his little daughter Jurbeni, who was taken by Rattud-Sonum.

HEADMAN LINEAGE, MAIN BRANCH

Sanggan, for his elderly father Jonia, taken by Earth-Sonum.

Guda, for the same Jonia, who was his uncle (*dadi*), to inherit some of his land.

Limodor, for his young son Guma, like all suicides taken by Sun-Sonum. One of the first local children to go away to school, he was miserable there and hanged himself.

Tabaro, for his adult son Rumbana, who also hanged himself and so was also taken by Sun-Sonum, after other Sora laborers in Assam entrusted him with money to bring home, and he somehow spent or lost it.

HEADMAN LINEAGE, GUDDARA OFFSHOOT
Sunamo, for his adult son Omino, taken by Rattud-Sonum.
Doneng, for his father Sundo, taken by Earth-Sonum.
Simpanto, for his young son Kandia, taken by Rattud-Sonum.
Kumbaijen, for his elder brother Sania, taken in middle age by Earth-Sonum.

BUYA LINEAGE
Sagalo was not yet able to commemorate his little brother Mando, who had died only a few days earlier, but there were two more bereaved houses in this small lineage. They were the following:
Ratoban, for his brother Palda, taken by Sun-Sonum when he hanged himself out of shame after sleeping with a prohibited cousin (his mother's sister's daughter, *mar-onsel*).
Ortino, for his young daughter Ipanti, taken by Rattud-Sonum.

OTHERS
Danasi, for his little daughter. This was a stray household with no other kin, and my friends did not know the cause.

I already understood that these causes of death were not random, and that individual stories were vital. Though the sample was small, I also looked for patterns in understanding the victims' susceptibility. I could not discern a pattern for gender, but there was certainly something about age. Rattud-Sonum attacked travelers on the path, who in this case were all young adults, and Wind-Sonum usually blew away children. Sun-Sonum by definition took victims of sudden violent death. The inclusion of a child was unusual, but the other three Sun victims were active young adults, at an age when they could well get into a situation of rockfall, illicit sex, or migrant money problems. There had been no victims of Epilepsy-Sonum (Kani-sɪm), and it was said that Sogad people were never "leoparded" (kɪnale), since they were protected by a special kittung in a big rock above the village. From these cases I also learned more about Earth-Sonum. It could cause symptoms of swelling or blockage at any age, but this list showed something that I later confirmed from my genealogies, that Earth-Sonum also took old people who had died gradually without dramatic symptoms, and I came to understand this as a way of talking about a full or completed life.

For several days people trekked downhill to markets to gather new cloths and pots or to negotiate for buffalo. On Thursday night Mengalu ceremonially cut the rope holding the eighteen rings, which would feature constantly in the days to come, and everyone danced long into the night.

On Friday Sundanto took me up a high mountain to hunt a peacock as a gift to little Guma, the schoolboy who had committed suicide. An animal for sacrifice had to be killed without spilling its blood, so that its soul could be directed to the intended sonum instead of going up "like smoke" to the Sun. This was easy with a domestic animal, but difficult for a wild one. Sundanto was skilled at chasing a peacock to exhaustion and killing it with a special club. Peacocks do not fly well, but just as we thought we had driven one to a summit with no escape it flapped ponderously to the top of another mountain. Our failure was embarrassing, since the Guddara people had caught their own peacock and were dancing it conspicuously on a pole around the fields below.

Karja Day 1, Saturday, 5 March 1977 (Full Moon)

Women from each of the eighteen "contributing houses" (tɪpna-siŋ) brought two large cooking pots, for rice and meat, swathed in new white or red cloths, along with small baskets of rice and quivers with dummy arrows (uded) to a spot outside the village. The pots from the main house were topped with Rijanti's precious lamp. The ancestor-men and ancestor-women then carried everything in a slow "sad" procession back into the village, with drums and oboes but no dancing, and laid the objects in a row outside the main house. This was the first of several symbolic entries by the dead into the domestic space of the village.

Ancestor-men sat in groups around pots of alin, each group chanting their own lineage's No-o-o song again. Mengalu rushed around, instructing everyone and organizing each household's contributions in his energetic upward-inflected voice, and counting everything carefully at every stage. Ancestor-women took a little rice from each of eighteen baskets and pounded it for a long time into a very fine flour, which they mixed with water and cooked into a gooey dough. They cut this into eighteen lumps that they sent back to each house to be eaten there, though not even Mengalu or Sundanto could explain the meaning of this. The orchestra continued unabated, but there was no dancing because it was still the "sad" first evening, though there was already a carnival air of joking. The ancestor-women lay down in a row to take a nap before the long night ahead, while the men repaired the bows. "Don't go tonight," Mejeru teased me. "The young ancestor-women will shoot at your penis!" There was a long pause while the men sat around another huge pot of alin. Some women nearby were discussing a visit to the dispensary in Puttasing, and asked me, "Can you give injections?" Mejeru told me how to reply: "Say 'I inject myself into young girls!'"

FIRST, OPENING TRANCE

In the slanting sun of early evening, while most men were still drinking up in the forest, I joined a small procession of women going to the cremation-ground of the Lower Village. Two teenage ancestor-women guided the old blind shamanesses Rijanti and Kuttumi down the steep drops of the terraced paddy fields. They were going to raise the dead. Little Guma's mother followed, lamenting fluently over the long evening shadows that lay across the silent fields. We cleared the cremation-ground of debris and helped the shamans down onto an old and tatty bamboo mat. They were joined by an apprentice, a young man called Dosinto, who sat between his teachers (fig. 1.7, p. 24). Stretching out their legs, the old women poured alcohol into leaves, muttered spells, and placed a laia-leaf parcel of rice grains between the first and second toes of each foot. Dosinto took the weight of the sword as they all three held it, eyes closed, and crashed it rhythmically into the ground.

The old ladies sang their invocation in unison, with Dosinto joining in hesitantly, and entered trance simultaneously. They were immediately confronted by a fierce Kond tribesman who blocked their path with his axe. Singing "Don't block me don't block me, Kond" (*dangdonging dangdonging, Kansid*), they distracted him with the leaf-parcels of rice, which they flung from between their toes. Once safely arrived in the Underworld they poured a circle of aba on the ground around themselves, then their ildas sang to announce their arrival before bringing on the sixteen people who were receiving a karja, along with a few earlier ancestors. Those of the main house and their lineage came first, followed by the others, lineage by lineage, with different sonums speaking simultaneously through Rijanti and Kuttumi. No one spoke through Dosinto, who was not in trance and looked uncomfortable. It was unusual for a man, and an adult, to be learning the funeral tradition, and indeed he gave up soon after.

When the drummers from the village approached, Sundanto chased them away to protect my microphone. Nobody was dancing, except for Jogoto, wearing an incongruous long military overcoat and twirling an umbrella. Two of the dead, including Ilesu from the main house, were supposedly victims of his sorcery—was he being provocative? He gave me a friendly (sinister?) smile.

The sonums spoke at length about the circumstances of their deaths. These were well known to everyone else, but for me their stories were only just developing. When Ilesu from the main house arrived, his wife fastened his old gold necklace round the shaman's neck.

"I've only just died and you're living with another man," he challenged her.

"He's my younger brother-in-law (*erisij*), I'm supposed to marry him!" she retorted.

The mood was somber but calm until the appearance of the little schoolboy suicide, when his mother renewed her desolate lamentation. Other children, victims of Rattud or of the Wind, were greeted by other weeping mothers, all in parallel verse using the distinctive lamentation tune. Rumbana, the suicide who had lost other people's money, was greeted with women's laments but also with a storm of indignation from men who had meanwhile appeared as if to greet him: "What happened . . . a thousand rupees . . . all gone . . ."

It had grown dark. Rijanti and Kuttumi sang a closing song in the persona of their ildas, while Dosinto listened hard and mouthed the words. They came out of trance, the orchestra struck up, some straw was set alight on the lineage's cremation-ground, and everyone danced on the embers. Mengalu led me up to his drinking site, from where we looked down on similar flames and dancing silhouettes on cremation-grounds around the village.

Groups of drummers and dancers flowed around the streets, wearing their best homespun clothes, some with bells, turbans, and bouncing egret feathers. A pack of girls wrapped in gleaming white cloths jigged up and down on the dry paddy fields, the cold light of the full moon made suddenly yellow by the flare of a fire stoked up to tighten a drumskin.

We had raised the dead, and they had followed us back to the village, but they had not yet entered their old homes. They would do this by bursting through the door after a sung dialogue, and later again by climbing up a ladder from the Underworld through the mortar set into the floor. In the paddy fields below the village the pyre-lighters (*siga*) had brought a thirty-foot ladder of bamboo cane from the forest and laid it on the ground. The pyre-lighters joined the ancestor-men in singing the No-o-o chant and splashing everyone with rice-flour water. Then some youths joined them in picking up the ladder and charging with it back and forth across the field at astonishing speed, to the accompaniment of a special ladder-charging beat. They then danced the ladder through the streets, thrusting it aggressively at bystanders. "If someone is killed, no one is blamed," Sundanto explained. "We don't give a police report, but just cremate them." This was how the shaman Rijanti had been blinded many years before. When they reached the main house they tossed the ladder onto the roof, where an ancestor-man caught it and laid it on the thatch, ready for the moment when it would be lowered into the house.

Humans had not always practiced cremation. Long ago when the first woman died, her husband did not understand what death was, so he just aban-

Figure 3.3 Dancers massing for the karja evening trance, Sogad 1977
Aro in bells and feathers in the foreground (right). Note the large children being carried in slings. The peacock has been stuffed and will be offered to one of the dead as an honor.

doned her corpse. Every day when he left the house for work, she returned to do the cooking. When he came home in the evening he asked his children who had done this. They replied that it was their mother, but he said, "Ah children, how can it be, don't say that, it makes me sad." When they insisted, he stayed behind one day to see for himself, and his wife did indeed come and start to work. He rushed up and threw his arms around her, but she turned to ashes in his embrace. Only then did he understand that the dead could not come back in their previous form, and that they had to be cremated.

This story portrays cremation as an essential act of transformation. The pyre-lighters were the agents of this transformation, and now the ancestor-men grouped themselves on both sides of the threshold of the house and began a sung dialogue in the same house-entering format that I had seen in naming rituals. Mejeru's team impersonated the pyre-lighters. "You're happy each time I cremate someone," they taunted the shamans, "because you'll pass leaves through a flame at their inquest and claim a payment in rice."

Pyre-lighters are always poor because of their contact with corpses, which is *upangge* (dangerous, infectious). "You're low-status (*oseng*)," retorted the group representing the shamans, which included Rijanti herself. "You can't face high officials as I can."

olongte nari' la janimain raji　　　　*olongte nari' la ganalmain raji*
olongte nari' la lajir mukoman　　　　*olongte nari' lakongjir mukoman*

the belted official greets me　　　　the be-sashed official greets me
the pointy-nosed race greets me　　　the high-nosebridge race greets me

The two sides sang competitively through each of the complementary roles in the karja: the lineage of basket weavers (kɪndal) who had made the shaman's mat, the lineage of potters (kumbɪj) from nearby Allangda who had made her lamp, the ancestor-women who had pounded the flour, the ancestor-men themselves . . .

Then the door was shut and barricaded. Rijanti's team started to sing outside in the persona of the dead householder Ilesu, demanding to be let in. I was inside with Mejeru's team, and a few minutes into the song, he started his reply in the role of Ilesu's widow:

agadillen la agadillen la　　　　*ad-labon do sambarin*
agadillen la agadillen la　　　　*tɪl-labon do sambarin*

boten pɪmpɪmtai boten pɪmpɪmtai　　*tungaren do la dinan ula*
boten pɪmpɪmtai boten pɪmpɪmtai　　*majaren do la dinan ula*

ayɪngen la gamai ayɪngen la gamai　　*kukuren la juri ñen*
ayɪngen la gamai ayɪngen la gamai　　*dumɪl do la juri ñen*

iñaiten gamai iñaiten gamai　　　　*sibrung do la goden*
iñaiten gamai iñaiten gamai　　　　*pangrung do la goden*

bogad peng gamlai bogad peng gamlai　*an-ubtar do la*
bogad peng gamlai bogad peng gamlai　*jenumtar do la*

it can't be it can't be, la　　　　you're under the earth, do
it can't be it can't be, la　　　　you're deep in the earth, do

who's knocking who's knocking　　halfway do la through the night, ula?
who's knocking who's knocking　　midpoint do la through the night, ula?

should I say, la, should I say, la　　it's my kukur-dove partner, la?
should I say, la, should I say, la　　it's my turtle-dove partner, la?

should I say la should I say la　　someone's come to pinch rice, do la?
should I say la should I say la　　someone's come to take rice, do la?

89

| I said perhaps I said perhaps | someone's come to poke into my flower, do la |
| I said perhaps I said perhaps | someone's come to eat my flower, do la |

Ilesu urged his children to build the embankment for a new paddy field. He himself had already entered the crops of his descendants, literally becoming their food:

| birinda kulen a-gadıllai ñen | birinda saren a-gadıllai ñen |
| I have become lineage food | I have become lineage grain |

Meanwhile the actual widow and her children were sleeping at our feet. Just as I had been divined over when asleep or dialogued over when too ill to speak, the person involved did not have to be the person paying attention.

This antiphonal debate was repeated for each of the sixteen dead people, with variations in kinship terms and situations: look after our children, my wife; plow our fields, my son; don't weep, don't be intimidated in the market, walk in the smooth center of the path not on the sharp stones . . . The stereotypical scenarios of relatedness were also a compendium of normative values. There was no reference to any cause of death, so the song was ultimately a device to allow the dead person to reenter their old house. After all sixteen roles had been sung through, Rijanti's team banged the door open with a sword and forced their way in.

The ancestors were now inside the house. They were followed by a crowd of dancers and drinkers who packed into every corner as the drummers, oboists, and horn players clambered up into the storage loft. In the small space left around the mortar, Mejeru's and Rijanti's teams sang about alin trees, the rice-flour water that represented milk, the ladder, the mat the shamans would sit on to trance, the ash of the pyre, the peacock that bestowed royal status on its recipient, the bael leaves that revealed the truth at inquests, monkeys that were long-lived because of their white hair, butterflies that were attracted to sweet alin before falling in and then coming back to life . . .

It was hard to record these fascinating texts against the drumming and laughter, but they contained the key Sora imagery of death, and also of the renewal of life. By now Rijanti's lamp had been lit, ready to illuminate the journey that she and Kuttumi would make to the Underworld, while a relay of ancestor-women tended the wick and fed it with special sweet-smelling castor oil. The pyre-lighters tore a hole in the roof and lowered the ladder into the mortar. In other villages I had seen this done by ripping the thatch open violently to a particularly frantic orchestral beat, but here it was done almost inconspicuously.

Karja Day 2, Sunday, 6 March 1977

Just before dawn Mengalu led the ancestor-men in the No-o-o chant again. The shamans sang a long list of previous shamans and ilda sonums, with the mountains where they now resided. Some sites like Samanti were forty miles away, far beyond the territory of the Lanjia Sora. The orchestra moved from one tune to another as the old blind shaman Rijanti danced and tottered round and round the ladder with the lamp on her head, and the pyre-lighters shinnied up and down the ladder. Mejeru draped himself in the clothes of the dead Ilesu and performed the high-stepping dance of pumping the bellows and the actions of Sun-Woman hammering embryos on her anvil, before chasing the fetus-swallowing python out of her forge.

The ancestor-men started a series of sixteen antiphonal songs about house building and domestic work, acting them out with axes, adzes, shovels, plow tips, and chisels that bit into the cow-dung floor. There followed sixteen songs about sowing, using baskets of various grains brought from each of the bereaved houses. The young ancestor-woman tending the wick was getting bored, but just as Mengalu was singing for the hanged child, Mejeru nodded off and fell over with a crash. Another young ancestor-woman holding an axe for the child started giggling, and the child's mother scolded her indignantly: "Don't laugh!" (*mangdong!*).

What were these pantomimes of establishing a new home? When I had seen the building song at children's naming rituals, I had assumed that the ancestor-men were constructing a house for the new namesake when he or she grew up. Now it was becoming clear that they were establishing a new domestic existence for the dead person, to replace the one he or she had left above ground. So maybe I had also misunderstood the mime of marriage by abduction in the baby's naming ritual, and that too took place in the Underworld for the previous namesake? To special wedding music, Dosinto, the apprentice shaman, took the lamp and led Mejeru by the hand as he carried a pot of alin to the prospective bride's parents. This was just the way Mengalu and I had each been danced on a bride abduction two weeks earlier, but this time there was no child. At last I understood Sundanto's point. The marriage, like the new house and the sowing of seeds, were all for the dead person: let go of your life above ground and start again (and indeed, the dead did sometimes send back messages about their further marriages and offspring down below; Vitebsky 1993: 187–95). This time the "girl" was a man in a skirt, with a padded blouse and big circular tattoos smeared in ash across his cheeks. They found her hiding in a corner and dragged her to the center, where she and Mejeru danced an exaggerated sex act.

SECOND, CENTRAL TRANCE

With occasional breaks, the dancing and singing continued all afternoon (Shamans to pyre-lighters: "When you go into the forest to cut the ladder, you'll be killed by leopards!" Pyre-lighters to shamans: "When you go into trance, you'll get stuck in the Underworld and die!"). As well as the ladder, the pyre-lighters had collected fruit and flowers from the forest, and they danced these under our nostrils and into our mouths. We were supposed to feign disgust, as these were the rotting flesh of corpses.

Toward evening the pyre-lighters unrolled a special new mat at the foot of the ladder, and Rijanti and Kuttumi sat ready to trance. This would be my second night without sleep, and the shamans had not taken a rest either. It was hard to hear the ancestors in the old ladies' faint, quavery voices against the drumming. As well as the sixteen people being commemorated, other ancestors came too with promises to look after them. The trance lasted over two hours. There were further songs about building and sowing. The pyre-lighters circulated their fruit and flowers once more, but this time they were fragrant (*serim*), and we had to inhale them.

Karja Day 3, Monday, 7 March 1977

THIRD, FINAL TRANCE

These flowers were part of the accumulating symbolism of a progression from death to new life. Toward the end of the night I could sense things drawing to a close. The two old ladies sat on the mat again, and the ancestors came for their final dialogue. The crowd had thinned out, and only close relatives remained. There was no drumming, so it was easy to record. But I was still more interested in songs than dialogues, and misguidedly turned the tape recorder off at this point to save scarce batteries. Outside in the predawn full moon there was the sound of numerous buffalo being killed with a blow to the skull from the back of an axe, to follow the dead to the Underworld. After the shamans had come out of trance the lamp was extinguished. Ancestor-women had been tending it day and night, so this was a significant gesture of finality. Men danced frenziedly on the wreckage of the ladder as the pyre-lighters hacked it into pieces before throwing the debris away. Sundanto confirmed my understanding: "Don't make us ill again, we've destroyed your path!"

The ancestor-men sprinkled buffalo blood over *sargia* leaves and sang the

Figure 3.4 Watching the dancers
A delegation from Sogad ready to go home after the funeral stone-planting for an in-law in another village. Other in-law villages are still dancing around them.

No-o-o chant again over the raw ritual, and later over leaf-cups of cooked meat. Marongger cousins from other villages danced buffalo of their own into the village to offer to our dead, then camped out in the fields cooking them. There were visits to houses, exchanges of meat, laughter around endless pots of alin . . .

Karja Day 4, Tuesday, 8 March 1977

In the very last act of the karja, Mengalu, Mejeru, and Aro sang a quick gabbled chant against sorcery and poured some aba into a caustic wild cashew leaf that had been stitched inside out (*opseng*) to represent sorcery's deviance. Mengalu handed it to me to throw away on the path. I held the leaf out to some women who shrank back, only half-laughing. The ancestor-men sang the final No-o-o song of the karja: "Who helped us to fast and stay awake? You, our ancestors!" Buffalo stomachs, buffalo flanks, buffalo heads, moved between houses, slung from poles between two carriers. The village felt exhausted, somnolent, and hot. Everywhere was filled with the stench of rotting or drying meat, stacked high up on platforms, and little leaf-parcels of food found their way to every drinking circle.

A year ago, when I knew so little language, I had experienced the karja in

93

Rajingtal as a confusing jumble of dancing, trancing, and sleeplessness. Now a structure was emerging. The karja was a powerful technique for controlling the movement and the agency of the dead, who were brought into the house, entertained there, and dismissed until the following year. Each of these three stages was matched by a trance (we're bringing you in; we're feeding you; now go away again). The entry of the dead was expressed in several parallel ways. They were raised from the Underworld at the same cremation-ground through which they had passed on the way down; as they arrived they spoke through the shamans to announce themselves. They were then led to the door of the main house, where ancestor-men sang their side of a dialogue to negotiate their entry. Once inside the house, their ascent from below was reenacted all over again up the ladder planted in a dip in the floor. The tatty mat of the cremation-ground was replaced by a fine new mat, and they spoke through the shamans again.

After this central trance, the current began to flow the other way as the proceedings moved toward a close. At the third, final trance the dead acknowledged that they had been adequately received, and their departure was surrounded by a symbolism of renewed life, as in the rotten fruit and flowers that became fragrant. After chopping up the ladder, the pyre-lighters also swept out all eighteen houses and threw away all the remains of leaves and offerings that had been given to the dead, thereby destroying any lures for their return.

Sogad was unique in the elaboration of the roles of all these shaman's assistants—ancestor-man, ancestor-woman, pyre-lighter, mat-weaver, lamp-potter—and I would never find another village in which each separate role stood out so clearly. There was an important relationship between the ancestor-men's songs, on the one hand, and the actual discussion that took place between husband and wife through the shaman's mouth, on the other. These formal songs, with their rigid parallel phrasing, as in the roles of Ilesu and his wife, were generic. They could do no more than sketch the outlines of what a husband or wife might say in such a situation, in the form of a debate where each side in turn made a conventional position statement. This is why Ilesu's wife could afford to sleep through them even when they were about her.

By contrast, dialogue between the living and the dead was not a debate between positions, but a conversation between persons. It took place in a language that was stylistically indistinguishable from conversations among the living. This was a reason why I failed to pay it enough attention till much later in my fieldwork, but also why it was ultimately so central.

The shaman made this dialogue possible through progressive stages of absence. She invoked her ılda sonums, and as she entered trance they responded with their distinctive signature tune; having taken over for a while, the ıldas too disappeared as the dead started to arrive. Now all the supporting formal structures of verse and music were withdrawn, and Ilesu's wife, like any other mourner, was left to face her sonums and talk to them on her own behalf. It would take much time, and many rituals and tape transcriptions, before I eventually came to see that the formats of verse, the signature tunes, the styles of dancing, and the specialist roles were all techniques of framing that led to this focal point: dialogues between the living and the dead, in ordinary, everyday language.

It seemed these dialogues allowed something to pass between persons that could not be said when they were all alive. Partly this was because the dead caused illnesses, creating an unavoidable need for negotiation. But I also picked up a clue to another aspect. From time to time, in an attempt to return hospitality, I would invite groups of Sora for expeditions to the coastal city of Vizag (Visakhapatnam), where we stayed in a university hostel on the beach. I was first prompted to do this by a conversation with Sundanto, when he said, "It's a pity you can't take us to see your country."

"Why can't I?"

"You're our brother," he replied, "but how would you stop the others from eating us?"

On one occasion, I left half the group behind in the hostel while I took the other half to the Vizag Post Office to phone them. None of them had ever used a phone before, and the result was even more of an entertainment than I had expected. They confronted each other with illicit affairs and other embarrassments that were known to all but could not normally be discussed, and they became so boisterous that the postmaster asked us to leave. I suggested that the phone made it possible to discuss embarrassing matters because they could not see each other's faces, and participants agreed. I later developed this insight: this was also how inhibitions were lifted once one speaker was no longer alive. Dialogues with the dead had an enabling function. A dead person still spoke for himself, but could be manipulated in a way that was not possible with a living person present in the flesh. His personality started to undergo a progressive simplification, and his agency, as a power to affect his descendant's life, also underwent diminution—while the agency of the living interlocutor was correspondingly increased. Years later, the shifting balance of agency between the living and the dead would become part of my interpretation of dialogue as also being a political phenomenon, linked to oppressive feudal power structures.

And indeed, history was happening on the last day of our *karja*. Unknown to us, a crowd of angry Sora armed with bows and axes had descended on a Pano settlement near Serung, in a kind of uprising called *fituri*, burning down the houses of the traders and moneylenders; two days later the commissioner for Tribal welfare looked for me in Sogad and took me in his jeep to inspect the damage. On the same day on our side of the mountains the block development officer had come up from Gunupur in another jeep to Puttasing to explain to people how to vote in the forthcoming election. This would be one of the most momentous events in modern Indian history, removing Indira Gandhi from office and leading to the end of her "Emergency." So far as I know, nobody in Sogad was aware of his visit.

By April 1977 I had run out of money and had a sore throat, toothache, septic cuts, a constant headache, and a weakness from hepatitis and malnutrition. The University of London noticed that their student was missing. I did not realize how much material I had collected, or its richness, and had a feeling of failure. One part of me wanted to stay here forever; another part was relieved that it was time to go home.

People came to me in a panic with land titles, police summonses, and forestry fines that they could not read, and I wrote many letters. Going past the police station in Puttasing I saw the usual depressing knot of petitioners, arrestees, and false witnesses, with the seasonal addition of people who had been caught distilling aba. I collected souvenirs: homespun loincloths and skirts, and home-hammered arrowheads. Some of my requests seemed strange: I wanted a particular old alin pot with a leak that had been cleverly repaired with beeswax ("No, I'll buy you a new one"), and an alin-strainer made of intricately wound palm-fiber ("Better get a plastic one from the bazaar").

In Sogad, Sundanto joked in front of his mother, "She'll be dead when you come back. She'll die tomorrow!" She did not seem to care, and many people made similar jokes. In Rajingtal, Asongroi's little girl Lokami chirped, "We'll be very happy if you come back." Inama's mother was like a skeleton covered with crinkled paper. Inama himself seemed thin and wasted, as people often did in the hot season, and had stabbing pains in his chest. I felt I would be grief-stricken if he died. "Don't cut the forest, don't collect leaves, don't distill aba!" he mimicked the officials, then added, "We sleep in the forest like lizards, like monkeys, like snakes, we plow in the rain at cockcrow, and they're sitting in a chair drinking tea!" His children with their bristly little heads climbed all over me while he rushed to fetch me a spear he had ordered from the blacksmith.

I flew back to England with the spear, stopped taking my tablets too soon, and ended up with falciparum malaria. This was the medical term for the sonums that made the British unable to govern this area in the nineteenth century (pages 131–32) and were still killing so many Sora today; but unlike my friends I received specialist treatment at the London Hospital for Tropical Diseases.

4

MEMORIES WITHOUT REMEMBERERS

Sogad, 1979

In February 1979 I returned to Sogad after having been away for nearly two years. My friends could not read, so there had been no way to give them advance warning. This was how their own reunions worked: a sudden reappearance, a gasp of surprise "Ai!," then embraces and narratives. In my case there were additional bizarre imaginings, fueled by the intrigues of Pano traders and others in my absence:

> Uda: The authorities came looking for you—we said, "He's gone to his woman."
>
> Sundanto: "He's dead," they said of you. "He's gone to a land inhabited by frogs and been killed by a bomb in Delhi."
>
> Dangdang: I dreamed of you, "He's dead," they said. I said, "What happened to our child?" I thought of you by night I thought of you by day.
>
> Pontia: The police said, "We'll arrest you for being friends with the sahib."

Dangdang and a man called Majji started singing:

a sintale ben do buñang len	we missed you, do, our brother
a dukale ben do buñang len	we lamented you, do, our brother
sinan angan idtai abgeje	when, when will you appear?
a bolongsi do mungkan la	his one-hand narrow face, do la
a banardub do mungkan la	his two-cupped-hands narrow face, do la
angan idtai abgije kani la	when will he appear, la
i desa lunglen do kani la	in our land, do la
i gorjang lunglen do kani la	in our village, do la
terdale a-gijeten o la	he bent down to see, o la
gemoiñle a-gijeten o la	he saw with joy, o la
a-resan onlenji kante la	our suckling babies, la
a-ungdran onlenji kante la . . .	our newborn babies, la . . .

Sora culture put an extreme emphasis on separation and loss. The phrasing may have been conventional, but it made me feel loved. Having begun as a wordless stranger four years earlier, I had become a person with enough speech, kinship, and shared history to be lamented.

The year 1979 was to become a great year of acceptance and discovery. I had been rescued financially by a research fellowship from Girton College in Cambridge, and while away I had been studying tapes and transcribing dialogues. I had also explored the relationship between the pairs of changing words in verse couplets (called *takudber*, "completing words"), and saw how the repetition of a phrase while changing only one term inside it directs attention to the words that do change. The words that matter are the words that are said only once. They do not gain their meaning in isolation, but in relation to a partner word. Regardless of whether they are synonyms, antonyms, or ambiguously both, the total effect is to enrich the meaning by turning everything into metaphor, so that each image feels three-dimensional or stereoscopic (Vitebsky 1978c): "we missed you we lamented you" gives a fuller sense of longing than either word alone; "our suckling babies our newborn babies," a fuller sense of their tininess and helplessness.

It was fortunate that I had made this effort, as I was immediately made to perform at a child's naming as an ancestor-man. I stood with Mengalu and another man outside the door as we sang our way through the roles of various ancestors who were preparing to break in, while Mejeru's team sang through the closed door in the role of the living householders, doubting the incomer's identity and seeking to be persuaded. I could now see how an oral tradition worked as performance. Like my other colleague, I joined in a split second after Mengalu started the first line of each couplet. I could not always keep up, but once he reached the first of a pair of important words, I could often predict its partner in the next line. It felt extraordinary and exhilarating to be actually doing a ritual instead of just observing, but also strangely normal, as if this was where I belonged. I followed the rhythm, intonation, gestures, and lanky leggy dancing of my role models Mengalu and Mejeru. At the same time I had to remember to keep changing tapes and batteries, to catch my own voice along with theirs.

Preparations were building up for the 1979 karja, and Mengalu invited me to join the team of ancestor-men for his headman lineage. Again, what more could I want? This year there were twenty-four people who had died over the past three years. Some had already featured in the karja two years ago, and were now receiving their third and final karja. Others were in earlier stages of postmortem existence. I hoped to study the differences between newer and older deaths. It turned out the formal features were not so easy to see through the surrounding emotion, but this too would become a source of understanding. This year's main house belonged to Tabaro, an elderly man in the headman lineage, and his wife Rondang. They were commemorating their only child, the suicide Rumbana. Rondang was a shaman of the healing kind, and thus very experienced in the despair of others, but she wept piteously throughout. Her name meant "Bag of Bones," and her ribbed bare chest matched her name.

I had heard Rumbana's sonum at the karja two years ago, speaking through Rijanti and defending himself over the remittance money he had lost in Assam. However, it turned out that his suicide had not been caused simply by losing the money. There was a double cause. While in Assam he had been present at the murder of a Nepali laborer, and the contamination had entered him and followed him home. A victim of murder or suicide requires a very difficult rescue from the Sun. Ancestor-men fire a stream of arrows into the sky to create a downward ladder, while indoors the funeral shaman ties a thread from the pitch of the roof and fastens a metal bangle or sword to the bottom. Sitting on the mortar for her trance, she then coaxes the deceased down the thread, through the metal object, and into her body, where he speaks. She then passes him on into the Underworld while an ancestor-woman sets the thread alight to destroy the upward return path. It seemed none of this had been done for that non-Sora in Assam, and the uncontrolled "frenzy" (*siara*) of his Sun-death was now at large in Sogad. Its first victim was Rumbana himself, but he had then become its agent, precipitating both the other suicides I had heard about in the 1977 karja: the incestuous Palda and the schoolchild Guma.

Yet there was something odd. That karja had been Rumbana's third and last, and subsequently he had even given his name to a new baby. So this year's karja would be his fifth—how could that be? He was supposed to be beyond this stage, yet his destructive impulse had continued, and he was causing further suicides. Unusually, his parents had started a second cycle of karjas for him, so that Rumbana would receive six karjas instead of three. "His father Tabaro walks around like a hollow grain-basket (*kultab*)," Sundanto told me. "His soul has already died."

I fasted, danced, and sang in their house for two nights without sleep. The shamans and ancestor-people subsisted on tobacco and alcohol. I did not smoke, but I chewed coffee beans to stay awake; they caught in my throat, so I had to drink more alin anyway. Here were all the stages of the karja I had observed two years earlier: the raising of the dead at the cremation-ground, the song duel before breaking into the house, the duplicate entry of the dead through the mortar and up the ladder. I took few notes and remember little except a feeling of euphoria, and also feeling the progression from death to new life again. Being bicultural was like being bilingual: entirely inside one culture at any given moment, but aware of the other and potentially able to switch. By now my notes were largely in Sora, but this was about more than language: I actually seemed to be able to live inside a foreign system of belief.

Just before dawn on the last morning, Rijanti brushed each one of us, ancestor-men, ancestor-women, and pyre-lighters, with a sword, down the back, down the arm. This was the *ardingen* to draw us back from the Underworld. Through such intense contact with the dead we had ourselves been in a sort of temporary death, similar to the state of a shaman in trance:

tungar a dina	*dayirai dayirai*
majjaran a dina	*dayirai dayirai*
rıngrıng a uyungen	*dayirai dayirai*
maraian a dina	*dayirai dayirai*
at midnight	come back, come back
at dead of night	come back, come back
at the midday sun's silence	come back, come back
at noon	come back, come back
dayirai dayirai	*asari nal ban*
dayirai dayirai	*kuttari nal ban*
i dong kudine	*sonumen a desa*
i dong rantune	*idaien a desa*
i dong gijgije	*mongol yung desa*
i dong gijgije	*mongol gaj desa*
anggere dajai maiñ	*bayiran a desan*
sungere dajai maiñ	*marantan a desan*
come back, come back	to the horizontal mortar
come back, come back	to the level mortar
don't go and sorrow	in the land of sonums
don't go and languish	in the land of ancestors
don't go and look	on the land of faint sunlight
don't go and look	on the land of faint moonlight
but ascend picking your way	to the outside land
but ascend sniffing your way	to the land of the living
akutamneten	*atarmal idaien*
bai'jatamneten	*apoppob idaien*

surda idaien	*akutamneten*
gugu idaien	*baijatamneten*

they have spat on you,	the termite-eaten ancestors
they have vomited on you,	the rotten-wood ancestors
the great ancestors	have spat on you
the grand ancestors	have vomited on you
	[this comes from a realm of decay, but is also a blessing]

dayirai dayirai	*asari nal ban*
dayirai dayirai	*kuttari nal ban*
kekerbɪj daija	*bayiran a desa*
kekerjub daija	*marantan a desa*

come back, come back	to the horizontal mortar
come back, come back	to the level mortar
come up with a whistle	to the outside land
come up with a whoop	to the land of the living

The separation of the living from the dead was even more emphatic than I had realized from the chopping of the ladder. Long ago in Rajingtal I had seen Ononti brushing her assistants with an iron arrowhead dipped in special water. Now I understood. As Rijanti ended her song over each one of us in turn, we bounded away with exaggerated energy, just as they had done in Rajingtal. We had indeed returned to life.

I also understood why the No-o-o chant was so slow and careful. We had sung it maybe ten times, taking fifteen or twenty minutes each time. Each time it began with phrases that were specific to the moment, before moving on to a list of ancestral names, which for the headman lineage of Sogad was exceptionally long.

This was the only chant where nobody ever joked or fooled around. Every name had to be remembered. The chant was the germplasm of the lineage, which would unfold through narrative, diagnosis, and dispute. As I compared it with my expanding genealogies on paper it became clear that male names were recited systematically twig by twig (*sipa*) and branch by branch (*tega*). Their chant and my diagram were alternative techniques of memory for the same structure. They both showed how the same repertoire of men's names was repeated down the generations, serving as a distinctive marker of a lineage. The simplest repetition was A son of B, son of A. This rapid repetition was made possible by short life spans, but the vagaries of demography made for many deviations. If one twig died out, its names reverted to the nearest twig, or failing that to the nearest branch. This was exactly how the inheritance of land and other property worked, though whereas property was divided equally between sons, the name would normally "emerge" in only one place. All of this was negotiated during dialogues between living and dead, and there could be many quarrels and disagreements.

Women's names came at the end, and the list was shorter. Their names did not stay long in a lineage, as an out-marrying daughter would generally pass on her name to a baby in her husband's lineage, who would later marry and transfer her name to the lineage of her husband in turn (Vitebsky 1993: 62). This transfer of her name confirmed that a married woman had completely shifted to her husband's lineage, but the process was gradual. The household's grain contained the soul-force of her husband's ancestors, and in the early years she could not climb into the loft to fetch it from the storage baskets; the first child she bore him might be attacked by her own resentful ancestors using Sun-Woman's python, as happened to the mother being treated by the stream at the end of chapter 2 (pages 65–66); and after death she would receive a duplicate stone-planting from her brothers' lineage and be enumerated for a while in both their No-o-o chants. Their dialogues might raise disagreements about which ancestors she would stay with in the Underworld, but whatever the destiny of a woman's name, it tended to be remembered in the No-o-o chant for a shorter period than that of a man.

I had collected a rich harvest of genealogies and recordings that would show how all of this actually functioned. What I needed now was somewhere quiet, with electricity, to study all this material. From late May to August I had business in other parts of India, and packed one bag of notes and another of cassette tapes—unique, irreplaceable material, including several days and nights of my own singing with Mengalu—along with the recordings of the 1977 karja that I had brought back to India for comparison. Photocopying was still unavailable, and tapes could be duplicated only in real time with elaborate equipment, so I nursed the bags carefully on my knee. But I was tired, and at a bus stop in Madras (now Chennai), the bag containing the recordings was stolen. I enlisted the embassy and the police, and placed ads in the newspapers. But there was no response, and my ritual chants were probably overlaid with film music and sold in the bazaar.

At the same time access to Soraland became administratively more difficult, and it seemed I might never see my Sora friends again. I spent the hot season in Delhi with my mind racing, cataloguing, listing, classifying, transcribing, drawing weird diagrams. There were inconsistencies in the genealogies. But

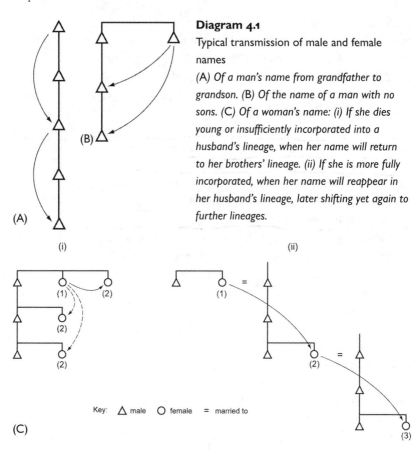

Diagram 4.1

Typical transmission of male and female names

(A) *Of a man's name from grandfather to grandson. (B) Of the name of a man with no sons. (C) Of a woman's name: (i) If she dies young or insufficiently incorporated into a husband's lineage, when her name will return to her brothers' lineage. (ii) If she is more fully incorporated, when her name will reappear in her husband's lineage, later shifting yet again to further lineages.*

Key: △ male ○ female = married to

also, what was the relationship between vertical and horizontal space? Which kinds of sonums could be held in pots, and what was the difference between their movement through the air and along a thread? What about blocking and opening, or rites of banishment and of induction? The heat of Sun-Sonum and the cool of Earth-Sonum? Contagion? Actions performed by day or by night? When we fasted as ancestor-men, was this to make us clean, or to make us less fleshly, or to share the ancestors' state of deprivation? If a sacrificial buffalo started as a stand-in (*apanadu*) for the donor, how did it also become a stand-in for the deceased when it was draped in his clothes, embraced, and lamented just before being killed?

Questions could not be asked directly, and "answers" could be erratic, and different again from patterns that emerged through cumulative observation. Some questions have never received a coherent answer to this day, and indeed, what counts as an answer? An otherwise systematic interpretation might come up against a subversive exception (pigs were always banished from the house—then why did Dumburu hang pots with pig's blood inside his roof?); and for some an answer was perhaps not possible: the numbers of leaves for offerings to each sonum seemed arbitrary, and perhaps the only point was that they should be different from each other.

I managed to negotiate a return in September, and I arrived with enhanced focus and determination. I made for Jamano's house, my old base in Guddara. It turned out Jamano had just died, coughing blood and suffering from what a doctor would have called tuberculosis. As with other such patients, I had earlier failed to persuade him to spend three months away from home in a hospital for the daily injections that might have saved him. I was close to his son Ranatang and to Jamano's brother, the funeral shaman Uda. They were part of the Sogad headman lineage, so I knew their family history very well. This was my chance to study exactly how his death would be interpreted (for a detailed analysis, see Vitebsky 1993: 99–146).

I had missed the inquest on the morning after Jamano's death, when he had spoken through Uda's mouth. Ranatang told me that his father's sudden collapse was due to Rattud-Sonum, as Jamano had passed one of their "police stations" (*tana*) shortly before his death. The inquest also revealed that the Rattud-people had been incited to act by Mengalu's sorcery. The full truth would be confirmed at the stone-planting a few days later. I was close to Mengalu, but here I did not know how to defend him.

I bought a buffalo and added it to twenty others contributed by Jamano's kinsmen. I learned something important about animals as stand-ins when all the buffalo escaped during the night, and Ranatang told me, "They haven't yet found the one with your face." On the day of the stone-planting I stayed close to Uda to follow every word of the dialogues. My buffalo had been found, and others would slaughter it for me, as it slipped from an identification with me to an identification with the dead man. While drummers and dancers swept back and forth beyond the door frame, there was intense concentration inside the darkened house around Uda. After brief appearances by preliminary sonums—ildas, former shamans, and Jamano's long-dead father—there was a fleeting, ambiguous appearance by Mengalu himself. This was his own living soul, which had somehow detached itself from his body and was speaking through the shaman. I had heard that this was possible for sorcery, but had never expected to hear it for myself. "Mengalu" croaked some unclear words about a land dispute and disappeared to a torrent of scolding. This was the living Mengalu's tactical error. The shaman Uda was the brother of his alleged victim, and the situation was skewed against him. Mengalu should have been present in the flesh to deny everything and take some control of the situation, but he had avoided this moment by going off alone up a mountain for the day.

Then Jamano himself announced his arrival. Instantly the women broke into uncoordinated songs of lamentation, while Ranatang urged his father, "One moment you were walking around, the next you were dead. Don't hesitate don't be afraid—speak out!"

"You died alone, no wife no daughter-in-law no daughter," added Jamano's widow. "Tell us how you died how you perished!"

Jamano was interrogated about his last moments: "When you died, whom exactly did you meet? . . . Tell us as a test (*tungjing*) . . . What happened next?" The tone was sharp until they were sure it was really Jamano speaking and not an impostor. Then they started to supply answers to their own questions: "What you said is, 'Hey children, my liver (*ugar*) is tearing my liver is sprouting out of my chest!' " Through the hubbub of voices, I could hear Jamano saying faintly ". . . then I vomited twice, I vomited on the ground beneath the veranda . . . 'Ow! they're prodding my anus like a buffalo, ow! my body is racked, ow! it's tearing apart,' I said."

Ranatang interrupted: "Was it Earth-Sonum Simu-Sonum? Our father's people our mother's people?—Or was it sorcery?" he shrieked hoarsely. "Speak out!"

Jamano did not answer, but continued to play on their pity. As so often, I admired the skillful emotional crafting of the collective dramaturgy: "I was sitting on the veranda. I cried, 'Help me Mandebo help me Sunamo, help me children, save me protect me . . . !' "

He was met with a chorus of sympathetic noises: "We couldn't hear, we were all in our separate houses" . . . "The Rattud-people pounced and beat him up without warning" . . . "Why didn't you put up a fight, why did you give yourself up to them?" and a growing pressure to identify the sonum responsible: "Did they drag you off as you hugged the main pillar of the house?" . . . "Which way did they take you after they wrenched you off the pillar?" . . . "Who was the main one to grab your hair, to get on top of you?"

There was a sudden attentive hush as Jamano whispered: "It was Mommo." With this crucial revelation, Jamano was starting to lead his mourners from his Rattud symptoms toward a motivation among the members of that collectivity. Mommo was a recent previous Rattud victim. As a new recruit, he had acted as the "front-person" (*abmang-mar*) for all the other Rattud-people, the "shadow people at the back" (*lub-dung-marenji*). In some inquests, like those for the little boy Mando or the young wife Panderi, the dead person was a pawn in the love life or political intrigues of others. By contrast, Jamano was a prominent elder with a lifetime's accumulation of allies and enemies of his own, and was the central actor in the story of his own death. This time the matching of symptom to motive involved a chain with several links. The dialogue revealed that Mommo had been incited by Jamano's deceased first wife, who turned up to confirm that she had missed him in the Underworld. Their pact had been incited in turn by Mengalu's sorcery, confirming Ranatang's suspicions and stoking him up to vengeful rage: "I'll slurp up all his blood, I'll slit his throat from ear to ear!"

First the sorcery attempt on Monosi, then the death of little Mando, and now Jamano's death; there had been other accusations and there would be more. I felt the noose closing in on the tragic figure of my quick-witted but wayward friend Mengalu.

The link to Mommo seemed tenuous to me, but it started a three-hour discussion that constructed an elaborate portrait of the dead man. His intimate relationships encompassed the love of his dead wife, the aggression of Mommo, and the enmity of Mengalu. Together they amounted to a summary of his life, and each had been fatal in its own way.

Jamano had been a senior member of the headman lineage and a prominent and moderate voice in village affairs. "If an official wears trousers if he wears glasses, you're terrified you're shaking with fear," he now claimed. "I warded off the officer-in-charge I kept out the police inspector, even though they speak government language they know Oriya language. Widowed women unprotected women never had to say, 'Issí! Why didn't you come to our rescue?' Hmmm, what have you all got to say to that?" I sensed Uda's own agenda here: his brother had been a big man, and everyone should know it. Jamano had indeed cushioned outside extortion with homemade debt relations at a more gentle rate of interest. The dead man spent a whole hour establishing a detailed public record of the money he was owed, with the story behind each loan. This was the moment for alleged debtors to object, but the discussion contained no serious disagreements. Monosi was not there, but when I later played him a recording, he was surprised to hear that he too owed a small sum, until he remembered that he had indeed borrowed money from Jamano several years earlier.

The line of inheritance was straightforward; these credits would now be inherited in equal shares by Ranatang and his younger brothers. There was also a consensus about the cause and meaning of Jamano's death, and it was now too late for Mengalu to contest his role. Nonetheless, there was still plenty to discuss, and the occasion contained the seeds of many other possible developments. This settlement of Guddara had been founded long ago by a branch of

Figure 4.1 Jamano's stone-planting: sacrificing the author's buffalo
Animals for sacrifice must be killed without spilling blood, to direct their souls to the
intended sonum and prevent them from drifting uncontained up to the Sun. Second from
left is Uda the shaman.

the headman lineage which had moved here across the valley from Sogad, and today's verdict was increasing Ranatang's desire for a complete split (though actually this never happened).

Within hours of dying, each person would become an interactive presence at their own inquest, and today's dialogue was a further development of that initial moment. A dialogue during the stages of a funeral differs from that during a cure, as it is the deceased rather than a living patient who is the center of attention. It is partly a discursive unpacking of the conventional elements in the sung laments ("What took you, I won't see your face again, now who will do the plowing?"), but its everyday prose format makes it more specific. Yet this is still not a fully freestyle expression of emotion, and one can detect recurrent patterns and concerns. Funeral verdicts and their dialogues are not only about grief and sympathy. They also interpret the past so as to control the future, by establishing how the dead person will affect the living, in order to control that effect. Jamano was a fresh and potentially virulent recruit to Rattud-Sonum. What was the next step in dealing with this fact?

The answer came in a chant that same day. As the twenty-one buffalo were slaughtered and dismembered nearby, the ancestor-men of Jamano's lineage formed two teams and sang a series of debates impersonating the dead man and various relatives. Having hidden during the inquest, Mengalu was back as the lineage's chief ancestor-man, but he was extremely tense, sometimes singing and sometimes bursting into tears and going away to hide while the song went on without him.

Eight times through the day they squatted in front of a row of offerings and sang the No-o-o monotone in the collective persona of Jamano's ancestors. I had sung this myself in the February karja, for this very lineage under Mengalu's leadership, but I had not been able to write it down, and now the tapes were lost. This time I did not join in, but recorded every word.

The chant immediately established Jamano's wretched, unrescued condition through a sundering from the solidarity and inclusiveness of his lineage:

our twin brother	our linked brother
our elder brother	our younger brother
our born child	our hatched child
reaching	merging
into our company	into our group
into our binding	into our bundle
let us comfort him	let us escort him
into our shared meal	into our shared food
our brother huddles	our brother cowers
in a hovel	in a shack
by a mean cattle-track	by a sordid cattle-track
a protruding-fanged sonum	a curving-fanged sonum
has snatched and eaten up	has snatched and drunk up
our born child	our hatched child

The rescuers would ransom Jamano using round, flat seeds from jungle plants, which are "deep language" (*jaru-ber*) for money, backed up with techniques of physical force and powerful speech:

all speak up	all speak out
we are right here	we are coming
wealthy headman	prosperous headman
circular-purse money	circular-purse cash
round *tarab*-seed money	round *tarab*-seed cash
let us hold our axes	let us grab our axes
let us brandish our swords	let us brandish our knives
let us speak like an advocate	let us speak for the defense

let us be forceful-mouthed   let us be forceful-toothed
let us lead him toward us   let us draw him by the arm
                                        toward us

Their rescue would be effective whatever the cause of death:

whether in Sorcery-House   whether in Kurab-House
whether in Sun-House   whether in Moon-House
whether in Manne-House   whether in Simu-House
whether in Bone-Scrunching House   whether in Bone-Grinding House
whether in Eat-Up-Victim   whether in Drink-Up-Victim
whether in Police-Station House   whether in Arrest-Victim House

One man explained to me, " 'Don't go and stay in Rattud-House, I beg you my child,' the ancestors are saying. They rescue him to go with his father his mother: 'My child has come back my brother has come back,' at the completion of the stone-planting."

The ancestor-men of this huge lineage went on to list the many hundreds of ancestors whom they were impersonating, in the order that I had already studied and mapped on paper.

In contrast to the negotiations and persuasions of dialogue, this chant was assertive, in a format that brooked neither contradiction nor failure. It transformed Jamano not just *from* the bad state of being a Rattud person but also *to* a good state of being an ancestor. This transformation operated in every domain at once: cosmological, as his ancestors moved him from one location on the landscape to another; ontological, as they turned him from one kind of sonum into another; and social, as they led him from the antisociety of his fellow Rattud-victims into their own company.

The word for transforming someone in this way is *tandi*, meaning "to rescue or redeem." This word implies a once-and-for-all change. Yet there was a problem. Every divination for illness reveals an attacker who has himself or herself already been through this redemption. Mommo and Jamano's wife had been similarly redeemed some time before they came back to take Jamano. How could this be? Sora say that the dead person spontaneously and perversely "wanders" or "reverts" (*gorod*) from his state of ancestorhood back to his membership of an Experience sonum. A sonum is often scolded: "Why are you making us ill? Didn't we give you a buffalo, didn't we plant you a stone?" and replies, "Yes but . . ." (*u'u do . . .*), followed by some excuse or grievance. However decisive the words and actions of the ancestor-men on the day of the stone-planting, these are more a declaration of intent than a final accomplishment, and the deceased person's transformation can remain painfully provisional. This is why illness and death continue to occur: there are always recently dead people who are not irreversibly transformed, and who thus keep on "reverting" and recruiting new victims to their Experience groups. ("Don't make her revert just because she's new," *ab-gorod-dong tabme gamle*, I heard one mourner say to a sonum.)

I could now link the distinction between funeral shamans and other sha-mans to the passage of time. Rituals of healing or acknowledgment are not moments when a dead person is transformed, but reminders that he is stuck in his current state. It is only at the stages of their own funeral that the dead can move on a step, and it is only these events that feature the No-o-o song, which is an explicit tool of transformation. This is why funeral shamans are so special, and why that song is sung so carefully at every stage of the funeral sequence. Whereas rituals of acknowledgment often do not need a trance, every stage of the funeral centers on a lengthy dialogue.

As I expanded my genealogies and pushed them back in time, attaching additional pieces of paper at the top and to the side, I made another important discovery. People talked constantly about the causes of recent deaths, but even though their names and genealogical positions were still well known, they could say nothing about the deaths of older ancestors. The more I explored family histories, the more it became obvious that within a few years the cause of death was forgotten. Why was it so important to know the cause of death in the early years, but not later? Even though I had performed the No-o-o chant myself and traced the transmission of ancestral names on my genealogies, there still seemed to be something essential that I did not understand. This something concerned time. In May 1977 I was still sometimes turning my tape recorder off to save batteries and cassettes when invocations gave way to dialogue; by September, after spending some weeks in towns with elec-tricity to play back my tapes over and over again, I was doing it the other way round. Everyone lived with a repertoire of sonums who were at diverse stages of complete or incomplete transformation. The whole system was a calculus of previous deaths. It was not the chants that were the heart of the mystery, but the dialogues.

I had accumulated many pieces of the puzzle but needed to find the key. What was the total panorama of redemption of all the sonums that af-fected one person or family? This was not the sort of thing one could simply ask—I had to see these relationships in action. The opportunity came when a baby in Sogad was diagnosed as being afflicted by Duri-sım (Lumbago-Sonum). I had seen this ritual several times, in the days when I was mesmer-

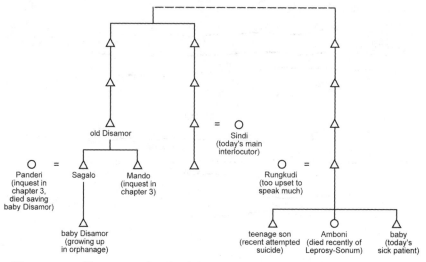

Diagram 4.2 Characters in Rondang's healing ritual

ized by the symbolism of invocations and paid too little attention to dialogues. Conveniently for my purpose, this ritual would gather many of the lineage's ancestors, regardless of the cause of their death. It would be like a condensed form of the karja, but rather than being confined to the dead of the last three years, I would be able to review an array of ancestors from various time-depths as they called in from various locations around the cosmos, each sending back messages that should match their degree of transformation or, on the contrary, reversion.

The shaman for this ritual was Rondang. The karja that year had been in her house, and I had fasted, danced, and chanted for her son, the suicide Rumbana, who had been triggering further suicides around the village. The sick baby belonged to the impoverished lineage of Sagalo, whose little brother Mando and wife Panderi I had heard at their tearful inquests and whose motherless baby Disamor I had helped to place in an orphanage. These were people I knew well and who welcomed me; the ritual required no noisy music apart from Rondang's own drumbeat, and my microphone worked perfectly. On a path leading out of Sogad, as the last drops of the rainy season pattered onto my open notebook, I felt completely integrated into this small, intimate banishing-rite (full analysis in Vitebsky 1993: 149–215).

The main people present were the baby's young mother, Rungkudi, and an older in-marrying widow called Sindi. Rungkudi was miserable and frightened. She had had three children. Of these, her teenage son had just attempted suicide (at the instigation of Palda, himself killed by the contagion of Rumbana's suicide), her little daughter Amboni had just died of Leprosy-Sonum, and today her baby was threatened. She would have to face her husband's ancestors, to whom as a young wife she was supposed to be deferential. Sindi by contrast was a confident matriarch who had raised her children, outlived her husband, and stayed on in his lineage. She did most of the talking on Rungkudi's behalf, as older well-established wives do. Both Sindi and the shaman Rondang were virtuosos in the old women's style of abusive backchat, and the entire event was an ironic sparring match between Sindi and her ancestors-in-law.

In all, nineteen dead people appeared, fifteen men followed by four women. The men appeared systematically, branch by branch, much as in a No-o-o chant. The first nine were long dead, and did not stay long.

"I'm Ortino!" announced one. "Come on, booze!"

"You see to this," Sindi replied. "I mean your nephews your grandchildren our daughters-in-law, make sure they get well. You sonums give us dysentery diarrhea, you take them you carry them off."

"Just say they're going for a trip to the Underworld!" the ancestor riposted.

"Pansia!" announced another. "Hoi there! Hey gai! Bring an umbrella!"

Various voices answered: "What umbrella? We can't afford an umbrella."

"Look," said Sindi, "because you lot plow on my back, I've got nothing, I've got no clothes or money . . ."

The ancestors established the otherness of their world through inversion: in the Underworld the seasons are reversed, so one ancestor complained that the baby's father had cleared a patch of jungle for cultivation without realizing that these were also the beanpoles supporting the dead man's ripening crops.

"Didn't you hear them crashing down oeeeeeeee a-boom?" he demanded.

"How would I hear?" Sindi retorted drily. "I'm deaf. If it went boom I wouldn't hear, if it went padoom I wouldn't hear (*boom dele jenang a'namdangai padoom dele jenang a'namdangai*) . . . Go on, drink up and piss off!"

As so often in dialogues with long-dead ancestors, there did not seem to be much emotion on either side. It was more as if it was safe to be abusive for fun—an old women's sport. As the dialogue shifted to more recent sonums, the tone changed dramatically. The tenth sonum to come was Sindi's own son Palda, who had hanged himself after an incestuous affair with a cousin. I had heard him speak through Rijanti's mouth at the 1977 and 1979 karjas. Rondang's performance was equal to Rijanti's. Palda came over as an obnoxious oaf, abusing his mother for several minutes while she responded sarcastically.

"Your tummy-button sticks out!" he declared on arrival.

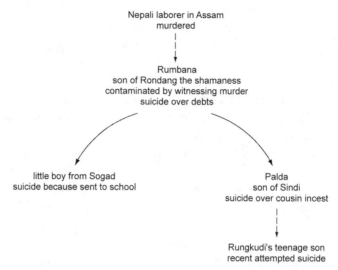

Nepali laborer in Assam
murdered

Rumbana
son of Rondang the shamaness
contaminated by witnessing murder
suicide over debts

little boy from Sogad
suicide because sent to school

Palda
son of Sindi
suicide over cousin incest

Rungkudi's teenage son
recent attempted suicide

Diagram 4.3 Chain of suicides

"So it might after giving birth to you," Sindi shot back. "I suppose that's why you're so clever? Up here or down below, we've got no sense, still fucking our sisters."

"It's just a quick down-and-up-again, mother, what does it matter who she is?"

Palda had been led to suicide by the sonum of Rumbana, the suicide who had hanged himself after losing other people's money in Assam. Since Rumbana had been the son of the shaman Rondang, the two women were bound together by a terrible shared experience. Surely she was not just a disinterested vessel, but I could only guess what distress or grim satisfaction Rondang was feeling as she incarnated the sonum of his next victim and acted out his slanging match with his mother.

The nastiness of Palda's appearance matched his continuing ability to harm. I had heard him too speak at both the 1977 and 1979 karjas, so he too, like Rumbana, had completed his three years. Rumbana's redemption from Sun-Sonum had been so incomplete that he had needed a second sequence of three karjas. Palda had not needed this extraordinary intervention, but his state was still sufficiently unstable that he had "reverted' to cause the near suicide of the brother of today's sick baby. Their mother accosted Palda. "Did your mother or father teach you to hang yourself?" Rungkudi demanded in a strangled voice, using a conventional idiom for a stupid action. "Don't you try to pass on your death again. I'm not joking, if you get my boy to do it I'll . . ."

Palda cut in. "Only the other day I almost made him hang himself," he confirmed. "I'd already made up my mind to destroy him . . ."

Meanwhile Palda's own mother, Sindi, was muttering sullenly in the background. "I always looked after you so well. How could we know? If only you'd said something! But you climbed up into the loft at dead of night: whose fault is that? I was sleeping outside on the veranda. You'd been acting strangely all day, not wanting to go to work."

"I did just what I liked and then hanged myself," he bragged.

"And unplugged my arse for police bribes!" she retorted. "I was a poor widow, your father was a pauper, do you think I saved up the money from his land?"

Palda stayed a long time before returning to the Underworld. The mood lightened with the arrival of his father, Sindi's husband, who had been dead for several years but had not yet faded into the characterlessness of a long-dead ancestor. They engaged in familiar marital bickering. This was a useful confirmation for me, as it showed a stage between the homogeneity of the long-term dead and the heartrending immediacy of those who had just died, a stage in which sonums retain their personality and their stories but are no longer distressing or dangerous.

Finally, four females came. Two of these, long dead, had little of significance to discuss. But two had died recently: Amboni, the sister of today's sick baby; and Sagalo's wife Panderi. Amboni had died of skin lesions, perhaps leprosy, and had received her first karja that year. Her appearance was aimed at her mother, who was surely expecting this moment.

"Mother?" the dead child whispered. Rungkudi started weeping silently. "Where are my gold nose-rings?" the girl demanded petulantly.

It was Sindi who replied. "They were so tiny, if I'd found them of course I'd show them to you. Oh my love my darling, don't cause your own illness in others. Can you say that your mother and father didn't do enough sacrifices for you? They didn't turn their backs or refuse to help you, did they? Think of all those pigs they offered, all those chickens, goats, buffalo, my lovely child . . ."

"Mother, you were horrid to me you scolded me, you called me Scar-Girl you called me Leper-Girl," Amboni accused her silently weeping mother. "You said, 'You're a big girl now, why should I feed you when you sit around doing nothing?'"

"She didn't mean it, she couldn't help saying it," Sindi said soothingly. "You were growing up and there were such a lot of chores to do."

"I want my necklaces," Amboni insisted in a querulous childish tone. "Why can't I have my nose-rings? I have to go digging, shoveling, and leveling fields in the Underworld, all without my nose-rings. I came out in scars all over; my fingers started dropping off. That illness was passed on to me in my mother's lineage, that's how I got ill. But my father's ancestors have rescued me."

"So don't pass it on," Sindi urged her. "Don't give it to your mother and little sisters!"

"If I grab them I grab them, if I touch them I touch them, if I pass it on I pass it on: that's how it goes." Amboni's reply summarized the entire Sora theory of illness and death.

"Your cough your choking, your scars your wounds, don't pass them on!"

But Amboni was already slipping back to the Underworld, with a parting shot: "My Mummy doesn't care enough about me!"

As with the arrogant Palda, so with innocent little Amboni: I felt strongly that the words of a freshly dead person also reflect the feelings that their mourners bring to the encounter. The child reproaches her mother with the cruel realism of what we might call the mother's own self-reproach: if only I'd known how ill you were, if only I'd been kinder . . . This pain felt by the living is matched by the fear that the girl will pass on her fatal condition to her family. This is a property not of her personality but of her cosmological state. Palda is nasty and Amboni sweet and vulnerable, yet as she herself says, this just is what newly dead people do. Both these dialogues reveal starkly how in rescuing the dead person from the Experience sonum that took them, the living are acting not only out of pity and grief, but also in order to protect themselves against future attacks. Through all the surrounding paraphernalia of chants, buffalo, blood, dances, leaf species, and signature tunes that I had studied for so long, the ultimate core technique of Sora religion is dialogue as persuasion.

The final sonum of the trance was Panderi, the young wife who had been killed by a Rattud-Sonum when she bent over to protect her baby Disamor. Her husband Sagalo had somehow quietly joined us. Sindi and her son Palda, Rungkudi and her daughter Amboni: here was a confirmation of how directly dead people turn up in response to the presence of someone whom they have the power to disturb, and also how living people come to meet their own so-nums. A trance is also a rendezvous.

Sagalo, like Rungkudi, let Sindi speak for him, and did not say anything himself. The dead Panderi began faintly, "It ate me up it drank me up, mothers."

"Ah my dear," responded Sindi, "it was so sudden, just like that, you . . ."

As she continued inaudibly, Panderi spoke again: "After I married into your family, mothers—"

"Yes, you said, 'This is my house this is my home,'" Sindi confirmed. "Didn't we do all your sacrifices? If only you'd been ill first . . ."

"It's not that, but your little grandchild would have been swallowed right up and I would still have been alive. I bent down to protect him, mothers, and they ate me up instead." Her voice rose. "I cried, 'Help me, fathers, help me! Aunts, uncles, mother-in-law, father-in-law!'"

"How could we see you?" asked Sindi.

Panderi became tearful. "'Where's my husband where's my husband, I want to be with him I want to speak to him!' I cried." Then dropping her voice: "They ate me up fresh-and-alive (*rongtapada jumlingji*) . . . your child your grandchild, they would have beaten him and snatched him, but I screamed 'U gai my baby, u gai my baby!' and bent down over him, so they ate me up instead."

"You can't say we didn't plant a memorial stone for you or do your sacrifices, can you?" demanded Sindi. Then in a vehement torrent she urged the dead woman, "Leave abandon that house that home, that place that location, that seat that site, leave it abandon it (*i-omdrenga i-omda kun a siing kun a kerun, kun a derakuna kun a tararangna, kun a tana kun a betuna, i-omdrenga i-omda*) . . . Say you're going to your in-laws . . ."

"Yes, my husband's ancestors have rescued me," Panderi cried. "But the Rattud-people won't release me, they won't let me go!"

"You should say, 'Let me go!' You should say, 'I've got my in-laws, I've got my brothers-in-law, I've got my new kinsmen, I've got my sisters-in-law!'" At that point Panderi's sonum left Rondang's body and returned to the Underworld.

Here was none of Sindi's earlier crudeness or sarcasm. The parallel phrasing that emerges in impassioned speech almost overwhelmed her last remarks, like a verbal battering ram to block out any counterargument. Panderi meanwhile reiterated the same message as at her inquest (page 81). The Rattud-people represented her brother's opposition to her marriage, while her husband's ancestors struggled to rescue her and take her into their own company. It was clear where Panderi wanted to go, but she had been dead only a few months and the struggle for her postmortem allegiance was still bitter and unresolved. Her case was still far from reaching consensus, and I wondered what she was now saying when she turned up in trances sponsored by her brothers.

I discussed cases with Sora friends, transcribed tapes, and collated them with my genealogies and recordings from other rituals, some involving the same people and some involving other lineages or villages. The pattern was

Figure 4.2 A married woman's soul returns to her home village
She will receive a duplicate funeral sequence from her brothers using part of the ashes from her cremation in her husband's village. The mood is very solemn; dancing and laughter do not begin until the stone-planting.

consistent, and within an overall spectrum I could now identify three distinct phases of a dead person's existence. The oldest ancestors had been dead for many years. Many had already given their names to their descendants, and others would do so soon. Most crucially, their redemption had taken full hold, so that they no longer perpetuated the cause or form of their own death. This was why that cause, like their distinctive personality, could be forgotten. They would have a drink, deny responsibility for their descendants' illnesses, and promise to protect them. These conversations were generally banal and flippant, though these old ancestors might give some useful pointers to the culprits.

The second phase included more recent sonums, like Sindi's husband, who retained stronger traces of their personality but were likewise no longer a threat. They too had been definitively redeemed and were receding, but their personalities were still vivid, and they had not yet been reduced to genealogical tokens. By contrast, recent sonums evoked distress, anxiety, or anger. They were dangerous, as they were still trying to perpetuate their own illnesses in others. This emotional intensity was linked to their cosmological instability, as they still reverted back and forth between being protective ancestors and agents of illness.

An ambivalence in emotional attachment was institutionalized into the foundation of Sora culture: the more you loved someone while they were alive, the more you might fear them once they had died. Here at last was a clarification of something I had sensed for a long time. There was a close correlation between the emotional tone of an encounter with a dead person, and the bringing of that person's cosmological transformation to completion. So it was all about time, and pacing. The three years of the karja defined the first, most intense phase of bereavement and were supposed to close it off. But people's feelings did not always correspond with this structure, and the balance between anger, pity, and fear might vary with relationships and with the cause of death—hence the long-term menace of the unrepentant suicides Rumbana and Palda, against the compassion for little Amboni and the loyal, self-sacrificing Panderi, who I guessed would not stay dangerous for so long.

The Experience sonums like Sun, Leprosy, and Rattud are just there, as the existential ground of existence. What matters is how people move between them. People can be redeemed into ancestorhood, but will slip back again to become the temporary carriers or agents of those Experiences. This was why redemption is not a single once-and-for-all event, as the ancestor-men optimistically asserted in our No-o-o chant, but a gradual process, a shift of emphasis in a person's nature between two idioms. The Experience and ancestor forms of sonumhood are not ontologically opposed entities, but two, opposed ways in which a person can perpetuate himself or herself in the lives of others. An unredeemed sonum uses aggressive active verbs for their encounter: "I grab," "I take," "I eat" (ñam-tai, pang-tai, jum-tai). It was only when they have stopped reverting that ancestors are able to pass on their names to a new baby, now using a middle verb form that implies mutual identification: añım-tenai, "I name [a baby] after myself" (Vitebsky 1993: 202–15).

The emotional swirl of real life makes this sequence complicated for the shamans to stage-manage—or rather, this is what provides much of their drama, including catharsis for their clients. Sonums evolve along with their mourners, and dialogue is a technique that helps them to synchronize their feelings and evolve in parallel. For me, this dialogue provides much of the ethnographic fascination, but for a long time it also made that sequence hard to perceive. Both the dead person and the mourners move though a progressive sequence of states; the dialogue between them creates a sympathy, almost a shared consciousness, which synchronizes their progress through this evolution. When there is a blip in this process the deceased presents it as a reversion in their own progress, while the living experience it as an attack. So the reason why it no longer matters to remember the circumstances of a death long ago is that the deceased and the mourners have helped each other to move away from the upset of the death. The sonum's new state can take over only gradually because the memory persists of what things were like before the transition. Reversions then appear as throwbacks or resurgences of these old memories; dialogue offers frequent confirmation of newer feelings to repress them.

It would be difficult to translate sonum into English, since no single word can encompass its multiple domains of meaning. One of a sonum's most important properties is to make the past shape the future through the way we think of it. It is as if the sonums themselves are memories, and the more traumatic and upsetting these are, the harder it is to stop them from hurting us. If, as a thought-experiment, we translate sonums as "Memories" with a capital M, then we can understand the Sora as saying that all illnesses and deaths are caused by Memories, and that it is these Memories that the shaman leads on stage to speak with their rememberers (Vitebsky 1993: 195–202). We have heard the Memory of Panderi conversing with her living rememberers as she expresses her own pain, her love for her husband and baby, and her rejection of her brothers. Similarly, Palda is a nasty Memory to his mother, while the old ancestors are Memories that have little power to distress or to harm, and can be safely insulted.

Sonums are not like our usual understanding of Memories as being contained inside the individual mind. Rather, as their location in points on the landscape makes clear, they roam at large outside the mind of any single rememberer. At the same time, they are thoroughly social, not only on the landscape but also in performance. A sonum is my Memory of a person, but it can also turn in conversation to address any one of the assembled rememberers in a manner specific to each of them and yet common to all. It is through this play between their interior and exterior properties that Memories are able to be both deeply intimate and publicly negotiable.

Living people engage with sonums in order to change them and to modify their impact. Memories fade (*masuna*) as their rememberers too change with time, recovering from their grief but also aging and finally dying themselves. So just as "remembering" is not so much a cognitive as a relational process, so too "forgetting" follows the evolution of social relationships. One by one, the qualities or attributes of the deceased fall away and are returned to the living, who then have less reason to talk with him in detail or with emotional intensity. His material property is divided early on between his heirs, while the cause of his death, and thus his association with an Experience sonum, is also immediately established. This is the most negative form of inheritance, but at first it is difficult or impossible to stop him from transmitting his suffering to others. If the series of three annual karjas goes right, as it usually does (except for Rumbana), then the deceased should emerge as a proper ancestor, still with personality and narrative like Sindi's husband, but with little or no tendency to revert.

A few years beyond this the cause of death is forgotten, as I discovered when making genealogies, and the dead person is no longer associated with any specific form of suffering. He is just an ancestor, and has nothing left to return to the living except his name. If the deceased is a child, the name usually returns quickly to a close sibling. Among adults, the timing or routing of a name can have elaborate emotional or tactical meanings. Occasionally the same name can "emerge" in two different places to bolster rival claims to the previous name-holder's legacy. In the dispute over Panderi it remained vitally important for Sagalo's side to sustain the validation of their marriage. When Panderi instructed her sister to marry him instead, I predicted that the dead woman would pass on her name to their first daughter. This did indeed happen, and so Panderi's name was captured by Sagalo's lineage. By contrast, an old patriarch like Jamano, with several descendants branching into sublineages, would probably wait several generations before his name is preempted by one branch to the exclusion of others.

The three years or so that it takes to turn a dead person into a full ancestor is paralleled by the period needed to wean a Sora child. This is also the number of years it takes for a child to talk, and before this age they will not receive a proper funeral, since they cannot come back and engage in dialogue. It takes a similar amount of time to become fully dead or fully alive, and in each case the process of transition is vulnerable to reversions: just as ancestors frequently revert, so many children die between the moment at birth when they are promised a name, and the festival some three years later when the name is definitively attached.

The naming ceremony uses the same funeral shamans, the same ancestor-men and ancestor-women, the same tunes, as the stone-planting and karja. The prose dialogues during the trance are similarly paralleled by the ancestor-men's sung set pieces. But there is a big difference. In the stone-planting and karja there was always a still group of weeping rememberers clustered around the shamans at the center of the swirl of revelers. But at the naming, the carnival mood inverts every morbid image from those earlier stages of the funeral. Nobody weeps, and nothing spoils the horseplay and laughter. The No-o-o chant confirms that this is a rite of transformation—one that I now understand as the final stage in the funeral of the *previous* name-holder, a stage that may have waited anything from a few years to a century for completion. While the karja ends with the dismissal of the dead from the house, in the naming, when the ancestor-men bang open the door and the previous namesake comes in, he never leaves. Through the baby's name, the ancestor finally comes home.

Yet the name is not quite all that is left of the person. The renaming is not a reincarnation, and there is no equivalent of the mainstream Hindu ideas of *samsara*, the cycle of rebirth, or *moksha*, the liberation from this cycle. It is definitely better to be alive than dead, and the dead do not attain a purification or release, but rather undergo deprivation and progressive attenuation. After stripping away the terminal illness, the fields and gold necklaces, and the name, there still remains an irreducible residue of the person that continues in an onward trajectory. I would sometimes ask an ɪlda sonum to bring me a very ancient ancestor, and would be told that he had died a second time in the Underworld and turned into a butterfly. I compared this with my genealogies and realized that the time when someone died again in the Underworld corresponded closely to the time when there was nobody left alive who remembered him in person, and even the successor to his name had died. It all made sense. Everything else about the deceased is brought back into the living realm except for a small core of what may be called his subjectivity. As they drift away toward butterflyhood, this subjective part moves beyond the reach of dialogue, and thus of knowability. A butterfly is a person who for all we know may never cease to exist, but who has no voice, no story, and no relationships. Butterflies are Memories without rememberers.

5

. . . .

YOUNG MONOSI CHANGES HIS WORLD FOREVER

. . . .

Where does a system like this come from? How do all these complementary roles come about so that everyone knows what to do, even if they argue about the detail? (Indeed, argument at that level is what drives the system.) How is it all sustained with no holy book and no one in charge? The whole is bigger than anyone's awareness or vision. No Sora sees their culture in the systemic manner of a researcher—they just live it and do it. This too is part of the mystery: how a traumatized person can become soothed after death, how lineages can reproduce themselves through renaming, how conflicting inquest verdicts can edge toward consensus.

Around 1980 I came across a remarkable paper by Freud, called "Mourning and Melancholia" (1957 [1917]). Whether acknowledged or not, this paper underlies most subsequent Western bereavement therapies. Freud sets up "mourning" and "melancholia" as two contrasting responses to loss. He calls "mourning" a "normal" condition that is resolved with the passage of time as the mourner's sense of attachment painfully withdraws itself from the deceased, maybe even finding someone else to love. He uses "melancholia" to describe a "pathological" failure of this process, in which the mourner loses the will to live, through an identification with the dead person.

When I first read this I was astonished at the resonances with Sora thinking. Freud's formulation reads almost like a direct translation of Sora animism into an alternative set of metaphors (Vitebsky 1993: 238–47). There is a similar intense attachment, based on memory, between the bereaved and the deceased, and a similar ambivalence between compassion and aggression. In normal mourning there is a gradual withdrawal that eventually leaves the successful mourner "free." In melancholia, on the other hand, the patient punishes himself in a "hysterical" fashion by overidentifying with the deceased to the point of taking on the same states of illness from which the deceased suffered.

This makes it clear that whatever else is going on, Sora religion is also a form of psychotherapy. But underlying this parallel, there is a crucial difference. The Sora system may be operated by living actors, yet it is represented equally from the perpective of the dead. Death is not an annihilation, but a separation in which both sides continue to exist and are desperate to communicate, and do so through the transmission and sharing of pain. For Freud (1957 [1917]: 255) the dead person "no longer exists," so that the bereaved person must either show a "respect for reality" or turn "away from reality" into something he calls a "hallucinatory wishful psychosis" (244). The Sora are equally sure about the nature of reality: the dead continue to exist, and they miss us as much as we miss them—or even more. Moreover, they take the initiative when they make us ill, thereby controlling the emotional tone of the relationship by forcing us to share their state. The whole process appears to be about how the dead feel.

For Freud, mourning and melancholia are alternative possible responses to bereavement. The psychoanalyst's task is to direct the patient away from the pathological response (melancholia) and toward the healthy one (normal mourning). The corresponding Sora contrast is between being trapped in an Experience sonum and being redeemed into the state of proper ancestorhood, and this is done by the deceased jointly with the mourners, conversing through the shaman. For the Sora these are not alternatives that exist simultaneously, but successive and inevitable stages in a process. Each person starts in an Experience sonum at the point of death, and each person is then gradually led into ancestorhood.

Both Freudian analysts and Sora animists emphasize the power of the past to affect our future, through intimate attachment between persons. The contrast between their models, which at first sight appear so opposed (whether the dead do or do not exist), actually takes place inside this assumption. For Freud, as probably for many readers of the present book, the idea that Memories have agency can be no more than a metaphor. Animist Sora seem to take this literally; because the metaphysics are reversed, so is the dynamic thrust of the system. The dead continue to have their own emotions and agendas. For Freud, the need for therapeutic work lies with the living, since only the living are real and the dead are contained within them as memories; for the Sora, the living and the dead are equally real and need joint therapy together.

Both psychoanalytic and animist healing are symbolic and performative. Being emotionally attached to Sora religion but quite comfortable intellectually with unresolved ambiguity, I never felt I had the need (or the right) to say that one system was more correct than the other. Looking beyond the contrast in metaphysics, I took these as alternative ways of pointing to a universal truth about human attachment. Certainly the relevant core literature in psychoanalysis and psychotherapy—Winnicott (1980), Bowlby (1980), Volkan

(1981)—encouraged this view. No Sora shaman has ever been challenged by a psychoanalyst (let alone a rationalist). The decisive challenge, both to the shamans and to me, has come from Christianity. For Christians, relations between humans are mediated by an attachment to divine entities (God and Jesus, called Jisu in Sora). These are not a simple alternative to sonums. The Christian model, which reached the Sora in Baptist form, offers another cosmology, other values, and another agency, which opens up other political possibilities.

I resisted engaging with the Baptist movement for a long time, and my involvement grew in a roundabout way. By the time I moved from Rajingtal to Ladde in 1976, and even before I mixed with the ancestor-men of Sogad in 1977, I was speaking everyday Sora quite well. I had notated the signature tunes of different sonums, but I could still grasp very little of what was sung to those tunes. Being trained in philology, I believed in mining texts for meaning. But how would I convert my recordings into texts? Ononti had been enigmatic, and Dumburu too did not explain what I needed. By September 1976, living with him on a remote rock slab on top of a cliff and weak with hepatitis, I knew I needed linguistic help. I thought of Monosi, but the thought was daunting. At our meeting in Bethany Bungalow in February 1975 he had seemed restrained and correct. I remembered Mel Otis's reaction to my inquiry about shamans; surely Monosi too would disapprove of my interests, to say nothing of rumors about the girls in Rajingtal.

So I was surprised and dismayed to hear that Monosi had just eloped with a woman to Assam. However, when I returned from the hospital three months later it seemed that Monosi too had returned. I went to find him at his home in an isolated house outside Ongara, a small village up the valley from Sogad and closer to the Baptist region around Serung. With barred open window spaces to let in the light, surrounded by its own garden of maize and papaya and its own small threshing floor, this was a delightful space that resembled a miniature mission bungalow. A little rivulet trickled down a drop between terraced paddy fields, where it was expertly caught and channeled in a banana stalk to provide a private shower. I would often come here to mull over my material away from the hurly-burly of Sogad, with its constant invitations to drinks at dawn, noon, and dusk and its hyperactive shamans.

Monosi was a small, muscular man in shorts and shirt, handsome with fading traces of childhood nose-piercings and facial tattoos. His mother was old and gentle, and his wife tall, imposing, and slightly sharp. There was no sign of the other woman.

In his own home Monosi turned out to be humorous, flexible, and a great storyteller. He was also an important public figure, and visitors kept dropping in to ask for advice about family, marriage, land, or officials. He knew a lot of myths and songs, but I was to discover two contradictory things: that he did not seem to know anything about shamans' chants because he had avoided them since becoming a Baptist over thirty years earlier, and yet that his father had been a shaman himself.

Sitting in the unusual privacy of his garden, I wondered why he lived so far outside Sogad. His answer went back to a key event in the village's history. Monosi belonged to the same lineage as Jamano, Mengalu, and Sidoro, the headman of Sogad, whom I knew as a cunning but rather withdrawn old man. But when the young Sidoro won the fight for the title in 1934 (as referred to in those old police records; see page 62), he became a vicious tyrant. "He had himself carried around on a litter like a raja," recounted Monosi, "and he was so cruel that people called him the offspring of a leopard and a cobra." Soraland was the first place where I understood how remoteness can encourage not only autonomy but also unchecked abuse; I would later see similar excesses in the remotest corners of Siberia (Vitebsky 2005).

There was something crazy about Sidoro's grandiosity as he claimed he could lay a line of silver rupees along the twenty-mile track from Sogad to Gunupur. He stole other men's women as he pleased, but if anyone else had a dalliance he would fine them, under threat of starting a police case: a fine for sex, a fine for distilling aba, even a fine for an allegedly stolen umbrella. In those days people did not have cash, so they simply could not pay. This was the point of the fine: in lieu of cash, Sidoro made them into bonded laborers (*kambari*)—in effect, he enslaved them.

"Think of Pasano the ancestor-man," Monosi said. "He's still poor, isn't he? His father took a loan of three rupees, at four annas [twenty-five cents] of servitude for one year. So he was a slave for twelve years." Headmen in other villages too had kambaris, but Sidoro was said to have had fifty men and women from his own village and even from his own lineage. I recognized an economic imperative in all this: paddy fields could generate a surplus way beyond the skimpy productivity of shifting cultivation, but needed outside labor beyond the scale of reciprocal work parties (*onsir*). To meet this, wealthy or aspiring men might have multiple wives. However, these produced multiple sons to split the inheritance, whereas kambaris gave their labor while leaving the estate intact. I knew one man who was the sole survivor of a village that was entirely wiped out by leopards. He fled to Sogad, and ended up enslaved. As he had no kin, Sidoro had other plans for him—to bury him as a human sacrifice under the hearth of a new house. However, the leopard escapee was

Figure 5.1 Sidoro, the old headman of Sogad
A studio portrait, probably from the 1960s.

having a secret affair with Sidoro's daughter. She overheard the plan, and together they fled to Assam.

Sidoro also had kambaris in remote hill villages that were often on the edge of starvation. He sent the wild men of Gailung, where Ononti had once warned me not to go, to descend as brigands on plains settlements at night and steal animals, brass dishes, and gold ornaments. During the hot season, when people slept outside, the Gailung brigands even kidnapped a plump child and cooked and ate him. I began to understand the old reputation of the Sora as a dangerous tribe.

"Sidoro was very spiteful toward us because Smallpox-Sonum took my father's close lineage-brothers, and he inherited their land," Monosi recalled. "He wanted to grab it off us. My father had this field in Ongara, so he built a house here to get away from him."

I could already feel a provocation coming in the narrative; and so it did. One day in 1944 Monosi's father, Bongalen, was plowing right up to the edge of his field and accidentally dug up some turmeric roots belonging to a man from Sogad called Gurpio. He went and apologized and gave back the turmeric, but Gurpio went to Sidoro and complained, "Look, Bongalen and his brothers have stolen my turmeric." Sidoro saw his chance. He conferred with his Pano barik and together they went to the police station in Puttasing to lodge a case.

The first Monosi's father knew about this was when the police walked up to Ongara and handcuffed him along with his two brothers: "You dug up some turmeric—come with us!" With Sidoro and the barik hovering in the background, they were dragged to the police station. The next day they were taken to Gunupur, and from there to Koraput, the district capital some 130 miles away. Their families heard nothing until three months later when the brothers turned up, having walked home barefoot along sharp, stony roads. Monosi was a boy then, but when repeating the story as an old man today he still cries. "My father hugged me and wept," he sobs. "His feet were in shreds."

Some time later, the quarrelsome Gurpio was killed in a fight at a stone-planting in Guddara. The killer hid in the jungle for some months, then emerged to do a deal with Sidoro that they would accuse Monosi's father of the murder. They even persuaded the dead man to confirm this accusation through the mouth of a shaman. However, a police inspector found no case against him, and he was released. Deprived of his prey, Sidoro targeted Monosi's elder sister, who was training to be a shaman. He sent the police, guided by the barik, to where she was working alone on a hillside. They kept her prisoner in the police station and raped her for three days. Having set up this situation, Sidoro then offered to intercede to get her released—for several hundred silver rupees, the cost of many goats and much jungle produce, which the humiliated Monosi and his father had to take to the Pano and the Komati traders in Gunupur. Monosi's sister was violated, and the family ruined.

But police are a double-edged weapon. Like sorcery sonums, they can turn against their handler and consume him. Sidoro's greed, arrogance, and multifarious intrigues had made him many enemies. When the headman of Ganudreb was murdered around 1947, the young Jogi Ganta, who was already the barik for Ganudreb and Rajingtal, conspired with the headman of Rajingtal to get the killer to say he had been incited by Sidoro. The case reached a senior police officer in Gunupur who offered to get it dropped—for a price ("There's been a report against you, but I can get the Circle Inspector to cancel it"). Fatally overestimating his own position, Sidoro shouted his habitual dismissal—"*Amen boten*—Who are you?"—and made as if to beat him.

The policeman kept his silence, but a few days later Sidoro was invited to make a formal visit to Gunupur. Blinded by his own self-importance, he went down the mountain as a great dignitary with a retinue of followers and camped on the outskirts of town. It was October, the rains were finished, and they had brought plenty of the new season's alin.

During the night, his kinsman Jamano had a dream. A shoal of fish was caught in a net, and while the little fish rushed about frantically, one big fish was trapped and could not escape. He prodded Sidoro, who was snoring heavily from his alin, and tried to warn him. But the headman merely snapped, "*Amen boten*, Who are you to scare me like that?" and went back to sleep.

The next morning, Sidoro prepared for a grand reception. He dressed himself in long trousers and a magnificent red turban topped with egret feathers, and draped himself in gold necklaces, heavy gold earrings, and the gold bangle of authority given to his ancestor—the spectacle of Tribal splendor that imitated the pageantry of royalty and whose mystique so intrigued outsiders.

As he was seated under a huge guava tree ready for his public appearance, his barik came up to him and inquired obsequiously, "Are you well, headman?" Then suddenly three policemen appeared. One held him round the chest while the others tied his hands and feet. They paraded him all round the town, proclaiming, "Behold, Sidoro the headman!" while Jamano murmured, "Brother, didn't I warn you?" The police summoned a goldsmith who removed every piece of gold from Sidoro's person and weighed it. The police made a meticulous list of every item, a total of 12 tolas or 140 grams. They gave the gold back to Jamano, and threw Sidoro into jail. The retinue straggled back up the mountain to Sogad, on the way evading an ambush by gold robbers, for the whole performance had been very public. Sidoro refused to eat prison food, so for three months his six wives had to trek up and down the mountain in relays with rice on their heads and cook for him in the prison grounds three times a day.

When Sidoro was released in December he found his houses and his wives in good order, with huge piles of grain and other accoutrements of wealth. Though his prestige in Gunupur was dented, he resumed his ruthless ways toward his own people. But the following March a neighbor fired a homemade gun into the air to announce a death, and sparks fell on a stack of thatching straw. A huge conflagration completely destroyed Sidoro's houses and store-rooms, which were grouped together like a little palace complex, along with numerous baskets of grain accumulated over many years of extortion. This was the end of Sidoro's pretensions as a petty raja. The Gunupur incident, including advocate's fees, was said to have cost him 10,000 silver rupees, and he also had to sell some paddy fields. The gold bangle of authority mysteri-ously disappeared in the fire, and his slaves drifted away with impunity. The grandest headman of the grandest village had been made by outside authority, and now he had been broken by that same authority. Thirty years later, in the mid-1970s, Sidoro seemed to me no more than an ineffectual old rogue who kept out of public life, though he still retained sixty acres of paddy field, about one-fifth of the cultivated territory around Sogad.

Administrators' reports, memoranda, and letters throughout the nine-teenth and early twentieth centuries (e.g., Mojumdar 1998; Pati and Dash 2002) give a stagnant and depressing picture. The raja of Parlakimidi was already fighting the British in 1766–68 and again in 1831 (Knight and Knight 2009: 67–68). In 1822 he committed atrocities "revolting to humanity," be-heading five Sora and displaying their heads as a warning on the four sides of the town (Ramamurti 1931: vi n. 2). The jungly Sora and Kond hills of the northeastern Madras Presidency were considered so remote, so unhealthy, and so difficult that in 1839 they were made into "Agency Tracts," where normal law did not apply, and a British "Agent" depended for law and order (and tax-ation) on semiautonomous petty rajas (*zamindar*, or "landholder"). The Sora were included in the Russell report of 1834 on royal misrule and Tribal un-rest, though this report directed much greater attention to the Kond because of their large-scale human sacrifice and female infanticide, leading to large British campaigns in the 1850s and 1860s to suppress these customs. In the same period, the Sora too were brought suddenly and violently under tighter control. The weekly market in Yaltap, which I started attending in 1975, had been established in 1863 (Carmichael 1869: 7) along with "a guard of twenty constables" (so it was a point of tension from the start, just as it was for the police inspector whose notes I read from the 1930s). The arrest in 1864 of a Sora headman led to armed clashes, with deaths on both sides, the punitive destruction of several villages, the establishment in 1866 of the police station at Puttasing, and the handing over by the raja of Jeypore of Sora resistance leaders for execution or permanent deportation to the Andaman Islands (Carmichael 1869: 246; Francis 1907: 258).

The Sora area has been perpetually marginal, first to the Madras Presidency, and again when it was incorporated into the newly created state of Orissa in 1936. Sora villages lie on a further internal border between Ganjam and Koraput Districts (since 1992, following further subdvision, between Gajapati and Rayagada Districts). Though there were some administrative differences between these districts, sources from the colonial period consistently reveal a relentless striving to squeeze revenue out of an underdeveloped area; competition between local rajas and the more distant British administration to get their hands on what little revenue there was; chronic indebtedness at all levels; feudal henchmen with grandiose titles, in effect licensed bandits, who extracted unlimited free goods and labor from the Tribals; freelance traders and moneylenders who exploited the Tribals even without the supposed legitimacy of such titles; and a resigned recognition that administration of any sort was possible only by relying on these go-betweens, even though the harshness of their extortions was the cause of the unrest that necessitated the employment of such people for its suppression in the first place. As late as the 1930s, "it was only with the help of bissoyis [a feudal title] and their retainers, 'who were more or less immune from malaria,' that the Government could 'exercise a continuous and effective control over the Savaras [Sora]' " (Mojumdar 1998: 132 n. 13).

Such feudal functionaries belong to Hindu Kshatriya castes. Whatever the chains of emulation or irony, socially they are very far from the Sora. The Pano, Christianized untouchables, are all too close. They were encouraged to settle throughout the Tribal hills by the British in the nineteenth century, supposedly as weavers to provide cloth (and I saw them still doing this in the 1970s, from cotton grown and spun by Sora women). Some Pano remained poor, like the men who bought up small loads of forest produce or the women who toured the Sora villages selling onions one at a time from a basket on their heads. But others wasted little time in humble weaving. They used their knowledge of the Sora language to move into trading and moneylending, and unerringly identified the most indispensable commodity at the heart of Sora culture: the buffalo of grief. There, they inserted themselves into the Sora's lives as monopoly purveyors. Every old person who wasted away after a lifetime of exhausting

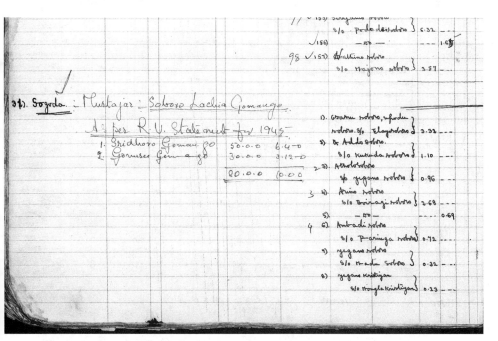

Figure 5.2 Register of rights, 1961

Start of the section on Sogad. The register still incorporates information from 1945, though this was obsolete even then, since Latsia ("Lachia") had died in 1934 and been succeeded as headman (gomango) by his son Sidoro ("Sridhoro"), who collected rent for the raja of Jeypore from his villagers. He is listed personally as having the suspiciously round figure of 50 acres and paying an annual tax of 6 rupees, 4 annas, and 0 paise. The columns against other names list supposed acreages. There were no records of individual plots, and villagers received no receipts (cf. Pati and Dash 2002: 395). All were illiterate, including the headman, who depended on his barik. This register was revised in the late 1970s.

labor on the hillsides, every strong adult whose red blood cells were finally overwhelmed by the malaria parasite, every undernourished child whose life gushed out during a few hours of diarrhea, threw their weeping family on the market for a series of ruthlessly overpriced funeral buffalo.

The Sora have rebelled from time to time by descending with bows and arrows on Pano settlements and burning them down, in regular *fituri* uprisings. There were fituris in 1928 (Knight and Knight 2009: 87), 1941 (Elwin 1945), and 1959, and again in 1977 while I was watching the karja in Sogad. There have been no fituris since, and I shall later argue that the spread of the Baptist church has made them unnecessary.

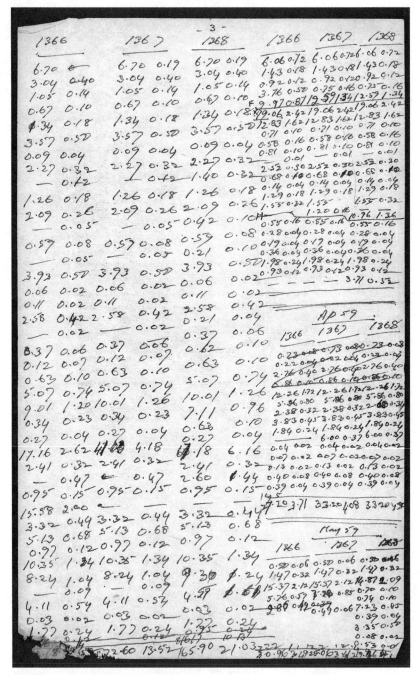

Figure 5.3 Revenue officer's calculations

Fasli years (an Urdu term from Mughal times) start with the monsoon and are 590 years behind the Gregorian calendar. Thus Fasli 1366 = July 1956 to June 1957. This officer would have communicated with Sora only through bariks.

By the time I arrived in the 1970s, the rajas had disappeared, and the oppressive picture in these nineteenth-century sources had at least partly softened. I had earlier thought of the Pano bariks as mosquitoes, casual bloodsuckers who spoiled what I—like some well-meaning government officers—imagined would otherwise be an idyllic world. These early documents do not emphasize the bariks, but I came to realize that they occupied a specific niche in an integrated political ecosystem, linked with headmen and police in a toxic nexus. These three roles seem to have evolved symbiotically after the Puttasing police station was established in 1866. The bariks were inserted between the headmen and the police, one for each village like the headmen. I saw them primarily as interpreters, but Bala, the bank manager, told me that they were appointed as police informers—in other words, to shadow the headman and control him on behalf of the state. The headmen imagined the bariks were "theirs," but actually they could be disloyal, as in the Judas bow by Sidoro's barik just before he was arrested and humiliated in town. This linguistic stranglehold provides the main explanation for the elaborate attempts by Jogi and the other bariks to get me removed from the area.

Until the 1960s, bariks and their assistants were paid a large sum of the villagers' grain each harvesttime for their "services." The grain was given via the headman, who received his own commission. The apportioning between all these people and their deputies and sidekicks was done publicly according to numerical formulae. In addition, villagers were still required to bring straw each year and thatch the police station as unpaid corvée labor, and any unused materials left over were taken and sold by the barik. Headmen might vary in personality, and some headmen and their close kinsmen did protect their dependents, as Jamano rightfully claimed at his stone-planting. But in principle this was still a one-way regime of extortion, without any of the redistributive function of a healthy tax system.

Within this unholy trinity, Sidoro had overplayed his hand. The headman was merely a Sora, and the weakest partner in a chain that passed up through the barik to the police, whose right of violence came from the state and was absolute. Extortion passed along the same route, from the little Sora through the headmen and the bariks to the police and other government officers like the forest guards or the revenue officer, who since the revenue settlement of 1961 kept the register of ownership of paddy fields. Any of these outsiders might target an ordinary Sora directly, but would still need to call in the barik to actualize their demands through the Sora language.

After the turmeric incident Monosi's father looked around for protection, and found it in the idea of literacy: if this is how the police and the ilda sonums get their power, why not do it for ourselves? There were no schools, so he sent his son Monosi, then probably around thirteen years old, to learn writing from Damano and another early Baptist pastor in the orbit of the mission bungalow in Serung. Monosi was a typical animist boy: "I would sneak out and drink alin, but they didn't punish me."

And so it was that young Monosi learned to write Sora in a phonetic adaptation of the English (Roman) alphabet. He still carries round with him, zipped into his Bible case, a tiny exercise book from that time. The large, childishly formed letters culminate in some hymns by Miss Munro, the Canadian missionary who also protected the Sora from 1946 to 1952 by representing them as their MLA (Member of the Legislative Assembly) in the state capital. Monosi sometimes sings me those early hymns, most of them long forgotten in the official Baptist hymnbook that has since taken shape through several editions. I knew the weighty Victorian Anglican hymns from my schooldays, but these were perky evangelical tunes I did not recognize:

sonum kudub gonglesida wan
sonum kudub gonglesida wan
miñam ling miñam ling
Jisun a miñam lingen
miñam ling miñam ling
Jisun a miñam ling

Chase away every sonum, father
Chase away every sonum, father
In the blood, in the blood
In the blood of Jisu
In the blood, in the blood
In the blood of Jisu

The new skill of literacy gave added attractiveness to these ideas. Around 1947 Monosi asked Miss Munro for something to read, and studied her 1939 translation of the Gospel of Saint John: "kɪnsale moiñlai, I was pleased with myself." He was especially fascinated by the role of Jisu's blood. "When I read 'unless you eat the flesh of the Son of Man and drink his blood, you have no life in yourselves' [John 6:53], I thought, 'This is just like our sacrificial buffalo!' "

iten absukateben? Jisun panang a miñamen
iten abbangsateben? Jisun panang a miñamen
a bangsa a miñam

bigada ijja
Jisun panang a miñamen

What heals you? Why, the blood of Jisu!
What makes you better? Why, the blood of Jisu,
His good blood.
Any other—no!
Just the blood of Jisu

"It means 'Only Jisu's blood has goodness (*benangsan*),'" he explained. "She saw how they killed animals and offered blood in leaf-cups. Seeing this, she didn't say, 'Don't sacrifice,' she didn't say, 'Give up immediately,' but said it through a song."

"How is this just like buffalo blood?" I asked.

"Jisu said, 'I cleanse you (*tablotamben*) not with money, not with food, but with my blood.' Just as we used to get well (*bangsalangle*) with the blood of a chicken or a pig, now we believe we've received goodness from the blood of Jisu (*anlen benangsan ñanglai*)."

Everyone who approached the Sora had put their finger on the vital role of blood: the Kond to feed human blood to their fields, the Pano for the profitable trade it supported in buffalo of grief, and now the missionaries. As Miss Munro had intended, Monosi had transferred the logic of sacrifice from one blood-filled being to another. Most, perhaps all, religions are based on blood sacrifice, substituting for a primal human sacrifice that the Kond still practiced until recently and that Sidoro the headman had planned for his slave. High-caste Hindu government officials want to suppress animal sacrifice, but the vegetarian offerings in their temples too are probably a gentler substitute for this. In the encounter between Christian missionaries and local religions throughout the world, this substitutive shift must have been accomplished many times. Rather than denying the power of blood sacrifice, missionaries trump it by arguing that Jisu does it better. There is no need for endless repetition, since he sacrificed himself once and for all, so that all we need now is to reenact this symbolically in the communion service.

The Gospel of John was the only portion of the Bible available in Sora then, and in describing Jisu's crown of thorns (19:2–5) it does not actually mention blood flowing. But this imagery already pervaded Miss Munro's songs, one of many Christian ideas that were taught before there was a text to anchor them. Thus, early Christianity was experienced almost like an oral tradition, but with a canonical book in the background, known only to outside experts.

This blood was the starting point for the tests that the teenage Monosi set for the new god: "I wondered, 'Does God know Sora?' " he told me. "I decided, 'If he speaks to me in Sora, then I'll believe.' But that wasn't enough. I said, 'That blood on the cross—is it really his blood? If he just says that God has forgiven me I won't believe, but if I see that, I'll believe. If he forgives my sin, then I'll believe. If I see his blood, then I'll believe.' When I prayed, I saw Jisu's face and heard his voice speaking in Sora. There was blood dripping down from his head: 'My child, your sins are forgiven.' He was a white man, so beautiful I wanted to embrace him."

Monosi learned fluent Oriya, which for Sora in this area remained an extremely rare accomplishment until the 1980s. In the 1950s he also learned some Hindi while working as a laborer in Assam. When the village council (*panchayat*) system was introduced after Indian Independence, Monosi was an obvious candidate for the new position of chairman (*sarpanch*). This system was designed to short-circuit previous local power structures like village headmen, which were branded colonial. It was obviously the future path to influence and money, and the old elites and exploiters rushed to seize the new positions (just as in 1990s Siberia, I watched old Soviet Communist Party bosses using their social capital to be reborn as heads of new private enterprises).

Like most innovations (except the Christianity that came the back way over the top from Serung and across the district boundary), the introduction of the panchayat moved up the path from Gunupur to Puttasing, reaching into the most remote corners of administrative space only gradually. When the Puttasing area first received its own panchayat in 1958, this included the villages around Sogad. The first panchayat chairman, "elected unopposed," was the Pano barik Jogi Ganta, the unopposable local agent of so much destitution, undernourishment, and early death.

The cluster of villages around Sogad, being one step further into the interior, were not given a separate panchayat until 1967. Unlike the long-Christianized area around Serung, almost the only Sora in the Sogad area who was literate and Oriya-speaking was Monosi. He got himself nominated as chairman—and so did Sidoro. A Brahmin official named Mishra invited them both to Puttasing and asked them as a test to read out a page in Oriya. Sidoro was furious: "*Amen boten*, Who are you to tell me to read this? You're just fit for plowing and cutting wood!" Monosi read it fluently, thus justly punishing Sidoro for forcing him to become literate as a child. When Monosi's term was over, Sidoro nominated himself again, absurdly signing his application with a thumbprint. He got the position when Monosi became ineligible for a repeat term, but the officials asked Monosi to teach him to write. Sidoro

Figure 5.4 Meeting of Puttasing district council, 1976

The secretary (literate) is Pano. All others are Sora. At the center, a council member representing a Sora village.

never managed more than his own name, finally admitting his inadequacy and handing the position back to Monosi.

I was not the first to benefit from Monosi's cleverness. While in Assam in the 1950s, he had read the Old Testament in Oriya and had founded a new church there. "I had a dream, like Joseph," he said, with his habit of referring events in his own life to a biblical template. "There was a huge assembly, all looking to me: 'What is to be done in our land? Why is Monosi silent?' Later I became the first general secretary of the Sora Baptist Association, so I believed more and more in Jisu." He became the youngest member of the select team that met at Bethany Bungalow to work on Bible translation. In the 1960s and 1970s he also became an informant for Indian and American linguists. Whether for the Bible Society in Bangalore, institutes of linguistics in Mysore and Hyderabad, or government offices in Bhubaneswar, Monosi was invited to answer questions as a cultural expert. Ironically, it was because of his skills as a Christian that he was able to purvey this "culture" to outsiders, even though he had himself renounced its beliefs and practices. Once, when he had explained his culture to the staff of a museum, who did not know a word of Sora, "they gave me a certificate to certify that I knew it!"

My quest was unlike that of any missionary, linguist, or official. At first Monosi did not quite understand what I was looking for, but he slipped easily into the role of informant. We started with Ononti's invocations from Rajingtal. I rewound the fragile little cassettes again and again, second by second, trying to catch the same word in the same line. I could work out some endings, but many of the syllables did not come together into words I knew, and I could not always be sure of word divisions. Monosi had been so saturated since adolescence with Christian formations that he too could not understand much. Yet some words began to emerge for him, and they awakened long-lost resonances from his father's chants ("Don't call the sonums for nothing, ka'ja gudingdong," warned his aged mother as we repeated phrases from my recordings).

I spaced these words out on a piece of paper, and started to fill in the gaps. Even the blind alleys were instructive. Why did Ononti include the command "write" (*idola*) in every line? What had to be written, and who was supposed to write it? This word was surely the key to the song, since it was repeated so often. I rushed to make connections with the magical writing skills of her Underworld ıldas, and it was only as the other words around them fell into place that I realized that i do la was meaningless padding, like "hey nonny no" in English folk songs. It was repeated so often because it meant nothing at all.

In other texts it turned out I had correctly identified some of the words, but had not been able to believe my own results. In the first tape I showed him, Ononti appeared to be singing "Don't block me, Kond," but surely this was not what she really meant? When I was with her in Rajingtal I had not understood this; by the time I heard it again from Rijanti in Sogad, I knew from this work with Monosi that the first obstacle a funeral shaman meets on the path to the Underworld is a Kond warrior brandishing an axe and looking for a human to sacrifice:

dangdonging je la Kansid	*dangdonging je la Kansid*
anggurang do la	*Kansid do gamtam*
anggurang je la kansid	*tikubang de la kansid*
	kansid do do la, jadi
don't block me je la, Kond	don't block me je la, Kond
axe on shoulder, do la	Kond, I tell you
axe on shoulder Kond, je la	axe-twirling Kond, de la
	Kond do do la, truly

These meetings with Monosi helped me in my performance as an ancestor-man. Sora has a huge vocabulary that builds compounds from simple roots, while the phenomenon of compound forms gives a double lexicon: "path" is *tangor*, but when added at the end of another word it becomes -*god*, just as *alin* (wine) becomes -*sal* and *enselo* (woman) becomes -*boj*. The second terms in paired lines of verse often do not belong even to this lexicon, and many seemed meaningless until Monosi showed me that some of them were from Oriya and some from other dialects and even other Tribal languages—in effect they were glosses.

I also started to get used to new Christian patterns. I do not know Hebrew but have studied Greek, and I recognized the origins of some of these from the New Testament. *Jadi* (truly) added a dimension of faith as it replaced *u'u* (yes) and is a translation of "amen," meaning "verily"; formations like *dele jenang den* (if it happened; i.e., "in that case") and *itenasen gamlenden* (why because) are also modeled on Greek particles or adverbial phrases that draw an inference and highlight the logical relationship between two clauses, rather than the animists' simple particle *do*, meaning "and."

Baptists created new abstract nouns by taking a verb and infixing the nominal particle -*en*-. The verb *rukku*, "to gather," was developed into *r-en-ukku*, "an assembly"; *ñang*, "to learn," gave *ñ-en-ang*, "a lesson." Speaker, prayer, parish, voluntary donations: whereas the old terminology of feudal government was borrowed from Oriya or Hindustani, the church had created its own entirely

Sora vocabulary, which was bureaucratic, and which—just as in bureaucratic English—drew the energy of a sentence away from verbs and toward these new nouns.

Before Christianity, no one had ever needed to say these things. Such linguistic changes went beyond the missonaries' more superficial problem of talking about olives in a land where these did not grow. How was this new language changing the structures of thought and of experience themselves, and where was Monosi in this? Monosi was helping me to understand Ononti's world and learning it anew himself, at the same time as having been an important agent in its destruction. He had himself helped the missionaries to coin new words. For the "lions' den" of Daniel he had suggested kɪna-siŋ, Leopard-House, from the place where Leopard-victims assembled after death. I could not decide if this was apt, profound, or comical. For those who were born Christian this would simply become the only meaning.

Miss Munro had been helped to learn Sora by the Hindu teacher Ramamurti. However, for composing hymns she mostly relied on Pano Christian advisers, who did not know about Sora parallel verse. Her hymns seem more like a translation from Sunday-school English. Their message was clear, but their repetitions ("in the blood of Jisu in the blood of Jisu") missed the metaphorical depth of changing one element in the second line.

"She didn't fully understand verse," Monosi agreed, "it wasn't till we started composing our own hymns that we did it properly." Parallel verse requires a particular rhythmical and melodic pattern, which could emerge only when Sora hymn-composers abandoned those alien evangelical tunes. They then shifted to the one tune that had been used by animists for work, love, and any casual thoughts, the only tune that had no connection to sonums. Variants of this tune float constantly over the Sora landscape, and now they encompass the words of hymns along with all other songs. The structure of the melody almost demands parallels in the words:

ersi kandring desa ban, buñangji	*pintu tulab desa ban, buñangji*
lumudamen desa ban, buñangji	*lumudamen desa ban, tonanji*
apaiyeten na jadi	*subsuben apaiyeten na jadi*
into the unclean jungle, brothers	into the sinful forest, brothers
into the dark land, brothers	into the dark land, sisters
it has sent us, na, truly	untruth has sent us, na, truly

The tune may be ancient and familiar, but it now carries new and subversive ideas. Untruth is not just what happens when people lie; it is a cosmic agent of destiny. The jungle, as the basic environment of Sora existence, is intrinsically contaminated with something called sin. *Lumud*, the ordinary word for "darkness," becomes a dirty state, so unlike the predawn "cock-crow" (*tartarim*) darkness of the Underworld, which is mysterious and sad.

Even now after they have been indigenized into parallel lines, Baptist hymns remain grammatically simple, with clear main verbs ("it has sent us," just as other hymns say, "I wandered I was lost") and second-person imperatives: singular when addressed as prayer to God or Jisu ("chase away every sonum"), plural when exhorting or instructing the congregation (many examples of "listen!" "see!"). There are few if any echoes of the first-person plural imperative of animist songs: "let us rescue him" (*atandiaiba*) or "may we be cool" (*sayud deaite*). I would later realize that this was consistent with the very different institutional structure of the church, which clearly separates instructors from instructees—a distinction that does not exist in animist ritual.

These main verbs are quite unlike the animist style in which no one is told what to do and the text is hard to explain or translate, as in Mengalu's chant to call up Leopard-Sonum:

1	*tengkurji*	*tengrapji*
2	*aile ñangle*	*aile mujñe*
3	*tam-kuRuan*	*tam-engeren*
4	*tat tat rade*	*dongdong rade*
5	*aile ñangle*	*aile mui'ñe*
1	carrying [victim] on [your/its] head	carrying [victim] on the back of [your/its] neck
2	who came and took	who came and snatched
3	like a hollow *kuruan* stick	like the numerous *enger* leaves
4	pull a *radé* creeper from afar	tug a *radé* creeper from afar
5	who came and took	who came and snatched
6	*tinji ba'din*	*galji ba'din*
7	*a jadrup' nam*	*a jadrep' nam*
8	*mittal barun*	*mittal aren*
9	*a jumamte*	*a gaamte*
6	nine striped	ten striped [*kina* means both "leopard" and "tiger"]
7	your jadrup' growling	your jadrep' growling [addressing leopard]

8	between hillsides	between slopes
9	who ate you up	who drank you up [addressing victim]

10	ba kına ben	ba kambud ben
11	sibırji	gobırji
12	tengkurji	tengrapji

10	your [plural] super-leopard	your super-bear
11	pinching with claws	dragging [victim] between [your/ its] legs
12	carrying [victim] on [your/its] head	carrying [victim] on the back of [your/its] neck

13	samda kului	gırda kului
14	aile ñangle	aile mujñe
15	tinji ba'din	galji ba'din
16	a ñangle na	a muijle na
17	rengkera bud	bongkora bud
18	a jumamte	a gaamte

13	scooping green algae from a pond	scooping green sediment from a pond
		[leopards are said to do this]
14	who came and took	who came and snatched
15	nine striped	ten striped
16	who took	who snatched
17	insect picking up its feet	insect lifting its feet
		[mosquito as warning of leopard nearby]
18	who ate you	who drank you

The verbs are all nonfinite, and the voice keeps slipping around, so that it is often unclear who is being addressed or referred to. The song is allusive rather than precise, not so much an invocation as an evocation, not so much a prayer as an impressionist mood piece. Its ungraspable syntax provides a setting for the dialogue in which the particulars of each case will be made specific.

The recording with the greatest impact on Monosi was the song that Taranti had sung for the peacock sonum as she squatted beside Gallanti to drive out epidemics. "You came to my house, it was dark, there was no path, you hadn't eaten," he later remembered. "I'd just broken up with that woman.

We went to sleep, and in the morning you played me that tape. She sang *agé-agé ogé-ogé*, and I was baffled—*what is this?!* But later she sang about spreading out feathers fanning out feathers and I realized 'Oh, truly (jadi), a peacock!' "

na yirtenai jadi	*piyurtenai jadi*
Komatin longlong nam	*bambaran longlong nam*
urbıl bed na langgin	*tarbıl bed na langgin*
nagade age age	*nage oge age*
nama nama nama	*nama nama nama*
name ama jadi	*ama e yu jadi*
bosondan Guddardan	*gonaitin Guddardan*
saring englai'lenai	*saring kilai'lenai*
Manengul manduyan	*Manengul tardungan*
saring englai'lenai	*saring kilai'lenai*
na, I return, truly	I whirr, truly
over your Komati village	over your Brahmin village
beautiful with unfolded feathers, *na*	beautiful with spread-out feathers, *na*
nagade age age	*nage oge age*
nama nama nama	*nama nama nama*
name ama, truly	*ama e yu*, truly
from smooth Guddara	from well-watered Guddara
I have flown	I have moved
from high Manengul	from airy Manengul
I have flown	I have moved

The song was exquisite, but for me it was one among many I was struggling to understand. For Monosi, it was an epiphany that changed his life. He had never seen Taranti, but he fell in love with her voice, saying, "I can hear that girl's soul."

Though I could not know this, I had introduced the beauty of this unknown girl's song at an unsettled moment in Monosi's life. He was reeling from the reaction to his elopement. The two of them had run away together to Assam for two months before he came back to face up to the denunciations and threats of disgrace from the Baptist leaders. "The pastor from Atarsing came to my house, the missionary David Hayward came to my house," he told me.

Figure 5.5 Taranti the peacock singer, 1976

"They prayed very much, and I did give her up." This episode had left Monosi feeling uncomfortable with the Baptist church, and with the pressure of a system that I would later come to call "pastor raj," the pastors' regime.

Monosi's elopement had been in 1976. His fascination with my recordings began in January 1977 immediately after he and the woman separated. By the time of the Sogad karja in early March, he was not simply waiting for me to bring tapes to his remote home, but coming down to Sogad to accompany me to rituals himself. While I participated, he took care to stand to one side. Yet while other Christians stayed away, Monosi was watching and listening. He started taking his own notes, and this was to turn into a lifelong project that came to parallel my own. Even so, Monosi has never ceased to read the Bible at dawn every day of his life. As David Hayward's wife, Ruby, told me recently, "If his faith hadn't been so strong he would have been seduced by the stuff you were taking him to." However, Monosi's faith did become more complex and nuanced. I was a counterweight to the missionaries, and not only because of my enthusiasm for the old culture: there were things he could share only with me about comparative theology and about his admiration for bold, strong women, who were usually animists. He watched Mengalu performing chants at the karja, fascinated to reflect that this was his own close lineage-brother. He completely forgave Mengalu's previous attempt to assassinate him by sorcery, and remembered instead how when he was a child Mengalu had returned from laboring in Burma during the war and washed him with the first soap ever seen. I noticed how Monosi's own speech and intonation were becoming more varied. It was strange and sometimes funny to hear his perfect bilingualism between didactic Christian harangue and a robust, humorous storytelling, which was less archaic linguistically but turned out to be just as witty as Mengalu's own. The songs he taught me also became more raunchy:

dedenai dedenai jampadi	part for me, part for me, tangled pubic hair
pirurui kaku nam gantenai gamte	your brother the flute says, "I'm coming in"

including a ditty sung by old women:

uda ola tojongling dete la kakung
aba ola tojongling dete la aying
aneng bandan lai'tule ontiden aying
aneng kuan lai'tule ontiden aying

[My breasts] have sprouted like young mango fruit, ola, when the leaves
   fall, la, brother

[My breasts] have sprouted like young aba fruit, ola, when the leaves fall,
    la, sister
the bird has plunged into my pot, sister
the bird has plunged into my well, sister

In March 1977, every village was holding its karja within a few days of the full moon, some of them simultaneously. I was invited everywhere; it was tempting to see everything, and it hurt to think what I was missing. I did manage to see enough to realize the range of variation in details, such as the diverse ways in which the ladder was brought into the house. The need to understand pulled me in the opposite direction: stay in one place and study it in depth. Sogad had now become my village, where I knew the most about kinship and who the ancestors were, so I had stayed and studied their karja. But I was still attracted by spectacle, and had already seen enough of Doloso's rituals in Manengul to know that he was the most theatrical and histrionic shaman of all. Could I also get there in time to see his karja?

I had first been led to Manengul by Ononti and had returned there several times on my own. Doloso had welcomed me at his stone-plantings. His assistant Rajani was also very forthcoming, but she was definitely his subordinate, and I imagined that by watching them I might learn something about a junior shaman's training. The moon was waning, and I feared I might miss the event, but there were reports of buffalo still making their way uphill, prodded by Pano, to be slaughtered. There was not a single Christian in Manengul, so there was no one there who could read a letter. I sent messages by word of mouth to ask about the date of their karja. The answers came at second hand and were not very precise, so it seemed wise to go immediately. I invited Monosi, who had not been there for many years since he had been chased out for evangelizing. After our two sleepless nights at the karja in Sogad we snatched a short rest in the afternoon, chewed some coffee beans as a defense against fatigue, and set out. It was Monday, 14 March 1977. Manengul lay high up on a ridge six hours' walk from Sogad, so it would be dark long before we got there, but I had a friend, Latsia, whose house we could use as a base. This trip was to have unforeseeable consequences that would ruin Monosi's standing in the church but fill his life with a different joy. It would also impel the most conservative animist village of Manengul toward the abandonment of their ancestors.

6

DOLOSO COMPLICATES THE FUTURE
OF HIS MOUNTAINTOP VILLAGE

Manengul, March 1977

There was no moon. My overworked flashlight batteries died, and we lost the path in the blackness. It was completely silent. As we scraped our way barefoot through thorns, I joked that we were following the narrow thread to the Underworld. Monosi wanted to veer toward the sound of frogs that had struck up from some paddy fields far below, but my knowledge of this mountain was more recent, and I was sure we had to keep climbing. The frogs faded, and we were beckoned at last by the distant throb of drums and A-E-A blast of brass horns.

The dancers were moving around in the dark as we burst into this high mountain village, stumbling over the boulders and huge drops between the houses. We had obviously missed the first trance on the cremation-ground, so there was no hurry as we made our way to the house of my friend. I introduced Monosi to Latsia, and we stacked our bags in a corner of his house, helped by his daughter Likini, a lovely young woman with an open, laughing face and huge round tattoos across each cheek.

Latsia's house was tranquil, and was being used by various recumbent figures to snatch some sleep away from the main house, which was not hard to find. While the orchestra thundered away in the loft, the shaman Doloso was dancing on lanky legs over his splendid and unusual brass lamp, fanning his hands from side to side (*birsaile*) and passing his hands and feet over the flame as a test (*jibjib*), or singeing the corner of each new skirt or loincloth before it was offered to the dead, I think to "cremate" it and send it on to its owner. He was a tall, lean man with unusually aquiline features and a sharp, compelling voice. Several of the dancers were men dressed in women's skirts and ornaments and with large female tattoos daubed on their faces with ash. Doloso seemed inexhaustible and even started pounding rice himself to make flour, before eventually handing the job over to an ancestor-woman to finish.

As he sang, Doloso was leaning forward to convey the words to his ancestor-man Palsi. The drumming never eased off, but Doloso sometimes also turned his head to sing into my microphone. He splashed the rice-flour "milk" over everyone and everything; he sang myths and narratives about a rabbit and a pregnant woman; together with Palsi, he "sacrificed" a buffalo made of dried mud by smashing it into fragments; and for each of the sixteen dead persons he sang their name and fed Palsi or an ancestor-woman called Soranti. Here was a reverse of the situation in Sogad: the ancestor-men and ancestor-women were reduced to a foil for Doloso's own prodigious activity. There was no sign of my friend the shamaness Rajani, whom I expected to see performing alongside him; I later learned that there were five funeral sha-mans in Manengul, and that the others had all gone on strike because Doloso insisted on doing everything himself.

As the orchestra played the cremation tune, the pyre-lighters carried the bamboo ladder into the house. Here in Manengul they did not push it vio-lently downward from the roof, but brought it in through the door, edging it through the packed crown of dancers before pushing it up carefully through the thatch:

barangko lingen idarko lingen	*tutumjing kolen jela'jing kolen*
up the barang-tree ladder up the idar-tree ladder	lizard-foot ladder gecko-foot ladder

Doloso suspended some edible seedpods from the ladder and then crouched at the foot of it to sing his way through a series of animals. Leaning toward Palsi, he named each animal before uttering its cry and pretending to eat the seedpods. Then he and Palsi stood up and twirled in opposite direc-tions. At each animal's cry, the ancestor-woman banged on the ladder with her stick to chase it away. The noises were uttered as actual words. The dove went *kurkur*, the chipmunk *jingjing*, the deer *pungpeng*, and the monkey gave a hoarse *kukokakai*. Another bird went *karipkarap*, and a snake hissed, while I could not catch the sounds of rabbit, wolf, leopard, and wild dog. "Eeee, I'll leave out the bear (*omdatai saluan*), you'll all jump on me!" Doloso said provocatively. "Go on, do it, do it!" the women clamored. The bear ran amok in the audience, and they did indeed jump on him and pin him down.

In other villages I had seen shamanesses step up one or two rungs of the ladder and sway in time to the music, but Doloso shot up and down the ladder over and over again, with a vigor that seemed almost superhuman. Everything

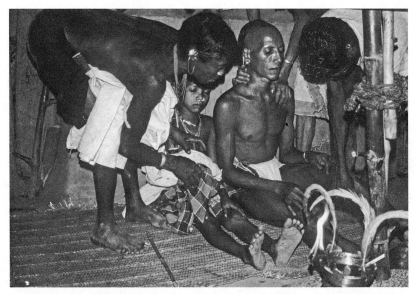

Figure 6.1 Unclenching Doloso and his daughter Ambadi, Manengul *karja* 1977
Their limbs have locked rigid. The lamp will light their way in the Underworld, while the
dead will climb up the bamboo ladder on the right before entering Doloso's body.

he did was hyperenergetic. This was totally his show, and Palsi was more his
sidekick than his dialogic partner. By keeping so much of the performance to
himself, he diminished that interplay of roles that had been so well developed
in the sung debates in Sogad.

Just before dawn I lay in a corner beneath the trampling dancers to grab
half an hour's weird slumber. The music ceased, and the house emptied for
the early morning gasal, and Doloso led me to his drinking group high up
on a mountain. By eight o'clock he was back sitting on the mat at the foot of
the ladder. This would be the main, central trance. Beside him, in Rajani's
usual position, sat his daughter, a little girl aged nine or ten called Ambadi. So
here was Rajani's replacement! This shaven-headed little figure, with tattooed
face, clad in a child-sized white homespun skirt and laden with gold and silver
necklaces, earrings and nose-rings, was going to go into trance alongside her
father! I felt extraordinarily privileged to witness such a perfect example of
training and succession. This was a threshold in the biography of every shaman, and was supposed to happen with girls such as Datuni in Rajingtal, but
I had never been around at the right moment.

Doloso started with long songs, to the same tune as the ancestor-men's sung debates in Sogad. There had been sixteen deaths, but they were being commemorated by relatives in thirty-six houses, who between them were giving thirty-six cloths, thirty-six of every kind of basket of grain, and thirty-six buffalo. Doloso varied the kinship terms and the conventional sentiments as he sang a separate song thirty-six times over the skirts and loincloths he had earlier singed. Then he sang over the baskets of grain, which he then poured into the mortar, where they piled up into a large heap at the foot of the ladder. He was like Prospero in Shakespeare's *Tempest*, conjuring up a world of sonums while keeping the theater totally under his command. Palsi was his Ariel, there to do his bidding, and Ambadi was his Miranda, the dutiful daughter who mouthed some of the words with him.

By ten in the morning, Doloso was ready to begin the trance. While an ancestor-woman tended his brass lamp, he began a long invocation, listing a range of local hills and sonum locations that were new to me. Doloso's shaman lineage differed from those of Ononti in Rajingtal and Rijanti in Sogad, and stretched in an unbroken line back to Sompa, the first shaman of all. As he uttered her epithet, Pubic-Haired Sompa, Sompa of the Coiled Pubic Tresses (Kurutij Sompa, Saekur Sompa), his voice trailed away, and his limbs locked rigid. So did Ambadi's: I could see how much genuine effort it took for others to bend the arms and legs of this small child.

The sonum of Doloso's teacher Disari sang her signature tune through his mouth and said reassuringly: "Ambadi is glancing fearfully *angari-tungari* from side to side, but we'll look after her." Each ancestor who spoke through Doloso was accompanied by a companion who passed through Ambadi's body at the same time but did not speak. As well as addressing the mourners who crowded around, the sonums in Doloso often turned toward Ambadi as if in a separate conversation, to confirm details of their relationship and their story: "Isn't that so, mother's elder sister (brother, father's sister, husband's second wife . . .)?" Here was an entire condensed education in kinship and history, with a fascinating level of detail. However, it was hard to hear or record through the drums, oboes, and shouting dancers, and Doloso was now too busy to lean specially toward my microphone. Women continued to pour into the house with more offerings. Doloso wore their extra necklaces and their extra nose-rings as the skirts and loincloths were piled higher and higher across his outstretched legs and Ambadi's. One sonum was being given a second series of three karjas, like Rumbana in Sogad; another, who had been taken by a Rattud sonum in Kond territory, was being used by the Kond as a human sacrifice in the Underworld and sang a special Kond tune, while a woman who was eaten by a leopard sang:

ajumete kana maiñ	*kuru maiñ ılan*
ajumete kana maiñ	*jeti maiñ ılan*
tatdtad rade kıdanten	*alabmoeten*
dongdong rade kıdanten	*atubobeten*

it ate me,	this furry-chested being
it ate me,	this unkempt-chested being
the creeping *radé*-plant tugger	seized me in its jaws
the *radé*-strand puller	bashed my head

Everything Doloso did was dramatic and flamboyant. Arriving sonums imperiously announced themselves and summoned their desired interlocutors: "Omino! Telenggu! Sondi!" A dumb woman mimed what she had to say; a victim of Epilepsy-Sonum acted out her convulsions; a small child who was not fully weaned clamped its mouth like a leech on a nearby woman and even on Doloso's own arm. When the dead sobbed, Doloso's eyes wept real tears, which dripped over the grieving relatives as they clung to him. At moments of extreme grief he would seize a mourner's head and bang it hard against his own over and over again. Doloso's sonums were more demanding than any other shaman's, keeping everyone up to the mark and complaining about the quality of everything—the grain, the alin, the cloths, the peacocks ("Did you just go and hunt a mangy rabbit?"). They were also more abusive: "Why have you given me poor millet, have your eyes turned inside out have your eyes been ripped out (*opseng-madlamji po egerda-madlamji po*)?" "Flabby-cunt woman gaping-cunt woman (*larbangtij-boj bungbungtij-boj*)!" The relatives howled, and the dancers jigged and loomed over our heads. The orchestra pounded away in the loft, and even through their own din they knew how to change their tune instantly. As soon as the sonum of a hanged man arrived, they immediately swung into the beat for Sun-Sonum: túmbulum! túmbulum!

Finally Disari, the former shaman, said of little Ambadi, "She's only a child, the journey is long and she can't manage all this work, so we're sending her back." Ambadi came out of trance and was helped up onto her feet. Later, four hours and forty minutes after he began, Doloso returned above ground. This maestro knew the owner of every cloth piled on his knees, without hesitation, as he handed them back ready to be offered again at a later stage of the performance. Though this was only her second trance ever, he told me proudly that his little girl had just been possessed by a succession of twenty-nine sonums.

There was no sign of Monosi. At the Sogad karja he had been by my side observing everything, but here I had not seen him throughout the night. There was no time to look for him. I followed the activities through the day as chil-

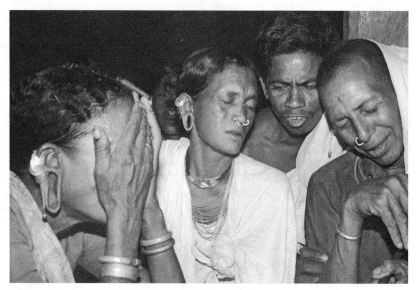

Figure 6.2 A client's anguish, Manengul karja 1994
The woman on the left is greeting a dead relative, who speaks through the mouth of Doloso (right). Rajani (center) is simultaneously channeling a different ancestor, who speaks to Palsi the ancestor-man.

dren bounced around and Doloso led a procession to dance the peacocks into every participating house, where they were "fed" with grain and alin.

Late in the afternoon, in his house, Doloso sang a lament for his own son, who had died when he was barely adolescent:

> *a mi-ol sangen danggara delam*
> *a bar-ol sangen danggara delam*

> you were young as a one-leaf sprouting turmeric plant
> you were young as a two-leaf sprouting turmeric plant

His pushy manner was suddenly transformed into tender grief as he draped the boy's clothes over the back of a buffalo. Here was the transformative, unifying, but also separating logic of Sora sacrifice laid bare: the buffalo had started with the donor's face (as mine had been described in Sogad) but was now being identified with the receiving sonum. Its death would then sunder it from the donor and leave it entirely with the recipient. The donor would have given himself, yet come out of it alive.

Doloso was an accomplished actor, but surely he was also expressing his own feelings. The effect was heartrending: I would gaze on your face and buy you presents, but all in vain. Why did my mother ever come here from Sogad? Nothing grows up here in Manengul except weeds. She gave birth to me, and I begat you, but you died. Whose fault was that? Maybe there was a failure of my seed: Falling-Grain Sonum (Balong-sım), or Premature Bud-Drop Sonum (Uralba-sım)?

arsukung ñanan	*ardaruij ñanan*	*ula*
tukıman a tangor	*ñalangan a tangor*	*ula*
tukıman a dirdir	*ñalangan a dirdir*	*ula*
arsukung godan	*ardarduij godan*	*ula*
tabaran tongñam	*rijoian tongñam*	*ula*

the monkey gait

the [monkey] leap, ula [i.e., narrow paths]

the red-ant path

the black-ant path, ula

the red-ant hobble

the black-ant hobble, ula

the monkey-bounding path

the leaping path, ula

the bo-tree walk on all fours

the hanging fig-tree walk on all fours, ula

angan maiatai uan nam

angan ganlotai uan nam

angan tabıbtai uan nam

angan jarutai uan nam

langga on ula

raja on ula

when will your father disappear

when will your father enter the earth

when will your father drown

when will your father go deep down

my lovely child, ula

my royal child, ula

iytai porıng biñ kurkurtamam

uang langga o'on

iytai porıng biñ daldaltamam

uang langga o'on

iytai porıng biñ jaljalam

ula langga o'on

iytai porıng biñ gijgijam

ula langga o'on

iytai porıng biñ abuma

o uang langga o'on

iytai porıng biñ abasiyam

o uang langga o'on

iytai porıng biñ jodsangam

ula langga o'on

iytai porıng biñ jodmedam

ula langga o'on

I would kiss you

dear lovely child

I would nibble you

dear lovely child

I would lick you	lovely child, ula
I would gaze at you	lovely child, ula
I would wash you	dear lovely child
I would wash your hands	dear lovely child
I would rub you with turmeric	lovely child, ula
I would rub you with oil	lovely child, ula

Through the night Doloso sat for the final trance to dismiss the ancestors, confirming the structure of the karja that I had worked out in Sogad, and just before dawn, as in every karja I witnessed anywhere, there was the sound of the buffalo being massacred throughout the village.

On this day, 17 March 1977, when Doloso, the ancestor-men and ancestor-women, the musicians and their instruments, were all brushed with a knife to retrieve them from contact with the dead; when the peacocks were burned on the cremation-ground, and the ladder from the Underworld was chopped up: this was the day of the election that Indira Gandhi lost. But from Manengul, nobody at all went to vote.

Much later when I discussed the Manengul karja with Monosi he was interested, but it turned out he had something very different on his mind.

"You remember that first night?" he said. "You'd brought some coffee beans. You went off dancing and drinking and recording, and left me alone in the house with that girl." How could I not remember Likini? So that was why he had not been around for Doloso's ritual!

" 'What are you eating?' she asked.

'They're medicine for staying awake.' I gave her some. 'Has anyone brought alin as a proposal?' I asked.

'Yes, people from Gailung, but I said no.'

'Why?'

'I didn't like (itsum) the Gailung man.'

I was flustered (gegeling). 'If another man asked you, would you like him?'

'Issí, no!'

Later I started asking her again: 'But I like you!'

'No, you're a Christian, and I'm tattooed and dressed in these ornaments, don't say that, I'm embarrassed (edte gamdong, garoj'ting)!'

That was that. But gradually, on the last night when they were slaughtering the buffalo, I said to her again, 'I like you (ñen itsum-tam).' " By now it was obvious that Monosi's use of itsum had developed to mean "love." He continued, "Again she said no. I said, 'Never mind for now, but later, I love you.' "

What did Monosi have in mind? An affair was called a dari relationship, and most marriages, especially among the poor, were simply long-term *dari* unions that had established a house and a hearth. More formal was a *pang-sal* (bring-wine), in which the boy's party would bring a pot of alin to the girl's father, as the Gailung people had done, either openly by day or secretly at night, suspending the pot from an arrow stuck into the thatch. If the family approved of him, they would drink his alin. A good trick was to use an old, weak pot and hang it over the door where someone would smash it with their head as they staggered out blearily before dawn, so that it flowed into their mouth willy-nilly. The most formal wedding was the elaborate "scatter-rice" (*sid-rung*), with dancing and a buffalo feast, usually confined to wealthy families. Any of these formats might be combined with an abduction, in which the girl was kidnapped from her home, but even here there were many consultations with go-betweens, and people were never married against their will.

I had been out following Doloso's every move, and had hardly seen Monosi since the karja. "No, I didn't tell you," he admitted, "but later I got my wife's agreement and went back again to Manengul. I spoke to Rajani's mother: 'I've got a wife and children, but I really love her, will you talk to her?'" I knew this was how it was done: I had consulted Inama in Rajingtal about a similar matter. "She did and the girl said: 'I like him, but he's Christian and I do rituals.' So I went to her house again, and spoke to her alone, 'Look, I've got a wife and children, and yes I'm a Christian, and I've just had that affair, but that woman has left now and there was no child. But I love you—what do you think?' She said, 'No, you're a Christian, it can't be, I'm embarrassed.'

"But as we kept talking, she became very friendly. She gave me her sheet to sleep on." A sheet can be used casually by any visitor, and I too had been hot-bedding with that same sheet. Yet it can be understood to mean more. Sharing a sheet was less obvious than sharing a necklace or cigar-holder (*odelpuden*), or touching the heel of the person in front of you with your toe when walking in single file. But the frisson was there: "From that I knew, yes she does love me."

Nothing is a secret for long. Her elder brother said, "Why not, if you love him?" Monosi's wife also approved. "Why not," she echoed, "I'd like her as my little sister. You don't have a son and I don't see the moon any more [meaning "menstruate"], so let's bring her to our house."

It turned out that Likini had also turned down an advance from another Manengul man, one of my drinking partners called Bambu. A few nights later Bambu took her down the mountain to Gunupur town, saying that Monosi was waiting for her there and had asked him to bring her, but actually aiming to spoil their relationship. When Monosi heard about this, he had a bad feeling and rushed down to Gunupur at first light. The moment he arrived, he realized something was wrong. "She was very ashamed and just looked down at the ground. I asked her for some water from the well, but she wept and said, 'I can't give you water from my hand, I've become unclean I've become dirty. Bambu did this to me. I did talk to you, but now I can't see you any more. We hadn't received a payment of alin from you, I did it out of love (*itsumen bate*)!'"

Monosi was devastated. "Why didn't you say so before, but just went off suddenly at night?" he asked. Likini did not answer. In the oppressive midday heat in the middle of an alien town, she turned away and went to fetch water. For a moment he thought of abducting her at the well, but feared that he would be beaten by Bambu or local thugs, maybe drawing in the police. He went home, and told his wife, "I did want her, but after this I won't take her."

"So is that all?" I asked. The narrative still felt as if it had an unfinished momentum.

"After that I had a dream," he replied. "She and I each carried a load of rice sheaves from her field to the threshing floor. I stacked mine neatly, but a bit of hers fell down from the stack. She stood very still and silent, and I picked them up and stacked them for her. The falling sheaves meant that she had slept with another man, but when she let me pick them up, that meant she didn't want any of those other men but her heart (*je'e*) was really set on me."

To divine Likini's feelings through a dream was one thing; to make it come true was another. Likini's father and brother were furious about her dalliance with Bambu, and forced the pace with catastrophic swiftness. Without telling Monosi, they invited her old suitor from Gailung to bring his kinsmen and abduct her, even though she had rejected his pot of alin. She fought and punched ("She's kicking my balls, she's going to kill me!"), so the next morning the Gailung man took her to Kulusing to find some female love-medicine (*monaboj-re*) to make her desire him.

In those days there were still no Christians up in Manengul or Gailung, but down in Kulusing it was already Christian territory, and this happened to be a Sunday. Likini asked to go to church with the women there, though this was an alien space. The congregation started singing a hymn about the death of Jisu: "They beat him and spit on him." This was one that Monosi had composed himself and sung to her. "I thought of him, my soul became confused," she told me later. "When the others were praying with their eyes shut, I slipped out at the back, I threw myself feet first into the well." An old lady saw it happen, and came running into the church to raise the alarm. The water was deep and Likini's feet were stuck in the mud at the bottom, "with bubbles coming *brr brr brr*" to the surface. A man went down on a rope and reached under the water to seize her by the hair. They brought her up with a rope round her waist and pressed her stomach, and water poured out of every opening in her body.

"Like a negative baptism!" I suggested to Monosi.

"*Jadi*," he reflected, "truly."

This was a gesture of despair, but perhaps also of anger. Likini had polluted the well, and the people of Kulusing blamed her Gailung abductor for bringing her. When she recovered consciousness hours later, she too rounded on him, saying, "Why did you drag me here? You knew I didn't want you—even if you kill me, I won't marry you!" Her father was summoned to a parley, but she herself paid toward the cost of cleaning the well with the gold necklace she was wearing.

I was filled with admiration for this determined woman, but I did not yet know whether the story would have a happy ending. Having recently danced a pantomime abduction myself, I was about to learn how it worked in real life.

"Her brother came to see me again," Monosi continued, "and I spoke with my first wife. We went together to see her twice: 'Come and live with my husband!' But she was still shy: 'No, no!' So we took three of my kinsmen and went late at night with a lantern and a flashlight. The others hid, while my wife knocked on the door.

'Who is it?'

'It's us.'

'Why so late?'

'We were on our way back from Gunupur and got delayed . . .' [not that this mountaintop was at all on the way between two low-lying sites].

"She thought, 'There's no food, I'll have to cook something,' and came out to fetch firewood. The moment she emerged, my three men grabbed her. 'U gai, why are you doing this?' she cried out. Her sisters came to the doorway. One of them confronted me on the path and picked up a stone: 'Why are you taking her? Did you bring us a pot of alin? Aren't you ashamed?' 'No, and I'm taking her. Go on, stone me, but I'm not ashamed!' "

Monosi has recounted the story several times over the years, sometimes with Likini interposing additional details. When his elders abducted Onai for him as his first wife, neither of the couple was really ready for it, and their marriage would always remain difficult, though as he said later, "She drinks alin and chews tobacco, but I won't divorce her. The two women get on very well, they don't quarrel." This time it was the fulfillment of his deepest desire—and of Likini's. This story forms the founding myth of their marriage. She says to me, in her Manengul mountain dialect and archaic female intonation, "I thought you'd been sent by the government to suppress our sacrifices.

I didn't know he was an important man and chairman of the district council, I thought he was your slave (*kambari*)." She laughs with a high-pitched whoop, "hi hi hiiii!" "And I didn't know what those coffee beans were, I was scared. I didn't eat them, but put them away and took them with me when I went to gather aba the next day. I showed them secretly to Rajani's mother: 'Look, the white man's slave has given me love-medicine, it's fragrant! What should I do?'" She laughs again. "But Rajani's mother said, 'No, it's alright to take love-medicine, if you love him . . .'"

The village of Gailung had a sinister reputation, but she dismissed the threats of sorcery from her rejected suitor. But her new Christian milieu sometimes gives rise to a darker sense of her own sinfulness, which I find uncomfortable to hear. In a low monotone (another distinctively female intonation) she once said, "But I did go with those other men, I went astray (*aro'ling*)."

The biggest threat to the marriage of Monosi and Likini came not from the jilted Bambu or the sorcerers of Gailung, but from the Baptist pastorate. Monosi had disgraced himself only the previous year with another woman, had been reprimanded, had recanted, and had been forgiven. This time he was not going to give up. Monosi and Likini have lived together ever since, and now have a grown-up son and daughter—but at a price. Despite his evangelical work throughout Soraland since the 1950s (which is how he knows so many far-flung villages and dialects), the pastors forbade him from speaking at church meetings. He was demoted from an elite position on the platform to the rank and file on the floor, and he could not receive monthly communion with the other baptized members of the church. He was dropped from the team of Old Testament translators, while Pastor Damano told his flock not to visit him and refused to christen his children by Likini. The public career of the most free-thinking Sora was sabotaged by the passion of his love life. This was the first incident that started me thinking about how the Baptist church had become a total institution, a regime of pastor raj.

I was widely seen as the catalyst of Monosi's bigamy. I would later become friendly with some of the pastors, especially the humane Dulupet and the saintly Pilipo, but at that time they were all unsure of a white man who was not a missionary but preferred the company of shamans; and their suspicions were reinforced now that I had corrupted one of their leading figureheads. By contrast, my stock went up among animists, and wherever I went around Soraland men in drinking circles would ask, "When are you going to fix me up with a lovely tattooed girl from Manengul?"

"I've known and talked with lots of women, but suddenly I merged with this woman (*abu'mu kan a enselon a dong jalai*)," Monosi told me. This beautiful remark was amazing—I had just learned a Sora way of talking about love at first sight. In the revelatory ecstasy of Monosi's telling, it seemed uncannily like his encounter with Jisu. And indeed he added, "This comes from God, but really it was through you that I married this woman! People are right when they say this about us."

Likini too became Baptist in order to live with him, and brought her father and all his household into the church with her. But it was not so clear what becoming Christian meant to Likini, and it was not until thirty years later, in 2007, that I asked her. By then, I had seen an entire generation convert, and my main quest had shifted to understanding what it felt like to undergo a complete change of belief during the course of a lifetime. "I immediately stopped drinking alin, and I sat in church," she replied. "My husband didn't drink alin or eat funeral buffalo, so I didn't either, out of shame (*garoj*)." This was not what I wanted: it was merely about changing habits, not belief. Surely there had to be more to it than this.

Likini's grown-up daughter Ponanti was listening. "He's not talking about eating and drinking," she said, and restated my question with a heavy emphasis on every word: "From. a. belief. in. sonums. how. do. you. believe. Christian. belief? How. do. you. change. your. thinking?" (*sonumen a dernan sering, ian gam Kristun derte? ian gamle ogandi nam bandate?*)

Likini gasped with the effort of thinking a totally new thought, and gave an exasperated laugh. "I'm a woman who does rituals," she repeated at last. "I eat buffalo meat I drink alin. But because he doesn't eat, I stop eating."

I could not see a way round this. "Do you really *believe* Jisu is the son of God?" I asked. This was an inappropriate question, which left Likini at a complete loss. For animists, before the Bible translators redefined it and gave it the ending of a reflexive verb, the root *der* meant to trust a person rather than to accept a proposition about reality. A similar shift of meaning happened to the Greek word *pisteuo* around the time of the New Testament. By habit Likini was a churchgoer, but intellectually she was an animist. Animists did not *believe*; they *knew* how things were, and especially how things were for themselves, since other tribes, castes, and races had different ancestors and sonums. The switch from knowing to believing, in which you must discriminate between propositions that remain true or false regardless of who you are, comes only with the new, Christian concepts of monotheism and faith.

Suddenly Likini began to answer in her own different way. Once in control of her own narrative form, she became fluent. "When my first child was in my womb, I suddenly felt a dislike for my husband. I couldn't bear him. I went to see my elder brother in Manengul.

'Brother?' I said.

'Huh?' he said.

'I don't like my husband,' I said.

'Why?' he said.

'Why indeed?' I said. Then I had a dream. I was carrying an old grain-basket, it was worn out, but I couldn't put it down. Then my brother said, 'Leave it behind, take a new basket.' So I picked up a new basket, and it was full of good rice. Then I woke up, and after that I liked my husband again."

The message was reinforced by another dream. Just before the birth she dreamed that her brother handed her a knobbly, bristly butid tuber, saying, "Little sister, this is for you, I don't have one of my own." Since he did not have a son, she understood that this tuber represented testicles, and she would have a boy.

I had learned to talk like an animist, but I was still a driven researcher, and now I was pushing her to make an unfamiliar connection. Likini's daughter too had been to school and was now a teacher herself. Both of us had put our question ineptly, in a modern way, and it was Likini herself who had turned it round. We had asked about the extraordinary historical shift of changing to a new religion; Likini had dreamed her answer in terms of a married woman's shift from her brothers' lineage to that of her husband. The more unusual experience was grasped by analogy with the routine one, and the unfamiliar domain of what one believed was referred back to the familiar territory of how one lived. I understood Likini's dream narrative as a parable. Her brother was releasing her to commit herself to her new marriage and her new son.

· · · ·

After that karja I continued to visit Doloso, and his local Manengul variants threw a revealing light on ritual actions I had witnessed elsewhere. One clue can open up a whole chain of inferences. Meanings may not be known or understood, but they can operate at a mysterious level below the threshold of awareness, where they form a coherent and consistent pattern that no one can articulate explicitly. The uncovering of these patterns is one of the re-wards of research. Thus, at a stone-planting or karja every household involved contributes a handful of their own rice to be ground collectively into flour. In Sogad I had seen how this was cooked into a cake, and a portion sent back to be eaten in each house. Doloso made it into an explicit human effigy, which immediately suggested that the descendants were absorbing something of the dead person back into themselves, in an act of symbolic cannibalism. This was confirmed when I was told that only men and in-marrying women ate this cake, and that it was strictly forbidden to the lineage's unmarried daughters. Of course! The effigy makes clear that the cake should be eaten only by those men and women who will go on to reproduce the lineage.

Doloso was not always a comfortable person to be with. Of course like any informant he was selective in what he told me. But he could also be over-bearing, with others as well as with me. It was said that his sister had committed suicide because he kept interfering with her choice of boyfriends. At her stone-planting she spoke through Doloso's mouth and asked who was drumming. It was her lover, so she called him over to share a gourdful of alin with her, saying, "Issí, I've gone down below! Drinking this with you is the only way we can be together!" Immediately after this dialogue the boy went out and hanged himself. The local interpretation was that he had imbibed the contagion of suicide with the shared drink, but I also sensed a ruthless emotional manipulation by the shaman through whom she spoke.

With his attempts to control his sister and his daughter, it was fitting that Doloso's main ilda was Pubic-Haired Sompa (Pubic-Haired Sompa, Sompa of the Coiled Pubic Tresses, Kurutij Sompa, Saekur Sompa). Sompa had so much pubic hair that she had to keep it coiled up under her skirt. Whenever she danced in the hope of seducing a man, this hair would uncoil and hang below her skirt, and her potential lover would run away. This left her feeling extremely lustful, and the veins in her head were throbbing bil bil bil with un-fulfilled sexual desire. In desperation she turned to her brother, saying, "Hey brother! The veins in my head are bursting: will the sun drown will the moon drown if we make love?" So she slept with their own brother, and her soul was cooled.

Sompa stands at the fault line, which among the Sora is so strong, between a woman's two lineages, that of her brothers and that of her husband. This tension is expressed in many ways, such as the prohibition on a young wife climbing into her husband's grain loft, the attack by her brothers' ancestors against the first child she bears for her husband's lineage, and the duplicate funeral staged by each lineage and the conflicting interpretations of Panderi's death and hopes for her baby Disamor's survival. Shamans marry cross-cousins in the Underworld, who in the terminology of the living are considered to be her brothers. So the jealousy of a shaman's husband is not simply against her devotion to any other man, but specifically against her devotion to a man who is a symbolic reflection of her brothers. Sompa's shadow lay behind the many failed marriages and semicelibate lifestyles of female shamans.

Around 1990 Ambadi became a militant Catholic and would have nothing to do with Doloso's rituals. "Trancing alongside her father is like having sex with him," Monosi explained, then as always finding a biblical template. "It's like Abraham and Sarah." To my understanding, she had taken the lesson of Pubic-Haired Sompa as a warning about the difficulty of finding a husband.

By taking Monosi to Manengul and introducing him to my friend's daughter, I had become an unwitting agent of Christianization in Doloso's richly animist world. Yet this would not be the simple Baptist story that was taking over in other villages of this area. The sorcerers of Gailung lost interest in Likini, but her old suitor and fellow villager Bambu still hankered after her, or maybe he felt humiliated as Monosi became a frequent presence in the village. When her family followed her into the Baptist church, out of pique he went down the mountains to seek out the Catholic fathers from Kerala, who until then had very little presence in the higher Sora villages. "They're much better," he assured his friends. "You can still drink, and go to rituals, and sleep around!" The rest of Manengul became an unusual outpost of Catholicism, and while other Sora migrated for work to Assam, Manengul girls started going as domestic servants to Kerala. There must have been pluralism in the air, as the headman of Manengul was converted around this time by a wandering Sarda Sora to a strange alphabet-worshipping cult that I would later go down to the plains to explore for myself.

So Doloso's master plan to keep everything in his own lineage, for which he had shut out Rajani, collapsed. I saw his karja again in 1994, and his 1997 karja was videoed by a visiting German psychoanalyst. Doloso was older and a little slower, but the performance was still superb and almost identical to what I had seen twenty years earlier. In this as in every other ritual since Ambadi's rejection, the person loyally trancing and dancing alongside Doloso was Rajani, who performed with far more enthusiasm than Ambadi had done. I felt sorry for Rajani, as he so obviously treated her as second-best to his own, lost daughter. Rajani, too, longed for a man, but Doloso demanded her celibacy for the sake of her calling. This was Pubic-Haired Sompa with a vengeance. At times, he would withhold her spiritual training, saying that she was unclean; at others he would try to separate her from her lover. During her first pregnancy he forced her into an abortion, which "scorched" (*yagale*) her womb and left her infertile.

I met Doloso for the last time in 1998, four years before his death. He seemed tired, and his pupils had the milky look of an old man. With a new openness, he gave me an explanation of his wall-painting, about which he had previously been so secretive. Apart from Rajani and the ancestor-man Palsi, I was the only person who could sing his sonum songs with him word for word (and certainly the only one who had studied them over and over again on a tape recorder). How awesome it had all been, and how silly it now seemed to the sari-draped Ambadi as she listened in casually from the veranda outside. The baby boy bouncing on her knee would never know that his grandfather had been one of the greatest Sora dramatists of all time. I was reminded of Prospero's final speech:

> Now my charms are all o'erthrown,
> And what strength I have's mine own,
> Which is most faint . . .
> Now I want [meaning "lack"]
> Spirits to enforce, art to enchant . . .
> And my ending is despair . . .
>   (*The Tempest*, act 5, epilogue)

"I was never really in a proper trance, I was just pretending," Ambadi told me nonchalantly from outside, within Doloso's hearing. "I did it because I was embarrassed in front of my father. I ate beef specially to disgust his ılda sonums and drive them away."

How could I not have realized the suffocating nature of Doloso's controlling nature? I later saw a production of *The Tempest* in which Prospero was physically confined to a wheelchair but exerted a total surveillance on spirits and humans alike through a battery of CCTV screens. It was as if Shakespeare had known Doloso. Doloso's daughter, like Prospero's, married another man to get away. I came out of the theater suddenly understanding Ambadi's new religion as part of this move, in which religious change can be a parallel to a family process, just as in Likini's dream. Ambadi had given me an important insight for my future fieldwork among the Christians: once radical alternatives become available, how many people convert not *to* a new way of being but *from* an old one?

7

. . . .

SHOCKED BY BAPTISTS

. . . .

Sogad, 1992 Onward

In February 1992 I was sitting alone on a high, exposed rock above Sogad, the village where I had chanted as an ancestor-man and finally worked out what went on in dialogues between the living and the dead. I had been away from the Sora for thirteen years. Many of my friends were still above ground, but during my absence Mengalu the ancestor-man and the old shaman Rijanti had made a final journey to the Underworld from which they would not return. The village had started to look very different. Thatching grass was now scarce, and the straw roofs and red-mudded stone walls were interspersed with rectangles of corrugated tin, covering houses made of home-baked brick and finished in glossy cement like non-Sora houses in the plains. These houses would be stifling during the hot season, but they marked the homes of upwardly mobile Christians. The hillsides, too, had changed. The jungle had been heavily cleared for woodcutting and overcropping: no trees were left standing above the shifting cultivation crops except heavily trimmed fruiting species like wild mango.

Far below, delegations streamed in single file from surrounding villages to a Baptist meeting, men in long, skinny trousers and shirts with their hair oiled down, women in saris of pink, orange, or electric blue, their breasts hidden inside short blouses. They were already too young to have been tattooed in childhood. Nobody was barefoot—all were wearing flip-flops. Some of the women toiled with loudspeakers and car batteries on their heads. A Baptist pastor walked unencumbered and alone, distinguished by his freshly ironed white *kurta* and *dhoti*, one hand holding a black Bible, the other a black umbrella against the sun. A white handkerchief peeped neatly out of his breast pocket.

Earlier, such a converging of processions from other villages could only have been of in-laws coming to a stone-planting or karja. But this was a new kind of meeting, and for a day it would actualize a virtual community of Sora Baptists. The guests did not brandish axes in a sweaty war dance or lead sacrificial buffalo into the village with an orchestra of drums, oboes, and horns. Instead, they arranged themselves in cool rows in a dry, out-of-season paddy field, shaded under a canopy of alin-palm leaves—wine trees turned to a new, teetotal use—decorated with streamers of colored paper. Men sat on one side and women on the other. Most were cross-legged, though many young women sat for modesty's sake with their legs straight out, already unaware that this was the shaman's trancing position. Combining Saint Paul (1 Corinthians 12:5–13) and wider Hindu custom, they kept a sari drawn over their heads most of the time, covering their faces entirely while praying, then drawing the veil aside as they looked up. The women did not cuddle and sprawl affectionately across each other but avoided contact; rather than being bounced on an adult's hip in a throbbing crowd of dancers, their small children were drawn into their mothers' subdued demeanor. In this new religion, it seemed, one scarcely participated with one's body at all. Or with one's face: years earlier I had sensed a restrained, closed expression on young Christians in the mission area around Serung. Now, even in Sogad, young adults whom I had known as animated children seemed inscrutable as I tried to discern signs of anger, grief, or tenderness behind their reluctance to laugh or cry. In these big public meetings at least, they had reverted to the frozen, thick-lipped look of photographs in early anthropology books, but without the technical explanation of a long exposure.

The scene offended my aesthetics and my ideology. It might have been appropriate in the villages around the mission bungalow in Serung, which had already been like this when I arrived in the 1970s, but here it was in the wrong place and among the wrong people. In the intervening thirteen years I had studied ethnobotany in Sri Lanka and nomadic reindeer herders in Siberia, built a career, and raised a family. Of course I had changed, but I had somehow expected my return to Soraland to feel like a homecoming, as if to my own people. Here, however, something seemed to have changed in the very notion of what it was to be a person.

The shock was also historical. In the 1970s I had regarded this new religion as a distasteful intrusion, and had expected that the church would wane with the government's increasingly tight restrictions on foreign missionaries. And yet I had also seen the self-assurance of the total Christian world around Serung. How could I have believed that this lifestyle would not also overtake the last heartland of their own animists, where Baptist churches had started as small meeting huts in every village and were now growing into grand cement edifices? My prejudice had led me to avoid Christian places and events, though in the 1970s I had attended one of David Hayward's smartly dressed Baptist meetings near Serung, provocatively wearing nothing but a loincloth and gold earrings. During the 1990s I continued to keep the company of shamans, drinkers, and sacrificers, but was increasingly confronted by Christian activity and discourse.

Gradually the researcher in me got the better of the reactionary, and I started to join in and take notes. In a typical Baptist service there is a raised platform across the far end of the hall. On the platform a solid wooden table is covered with a white cloth, and perhaps also with a bouquet of plastic flowers. This is not an altar but is for laying out books and papers. Jisu calendars, and maybe a clock, hang from the wall. The floor is usually of smooth black cement, with guidelines in dark red defining a gangway between the men's side and the women's side. The pastors and their assistants on the platform are all men (it is said they can also be women, but I have not seen this), and mostly quite young.

The meeting usually starts with a long discussion of who will do what during the week or at future meetings. Long before the start, and again at any pause, a voice may start a hymn, everyone starts clapping, and some men start drumming on a muringga, a long, two-headed drum that is deliberately different from any of the drums used in animist ritual. Especially among young women, the singing can continue for hours after the agenda has been completed and the platform people have departed.

As with the old religion, so with the new: it has taken me years to work out what was going on. The logic of sonum encounters yielded a volatile, fluctuating religiosity, mainly as a response to the unpredictable incidence of illness and death. Baptists have abolished the rituals of stone-planting, divination, and healing, all responses to unscheduled events, and introduced new formats based on regularity: early morning prayer, daily evening services, main Sunday services, monthly communions of the baptized, and periodic large meetings (soba, from Oriya sabha) like the one today. A sheet with Bible references for study is printed and circulated in advance for every day of the coming year. Of the life-cycle rituals such as baptism, naming, and marriage, only burial can escape this time-tabling. For Sunday services the Pastor's Handbook (Gupamar a Danardi-Ol) specifies a meticulous schedule (in Sora):

TIMETABLE OF SUNDAY WORSHIP

	Time	Worship
Children's Time	07.30 AM–08.00 AM	
	08.00 AM–08.30 AM	Lesson
	08.30 AM–	Pause
Brothers' Time	09.00 AM–09.40 AM	
	09.40 AM–10.00 AM	Beginning of the service

	10.00 AM–10.30 AM	Lesson
	10.30 AM–10.40 AM	Collection and thanksgiving
	10.40 AM–11.00 AM	Announcements and prayer
	11.00 AM–12.00 AM	Main lesson
	12.00 AM–	Pause
Sisters' Time	02.00 PM–02.30 PM	
	02.30 PM–02.40 PM	Beginning of the service
	02.40 PM–03.10 PM	Lesson
	03.10 PM–	Pause

Even though young people have watches and can read them, few services stick closely to this, and lessons are often very long. Monosi is scornful of the overkill in the Sunday schedule: "Why salt the same vegetables three times? They become bitter . . . If you pound the same rice over and over, you just get flour." Men and women may be present throughout, but the program is especially demanding for women, who must first bring their children to the children's service and then come back for the women's service, sitting for hours with no back support and feeling anxious about their children's behavior. The children's lessons are aimed mostly at their parents. In Rumbatti village, birthplace of Paranto's mother before there were any Christians there, I heard lessons based on "A rod and reproof impart wisdom, but a child who is unrestrained brings shame to his mother. . . . Discipline your child, and he will give you rest; he will bring you happiness" (Proverbs 29:15–17); and later, "The one who spares his rod hates his child, but the one who loves his child is diligent in disciplining him" (Proverbs 13:24); "For what son is there that a father does not discipline? But if you do not experience discipline, something all sons have shared in, then you are illegitimate and are not sons" (Hebrews 12:7–8). This was not at all how Paranto had been brought up.

Women on the floor drooped listlessly while men on the platform harangued them with disciplinary messages from the ancient Middle East. Bodily discipline was hard to maintain. A microphone conveyed the preaching above the squalling children who flopped across their parents or writhed on their laps, while the adults whispered to each other in a constant babble. A marshal patrolled the aisle holding a stick and a whistle, classic props of the Indian chowkidar, or "watchman." He was a local Sora, but his khaki trousers, bushy mustache, and bristly chin gave him the un-Sora look of the military Paik caste, while a white handkerchief peeping from his trouser pocket echoed the pastor style. He scanned from side to side, sometimes looking serious, sometimes grinning. As well as leading a toddler to its mother he used his

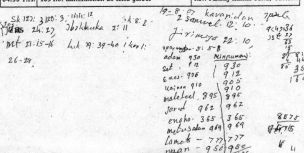

RS. 28 584.

TARIKO : 11.03.2007 ADDIARAN ADINNA

Time	Item	Speaker
08.30 A.M.	Manoih dage kaninkinan	
09.15 A.M.	113 No. Kaneken do Gamangtungan agarbran	Rev. Mohipal Karjee
09.20 A.M.	Bethany Bungalow Apsele idsumtaniyan	Rev. Pratap Jena, Cuttack
09.30 A.M.	Hanangan : Sanengseng darakunaban ayerba, ଏଶ୍ୱ ଈଦୁ ଶିଦ। Philip 3:12-14	Rev. Upendra Kumar Pancha, Nuagada
10.30 A.M.	Garsileban do idsumtaniyan	Pastor Krusaram Karjee
10.35 A.M.	Asumaranji apsele garberan	Mr. Amino Gamango, Scripture Union
10.40 A.M.	Ganadalm beranji	Mr. Livingstone Gamango
10.50 A.M.	Kanenkenan	Serango Christian Hospital
11.00 A.M.	Hanangan : Lua nebanji adra'lin janangden ....Gamangtung lingan hen moihtinai, ଥପ୍ଵଓ ଈମୁଶି ବୁଷ ପୁଷ୍ଟିତ ନୃଢିକ.....ଓଥାଓ ଶୁ ସଡାଥୁଡ୍ଜକ ଠାଚ୍ଚ ଥାନନ ଈଶିଟ। Abakuk 3:17-19	Rev. Saras Kumar Mandal, Kolkata
12.00 A.M.	2 No. Kanenken do sittagar	Rev. Saras Kumar Mandal, Kolkata

ORUBAN AULLI

Time	Item	Speaker
02.00 P.M.	1 No. Kanenken do Gamangtungan agarbiran	Rev. Pirat Sabar
02.05 P.M.	Kanenkenan	Souri Child Dev. Centre, Souri Colony
02.10 P.M.	Hanangan : Kristu Si'ng birindan, ଶୁଷ୍ଟିଦ ଥଶିକାଇ	Rev. Stephen Abraham, Chennai
03.10 P.M.	Garsileban do idsumtaniyan	Pastor Pradhani Mandal
03.15 P.M.	Asumaranji apsele garberan	Rev. Enosh Raika
03.20 P.M.	Ganadlam beranji	Mr. Titus Raita
03.25 P.M.	Soban asaninsinan	Mr. Joseph M. Bhuyan
03.30 P.M.	Hanangan : Estor a surped-damna mandrengnan, ଏଛଉକ ଘମଏଓ ଘାଚନ, Estor 4:16	Rev. Pankaj Kumar Sahu, Cuttack
04.30 P.M.	103 No. Kanenkenen do sitta garber	Rev. Pankaj Kumar Sahu, Cuttack

Figure 7.1 Program of church meeting, 2007

By now, such programs are computer-printed. Monosi has annotated this copy with Bible references (top) and calculations of the 900-year life spans of Adam, Seth, Methuselah, etc. (bottom).

Figure 7.2 Sermon from the platform, near Manikpur 2005

stick to tap anyone who nodded off, and sometimes he sat on a chair in the open doorway, conspicuously controlling the exit.

Was it my prejudice, or was there a connection between the flagging attention and the structure of the event? Coercing people's attention is never an issue in animist ritual, where no one person (except for me) listens carefully to all the words from start to finish. It had taken me years to work out while being distracted by a rich encrustation of signature tunes and esoteric poetics, but the framework is actually simple: summon the sonums (with checks to confirm their identity), recite their story or debate with them (possibly raising many side issues), feed them, and dismiss them. This structure creates rises and falls of dramatic tension by which people vary their level of engagement. Chants and dialogues can last for hours but people wander off, interrupt, or snooze while waiting for moments of particular personal interest. However, in church, everyone is supposed to be in a uniform state of permanent high alertness. When attending regular services I could not locate the climax or point at which something actually happened. In the printed record sheets that are filled in for every service, I saw that each sheet was headed in English: "Karanjasing area—An unit of Soura Baptist Christian Mandali Sammiloni

Bethany Bungalow Serung Gajapati—Societies registration No 8445/798."
Then in Sora:

SUNDAY SERVICE TIMETABLE
Congregation branch: . . .   Date: . . .
1. speaker/preacher   2. president   3. secretary I [for writing
                                                                                 minutes]
4. secretary II [for   5. treasurer
    correspondence]

1. Opening of service by secretary
2. Leading speaker's time
3. Lesson time
4. Prayer to conclude the lesson
5. Prayer for collection and first fruits
6. A little free time outside
7. Parish announcements
8. Prayer for the sick
9. Lesson given by Mr. . . . [so this is always a man]

LESSON

10. Prayer to conclude the lesson
11. Prayer for voluntary donations
12. Free speaking time
13. All stand and sing
      Timetable may be changed in case of need

This detailed program revealed how much my view of what ritual is, or should be, had been conditioned by my association with shamans. I was looking for the wrong thing. There is indeed no climax: this is just what the Baptists have abolished. Though it would make no sense in animist logic, this is a ritual with no turning point. It is a powerful moral theater that changes much of the point of an animist ritual event. Where an animist ritual persuades by negotiation, a Baptist service persuades by assertion, like a political speech. It is not so much a ritual as a rally, and the expected response is acquiescence and a feeling of belonging. As I started attending church, I found myself inside a new kind of performance in which dialogue is replaced by monologue and one participates not by speaking but by being spoken to. Instead of squatting close around a female shaman and conversing with the dead through her body, one sits on the floor to be taught and exhorted by male preachers from behind a raised table. There is a corresponding rearrangement of the roles of layperson, specialist, and otherworldly entity. Dialogue through a human intermediary (shaman) with an entity (sonum) has been replaced by a monologue by an intermediary (preacher), conveying a message *from or about* an entity (God or Jisu).

Every rhetorical device becomes correspondingly different. The Baptist style avoids the excited interjections of ordinary conversation—*U gai! Iten do!?* (Wow! What then?!)—and narrative devices like "I said . . . she said." Biblical quotes often take the form of instructions or exemplars from didactic texts like Proverbs or Paul's Epistles. There are repeated parallel phrases, but these are not the stereoscopic metaphor of animist rhetoric. Rather, the repetition urges the audience to acquiesce while preempting their answers: "Do we lie? Do we steal? Huh? Huh? No, brothers! No, sisters!"

Words are not whispered or wept, but uttered in a new hectoring intonation that offers no right of reply. It is hard to remain interesting without a climax, and without the controversy or opposition inherent in dialogue. The printed agenda and the day's Bible readings are just brief prompts. The rest is left to the improvisatory skill of men who may lack the interactive tradition and humorous creativity of an Ononti, Doloso, or Rondang. The verse of Christian hymns has a tighter syntax than animist incantations, but by contrast the prose of Christian sermons is often very unfocused: "We think, why so much in our house, why is there so much illness?" a deacon declaimed loudly. "Have we forgotten something here, God? What am I like? As for me, what I did before, and what I did in between, and what is now—" He broke off, and suddenly dropped his voice. "But we [inaudible] God." Then loudly again: "Therefore, my brothers, it is with love like that, therefore gradually our work, well, it will be turned upside-down . . ." (*Ellen oganditebe, itenasan dakadne singlunglen, iten asen dakatne banimbimen—tenne karaniden jenang dete, Kittung? Ñen iten amrid daku? Ñen apsele iten lɪmlai abmang, do tarandi lungen iten lɪmlai, do iten daku—*[suddenly quiet]*—do ellen Kittungen a dong* [. . .]. *Kan asan tɪmyɪmdam buñangñenji, gamlenden kan amrid daku, kan asan dɪrga dɪrga baralen, iten, anopsengen dete . . .*)

One can imagine an old animist woman like Sindi butting in with "Hurry up, get on with it, piss off!"

The monologue format, precise scheduling, and policing of behavior prevail because authority comes not from trance but from writing. Biblical texts are not open to negotiation, since the only discursive talk comes from the platform men, who are the authorized interpreters of their own discourse. This is a development of the old religion's fetishization of writing, but there the literacy of ɪlda sonums served to facilitate the articulateness of oral dialogue. Animists did not understand what was being written in those Underworld police station logbooks, except that it gave the writers power over those who were being written about. By the 1990s, the growing literacy of young Christians was making the old-timers' awe at the mystique of writing seem absurd. They had captured this power directly, by mastering it themselves. Yet mastery of the written word is still patchy. People stand up in church to read a sentence aloud, hesitantly and repeatedly, following the catechist phrase by phrase. Even senior churchmen often stumble when reading aloud and say the wrong word (*tanongba*, "husband," for *tanoltol*, "ornaments"), and I can read upside down what they have just written faster than they can read their own handwriting the right way up. So Christian leadership is still a culture of oral competence, extemporized around a written core, which is a monopoly that remains technically difficult even for the monopolists.

In Europe the shift to Christianity took place over centuries "with the slowness of a glacier" (Brown 1995: 9), and the process of eliminating "pagan" elements has never been fully completed (e.g., Burke 1978; Favret-Saada 1980; Lindquist 2005). Modern evangelical movements are in a hurry, and in this rush the Sora Baptist style often feels inchoate, with different aspects of doctrine and emotions still in the process of being formed, unevenly, at different paces. However, the institutional structure developed rapidly and confidently. In 1992 the complete Sora Bible was finally published, and the scene on which I gazed down that morning was the culmination of a process that had been accelerating for a century since the missionaries' first tentative appearance down in Parlakimidi around 1900. Damano and Monosi, who had been the translators' main Sora helpers, were forerunners in the growth of the Sora Baptist Association from 1,500 members in 1958, 400 of whom were baptized, to 180,000 members today.

Just as I was arriving in the 1970s, foreign Christian missionaries were losing their permits under pressure from Hindu nationalist politicians, and by around 1980 the last of the Canadians were gone from Serung. Yet long before then they had set up a structure of Sora pastors (*gupamar*, "herder"). Today, each pastor looks after one of thirty-one parishes (*palli*), amounting to a total of some 800 village congregations (*renukku*, "gathering"). Pastors are assisted by deacons (*gankɪlmar*, "service man"), and beneath them, each village church has a catechist (*ñangñangmar*, "teacher") as well as secretaries, cooks, and other paid workers. In addition there are free-ranging evangelists (*bangsanoplingmar*). This structure is complemented by the Sora Baptist Association (*kenudduai*), based at Bethany Bungalow, with president, treasurer, general secretary (Monosi was the first, from 1971 to 1973), committee, bank account, budget, and annual report. The territorial hierarchy of association, parish, and congregation (*kenudduai, palli, renukku*) is a bureaucratic concept, which is equivalent in civil administration to *zilla*, subdivision, and *tahsil*. From the Baptist Association as the overarching unit, through the parishes and down to the village church, the structure is hierarchical and segmentary, and church events reinforce this cell-like structure at every level. This is a completely different principle from the organic complementarity of roles between healing shaman, funeral shaman, ancestor-man, ancestor-woman, and client.

Big rallies, visiting preachers, the transfer of catechists from one village to another, all encourage uniformity of doctrine and procedure, in a way that is very far from the individual inspiration of the shamans, who did not compare notes. Even so, there seem to be no agreed answers to such dilemmas as Why is it wrong to cry "Hallelujah" like a Pentecostal? Why does the beast in Revelation have ten horns? Did Eve have sexual intercourse with the serpent to give birth to Cain? Why could Solomon have a thousand wives, and I'm not allowed to have two? These are serious questions, but few pastors and fewer catechists are well enough trained to match the monopoly of knowledge that they claim. Often the response to parishioners who ask difficult questions is an angry "Who are you to ask?" (*amen boten*) or "Hey! Are you testing me?" (*ai! tungjing-ting po?*). Many laypeople have their own Sora Bibles, but no commentaries to guide interpretation or debate. Allaby the intellectual published a commentary in Sora on Saint John's Gospel, but this has disappeared from circulation, and the only copy I have ever found was in the Haywards' house in Vancouver. They gave it to me, and I passed it on to Monosi, who may well be the most attentive and thoughtful reader that work will ever receive.

Unlike the headmen and bariks who were imposed from above, pastors are selected by the parishioners themselves. "Lutherans require pastors to have a master's or bachelor's in divinity," David Hayward explained, "but our leaders are grassroots, local. It was more important to have them pious than educated."

"Isn't there a risk that they will be ignorant or naive?" I asked.

"Yes, but they're recognized by their community as a leader. And they can go for further training." These are the pastors who go outside to Bible training college, and whom Monosi denounces for their arrogance (*kinsa*) and what he thinks is their unjustified claim to the title Reverend.

The early pastors were independent and high-minded. They decided they would no longer accept foreign money, but would fund the church entirely from a tithe of 10 percent of the parishioners' harvest: God made the harvest, so one should give some of it back to God (this is an unacknowledged parallel to the animist idea, which I worked hard to demonstrate to Monosi, that their crops are nourished by their ancestors to whom they likewise owe a debt).

This was Damano's position, but it was not a simple decision. "When I was new," David Hayward told me, "I thought so-and-so is in debt, he needs money, so why not? But Perry Allaby said, 'No, it will set a precedent.'" How well I understood that dilemma. David continued, "They also asked for money to go out from Serung to the villages, and again Perry said, 'No, seek God's kingdom first.' Mel Otis too opposed outside aid; he said, 'Don't give motorcycles to pastors,' and he was right."

However, some of the more recent officeholders of the Sora Baptist Association have had "grandiose schemes" for the missionaries to finance, while seeking to retain autonomy of action and judgment. This tension is perhaps inherent in any process of decolonization: the Haywards have been welcomed on their occasional return visits with great honor, but when they wrote from Canada to suggest that the Baptist Association high command's punishment of Monosi was too harsh, they were told firmly not to interfere: "It's our church now."

That early high-mindedness was not easy to sustain. The pastor in 1992 was walking to the meeting aloof and unencumbered, cool and clean. Probably no Sora had ever walked this way before there were pastors. Where did his style come from? The accusation of kınsa, "arrogance," which animists and Christians alike throw at pastors, is not about a new affectation, but rather has become focused on a new category of person. Pastors take over many aspects of two kinds of power that were previously separate, those of the headman and the shaman, corresponding in principle to many similar structures in India that distinguish king from priest, temporal from spiritual power. With their fastidiousness and disdain, pastors also incorporate a new bourgeois aesthetic derived both from the missionaries and from the spreading middle-class values of the town.

The Sora headman's position is founded on wealth and coercion. High-caste government officials, Pano bariks, and Sora headmen all behaved with kınsa, secure in their domination, and the church's hierarchical structure contains the potential to encourage headman-like behavior as it funnels power and wealth up a hierarchical pyramid.

To the extent that the pastors replace the shamans, this is by contrast rather than by resemblance. Shamans may wield extraordinary spiritual and psychological influence, even processing inheritance among the richest headmen, but they are not directly involved in politics, and are usually poor themselves.

The more important funeral shamans are generally women, while the pastor is always a man. A shaman wears ordinary, grubby clothes and works like an ordinary person, but a pastor generally does no manual labor and wears a uniform of freshly laundered and ironed white cotton like a Brahmin priest or a politician. His performances are less fleshly than the shaman's. While she may be embraced by howling mourners, he remains separated behind a table; he does not embody those they have loved nor enverb them in his speech but instead is a conduit for the words of God and Jisu, from whom he, however, remains distinct, with no sense of impersonation.

So long as the state reached the Sora through the filter of feudalism, the remoteness of Soraland amplified its malign aspects and subverted its benign ones. Vicious police and opportunist forest guards frustrated the best intentions of honorable government officers, who were trapped in a deadlock that reached back to the mid-nineteenth century and lacked the local knowledge or logistic reach to bring them to task. During the 1970s I had many discussions with police chiefs, revenue officers, medical officers, magistrates, and intelligence officers, enjoying greater access to such people than I could have in my own country. Our conversations were sometimes uneasy, and there must have been things going on of which I was unaware; but I believe that many were sincerely trying to do their duty and improve their citizens' lives. None spoke Sora, and all came up against the wall of the bariks.

However, on the map Soraland was not very far at all from some big towns. In the 1980s the gap between political space and physical space suddenly collapsed. During that summer of 1979, when I was singing as an ancestor-man and sacrificing a buffalo to Jamano, the Lanjia Sora Development Agency was established. Soon after, the uphill track from Gunupur to Puttasing, with bridges and escarpments washed out each rainy season, was surfaced into a permanent road. I had often trudged along this route, carrying a much lighter load than my Sora friends but more rapidly becoming exhausted, and had once been wafted over these obstacles in a sturdy government jeep in which the familiar places for washing and resting slipped by almost unnoticed and even the strenuous slopes felt luxurious in first gear. By 1992 the route was served by a battered old bus, and the road was maintained by teams of Sora men and women breaking stones and laying them under the eye of an Oriya overseer in shirt and skinny trousers, while monumental black-on-yellow signs painted on rocks listed the project budget and the dimensions of the road.

From 1984 Rajiv Gandhi poured money into local Tribal development, especially for roads and schools. He strengthened *panchayat raj* (rule by local council), and made the panchayat the conduit for this money. ("Just after

I stopped being chairman!" Monosi observed wryly. "In my day members were paid one rupee per meeting; there was no other stipend. When I went from Sogad to Gunupur on foot, I was given ten paise [cents] per kilometer—three rupees for thirty kilometers.")

Schoolmasters had been posted to large villages like Sogad and Rajingtal as early as the 1960s, and I had occasionally seen these lazy teachers in the 1970s. Those of higher castes were repelled (kırıleji) by Tribal life and were permanently absent, while some local Pano stayed, sometimes taking advantage of the Sora girls rather than teaching children. By the time of my return in 1992 there was supposed to be a school in every village. In Sogad there was nearly universal attendance, and there had been a boys' hostel since the mid-1980s.

The government was catching up with the missionaries, but with a difference. Sidoro had been hostile to schooling, fearing that young people would become Christians and move beyond his control, as the people of Ongara had done under Monosi's initiative. However, he had not foreseen the language revolution. The church had made young Sora literate in their own language, even if there was nothing to read except the Bible and the letters of Christian migrants writing home from Assam; but it was school that taught them to speak, read, and write in the state language, Oriya. The bariks were suddenly revealed as having only one skill to underpin all their other techniques of intimidation and fraud—a monopoly on interpreting between the two languages. They disappeared more totally than the headmen, who, though they had partly been the bariks' puppets, still owned much of each village's paddy land.

It was only after my return in 1992 that I started to develop a historical perspective on all this. Through the gap of thirteen years' absence I came to understand that what I had witnessed in the 1970s had been the last vestige of a regime (raj) of headmen and bariks. The headmen had been established as a system of indirect rule in the furthest hinterland, a proxy for a powerful but distant British raj; now the power of the headmen had faded (masunale), and the independent Indian state was entering a phase of more direct rule.

The disappearance of feudal structures also undermined the privileged relationship that shamans had enjoyed by marrying the castes of rajas and their henchmen in the Underworld. Among the symbols of power in their wall-paintings, leopards and pythons were becoming physically extinct through deforestation, but rajas were becoming demystified. In the world of the next generation only the bureaucrats and armed policemen would remain, and even these would become diminished by a general participation in democracy and a diversification of power.

Where funerals had been the main gatherings and the main call on the

Figure 7.3 Baptist wedding invitation, 2009
"Invitation to holy wedding—come at 8 o'clock in the morning—Therefore what God has joined together, let no one separate (Matthew 19:6)—In the name of Jisu, many greetings . . . I invite you because . . ."

family economy, now all this was being directed toward weddings. During the 1990s, *dari* unions were increasingly branded as shameful, even illegitimate. A *dari* marriage was cost-free, but a formal wedding (*sid-rung*) was coming to resemble a classic Indian wedding, and was becoming correspondingly expensive. The cost of sacrificial buffalo continues to be cited as the main economic incentive for conversion to Christianity; but actually, just as weddings have taken over as society's most important ritual, so have they become the main drain on a family's economy.

Animists, too, had a wedding season around January–February, in the cool weather following the bounty of the harvest, when they would catch up on any unfinished stone-plantings. They took care to complete their weddings before the month of blood (*miñamgaj*, around February–March) leading up to the karja, but Baptists continued their weddings until well after the March full moon. By around 2000 during this season there were Christian weddings almost every day.

During the 1990s these had already developed a format of printed invitations, palm-leaf canopy, men and women sitting separately, loudspeakers, and Christian speeches. Yet they still sometimes retained pre-Christian features, such as men dressed as women throwing clouds of ash.

By 2009, such uncouth performances had completely disappeared. That year I went to a Baptist wedding between a Sogad boy, a nephew of Doddo the oboist, and a girl from Borei who was a niece of Sojono. Both the families were my old friends, and I felt very welcome. We found Sojono and some other Borei men sitting on white plastic chairs outside the church hall. Inside the hall, women were sweeping, but one of them rushed forward to wash our feet with warm water, an important biblical gesture of hospitality. Other women nearby were carrying sacks of provisions on their heads or cutting up drum-head cabbages (new) with the sharp rims of metal mugs (also new). Men were playing muringga drums, but the main dancers were girls, taking little steps from left to right and moving with arms linked behind each other's backs in groups of two or three, like tribes from central India. Boys danced separately, combining traditional Sora footwork with upraised arms like Hindi film dancers. One man brandished a hymnbook aloft, and everyone was singing to the standard non-sonum tune. These were not special wedding songs, but regular hymns speeded up for dancing: "Jisu suffered on the cross . . . Jisu pitied us . . . he shed his blood for us."

I visited the bride in her home, where she seemed very subdued in a yellow sari; then I joined the Sogad people where they had borrowed a house outside the village. The groom stood in white trousers and shirt, with a stomach upset and looking rather ill. When he was ready we set off in procession, walking in single file along a thin raised paddy embankment without music or dancing. We were a marriage party entering from another village, but we did not make our arrival into a performance.

People were gathering in a big dry paddy field where rice-straw had been spread under a canopy of alin-palm leaves. Loudspeakers were still playing Indian film music, at the same time as a group of girls sang Sora hymns and clapped to the beat of a muringga. The ambience was very Christian, but there was a sprinkling of animist faces. We sat on the men's side and made ourselves cushions of straw in a conspiratorial huddle while Doddo giggled and regaled me with tales of everyone's illicit affairs. There was a core of close relatives toward the front, but also a large penumbra of spectators, perhaps not fully invited, who did not quite sit down. The bride and groom sat at the front facing the dignitaries, now both in white, and she with her head covered and attended by two bridesmaids in yellow saris. On this level field there was no platform, but a long line of chairs facing them. One by one we were loud-speakered by name to join this row, until we numbered about thirty guests of honor. As each person came up, he went along the row of those already seated, shaking hands with each person. There were no women, and the mothers of the couple in particular were occupied with cooking.

The pastor was instantly recognizable as the only person in a white dhoti outfit. As he took his place at the center the film music stopped, and the church secretary of the host village, Borei, started a prayer. I looked down the line and saw that even Doddo's head was bowed. The secretary continued at length through a numbered agenda, following the template from the *Pastor's Handbook*: who was marrying, who would witness, read, and sing. The pastor was Enusai from Karanjasing, who announced the legal requirement, increasingly feasible since the introduction of birth registration, for the boy to be aged twenty and the girl eighteen.

Triggers for teaching, as prescribed in the *Pastor's Handbook*, came from quotations such as "A prudent wife is from the Lord" (Proverbs 19:14) and "Who can find a wife of noble character? For her value is far more than rubies" (31:10). The service seemed a close translation of the English Protestant marriage: "Do you take this woman . . . ? . . . I do . . . And will you keep her close all your years . . . ? . . . I will . . . For richer for poorer, in sickness and in health . . . With this ring . . ." And finally, "In the name of the Father, the Son and the Holy Spirit and according to government law, in front of everyone here I declare these two to be a couple." Register, signing, witnesses. So here, in a life-cycle ritual if not in a regular service, was a Baptist moment of transition.

Others on the platform corrected the pastor when he occasionally stumbled, but away from the text he was very fluent. The main lesson was based on Hebrews 13:4, which begins, "Marriage must be honored among all and the marriage bed kept undefiled," and adds more menacingly, "For God will judge sexually immoral people and adulterers." Chastity had become a religious value. Enusai occasionally paused to address the assembly, "Eh brothers, Eh sisters?" or to repeat a phrase in Oriya.

A girls' chorus struck up a song, to the accompaniment of a muringga drum and a harmonium, while the bride cried and sagged on her feet, supported by a bridesmaid. They were reading from a computer printout of twenty verses, which offered a blend of traditional and bureaucratic idioms. The first verse opened with the prayer format, almost unknown in animist poetics, of a direct request. The melody was the traditional non-sonum tune used for love songs, work songs, or comment-on-life songs. The first verse was in the traditional style of parallel phrasing:

e ganugu Kittung amdanga la	Eh great God listen, la
e tanimyim Jisu a sintam la	Eh dear Jisu, we thank you, la
e marid janggara gadlamtam la	Eh Holy Spirit we inform you, la
garbernalen amdanga la Kittung	Hear our prayer, la, God
surpidnalen amdang ga la Jisu.	Hear our offering, la, Jisu.

But in the second verse each line supplied information that was additional but not parallel or stereoscopic. The elevation of the precise date into a subject for song was a Christian-modernist touch (cf. Schieffelin 2002):

ɲagi tariko lingen, Kittung	On the third date, God
bagu anggaij lingen, Kittung	In the second month, God
bagu ajar tinji miñum lingen	In the year two thousand and nine
anosaij nam mannileji la, Kittung	They obeyed your law, la, God
renukkun janang mannileji la.	The congregation, that is, obeyed it, la.

A later verse reverted to parallel phrasing with the traditional image from old songs of the pairing of doves as the basic metaphor for faithful love:

nami aɲam lingen e Jisu la	Right now, e Jisu, la
Sara tonan len a dong la	Sarah our sister, la
Joɲaso ream len a dong la	Joyaso our brother-in-law, la
kukuren jenuri jurile la	Has been paired as a kukur-dove, la
dumulen jenuri jurile la.	Has been paired as a turtle-dove, la

Near the end, the song moved to the imagery of separation that also pervades Sora singing about emigration and death:

e tanımɲım dam la o'on amen	E dear child, la
bolongsi mukka nam aggijai la	We won't see your one-hand-narrow visage, la
banardup mukka nam aggijai sanggo	We won't see your two-hand-narrow face, friend
nami sering rıngrıngte la sanggo	From today it is silent, la, friend
nami sering kadingte la o'on	From today it is hushed, la, child

The bride's father gave each guest of honor a folded paper containing a ten-rupee note (the first time I had been given money by a Sora). The girls sang more songs, and draped garlands and scarves around the bride and groom. The audience applauded (the first time I had heard this), and the bride's family fastened a watch around the groom's wrist. I was seeing for myself how the old Sora pattern of bride-service was shifting toward the wider Indian pattern of dowry. Bride-service matched a society without cash or consumer goods where the main resource was simply one's own person and the boy would work as an unpaid laborer for his new father-in-law. In the Bible Jacob had done so (Genesis 29:18–21), but this was not mentioned, and one of Pastor Enusai's lessons worked against it anyway: "When a man is newly married, he need not go into the army nor be obligated in any way; he must be free to stay at home for a full year and bring joy to the wife he has married" (Deuteronomy 24:5). This lesson certainly fell on stony ground, since no Sora could afford to do this.

Everyone sat cross-legged on the ground for the feast, which of course contained no sacrificial meat. Enusai changed into his black trousers and white shirt, and roared off on his motorcycle without joining them. Afterward people flopped and visited relatives' houses, where—despite the earlier reading of the wedding at Cana (John 2:1–11)—they were served tea rather than alin.

In the evening the bride was escorted to her new village of Sogad, though without the music and dancing that would have accompanied an animist procession. The following morning prerecorded loudspeaker hymns started up at dawn, and by midday the bride's family arrived in Sogad for a duplicate event, just as had happened in animist times. Again, the bride stood, sagged, and cried while the gathering clapped in time to hymns. Men (hardly any women) went up and gave offerings of ten or twenty rupees, which were announced by name. The serious work had been done yesterday, and today there was no pastor, only catechists. Monosi and I had also been scheduled to make speeches as elders of the host village, but their lessons went on for so long that our turn never arrived ("It's already evening!").

Weddings are the most comfortable Christian events for me, since many people are invited up to the platform, even animists. However, one aspect is not comfortable. The selection of biblical quotations, the women's silence, and their veiled heads all seem very masculist. The sermons to welcome the bride to Sogad seemed rather stern, with yet more about whoremongers and adulterers: God judges them, obey your husband, God judges those who do not have a Christian wedding . . . Even when I prompt them, I have hardly ever heard a woman express any opinions on church administration or doctrine, even though (or perhaps because) they are the objects of much of these domains.

Perhaps too this is the reason why the *Pastor's Handbook* devotes so many more pages to the marriage ceremony than to any other occasion. This seems to be a focal point for an assertion, both of a control over women's sexuality, and of a difference from how things were done before. The sexual goings-on in Doddo's gossip as we sat under the canopy were precisely what the lessons by pastor, deacon, and catechist were trying to suppress. The dancing was joyful, but the sexes were separated, and the erotic resonance of an animist wedding was absent. There was no carnival, no transvestism, no obscene miming or suggestive songs, and no rubbing of the couple's thighs with turmeric. There was a mention of legitimate sexuality in the service of fertility ("Be fruitful and multiply," Genesis 9:7), but with no link to ancestors, even though this link is very strong in the Jewish culture of the Old Testament. This disjunction lay at the heart of Sora Baptist thinking, and it was a puzzle that I was to spend many more years trying to understand.

Marriage had become an arena for the assertion of new values, through a new discourse of discontinuity as well as of restraint, abstention, and control. The didactic style of the pastor's rhetoric, too, emanated a sense of values by instruction rather than by the consensus that arose gradually out of dialogue. This new authoritarianism provided an uncanny echo of the orders barked out by teachers at school. Both school and church worked against previous styles of child rearing and socialization, and used teaching as a tool to make young people utterly unlike their parents. With my enthusiasm for the inner soft-nesses associated with the rough edges of animist life, and still chafing at the pastors' punishment of Monosi, I could see all this only in terms of constraint, restriction, and loss. It would take many years of studying the Christian life-style and the history of how it came to be adopted before I was also able to see this the way young Sora themselves saw it: as a liberation. This insight would also show me that this liberation works best in terms of relations with the outside world, but there is a price to be paid on a more intimate level.

What I did already understand was that the Baptist marriage ceremony represented an orientation away from the past toward a future. Yet what kind of future? With the rejection of ancestors, it was also an orientation away from the idea of an afterlife, or at least of an afterlife based on social relations. Whereas funerals are largely focused on older people, school and weddings are aimed at the young, as the age group that is open to teaching and change. Even while pastors in the 1990s were still trying to educate old animists out of their drinking parties and dirty jokes, they realized that the future lay else-where, as should their efforts. For children the school, for young adults the church: these were already functioning in each village as a youth club, severing vertical relations between the generations, sucking social interaction out of other spaces and drawing young people out of the family homes that had pre-viously been the only form of indoor space. Some schools became boarding schools, while the church became a men's house till late at night, sometimes with sleep-ins in the church hall. Though schooling was officially secular with Hindu undertones derived from national Indian culture, peer-group pressure ensured that Baptist forms of rhetoric seeped into every social space. In this fully indigenized church, foreign missionaries were no longer necessary.

Schooling was joining forces with Christianity to make the succession of shamans impossible even while there were still clients who needed them. In Manengul, Doloso lived on until 2002. Without his daughter Ambadi his tradition has been continued, half against his will, by Rajani, but her client base has shrunk and shrunk. The karja was the copestone of the entire edifice of Sora religion, but it required enthusiastic participation by the entire village community. From thirty-six contributing houses in the Manengul karja of 1977 there were seventeen in 1999 and only two in 2005, one of them being Rajani's as she commemorated her own recently deceased husband. The demise of Doloso's tradition was not simply a consequence of his personality or his family situation. Rather, it is one exemplar of a historical shift that was going on in front of my eyes. There must always have been complex demographics of succession among shamans. Yet a historical process is vaster than any personalities, configuration, or agency, and the system was losing its resilience. In Ladde, Dumburu's son Arambo, who had been so open to sonums as a small child, was approached as an adolescent by a kittung who stepped out of a large rock. This kittung made him drunk with strong aba and invited him to follow him into the rock. Arambo refused, and instead surrendered himself to an alternative vision of Jisu robed in white, with holes in his hands and a crown of thorns. He was baptized in 1999.

One day in 1994 I met my first shaman, Ononti, on the path, still barebreasted in the manner disapproved of by Baptists and Hindus alike. She had shrunk and was looking frail. I asked her when she was doing her next ritual.

"I've given up," she replied. "My ilda husband has divorced me. My sonums say I'm dirty, they say I smell jungly, they say I eat buffalo, they say I drink alcohol." She had also had her gold necklace torn off her neck by youths, a sign of disrespect that earlier would have been unthinkable. I had never heard of a shaman giving up like this. I remembered her pride, and felt that something drastic must have occurred. Ononti's close friend and junior colleague Maianti had been killed by sorcery, and Ononti had never recovered. Out of the circle of forceful, independent women who had surrounded Ononti, Maianti's little girl Datuni, who had watched Ononti so intently, had been lost to the world of school.

Shamans, especially women in the funeral tradition, were supposed to start their training as children. I had never witnessed a moment of initiation, in which years of dreams and of sitting alongside a teacher culminated in an occasion called *raptulsing*, where the shaman flung herself off the roof of a house while in trance to demonstrate her trust in her ildas. How could any of this happen in a community where girls go to school? The sonums of Rajingtal were unusually persistent and were now appearing in dreams to persuade my old friends Gallanti and Taranti, who had sung the peacock song that so affected Monosi, to extend their repertoire to the funeral tradition. In 1994 I witnessed an extraordinary event in Guddara, a vital moment in the initiation of a woman called Sompani. This was not a child dreaming of courtship in the Underworld, but a single mother with an adult son. Perhaps shamanizing had always been her destiny, as she had been named in childhood after the primal shamaness Pubic-Haired Sompa. Rijanti and Kuttumi, the funeral shamans of Sogad or Guddara, had long since died, and even Uda had gone since my visit two years earlier. There was no funeral shaman left in Sogad except a woman called Sindai, though there were still quite a few animist clients. The old shamans' ıldas were powerful and demanding—who would attend to them?

In a crowded, darkened house shielded from the midday sun, I found Sompani sitting beside Sindai. Sindai was in a full trance, but Sompani was in an unconsummated half trance. Uda's sonum son had already become her new husband, and was calling her from the Underworld. However, Sompani was unable to go down there. Women propped her up as she sank back against their shoulders, her torso drenched in sweat and tears trickling down her cheeks, unable to take the plunge or utter a word. A succession of sonums spoke through Sindai, commenting on the situation. The recently dead Uda was the most prominent. Sindai convincingly reproduced his high, sharp intonation as he criticized Sompani's new wall-painting. He also called me over to complain that I had not sent a buffalo to his stone-planting ("How could I know?" I protested. "Nobody wrote to me. I often thought about you but didn't know you'd died . . ."). Some ordinary ancestors came too, and Jamano defended me from Uda's reproach: "Pirino did give a buffalo at my stone-planting!" Uda's main message was that Sindai needed a colleague to trance alongside her. Several famous shamans from long ago came one after another singing their signature tunes, while the women huddled around urged each of them: "She must sing! Make her sing with you!"

Uda returned to sing again through Sindai, who turned her head to address his words to Sompani directly:

Let us show you	let us guide you
Poisonous snakes on the path, my love	venomous centipedes on the path, my love
You're dazed with fear	you're rooted to the spot
Come to us, my darling	reach out to us, my darling

The session was a failure, and broke up leaving Sompani wretched and exhausted while the men dispersed for their evening alin. After dark the ses-

Figure 7.4 Sompani weeps as she fails to enter her first trance, Guddara 1994
*An ılda is speaking through the entranced Sindai (left) and encouraging Sompani along
the path to the Underworld.*

sion resumed. There was the same buildup of tension and frustration, until
suddenly Sompani herself started singing:

Don't block my lovely path	don't block my beautiful road
Will I ever see you again, my darling	will I ever reach you again, my sweetheart?

Her own sonum husband started speaking fluently through her mouth,
surely also echoing some of her own feelings: "My father Uda was very sad
down below, he'd found me a new shaman for a wife, he wasn't sure if she
could do it, at first I was shy too to work with her . . ." Sompani had just become the next funeral shaman of Sogad.

Sompani's moment of initiation was two years after my first return to
Soraland in 1992. After the sermons at that Baptist rally I joined the lineup of
dignitaries to receive the handshaking that was introduced by the Haywards
and now concludes every Baptist event. The congregation filed past, men first,
then the many young women looking downward, each hand at a different temperature as they held each male hand in turn. While hymn singing continued
to one side, and loudspeaker film music to another, we sat outside on the
ground in rows, men and women mixed, to be fed on rice and goat-meat,

187

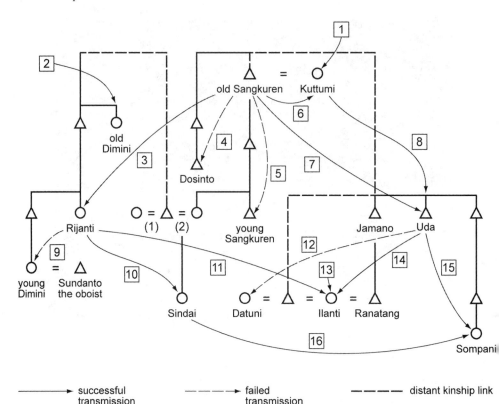

served on banana leaves with newly coined Christian courtesies (*absuyim*, *sintam*, "please," "thank you") and washed down with weak sugared tea and powdered milk.

Just before dusk I discarded my long trousers, shirt, and sandals, changed back into my loincloth, and climbed up through the forest to join my other friends at their evening gasal on a high outcrop of rock. I sank back into my comfortable animist habits, reveling in my hardened bare feet and the rough stone of the seat, and washed out the taste of the tea with alin, "Kittung-Woman's breast-milk."

Already in 1992, there were fewer drinkers and fewer young men. Having been away for thirteen years, I felt not only the shock of the new but also the loss of the old. Mengalu and Dangdang, the most humorous and affectionate of the ancestor-men, had died, also without successors. My surviving friends had reacted to my absence by playing with wild rumors of my death, just as people had done when I went away in the 1970s: " 'He's been shot,'

Diagram 7.1 How Sompani inherited the vocation of funeral shaman

Building on the schematic model of diagram 1.1 (page 30), now seen in practice in Sogad and Guddara. Each shaman marries an ɪlda child of their human predecessor, and may also acquire a whole team of other ɪldas. A tradition can be shared among several successors, and a shaman can accumulate ɪldas from different sources.

[1] Kuttumi brought her own ɪldas from Gailung when marrying in, before also acquiring local ones from her husband. These included Pubic-Haired Sompa, until then invoked in Gailung and Manengul but not in Sogad.

[2] Old Dimini somehow acquired ɪldas from Karanjasing before that village went fully Christian in the 1960s. I do not know where they went after her death—probably to Rijanti.

[3] Sangkuren and his pupil Rijanti were each in turn the mainstay of village funerals for decades.

[4] The ɪldas rejected Dosinto, whose failed attempt in 1977 can be seen in figure 1.7 (page 24).

[5] Old Sangkuren hoped to pass his ɪldas to young Sangkuren along with his name, but the young man died in an accident in Assam.

[6] Old Sangkuren shared his ɪldas with his wife Kuttumi, and they were said to be a formidable partnership. After his death, as I saw, Kuttumi regularly tranced alongside Rijanti.

[7] Old Sangkuren trained Uda in dreams from the Underworld after his death.

[8] Kuttumi trained Uda while she was alive, and he now has her ɪldas from Gailung as well as Sangkuren's.

[9] Young Dimini refused the ɪldas' approach and survived their attempts to drive her mad when she resisted.

[10] Rijanti trained Sindai while she was alive.

[11] She also trained Ilanti while she was alive.

[12] Datuni had been Ononti's pupil as a child in Rajingtal (figure 1.9, page 29), and moved to Guddara on marrying. There was talk of reviving her childhood vocation by marrying a sonum son of Uda, but this did not happen.

[13] Ilanti brought her own ɪldas from Regei'sing when marrying in.

[14] Ilanti combines several streams of ɪldas but did not become a central figure after the deaths of Rijanti and Uda.

[15] Uda later trained Sompani from the Underworld (chapter 7, pages 186–87) and gave her his ɪlda son in marriage, 1994.

[16] Sindai trained Sompani while she was alive in 1994. They are still close and sit together for trances. Sompani will surely have no successors and is probably the last Sora shaman ever to be initiated.

they said . . ." " 'His countrymen wrote it in a letter to Monosi,' they said . . ." "We were very sad, we couldn't eat . . ." They blended me with Rajiv Gandhi, who had been assassinated by a suicide bomber in Madras on the night of 21 May 1991, only hours after he had addressed rallies of Sora in Gunupur and Parlakimidi: "We cried (kudilai) when we heard. He looked like you, he had light skin and a pointy nose. 'How could someone kill our brother?' we said."

The handsome Ranatang looked old and worn, suddenly resembling his father, Jamano, whom I had known only at the end of his life, just before the funeral that had provided me with so much valuable research material. Jamano's brother Uda too, through whom he had spoken in trance, was now a small, shriveled figure suffering from the same tubercular cough that had killed Jamano. He was soon to follow him.

Jadi po, asked Ranatang, "Is it true, Christians say their Kittung made people simply by speaking words instead of giving birth to them?"

"They say there's only one Kittung, and he's male!" wheezed Uda. "But look around you: everything you see, animals, trees, mountains, sky—they all came out of God's vagina. Why do you think the world stays the same now, and no new kinds of things are born? Because her very last offspring was fire, and it scorched her clitoris. 'U gai!' she yelped, 'I'm not giving birth to anything more!' "

The fire flickered on their dear, familiar faces. Frogs croaked around a darkened spring nearby, site of an Earth-Sonum that watered the terraced paddy fields below, but had also taken my witty young oboist friend Sundanto, with his puffed cheeks. Fireflies winked infinitely into the void as the rock fell away toward the faint hymns that still wafted up from the invisible church. Many Baptists were my friends too, but would I ever understand them? What were they trying to do?

8

CHRISTIANS DIE MUTE

Because the dead so soon grow cold.
—Oscar Wilde, *The Ballad of Reading Gaol*

Remembering makes you ill.
—A young Sora Baptist

I was to gain an important insight on the last day of that 1992 visit. The short trip had several intimate and moving moments: in Rajingtal my old shaman, Ononti, held my hand and head-banged me, and Asongroi clasped me long and tight to his chest. But during my long absence, my very first Sora friend, Inama, had died. I had not known, since no one in his family could write a letter, and so I had not sent a buffalo to join the twenty-two others at his stone-planting. In the few minutes before I was due to leave, I found myself alone with his son Paranto in the dark interior of the very house where I had begun my life with the Sora seventeen years earlier. Paranto was now grown up, with children of his own, and had become a Baptist.

We sat in silence, both full of memories, until I asked, "Where do you think your father is now?"

"He may be up in the sky with Jisu," he replied quietly, "or he may be down in the Underworld with our ancestors. How can we tell? We don't talk to them any more."

Suddenly he flung his arms around my shoulders in the darkness, and started to sob:

You're going to a far place	You're going to a distant place
You're going where I can't feed you rice!	You're going where I can't pour you water!

These verses were in the format and had sentiments of the old funeral lament, which the Christian Paranto had not uttered when his father died. He had not joined in his father's cremation or the planting of his memorial stone, and had not greeted him when he came back to speak in Ononti's trance. Yet something about this moment made it possible—maybe even necessary—for him to utter those words. Years ago I had gone away, probably forever. Now, after his father's death, I had reappeared and was going once more, perhaps forever. As he waited for me to leave, it was as if Paranto saw his father dying all over again.

In the dazzling sunlight beyond the open doorway, past the coconut tree that I had helped father and son to plant as a seedling and that now towered eighty feet above our house, the forests and cliffs that held the sonums of everyone who has ever lived here lay baking in the deserted midday heat of the "silence of the sun," *ringring a uyungen.*

Then our private moment was over. A crowd of friends and relatives burst into the house to wave me off. Among them was Paranto's own little boy, who was called Levisto (Livingstone) but who looked just like his grandfather Inama, whom he had never known, alive or dead.

It was in that instant that I started to realize how much I needed to mourn a world I had loved, a world that had shaped me for much of my adult life. Here was a young man who was barred from speaking to his father by the abolition of dialogues with the dead. Outside our darkened house was a landscape populated by innumerable ancestors, but that was rapidly becoming treated as if spiritually uninhabited.

I was used to Monosi's Christianity as something exceptional among my close friends, but now this new religion had taken over my primal family. This moment with Paranto opened up a new mystery that would take my quest for understanding into unexpected territory. Having spent years writing and lecturing on the sophistication and therapeutic benefits of Sora dialogues with the dead, I now had to start again in midlife. My entire scientific quest was taking off anew—and not in a direction I wanted. How could people willingly give up something that was so fulfilling?

I could not solve the puzzle by turning to a wider Christian literature, or by asking the retired missionaries in Canada. If I relied too much on outside sources, or on my own knowledge as a non-Christian but educated European, I would contaminate this process of discovery by prejudging the outcome or the meaning. I had to understand these Baptist practices as a *Sora* religion. As with the old Sora animists, I would have to decode their rituals and link them to their social behavior to understand how they used biblical stories and teachings to create a world of their own.

Whether in the Roman Empire or the twenty-first-century jungle, Christian conversion gains its significance, and its ritual and cognitive shape, from what it replaces as it absorbs, transforms, or rejects elements of an older religion. Paranto understood my question (*Where* is your father?) because he grew up thinking of the dead as being somewhere in particular, in specific locations. But he no longer knew exactly where his father was, and thereby he had also lost something else he would previously have learned from dialogue: *how* his father was. Paranto's distress revealed not only an absence of certainty about death, but also a suppression of communication among a people for whom dialogue had been so central. Christianity did not silence religious discourse—the platform men in the church could monologue at great length—but it did mute debate. When members of the congregation were invited to speak, it was not to argue their own contrary position, but more to read out a verse or prayer that was pre-scripted or to give the required yes or no to a rhetorical question.

What was the lure of this new way? As an anthropologist, I could not accept what the missionaries themselves might claim: because it's true. How could the old world collapse so suddenly, and why did it do so now? At the wedding in Borei I met Sojono, whom I used to visit on the path up to Ladde but whom I had not seen for two decades. "I used to go for rituals," he reminisced, "and you remember we used to drink together. I thought about my life: it was difficult. If my wife was ill I'd go to a shaman, take this much grain, then we'd have nothing to eat. When I looked after her, I couldn't even work. And it wouldn't have done to beg. Now I don't have any of that."

Christianity gave release from poverty and hardship. This economic rationale is argued by Christians at all levels from missionary to pastor to paupers like Sojono, who all invoke this reasoning, often dwelling on the high cost of sacrificial animals and replicating the arguments of Hindu officials. I could not deny any of this; but rituals were part of a broader moral and social economy. They were also how Sora shared meat, and they were surely no more expensive then modern clothes, weddings, and motorcycles, or the overhead of sending children to government boarding school.

This argument also does not acknowledge the progression of the funeral sequence, in which sad memories are transformed in order to make one well again. Even if one believed in only one God, I still could not grasp why it was so important for Christians to sever ties with the dead. So instead of debating whether paganism or Christianity brought more wealth, I asked about mourning.

"No, we don't grieve for our ancestors," Sojono replied. "We did before, because if we didn't do rituals we'd fall ill and our crops would burn up with drought. Now we don't mention them, just God and Jisu. We don't talk to our ancestors, we don't call them. We used to ask them to protect us, but now the dead are embarrassed to come to us, because we call on Jisu instead."

Sojono's answer suggested another reason why my older friends might be

Figure 8.1 Baptist graves outside Sogad, 2007
Inscriptions are in Sora or Oriya. The most legible one (center), *for Malingo Raika, says "repent"* (abyarjin).

afraid to die. In the old Sora world death was a state of separation in which the dead craved acknowledgment and kept bringing themselves to the attention of the living. Among animists, their need to talk was matched by an equal need in their children. But now the parents of young Christians anticipate reaching out from the Underworld for dialogue but getting no response.

The absence of long-term engagement with the dead is already clear at the moment of burial. Baptists will need their bodies again when Jisu returns, so they reject the animist pyre and bury the dead instead. The word for an individual grave, kıntalod, is the same as the old word for a lineage's collective cremation-ground. Sora graves are tombs, built up out of brick and finished off with cement. They are placed singly or in clusters (not necessarily of kin) beside paths, on waste ground near villages, or in their owners' paddy fields (a wider Hindu practice). Scraped into the cement, in Sora or Oriya lettering, is the dead person's name with the dates of birth (guesswork for older people) and death. Reflecting on this, I went back to some clusters of animist memorial stones and tried to find out which stone had been planted for whom. When people could not remember, I tried to identify stones I had helped to plant years ago, but my memory was no better. I was missing the point. Despite the permanence of the memorial stones, and however much mourners may embrace each stone and weep over it at the time, once the stone is planted, its identity rapidly sinks back into the jumbled heap. A stone cannot evolve, but the dead will, as they manifest themselves as symptoms in living people's bodies and voices in the mouths of their shamans.

Baptist graves are a new site for a new form of neglect of the dead, who are now quite literally mute. The identity-card content of their inscriptions is not developed discursively—and certainly not by the dead themselves, who have lost their subjectivity along with their voice.

At a burial, a catechist, deacon, or preferably pastor officiates. There is no drumming or dancing. Women weep, though pastors disapprove and say that the deceased has gone to a better place. The *Pastor's Handbook* devotes five pages to weddings, but offers only ten lines for a funeral. These are nothing more than biblical references, with a mere four references for the moment of burial itself: 1 Corinthians 15:51 ("We will not all sleep, but we will all be changed"); Job 1:21 ("Naked I came from my mother's womb, and naked I will return there"); 1 Thessalonians 4:14–18 ("God will bring with him those who have fallen asleep as Christians. . . . Therefore encourage one another with these words"); and 1 Timothy 6:7 ("For we have brought nothing into this world and so we cannot take a single thing out either"). Though pastors make lengthy speeches at services, weddings, and church rallies, there are no lengthy graveside speeches about the dead person. The officiant will speak to the family to confirm the dead person's record of church attendance, but there is nothing that corresponds to the detailed exploration of his life and relationships through animists' dialogue.

For Monosi, who is convinced that the quality of church officials has declined anyway, this is not enough. "It's very necessary to make a speech about what the dead person was like, how they lived," he told me indignantly. "We won't meet them tomorrow, we won't meet them ever." Sometimes he tries to speak of the dead by the graveside, but feels he is being hurried away: "It's nearly nightfall, let's go," he mimicked. "The pastors just read and go. Damano was serious, he really used to comfort the bereaved, but now they're just interested in weddings where they get fed well and paid lots and don't have to look after anybody!"

The aftermath of the Baptist burial suggests a tension, with pastors chivying one way and people pulling in another. The family may put out a bowl of rice each day for three days, like some animists, and those who did not view the corpse may feel the ghost (*kulman*) tugging at their arms. Some people do nothing on anniversaries, Christmas, or Good Friday, but others go to the grave to clean and repair it, pray, lay flowers, light lamps, and lament. Baptists are aware that Catholics do these things more elaborately, and this is one reason why they sometimes defect, even though the Catholic mission is some way away in the plains.

When the body is laid in the tomb, flowers are put in the dead person's hair, and the body is covered with money and with newly bought clothes. This much is allowed by the pastors. But sometimes, against pastors' instructions, mourners bundle up the dead person's old belongings (sandals, clothes, comb) to bury these too. This is rationalized as follows: "He touched it, we may see it and feel sad." But there is also a more menacing rationale: "He may come back looking for it." These reasons show two different ways of dealing with the animist logic of attachment now that there is no framework for containing it. The personal belongings are buried not in the actual grave but in a separate hole nearby. The way I understand this is that new clothes can safely be put into the grave because they have no history, but the personal effects are more complicated and dangerous because they are a bundle of the dead person's attachments. The burial of used clothes is reminiscent of the "jungle funeral" that animists give to people killed by Epilepsy-Sonum or Leopard-Sonum. Those sonums are so contagious that relatives dispose of the victim's gold and even their fields to remove every source of dangerous attraction (*ud-saga*). But here, in an uneasy compromise, the belongings are ambiguously half-separated from the deceased.

Sojono could even envisage himself as one of these rebuffed ancestors: "My children talk to me when I'm alive, but once they bury me? We used to embrace the shaman and weep, asking 'Which sonum took you?' But now we lament at the burial and put in cloth, but we don't lament any time later, only then. No lamenting on the anniversary, just renew the white paint if we can afford it. No!" he contradicted me. "No praying or recycling of the name! When I became a Christian I abandoned my father, my grandfather."

This was like an emergency triage: you can lead your contemporaries and your children to Jisu, but if your parents are too slow to follow, you simply abandon them (ironically, I later transcribed this recording with Monosi in an Indian city apartment we rented from American Mormons, people who will retro-baptize *anyone's* ancestors). Paranto's tears revealed his confusion about how key emotion words like *sinta* (feeling the sadness of loss) actually work for him. Animists and Baptists have sharply opposed views on this. Animists say that holding dialogues with the dead "cools" your sinta, that is, eases and reduces it. This is what Paranto would have said as a young animist; but recently he explained, "I don't talk to my father because it would make me feel sad. If we talk again and again, we don't stop sinta-ing."

"No, we don't feel sorrow," Sojono confirmed, "we don't remember them. If we remember them, we fall ill: 'They're talking to me again, they're paying me attention again,' the dead person says."

I found this view widespread among young Christians. "Remembering makes you ill," said another bluntly. This is exactly how the animist system works, except that animists think that remembering is necessary and un- avoidable, and would not agree as he continued: "The Bible says forget and rejoice."

Here was a challenge to my psychotherapeutic interpretation. Even if I had successfully shown how Sora shamans and Western psychoanalysts teach us the same lesson about attachment and loss, could I assume that this is a human universal? The Baptists really did not believe this. Would I have to re- sort to claiming they suffered from repression? (And even now, having thought about it for a further twenty-seven years, have I fully shaken off this prejudice?)

During the 1990s the spiritual experience of Christianity remained obscure to me, but the social and political reasons for its spread became very clear. Again and again, I was given Sojono's rationale. The old religion was linked to hardship and humiliation, and both were being thrown off together. The old-timers drank, danced, and laughed, and huddled under the protection of their shamans' high-caste familiars. But those Hindu sonums also come from the same wider world that held Tribals in distressing contempt. In trying to join that world, young Sora were turning this contempt back onto their parents (and my sympathy for the old religion sometimes made me feel in- cluded among them). The next generation turned up in government offices with sleeked-down hair, mustaches, white shirts, long trousers, and shoes, and were offered a chair. As one young man put it, "We used to be treated like dogs, but during the last election campaign the raja of Parlakimidi dined in our church."

In turning their back on the cries of the dead, young Sora are erasing their parents from their own identity. The biblical commandment to honor one's father and mother (Exodus 20:12) conflicts with the scramble to achieve social and economic advancement, and I felt that this contempt was a defense against the unacknowledged pain of having to abandon them. Their parents' economy, burning their bodies out on jagged mountainsides to raise scanty neolithic crops and dying at forty; their hardened feet cracked from clamber- ing over abrasive rocks, and their lanky shanks exposed under tattered loin- cloths as they stand obsequiously seeking an audience with disdainful high- caste officials; their awe at literacy and at the snatches of garbled Oriya uttered by their shamans' helper sonums—all of this can only appear pathetic to their children who write Oriya at school, wear smart clothes, and fix their eye on government jobs.

By the 1990s most young people were becoming Christian through peer-group pressure at school. Today, young people within the Baptist heartland who are born into Christianity know no other life. They often repeat Sojono's economic rationale, but they have never lived the animist economy or spirituality themselves. They know almost nothing about their grandparents' lives and have been told simply that they were poor, walked in darkness, and worshipped devils.

By contrast, earlier Baptists started their lives as animists and passed through powerful transformative experiences. Many early pioneer conversions took place in a moment of despair, and narratives dwell on disappointment with sonums when loved ones die. For animists, dialogue is the great healer. But when it fails to assuage grief, it also exposes one's helplessness in a way that links the existential to the political—a small personal reflection of a wider collective humiliation and helplessness. When the consolation of dialogue fails and is overwhelmed by anger, conversion emerges as revenge. In 1994 a man from Kumbulsing called Omino told me, "I entered Christianity two years ago, out of sadness. My child had burned his hand. They treated him in hospital in Gunupur, but however many sacrifices I made he still died. Then the Christians invited me to their church." Old Oransu of Rajingtal had been a very early convert, of the same vintage as Monosi. Just before he died he told me, referring right back to the 1940s, "I adored my first wife! When she was dying after childbirth I sold all my land and gold to pay for sacrifices. My sister Dubari was a funeral shaman, she was Ononti's teacher. But when my wife died I was furious, I smashed my sister's sonum-pots, saying, 'Why didn't you save her?' My sister said, 'The sonums of all the old shamans will come and get you!' I said, 'So what, let them!' "

"Two days later," he continued, "a Pano man, Pitoro Surjo, came by. He sang about Jisu feeding us full and said, 'If I tell you to become Christian, the bariks and headmen will kill me! But come over to Serung and see for yourself.' Pitoro sponsored me to convert. God made an effigy (*kundaj*), Adam, and breathed life into him. Cows, pigs, goats—they were all in pairs and he put them in a big boat, but Adam was alone and sad, just like me. Then I thought, 'We eat poor food, we don't know writing, we live in fear of police and leopards—why not go over to the Christian religion (*darma*)?' "

It makes no sense to ask a Sora whether the Bible is myth or history. For a rugged old-timer like Oransu, with little exposure to Bible classes, Adam could easily find a place on Noah's ark. More importantly, such narratives are set in a new discursive structure of rupture and discontinuity, in which everything falls on either side of a watershed: before and after conversion.

A key figure in the development of this discourse was Monosi's old mentor Damano. As early as 1965, when he was pastor in Karanjasing, Damano chased Jogi Ganta out of his position as the village's barik. Jogi still held Rajingtal in an iron grip in the late 1970s, and this was one source of my troubles with the local police. In the villages that remained animist, the bariks did not lose their power until the 1980s, when the combination of Christianization, schooling, and development projects broke the monopoly that had depended on the animists' isolation. Jogi lodged a case complaining about the loss of his "rights" in Karanjasing, but even though he was hand in glove with the police, his case came to nothing.

This incident was a harbinger of things to come. As I collected more stories about Damano, a clearer link began to emerge between spiritual change and political liberation. The cruelty of Jogi the barik and Sidoro the headman did not simply arise from personal nastiness, but were a manifestation of the cruelty of an entire world. Officials sometimes asked me to help devise policies to help the Sora, but seemed to think the Pano could somehow be left out of the policy. I then felt compassion for the Pano too, since they were (supposedly) forbidden to own land and had nowhere else to go. To sustain an unremitting dislike of them, the Sora had to attribute to them a hateful racial essence (even while admitting that my Pano friend Prakash was a good man—but he did not need to trade, as he had his own fields, downhill where this was permitted).

The problems of the Sora have systemic, even global, roots. K. S. Singh (1985) divides Tribal politics in colonial India into three phases. These fit well with the Sora. The 1790s to 1860 saw the rise and consolidation of British power. From 1860 to 1920, merchant capital penetrated the Tribal economy and took away much of their forest (actually deforesting much of India to provide wooden sleepers for railways; Gadgil and Guha 1993). It was right at the beginning of this period that police stations, weekly markets, and more intrusive taxation were violently established in Soraland, followed rapidly by the outflow that continues to this day of migrant labor from the newly land-starved subsistence economy of central Indian tribes to the newly labor-hungry export economy of the Assam tea gardens (Jha 1996). From 1920 to 1947, some Tribals were drawn into the growing Indian nationalist movement and even into separatist movements of their own, though the Sora do not seem to have been involved in these movements directly.

After Indian Independence the new Congress Party government outlawed the institution of *kambari*, the bonded laborers or slaves of the big headmen—

locally, through the Orissa Debt Bondage Abolition Act of 1948, aimed particularly at this southern corner of Orissa (Pati and Dash 2002: 113). The manumission of Sidoro's kambaris would have happened by government decree if they had not walked away anyway after his palace burned down. But there was a justice in the timing of all this, symbolized perfectly by the mysterious disappearance in the fire of his gold bangle of authority. Around this time Damano met some Sora from the more cosmopolitan Titinsing area down in the plains, who were singing in the weekly market at Rayagada:

nam sering nam sering	*jijiang kambara marilo bu*
nam sering nam sering	*red'red'ang kambara marilo bu*
nam sering nam sering	*gıdrarung kambara marilo bu, buñang*
From today, from today	firewood-tying slavery is finished, bu
From today, from today	firewood-bundling slavery is finished, bu
From today, from today	slavery for rice-handout wages is finished, bu, brother

Damano adapted this song into a new hymn that spread rapidly, a variant of which remains in the hymnbook (No. 101):

nam sering nam sering	*Kittung la ompuling mailenai*
nam sering nam sering	*Kittung la tegan tegaling la*
nam sering nam sering	*Kittung la maidan maidaling la*
nam sering nam sering	*Kittung la a bu'di bu'diling la*
nam sering nam sering	*Kittung la je'en je'eling la*
nam sering nam sering	*Kittung la anuyıp uyıpling la*
From today, from today	I have joined God's group, la
From today, from today	I have joined God's team, la
From today, from today	I have joined God's circle, la
From today, from today	God's intelligence has given me intelligence, la
From today, from today	God's soul has given me soul, la
From today, from today	God's alertness has given me alertness, la

The phrase *nam sering*, "from today," is common in songs about partings, as in funerals, weddings, or laments when young people leave to work in Assam: "from today your face is hidden your face cannot be seen, from today our house is silent our house is deserted." The antislavery singers caught the era's mood of sudden and irreversible liberation and gave the phrase a defiantly optimistic political twist. But Damano went further. The song about the end of slavery said only what the liberation was *from*; Damano's adaptation also said what the liberation would lead to. His song showed the way out of the wretchedness of feudal exploitation by exposing the old religion as complicit in that wretchedness. Baptist Christianity would not only bring liberation from a cluster of oppressive entanglements; it would also complete the rupture by establishing a new time that would turn the Sora into new persons with a new relationship to a new divinity.

Damano's song was not composed for him by a Canadian missionary. It was created by a Sora, and it refers to an event, not long ago in Israel, but here and now in India. He was one of several Sora Baptist leaders, including the younger Monosi, who indigenized what the missionaries had brought them. But Damano was the most militant, not just a pastor but also a prophet. He denounced drinking and smoking, but also the homespun loincloths and skirts and the gold and silver ornaments that Miss Munro considered so charming. He refused to baptize anyone who wore traditional clothes, and it was he who insisted that women should wear saris and cover their heads.

Why are dialogues with the dead such a threat to this agenda of rupture? Whether one believes that they assuage sadness or stoke it up, what matters is that even while regulating its pace, they sustain attachment. As Sojono explained so clearly, the dead respond to attention. This surely explains why the pastors are uncomfortable about graveside lamentation. By giving grief articulate form, it is as if the lament calls the sonum into presence—perhaps even wishes it into existence.

As our discussions continue beyond four decades, Monosi has recently developed Sojono's point in a startling direction. He agrees that your children are very close while you are alive, but that after you die they cannot talk to you and so they ignore (*maioteji*) and forget you. But now he adds something extraordinary. Under Christianity, he now thinks, the dead also forget us, in a "total forgetting" (*atakud karida*). Sora thinking has continued to evolve beyond the simple optimism of the early missionaries. A Sora philosopher has taken the depersonalized Christian notion of eternity and blended it with the mutual relationality of animist forgetting.

Back in the 1930s and 1940s Miss Munro used to say, "Wear your costumes and ornaments, do your dances!" She required only that converts should give up blood sacrifice. Like many missionaries (and government folklore departments), she thought that "culture" could be separated from "religion," and that the former could be preserved and the latter abandoned. Few anthropologists would agree; nor did Damano. With his deeper inside knowledge, he understood that religion lay at the heart of the culture, and decided that everything had to be changed, root and branch. Miss Munro's nursery-school style dwelled on sweetness and light; Damano dwelled on the sonums' dark side. Chief among his targets was alin. As one of his own hymns puts it,

alin ja kadabtai	*aban ja kadabtai*
pogan ja kadabtai	*aban ja kadabtai*
koran ja kadabtai	*idal ja kadabtai*
kınsa ja kadabtai	*idal ja kadabtai*
gatarsin goiberan	*omdale sidba!*
guaren singkuden	*omdale sidba!*
nami sering nami sering	*Kristun a tangoren ñatenai*
nami sering nami sering	*Kristun a sa'kai sa'kai'tai*
nami sering nami sering	*Kristun a roi'tad gantenai*
I renounce wine	I renounce liquor
I renounce tobacco	I renounce liquor
I renounce anger	I renounce envy
I renounce arrogance	I renounce envy
playing, joking—	abandon them!
stone-planting, memorial stones—	abandon them!
from today, from today	I walk the Christian path
from today, from today	I witness the Christian witness
from today, from today	I enter the Christian straightness

"All those bad things came from our ancestors, just like robbery and sacrifice," another pastor explained to me. Even playing? Yes, the giggling and erotic horseplay during work parties were on a par with the seven deadly sins!

It is true that alin is a contributing factor in quarrels and homicides, but alin intensifies everything, even reconciliation. "Suppose we've had a big quarrel," explained the teetotal Monosi, "then I bring alin: 'Drink, brother!' 'Ooh, that tastes good!' The quarrel fades, the nastiness (*ildagi*) fades. Similarly, however wretched a sonum, if it gets alin it feels happy (*moiñte*)." Miss Munro used to say, "Drink your alin in moderation, it's pure from the tree and your lips don't touch the spout, you only mix tree bark" (little did she realize how intoxicating those creepers could be!). But Damano understood the deeper meaning of alin: like sung laments, it attracts the dead. If you let the sonums back in, they will never let go again. "It's the sonums' big need," Monosi explained. "There can be meat, rice, a shaman sitting there ready, but if there's no alin, nothing can happen."

Baptists look puzzled when I point out that Jisu too used to enjoy an occasional gourdful of alin. No wonder: when I searched the Sora Bible I found that social drinking (*gasal*) had been systematically rendered as "getting drunk" (*taraj*). This message is further confused by Miss Munro's 1939 translation of "wine" not as alin but as "fruit juice" (*gu'ur-dan*, which is something the Sora do not drink), while in the more recent edition it is "grape juice" (*drakia-dan* or *drakia-sal*). Thus, Ecclesiastes 9:7 tells us to drink our grape juice with a happy heart, in Psalms 60:3 God makes us drunk with grape juice, at the wedding in Cana Jisu turns water into grape juice, and at the Last Supper it symbolizes his blood. The Sora do not have grapes, so it is even more odd to be urged so insistently not to drink their juice, or to read in Revelation 17:2 that it is the intoxicating product of the fornication of the whore of Babylon.

Church officials are greatly concerned with the perennial threat of backsliding into immoral behavior. For today's youth, alcohol bears no trace of its former link to sonums. Instead, it is associated with forays for hooch in the back streets of town. But for older people who grew up as animists, it implies communion not only with the living but also with the dead. Damano's prohibition was not simply to avoid intoxication or the nourishing of sonums, but to break the possibility of any engagement with them. This prohibition entails a huge change in the foundation of human relationships. It hits directly at our compassion for the dead and at the solace that we offer to them, and to ourselves, by communicating with them.

Damano had been a *buya*, a priest of his village's local kittung, the entity that provided the missionaries with the Sora word for "God." He smashed and burned his sacred pots, a life-changing act of the kind that a missionary described in a newsletter of 1948 as a "quiet, simple ceremony" that had just been performed by eighteen lay families in one week. The ceremony of "pot-removal" (*tab-dang*) still occupies far more space in the *Pastor's Handbook* than all funeral rites. Damano's conversion was so fervent that he reenacted it in front of a missionary's cine camera to make a propaganda film called *From Darkness to Light*. It is said his offended kittung drove him crazy as a punishment. As he grew more fanatical and *sanapyu* (uncharitable) he spoke like flaring fire (*ñamangtudte berre*) and quarreled with the missionaries, while his rigid response to his son's bigamy led the boy to boycott his funeral.

But Damano was right about alin. Miss Munro had dwelled on sacrificial blood, but Sora religion also depended on the enlivenment of plant juices, combining life-fluid with intoxication. This was the same combination of blood and fermented vegetation that lay at the heart of Jisu's Last Supper. Each fluid beckoned humans with its own version of the divine, but in Soraland the sonums were always lying thirstily in wait. Damano needed a symbolic substitute, not just for Jisu's blood but also for the communion wine—a substitute for the substitute. Today Baptists manage communion with fresh un-fermented juice made from the red *sunsuni* seedpod. Monosi is more flexible, and when I took him to communion in an English cathedral in 2010 he drank his first sip of alcohol in nearly seventy years.

During the 1990s the landscape was busy with acts of severance. When I saw memorial stones dismantled in the 1990s by young Baptists and reused as cattle fencing, I felt a shock of blasphemy. I could not help my response at that moment, but later realized that this was just a sign that the stones had become irrelevant. Yet demolition can also be aggressive and contemptuous, and the sonums may strike back. One day three men cut down some trees by an Earth-Sonum spring, and all died soon after. Another man cut down an enormous tree by another Earth-Sonum spring to make a paddy field. With each blow it squealed like a pig, and he fainted on the spot. Another man and his wife dropped dead after axing another screaming tree, but Jisu brought them back to life. While the man was unconscious he saw the Earth-Sonums, who said, "Why did you do that?" "I didn't know," he replied. "You knew about us until you became Christian—now you'll have trouble!" But Jisu sent an angel to argue with the sonums, pleading, "He's doing it to grow food, let him go."

The angel negotiated away the desecration with a subsistence rationale, but that sacrilege was not only in the violence against the tree but also in the annihilation of a particular complex of meaning. Earth-Sonums embody the memory of an entire cosmology embracing subsistence, inheritance, and personal destiny. Ancestors in the Underworld are distributed under particular Earth-Sonum sites, from where they legitimate the continued cultivation by their descendants of land around those sites. Their placing amounts to a system of title-deeds (Vitebsky 1993: 219–24). In the 1970s this placing was still an important topic of dialogue and dispute, although already officially superseded by the government's 1961 register of rights. Today young Baptists do not know the locations of Earth-Sonums (or any other sonums), and use only paper documents. As for spatial representations, the ones they study most closely are maps of the Holy Land at the back of the Bible. As an image of sacred space, these maps replace shamans' wall-paintings. But while shamans travel to the Underworld every day, no Sora has ever visited Israel. Most Sora Baptists do not realize that Israel is still there and that there are still Jews today, far less that they are not Christian. There is room in Baptist cosmology for past wisdom ("What we have heard and learned—that which our ancestors have told us": Psalms 78:3), but these ancestors are ancient Jews, while their own Sora ancestors have nothing worth teaching them. Only the more subtle Baptists get my joke that they know more than I do about my Jewish ancestors

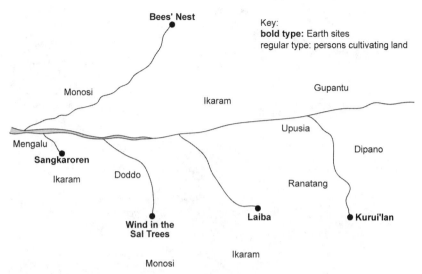

Map 8.1 Some Earth-Sonum sites and their cultivators, Sogad 1979
*Earth-Sonums were located in water sources, and contained groups of ancestors.
Cultivators' claims to nearby irrigated fields and shifting cultivation plots were negotiated
and justified through dialogues with those ancestors. Today, irrigated plots have individual
paper title-deeds, while hillside patches are leased from the government (chapter 10).*

5,000 years ago whom no one has ever met, while I know more than they do
about their own grandparents who were my friends.

Missionary discourse uses analogy to convert traditional Sora symbols
along with Sora people: the 1948 newsletter that describes a shaman burning
his sonum-pots sees the reflection of the fire as representing love and hope
in his shining eyes, and asks readers to pray that the Sora's hearts will be
filled to overflowing with love for Jesus so that their alin pots, forgotten, will
overflow in their palm trees. Some missionary accounts are compassionate
and denigrating at the same time. In a 1958 newsletter to Canadian supporters, Perry Allaby's wife, Edith, described "an image that only demon worship
could bring forth," a widow weeping at a stone-planting, where the supposed
arrival of her husband's sonum only brought her "fresh grief" and left her
in "utter, hopeless loneliness." Without ideological sympathy and years of
tape-recording, how could she ever have imagined that others might see this
dialogue as a great psychological and spiritual achievement? By contrast, a
meeting of the Sora Association had "a well-planned program": "Oh, it is a
happy time! . . . There is laughter and fun! . . . There are drums, and cymbals,
too, but how different when used to accompany voices uplifted in praise to

Figure 8.2 Dave and Ruby Hayward, retired missionaries, Vancouver 2009

God!" These documents do not give the words of any Sora themselves, whose misery or happiness is inferred for them.

Is separating Paranto from his dead father an act of extreme loving kindness or extreme mental cruelty? Following anthropologists' traditional suspicion of missionaries, I too have sometimes seen them as predators like viruses, infecting other minds and reconfiguring their spiritual DNA to resemble their own. Yet the missionaries I have come to know best, Dave and Ruby Hayward, were not agents of mental cruelty but people whose hearts did indeed overflow with love for their Sora congregation. I had not met them since they left India at the end of the 1970s. In 2009, though in their eighties and well aware of our different views, they very generously invited me to stay at their house in Vancouver ("How will we recognize you at the airport if you're not wearing a loincloth?"). As well as reminiscing and discussing theology, they also shared their archive of old missionary reports and newsletters. The tone of their forerunners' writings confirmed the character sketches I had put together from Sora friends: Miss Munro innocent and optimistic, Perry Al-

Figure 8.3 Baptist girls, 2013
Showing a contrast outside with the restraint encouraged in church.

laby intellectual and waspish ("He never ate our food, even on tour"), and the bearded, intense-eyed Mel Otis (he who refused to talk to me about shamans on my first day in Soraland), ascetic as a monk.

Yet even the kind Haywards, the Sora's favorite missionaries, who walked everywhere, mixed freely, and ate Sora food, advocated the abandoning of ancestors. If you believe you have found the unique truth, how can you not urge this insight on others? My position—and the role that sometimes falls to me—is to serve as a link to these ancestors. It is not only for Paranto that I have sometimes become a living reminder of a dead friend. Whenever I return, the elderly widows of Mengalu and Majji still seize my head in both hands and bang it repeatedly against their own. Young people would be too embarrassed to make this archaic and expressive gesture, but they are left without a substitute. As I approached Ranatang's house for the first time after his death, his daughter—a young Baptist in a sari—ran up and clasped my hand to her forehead, squeaking and gibbering wordlessly for a full minute before running away in confusion.

Holding a person's hand to one's forehead is a conventional Sora greeting, but the girl's inarticulateness hinted at something more: the lack of opportunity to engage her father directly in dialogue, and my role as his substitute.

Like Paranto's tears over his father, Inama, such episodes (and there have been others) happen after I have been away, sometimes for years at a time, and they seem to be triggered by the combination of my sudden reappearance with my closeness to someone of my own generation whom they loved and who has died during my absence. I become identified with the dead person, and our chaotic emotional moment replaces the more structured format of dialogue with the deceased.

The dead may resist neglect more directly by the way they appear in dreams. Animists too dream about them, but among Christians this is the only way the dead can reclaim something of the voice that was muted by their attenuated funeral. Paranto has a recurring dream in which he sees Inama dancing with his friends, oblivious to his son and out of reach of any conversation, on a path that leads down an abyss into the Underworld. Above him rises a path to a gate in the sky. Paranto is unsure about the value of these paths: sometimes the upper path seems easier, so he feels his father should avoid the lower one; at other times the upper path seems too difficult, so that his father will inevitably go down below. Sometimes Inama speaks.

"It was as if we were meeting in waking life," Paranto told me in 1994 after one such dream.

"'You've died, where have you come from?'

'I'm not dead,' he said. 'I remain, I exist (ñen dakutenai, ñen daku).'

I got up and looked around: it was the middle of the night—[amazed tone] there was nobody there! I cried, I was very sad: 'I thought you were dead!' I met him under the tree on the way to his favorite drinking place.

'Ai! Where are you going?'

'I'm just wandering around.' He looked just as he had when he was healthy.

'But how come your body was so sick, and now you're healthy again?'

'It's alright, I'm fine now.'

I looked around, there was nobody there."

"Were you frightened?" I asked, thinking of the dangerous existential state of recently dead sonums as they pass on their illnesses.

"I was, but he didn't scold me and didn't harm me. He just said nice things to me."

Was this a realistic continuation of Inama's gentle personality, or was it Paranto's Christianity that tipped the balance between the tender and aggressive aspects of a dead person's attachment to the living? "I've met him three times. We just talked, and sometimes we cried together. He tells me to get on with the plowing. Once I saw him with that old man from Sinjangul who's recently died. They were living together in a shelter made just of straw. It was far down in a deep gully, the way there was steep and difficult, I didn't go all the way down. I recognized other dead people. Some of them didn't have houses at all but just sat by the side of the path eating out of a trough like pigs. But my father and his friend were alright."

Paranto is a regular churchgoer, and his dreams blend elements of animist and Christian imagery. His father's ambiguous position seems to combine the path to the animist Underworld with the tension between the broad and the narrow paths in Matthew 7:13–14. This dream has probably been conditioned by church sermons: old Oransu had similar dreams in which an abyss big enough to swallow mountains stood in contrast to a path up to a door of gold and silver in the sky. In Paranto's second dream I recognized a description of the homeless dead, cowering "in a hovel in a shack" (*tupusing lungen gabolsun lungen*), as I myself had sung when performing as an ancestor-man. These are people waiting for a stone-planting ceremony to transform them into the next stage of sonumhood. For the animist dead, this is a routine phase. Those whose Christian children will never give them that stone-planting may remain in this unfinished state forever. Inama's situation seems ambiguous: has he gone up to Heaven or down to the Underworld? If down, he resides in a scrappy shelter, but his situation is not as bad as some other people's.

Many people meet the dead in dreams. I too have dreamed about Inama, whose voice I can still recall. I also dreamed that my own father telephoned me after he died, restored to health like Inama, but do not remember anything of what was said. My wife had a dream encounter with her dead mother, who uttered only one brief message asking for a place in our home. Perhaps it takes a Sora with an animist upbringing to dream such elaborate verbal encounters with the dead, and for these to become an integral part of his life-story. Paranto's dream reactivates the format of dialogue between living and dead that has been suppressed by the church; and in the absence of a waking performance through a shaman, the dream supplies both sides of the conversation. The dreams give Paranto the reassurance he yearns for, and which his Christianity is unable to provide. Inama is now well, he is still benign, and he gives normative instructions (get on with the plowing). But it is not quite Jisu who has brought about this restoration: just as the dream substitutes for dialogue, so it presents Inama as if he has been through the transformative stages of an animist funeral, which allow him to emerge as a guiding ancestor. Since this encounter is not articulated in a public arena, it remains private to the dreamer and those whom he tells.

A similar need for reassurance can also motivate a dream about someone living, where it can likewise find its outlet in a private conversation. Many years later I reminded Paranto of how his father had dreamed about my return from hospital in the 1970s when he thought I had died. "I've dreamed about you too," he replied. "Once you'd been in my house but moved on before nightfall. That night in the dream I said, 'Why did you leave me, I told you to sleep here, you're tired. If you're angry with me I won't know what to do.'"

"How could I be angry with you?" I protested gently.

"I feel a lot when you're around," he said, "because you're my *dadi* [father's younger brother] and it makes me think about him."

9

REDEEMERS HUMAN AND DIVINE

The new Christian ideal requires a new kind of person. But how does one make a new person who is not built up through relations with numerous ancestors? How does that person even acquire a name?

In February 2009 I witnessed the naming of a Baptist baby, the grandchild of Gallanti. Gallanti had taken over as funeral shaman of Rajingtal after Ononti became estranged from her ilda-sonums (page 185). Gallanti had then taught Lokami, who by now had emerged as the greatest shaman in the region. But religious conflict had split Gallanti's family. Her young son Labaiño had been appointed a Baptist catechist. Though he tolerated his mother's wall-painting in a separate tumbledown hut, he would not allow her to sit and trance. I remembered the extraordinary sight of Gallanti in her prime thirty years earlier, breast-feeding baby Labaiño during her trance.

Gallanti looked frail and sad. As she picked at a thorn in my foot, she said quietly that she expected to die soon.

Labaiño was friendly, but uncomfortable when I praised Gallanti. Catechists lack the clout of pastors and are their anxious dependents, easily demoted for having a deviant in their close family. It was like having a witch for a mother. He was particularly concerned for his image on the day when his baby son would receive a name in front of a full congregation.

The ceremony was to be conducted by Abraham, the catechist of Pattili, and Buyajo, the deacon of Abada. I found Buyajo sitting on the floor of the meetinghouse with other officials, writing his speech. An older man with an alert face and a small mustache, he was the senior person present and the only one wearing a white dhoti. They were well aware of how close I was to the shamans of this village, and watched me uneasily as I took notes. I saw the duties filled out on the Sunday calendar for the whole year to come, which included frequent mentions of my nephew Paranto. I felt I was flying near the candle flame of power, though these people could not conspire and damage me as the bariks had done in an earlier era.

Six men walked onto the platform in the church, shook hands with each other, and sat down on chairs. Below the platform the floor was full, though

Figure 9.1 Labaiño the Baptist catechist, 2009

there were many more women than men. "Ladde secretary, Pattili chairman, please come up," they announced, naming several men by their positions. I was happy not to be invited onto the platform this time but to remain on the floor, on the male side opposite Gallanti.

Abraham opened the meeting, announcing the congregation's registration number, the qualifications of the church officials present, and the numbered items on the agenda as specified in the *Pastor's Handbook*:

1. Convenor's announcement
2. Beginning of service
3. Questioning of father and mother
4. Naming the child and consecrating the child
5. Lesson
6. Pause
7. Greeting/receiving (*olong*) the child

The aesthetics of bureaucracy led to a lengthy apology for possible violations, as Buyajo continued: "If I've made a mistake with the agenda, please

Figure 9.2 Labaiño as a baby, 1976

Figure 9.3 Gallanti continues to maintain her wall-painting, 2009

forgive me, and may God forgive me . . . This is all in the name of Jisu . . . I don't know, I have no skill . . ."

During the whispered consultations of the men on the platform about the order of events, the parents sat on a mat on the floor, looking up at the platform, Labaiño's wife holding their baby and wearing a white cloth over her head: "These two have gained a child from inside the womb . . . we have come together to give the child a name, so let there be much prayer and glory to God . . . We thank you, God. More than the sea is wide and deep, more than the countless grains of sand, you love us even more than that . . . Let us stand and sing hymn No. 1." This was followed by the Lord's Prayer, muttered by the entire congregation with eyes closed, mostly uttering the anchor words at the start of each phrase (in English this would be "our . . . who . . . thy . . . on earth . . . give us . . . and forgive . . .").

There were announcements, including instructions for attending a forth-coming rally: "The authorities have introduced a ticketing system. You must have the signature of your pastor or area secretary, stamped with a seal, other-wise you'll be thrown out or arrested. All sorts of people hang around, there are fights." This was a reference to violent clashes at previous events with anti-Christian groups of Hindu fundamentalists (chapter 11). But this was com-bined with another agenda: "Boys and girls go to the cinema together. They go off dancing and do dirty things." "Dirty things" were what made animist funeral gatherings such fun even without the cinema, but at this rally each village would have an all-night watchman to prevent his own young people from misbehaving.

The pastor repeated these instructions for nearly an hour. It seemed that women in particular could not be expected to understand the concept of paper permits. Then the meeting resumed its main purpose. The mother handed the baby to the men on the platform, and Labaiño handed them the name on a piece of paper: Subijito. This was a Sora pronunciation of an unfamiliar Oriya name Subha Jita, meaning Good Life, and they read it with difficulty.

The ceremony followed the *Pastor's Handbook*, with its three pages of refer-ences, quotations, and exegesis for naming a child. Half a page is devoted to the pollution of women after childbirth (Leviticus 12:1–8; Luke 2: 21–24), so far removed from Jamani's casual labor in our little hut above Ladde, and not actually observed by Baptists, especially the sacrifice of two doves to cleanse the mother, which Buyajo quoted approvingly. Other references were more odd, such as verses about Pharaoh's and Herod's birthday parties (Genesis 40:20; Matthew 14:6). These are actually inauspicious if one reads further, since both lead to a brutal killing. The sayings of Jisu seemed more whole-some: "Whoever welcomes a child like this in my name welcomes me" (Mat-thew 18:5) and "Let the little children come to me and do not try to stop them, for the kingdom of God belongs to such as these" (Luke 18:16). The following verse (18:17) was particularly significant: "Whoever does not receive the king-dom of God like a child will never enter it." This was developed by the only paragraph in the written instructions that is not a direct paraphrase from the Bible, but a broader statement of ideology: parents must observe norms of good behavior, since "whatever a child sees and hears, its life (*mandreng-na*) will come to match that exactly."

Here was a new theory linking childhood to moral development. Animists carried their babies pressed to their bodies for three years, but they had no theories of child psychology. Dialogues with the dead show how much animist social identity depends on verbal articulateness. Babies cannot speak, and the corresponding limitations to their being are sadly revealed in their skimpy funerals. This was the first time I had heard infant experience reflected on at all, let alone viewed as significant enough to be the cause of adult behavior.

Meanwhile the audience shuffled restlessly on the floor, and said nothing. A marshal with a stick tapped dozers, women probably exhausted from work and boredom. Apart from watching and taking notes, there was nothing for me to do either, and I missed singing and dancing with Mengalu.

After the congregation had queued up to shake hands with the men on the platform, they sat in rows in a dry paddy field for a meal of rice and curry. There was no special place for Gallanti as the baby's grandmother. While she sat with others outside I was called into the meetinghouse, along with the other male VIPs, to be served by young women. I felt disloyal abandoning my old friend. Her tiny, archaic figure embodied not only a cultural gulf but also a financial one in the new dual economy where money circulates at two separate velocities. That same week I went with Gallanti to a wedding that cost many thousands of rupees, and in which the pastor was paid many hundreds. At the end, we lined up to present cash to the newlywed couple. As other young people put in tens and twenties (and I put in a fifty: it had to be more, but not ostentatiously more), Gallanti carefully unwrapped two single rupee coins from a torn rag.

Unlike a regular service, the naming ceremony was one of the few Baptist rituals that effected a change. But this was not simply a consecration of a baby to God, as in a European christening. It was also an act of severance. Baby Subijito's orientation was not to a lineage but to a congregation. Here was a vision of children as the future of society, but not by the animist logic of lineage continuity and recycling. Damano's rupturism was inserting itself right into the family. Where was the precious ring, supposedly saved from the previous namesake's funeral? Where was the song of the ancestor-men knocking at a closed door? Where was the trance, to pass on a name—so specific, so precious, shared with namesakes past and future? Over nearly forty years I have recorded thousands of Sora names, almost all of them (even rude nicknames) inherited from ancestors. Baby Subijito was starting as an ancestral *tabula rasa* and would acquire none of the identity markers, the constant reminders from predecessors, the cumulative involvement through ancestor-induced illness, which constitute so much of an animist's biography. Instead, his person would grow through regular Christian events: daily readings and prayers, Sunday services, and interparish rallies that he would attend holding a signed, stamped ticket.

Between Subijito and God, between the individual and the church congregation, the lineage with its catalogue of ancestors was falling out of sight. Young Christians often genuinely do not know the names of their dead grandparents. Christian names take no cue from the family past, and cut the child off from family history. Being drawn from characters in the Bible, they are not repetitions of a previous person but references to a role model whom nobody has met. Though the choice of Subijito was not biblical, and the church officials found it eccentric, it is similarly nonancestral and represents a new trend to choose cosmopolitan names that may be Oriya or even names of Hindi film stars. As such, it anticipates the non-Sora name that the child is likely to receive in school (page 252). This was all the more reason for Labaiño to be embarrassed by his primitive animist mother; but though he would surely deny this, his baby's high-status Oriya name also matches the naming of her ılda husband in the Underworld. Indeed, he updates this relationship: rather than marrying Oriya high castes in the form of ılda-sonums, his child will become like an Oriya himself.

During the 1990s I felt I was learning the Sora language afresh, confronted with a new vocabulary that reflected a changed understanding of human feeling and action. Apart from representing the metabolism that keeps us alive, the animist *puradan* (soul) can become happy or sad, hot with agitation or cool with calmness, and in extreme distress it can even escape the body and get lost. But all these happen in terms of an interpersonal situation. Unlike Freud's psyche, the puradan is internally undifferentiated and does not have internal divisions corresponding to an id, ego and superego, or conscious and unconscious. Any conflicts or contradictions that it experiences take place in relationships with others.

Baptists create a new kind of person who is more separate and has a more complex internal psyche. The new Baptist vocabulary locates emotional states inside the person rather than in the interactions between persons. What was previously projected outward is now introjected inward. This shift has intensified in recent years. In her 1939 translation of Saint John's Gospel, Miss Munro kept to the simplicity of *puradan* to gloss both the Greek *kardia* (heart) and *pneuma* (Holy "Spirit"). But recent translations (by Canadian missionaries who presumably knew Greek, working with Sora informants like Damano and Monosi) have developed a more differentiated terminology, by picking up earlier terms that were known from cutting up animals but whose functions were vague. Now the biblical *kardia* (heart) is translated sometimes as *ugar* (John 13:2, 16:6), sometimes as *je'e* (John 12:40, 16:22). These are old animist words: *ugar*, in this case, seems to mean "liver" as a seat of feelings, while *je'e*, often linked to energy and enthusiasm, is generally said to be higher up in the chest. Use is inconsistent: in Mark 12:30, *ugar*, *puradan*, and *je'e* emerge as the terms for loving God with all your heart, soul, and mind (Greek *kardia*, *psyche*, and *dianoia*). Spirit (*pneuma*) is now translated by another word, *janggara*, which is also quasi-anatomical and equally imprecisely located. The literal, animal-butchering word for "heart" is *tamongkum*. Among animists I never heard this used as an emotion word. I cannot find it in the Sora Bible, but it has become important in sermons following calendar pictures of Jisu holding his chest open (just like Hanuman the monkey-god in Hindu calendars), perhaps reinforced by schoolroom diagrams of the circulation of the blood: "Jisu gave blood not only from his veins but also from his *tamongkum*."

Where animists map their social relations and emotions onto a shared sonumscape across the fields and mountains, the elaboration of this anatomical vocabulary emphasizes the Christian person's differentiated interiority. Previously creatures "lived" and were "alive" (*meng*, *ameng*), but the abstract word for "life" itself, *mandreng*, as in "everlasting life," *er-añiden a mandreng-na*, had to be coined as part of a new Christian metaphysics. I had often heard old-style women call out to each other across the mountains, E *mandreng!* (Hey woman!). It was only during some embarrassed giggling while I was interpreting in a city hospital that I discovered this was also a women's euphemism for vagina ("My *mandreng* is sore"). This meaning was surely unknown to the missionaries, but they may have been guided toward the word by an implication of deep interiority and origin. As Monosi reflected, "We gain our mandreng (life) from our mother's mandreng (vagina)." In Christian usage *mandreng* usually has the suffix -*na*, meaning "the very one," which further emphasizes its meaning as an absolute core.

I have tried to get a precise sense of these words from many people, but even Monosi's explanations are confusing. "We can't find the ugar, it's just a word. Sometimes you kill a chicken or a snake. The ugar is what twitches after—it's in the body, it's in the blood. Its puradan and je'e have already perished. That's also the mandreng in the blood. The je'e has died along with the body, it's like breath [*ranggi*, also meaning "wind"]." Then, contradicting himself, he added, "When you kill a snake and its tail still twitches, that's its mandreng."

This was baffling. Another time I tried switching from the language of anatomy to emotion. "Where do you feel feelings?" I asked.

"In the ugar, in the je'e, but really the ugar. Where the tamongkum is, the mandreng-na, that is the ugar. Feeling is in the mandreng."

His explanations blurred together the entire vocabulary! "Are ugar and mandreng different?" I asked. "The words are different, but the meaning is the same," he replied hesitantly.

This was so unlike Monosi's usual precision, and I imagined the missionaries having similar inconclusive conversations as they struggled to render Greek terms for "soul" and "spirit" consistently into Sora. It was not that Monosi (of all people) was incoherent; rather it was a reminder of how complicated it is to participate in the creation of a new ideology, and to use it with conviction to live one's life and feel one's feelings. Animists might give very diverse accounts of the sonum-world, but they used sonum terminology with confidence; by contrast, this feels like a reminder that the Sora Baptist movement is a new religion, still under construction. These quasi-anatomical terms now have to perform a function that has never before existed in Sora thinking: they have to originate emotion from within the person.

Animist emotionality was highly interpersonal, created and negotiated through views of one's actions that emerged in gossip, drinking circles, or dialogues with the dead. This thoroughgoing exteriorization left the self as a black box—or rather, there was perhaps no animist concept of an internal, core *self*. The new Christian interior location has become a site not only of emotion but also of a new kind of moral responsibility, creating a different, self-conscious Baptist person who is subject to inspection (*melmel*, previously applied to reading omens rather than persons) and judgment (*bisara*, an Oriya word previously used for a formal dispute or debate in front of a village council or outside official). Their differing metaphysics left both animist and Baptist persons incomplete or unfinalized, but differently so. The animist is incomplete until the postmortem diagnosis summarizes that person's relationship with others; the Baptist person is incomplete because of an internal moral failing. Both require work, but unlike the grumpy reproaches of an animist ancestor against which one defends oneself robustly and indignantly, this new judgment has an absolute quality: the Baptist self is in need of moral improvement as it tries to measure up against the tamongkum of Jisu himself. As the calendar picture of his sacred heart shows, his internal organs resemble ours physically but shine with a moral radiance.

This morality creates a new domain of sincerity and hypocrisy. Even in animist thinking there was already a gulf between performance and intention, through lying (*subsub*) and deceit or cheating (*jolda, tontoro, bukai*: "You speak tasty words, but how do I know what is in your ugar?"). But the biblical translation of "hypocrite" as merely a "deceiving-man" (*jolda-mar*) misses the novelty of hypocrisy as something arising from a measure of sincerity that is absolute and nonnegotiable. Scheming headmen, Pano traders, high-caste officials, even one's own animist companions—all may deceive you, but they are not hypocrites, because they promise nothing more than they deliver. When that naughty shaman incarnated a dead husband in order to sleep with his widow, this was just a funny story; but scandals surrounding pastors (pages 256–57) signify a newly disturbing hypocrisy. Denunciations from the church platform partly resemble the old animists' public accusations of sorcery, adultery, or any other cheating. But now there is more: one must also judge oneself introspectively. Thus 2 Corinthians 13:5 says *tungjing-dam-na-ben,* "examine your<u>selves.</u>" Even if this reflexive form had been grammatically possible for animists, it could not have had such an interiorized meaning.

Laypeople are tested for sincerity when they present themselves for baptism, with the same word (*tungjing*) that animists use to test the identity of sonums who come for dialogue. But now they are tested for sincerity rather than for identity. The pastor asks the secretary of the village church these questions: Does he attend church regularly? Does he join in praying properly? Does he give offerings and tithes? Is he sexually correct? Does he avoid tobacco and *alin*? This much concerns observable behavior. But the pastor also asks the candidate: Do you *really* believe (*jadi ná*)? Did Jisu die for you *jadi ná*? Has God taken away your sin *jadi ná*?

This probing is tougher with young men who are likely to play a part in public life than with little old ladies who get baptized to avoid embarrassing their children. Monosi described his own baptism by the missionary Perry Allaby, dating it with typical precision to 8 February 1953, and the sharp, searching questioning by Miss Turnbull and Miss MacLean (both strangely pronounced): "'How did Jisu give to you?' they asked, holding out their hands. 'Like this?' 'No,' I said, 'I prayed, then I felt it <u>inside</u> (*imlɛnai*).'"

The interrogation tests faith, but there are correct answers, and one can cram for the exam. It is because it is so difficult to sustain and verify inner sincerity that the church resorts to external forms of surveillance, denunciation, and demotion from the platform.

"How can we know if I really believe or I'm just pretending?" I once asked Monosi.

"We don't know, but right now we believe you. Later a person may bigamize or steal or be arrogant (*kɪnsa*), and Sora will say, 'Issí, he's lapsed, he's become corrupt (*masunale, ildagi dele*).'"

"Your faith may not change even if you do these things," I objected. "You had two wives at once, but never lost your faith."

"That's true!" he conceded. Monosi fell further than most from the platform, though people never ceased to turn to him as a wise man.

Monosi is sincere in his sense of his own "sinfulness," *pintu*. This is different from a Sanskritic Oriya word, *papa*, by which animists understand a contagion or infection that brushes (*gatar*) the person from without. That is an automatic mechanism, a supernatural equivalent of treading accidentally in excrement, and *papa* is removed through ritual washing and cleansing of one's outer surface. But Christian *pintu* is an internal condition. Instead of fearing spiritual attack from outside, Baptists worry about their own inner deficiency, as when the formerly carefree Likini regrets her promiscuous youth.

The word *pintu* had long featured in hymns and sermons, but its significance must have been unclear until the 1970s when the translation of Genesis closed the gap between Jisu who redeems us from sin and Adam and Eve who dropped us into it in the first place. Sin was now revealed as an inescapable existential state. I once heard Monosi musing in moral anguish, "What will happen to us bigamists when Jisu comes back?" "God's will," replied Oransu, the unrepentant old Baptist polygamist. "Maybe I'll go to the Underworld instead of Heaven." He chuckled and added with an old-timer's robustness that would be beyond the repertoire of a young Baptist today, "But I don't care, at least the company's good down there. And my wife—I never loved anyone like that again! I had six more wives after her, sometimes two or three at a time. The pastors didn't like that, so I said, 'Alright, I'll join the Catholics, they'll welcome me with garlands.' The pastors didn't bother me after that!"

Monosi had his own problems with the pastors, and laughed heartily. But I believe his anguish was genuine. Oransu had not had a mystical experience like Monosi's vision of Jisu's crown of thorns: perhaps the love of women was enough. When sleeping in church halls I have sometimes seen men wake before dawn, muttering and imploring God or Jisu in a frantic, whispered ecstasy. Monosi listed forms of mystical experience: "a feeling, a dream, a waking vision, or we faint a bit like a fit" (*imnan ode, genimte lungen ode, tanalmad, ode satunglangte aji bayan amrid*), or an ecstatic state called *umpul*. "Once I was very sick," he told me in 1998, "and after praying a lot I lay face down on the bed. I wept copiously, slapping the bed, slapping my chest. I shouted 'Hallelujah' over and over again. An hour later I came to, I wept a lot and immediately felt joy, as if an *umpul* had entered my body. It was as if my *ugar* and my *puradan* and my hair were standing on end. I returned some medicine unused to the pharmacist and got my money back!"

What kind of divine madness was this? Was there a connection with animist forms of altered consciousness? I reminded Monosi of Taranti's peacock song on the tape that had so enthralled him twenty years earlier. "The feeling that she had when she was in trance, was that the same or something different?"

"That was from her ılda sonums," he replied hesitantly. "Mine was from God and Jisu." He thought a moment and added, "But the feeling is the same. How could it be different? It must be the same. There are lots of sonums, lots of gods (*kittung*). I've read in Oriya that there are 33 × 20,000 gods, which is why I composed a Christian song to Taranti's peacock tune: Kittung Kittung Kittung, you are the great Kittung, you are the hidden Kittung, of all the 660,000 Kittungs, you are the *Living* (*ameng*) Kittung."

This was not quite what I had expected. I understood that animists feared uncontrolled possession, but also knew that they suffered little from it, probably because all spiritual communication is channeled so narrowly through dialogue, in which only the shaman goes into trance. A shaman's practice is steady and competent, not wild and ecstatic. Her trance is induced deliberately and is more stable and directed than a violent umpul fit. Baptists are caught in a tension between inspiration and sobriety, in which their moments of ecstasy are private (like their dreams about the dead) and not institutionalized. In the pastors' bureaucratic cosmology, ecstasy is highly suspect because it lays one open to the wrong beings. One year at Pentecost, I was told, a fight broke out in the Rumbatti Baptist church when half the congregation became possessed, beyond the control of the marshal with the stick and the mustache. When the preacher shouted, "This is the work of the devil!" they answered back, "No, the devil is you!"

For Monosi it was not that Christianity had introduced a new kind of experience. The essential difference between his ecstatic experience and an animist trance lay not in the experience itself but in the source: his umpul was from God.

So what kind of being is the kittung of the Christians?

Miss Munro had come to Sora via Oriya, with Pano Christian interpreters. Old missionary documents contain numerous regrets at the insincerity and deceitfulness of Pano converts, and she was determined to learn Sora. To translate "God" she wanted a true Sora word, rather than taking a Sanskritic Oriya term for the supreme Hindu godhead like Ishwar or Bhagavan. She adopted the Sora word *kittung*, that class of beings that claimed Damano as a priest (*buya*). Unlike sonums, kittungs do not attack humans and generally have little interest in human affairs. Their rituals are seasonal rather than responses to a situation, and they do not speak or put their priests into trance. Kittungs made the world, as many origin myths recount, with male and female aspects often blurred into one single kittung. But then the animist kittung withdrew, becoming what theologians call a *deus otiosus*, an "inactive god."

But Miss Munro's Kittung (now with a capital K) was far from otiose. He replaced sonums as the active principle in human life, only with none of their negativity. His functions were qualified by terms translated from Hebrew and Greek, each carrying its own resonance. Lord God (Gomang-tung) was a new term that picked up the hierarchical feudal idiom of headmen, rajas, and Hindu gods. The Living God (Ameng-Kittung) is a special Christian formulation for a being supposedly more authentic than gods inhabiting stones and idols. But for her first translation, the 1939 version of Saint John's Gospel that so influenced the young Monosi, Miss Munro chose Creator-God (Gaddıl-tung). As a term meaning both "to cause to come into being" from nothing (Latin *ex nihilo*) and "to mold an existing substance," this term suited the opening lines of John's Gospel: "The word was with Gaddıl-tung. He gad-dıl-ed everything . . . from him life itself was gaddıl-ed." In recent editions Gaddıl-tung has been replaced by the simple word Kittung, a generic term that instead emphasizes his identity as the one and only God.

Another property of the new God was absolute goodness, an attribute that had never before been credited to any beings, whether human, sonum, or kit-tung. So which being could carry the burden of representing evil in a new, equally absolute sense? Unlike the kittungs, there were no beings in the old cosmology from which to derive or develop this term, unless this was to be the entire realm of sonumhood. In early hymns and in a notebook from Mono-si's adolescence I have found the singular form *sonum* for the devil. Sonums were no longer to be morally ambiguous or open-ended, like the living Sora humans they once were. This was the first step toward the complete ignorance among today's young Christians—and even Monosi's uncertainty—about the soul-force that ancestors put into crops and the identity they conferred onto babies through their names, seeing them instead as nothing more than parasites. Monotheism was bringing the Sora a dualism between good and bad that they had not thought of before—or rather, that they had previously perceived on the political plane of traders and police, and dealt with on the spiritual plane by co-opting their oppressors as shamans' helpers.

But the devil is not just a dead human ancestor or one of the previous reper-toire of collective sonums like Sun, Earth, and Leopard. The cosmic drama of Christianity requires him to be a strong character to counterbalance God, and moreover an unwaveringly negative agent. The eventual solution was Duaing-sım, the Bad Sonum. *Duaing* is the ordinary word for a "bad" person, anyone from a naughty child to a wicked exploiter like Jogi Ganta. However, this left the moral status of other, ordinary sonums unclear. Bambu of Manengul, Monosi's old rival for Likini's hand and my Catholic drinking partner with cheerful animist tendencies, tries to rehabilitate ancestor-sonums by telling me that they are different from Duaing-sım. The point of his argument is to separate sonums into good ones and bad ones. But even this rationalization is rooted in a dualistic Christian framework. The point of the old religion, on the contrary, was to blend them in a moral universe where good and bad, kindness and aggression, were not properties of different beings but coexisted in all of them. When Baptists merge them in a different way by insisting that all sonums are bad, they can end up in deep water. Much of the regular preaching is done by young catechists like Gallanti's son Labaiño, who are not sophisticated theologians:

"Is it true that all sonums are bad?" I ask them.

"Yes, jadi! They demand things from us and make us ill."

"But your father and mother are good?"

"Yes, very good."

"But after they die, they will become sonums?"

"Yes."

"So suddenly these good people will become bad?" Silence, and an embarrassed laugh.

Monosi finds this Socratic teasing very funny, but he too does not have an answer. Christians continue to fall ill and die: how and why does this happen? One explanation draws on *rugam*, a Sanskritic term for "disease." This is a vague word that implies no quest for causality, making it very suitable for post-sonum medical aetiology. If you have a rugam you go to the dispensary and get a pill or an injection. The rugam may have a cause, but it is someone else's job to know about this: a compounder, nurse, doctor, or pharmacist. These people know about the "insects" (as germs are called) that get into our bodies, and peripatetic government health workers and vaccinators, men in trousers and ladies in saris, occasionally turn up on verandas in remote villages to reinforce this message.

This view of causality does not leave any room for sonums, and does not need them. You do not seek a cause unless something about the situation leads you to move on to a divination. The church originally prohibited dialogues between the living and the dead because dialogue reinforces their mutual attachment. But as the prohibition becomes more effective, dialogues also become more pointless, as there is nothing left to discuss. Among animists, every time anyone dies or just has a stomachache, the sonums are there as a focal point of causality and negotiation. But Baptist teaching blocks this logic. Just as the Baptist funeral prevents the living from knowing anything about the dead, it also prevents the dead from having an effect on the living.

For animists, a healing ritual is a pivotal moment in making a deal: you know if the sonum has accepted your sacrifice not only from how the conversation proceeds but also because you get better soon after. In the 1970s I used to take friends suffering from tuberculosis to the city for treatment (unless they refused, like Jamano). Each time they were told to stay there for three months of daily injections. Quite apart from being reluctant to neglect their work for more than a day, they could not understand a cure that did not succeed (or fail) immediately. They insisted on going back home, to feed the sonums of previous victims with more sacrifices and infect others around them, eventually dying themselves and being diagnosed as the cause of yet more coughing and dying.

Old-timers too sometimes went to the government dispensary in Puttasing, where they happily accepted its medicine without explanation. The mission bungalow further away in Serung also had a Christian hospital that grew over decades into a major regional facility attracting animists, Christians, and Hindus alike, whether Sora, Oriya, or Telugu, and sometimes converting them with its demonstration of the power of God and the kindness of Jisu. Animists did not care about reconciling the two kinds of causality, and backed up the dispensary medicines with sacrifices as usual. "If you just eat medicine you eat alone," Ranatang scoffed. "If you kill a buffalo everyone joins in!" Monosi supplemented this robust remark with a finer analytic insight: "The old Sora see illness as coming from outside the body, so if we all eat together the person gets well. Christians say illness is inside the person—so it's pointless for everyone to share the medicine!"

The decline of sonums has led to a lacuna in causal explanation that hospital medicine does nothing to remedy: whom should we blame for the illness if not the dead? One answer is that there is an intentional agent here among the living, and my impression is that sorcery suspicion has expanded greatly among Christians. As well as the usual slow-acting *tonaj*, there is also an increase in *bano*, an Oriya kind of sorcery that works instantly, "like an arrow." For animists, sorcery allowed much social conflict to be aired, but it merely embellished a more basic causal mechanism. An inquest might reveal that the sonum that took the deceased was "incited" or "hired" (*baiñ*) by a living sorcerer, and this was how Mengalu became implicated in so many deaths, but the sonums also had more fundamental motives of their own. Baptists, even where they suspect sonums, cannot do anything with this idea. Sorcery fills the gap.

Injections, insects in the blood, high-speed sorcery: why not simply blame God or Jisu, just as one previously blamed sonums? All my inquiries ultimately come up against the idea of God's will (*Kittungen a itsumen*). This phrase may be uttered casually meaning "just so, who knows," or it may serve as a serious theological conversation-stopper.

The will of God poses a special problem in a society that until recently put so much emphasis on narratives of causality. The idea of God's will contains no mechanism to explain how God kills, nor much about his motivation. It thus gives little indication of how he could be blamed, and what for. At the time of affliction people may address a rhetorical question: "God, why . . . ?" They may even scold him vehemently: "If it's a sonum, why didn't you block it? If *my* blood is sick, why don't you heal me with *your* blood? If it's sorcery, why not remove the dart? Or if you're testing me (*tungjing-ting*) like Job, then just lead me off (*orung-ing*)!" There is, however, no systematic logical thread of anger or disillusionment, and one is compelled to subside into acceptance. God does not "eat" (*jum*) or "take" (*pang*) people like a sonum, but "leads" them (*orung*). He thus avoids being identified as the perpetrator of the event, but rather emerges as an ameliorator or rescuer, a kindly role that is even more explicit with Jisu. Even when he "leads" someone off as punishment, there is an element of justification, as when God "led" off the good-hearted Pastor Pilipo in a road accident (page 258) because he mixed with Pentecostals.

This vision implies trust in the wisdom of God and Jisu to be always justified. But this absolute rightness is a totally new idea. For animists, causality implied the possibility of challenge. Any being who is a cause of our suffering does it with a kind of intention that is like our own and can therefore be understood—and countered. In removing God and Jisu from comprehensible causality, Baptists also remove them from the challenge of dialogue and from the earthy, belittling banter with dead humans: "Ai! Aren't you ashamed? Now you're demanding a buffalo but I remember how you used to shit . . ." Communication with God or Jisu is not a context in which to be flippant or obscene.

The will of God is not like any intentionality that we can understand with reference to ourselves, as frail creatures having needs. Unlike humans both living and dead, God and Jisu have no hunger, no longing, and no needs. These are of course the elements of shared humanity that enable us to relate to sonums. Jisu's partial humanity is of a special sort. It is free from human sin—and from the cadging nature of sonums. He is not short of food or clothing, not attached to his old earrings and necklaces, not jealous that somebody else has inherited a patch of land. He does not need anything at all, and certainly not anything we can give. In animist sacrifice, animal blood is shed to assuage the neediness of sonums. But Jisu only gives. His blood flows in the opposite direction—not *to* him as a hungry sonum but *from* him as a willing sacrificial animal. This is a generosity arising from surplus, the concept of divine grace.

The half-human nature of Jisu reveals most clearly how the tone, and even the logic, of a form of Christianity can be molded by the specifics of the animism that it replaces. As well as being contrasted with sonums as all-good, he also replaces the ildas, the shamans' Underworld spouses who command other sonums to come and negotiate. The same Omino who converted after his son died from a burned hand also told me, "I was walking through the jungle when I met a were-leopard. It was a Kond one, very dangerous, but I prayed to Jisu and it didn't harm me." Here, I believe he was casting Jisu as a great protector, a super-ilda. Just like an ilda, too, Jisu belongs to another race that is normally unapproachable but whose protective power when co-opted is very great. Ildas belong to the same Kshatriya castes of rajas and policemen who persecuted the old-time Sora; Jisu, even more powerfully, is a white-skinned European, like the missionaries who promote him and claim to be on the Sora's side, and like Dumburu's idea of kittungs as white typists. I now realize that whenever I was sent to intercede with police and forestry officers in the 1970s, I too was being used as an ilda.

Jisu's suffering, too, is felt in a distinctive Sora way. So many Sora visions of him show the crown of thorns, the moment of suffering and bloodshed that equates Jisu most directly with the buffalo of grief (*dukabong*), which is dressed in the clothes of the deceased, embraced, and lamented. I suspect that this is a transformation of the Sora way of feeling pity for their dead. This hunch is confirmed by the old Sora word *ab-asu-yim* (cause-illness-feeling), which is a very revealing counterpart to the Greek *sym-pathy* or Latin *com-passion*, which both mean "a suffering with." Where the Greek and Latin leave the two sufferers alongside each other, the Sora makes their relationship causal. When animists feel sympathy for a dead person, this feeling makes them ill with the same symptoms, activating a vulnerability that Freud understood so brilliantly, and that Sora Baptists divert from dead humans (where sympathy functions as a contagion) to Jisu, where it can do them no harm.

Bloodshed, sin, love, trance, dialogue, denunciation from the platform: all tensions and passions are ultimately resolved over time. The analysis I had developed by 1980 portrayed dialogues with the dead as a close parallel to

Freudian bereavement therapy. Both these insights into human emotions appeared as monumental achievements of human understanding, each formed quite independently and each appropriate to its own cultural milieu.

I still believe this. But introducing Baptist doctrine as a third element subverts my earlier tendency to conclude that the parallel between animism and psychoanalysis necessarily points to a human universal. Despite their opposed metaphysical assumptions (the dead do or do not really exist), these two systems of thought are very similar in their emotional orientation, in which the world is driven by attachment between humans, and memories of the dead are how this attachment operates across time.

The cosmology of the Sora Baptists differs profoundly from both of these, because it is not based on human attachment as the starting point and end point of existence. When Baptists love each other, or feel attachment (including feelings of intimate hostility), I cannot say how far this is the same emotion or experience as among animists. Firstly, these feelings are not expressed, discussed, made public, and processed through the same performative techniques. Secondly, they also have a point of reference in a love between humans and God or Jisu, as a kind of ideal template: thus, Monosi sees his love for Likini not just as an attachment between humans, but also as God's work. Animists would agree with Freud about the importance of attachment but disagree about whether other entities exist beyond life in this world; on the other hand, they would agree with Baptists about the existence of otherworldly entities but not about what these are, and thus about where to direct their feelings of otherworldly attachment. Finally, Freud and Baptists would disagree both about the existence of otherworldly entities and about where one's prime attachment should be directed.

Another, quite unexpected consequence of making a comparison with Baptists has been to reveal the profundity of the animist system, not only as a psychology but also as a theology. Animists and Christians agree that human existence contains a suffering that cannot be avoided at the time but can be mitigated retrospectively. They disagree about the cause of that suffering and about the authority and charisma that can put it right, but both call this process of spiritual salvation by exactly the same word, redemption, and both derive this term metaphorically from a financial transaction—the redemption of a mortgage or loan, or the ransoming of a person from captivity (e.g., Exodus 21:8). This is the verb tandi. The Sora New Testament uses this word to translate the Greek root lutro (e.g., Matthew 20:28, Mark 10:45, 1 Timothy 2:6). Just as my team of ancestor-men in the 1970s sang of buying back the deceased with round-seeded money plants while buffalo were slaughtered next to us, so 1 Peter 1:18–19 says that redemption takes place not with mere silver and gold but with the blood of Jisu as a lamb. Whatever the differences between modern Soraland and ancient Israel, they are both societies with political domination, money, and edible animals. There is no mistaking the link between slavery, finance, and blood in a hymn composed by Monosi himself (No. 173):

Janggaran batten teniylung a delin,
Miñamen batten teniykuij a delin.

With your soul you paid the initial deposit for me,
With your blood you paid off the full payment for me.

Monosi sees the sacrifices of animist Sora religion as similar to the Old Testament, with both religions at a similar stage before the coming of Jisu. This view seems reasonable for sacrifice, but I am convinced that redemption was already the main point of the animist religion, and he is now becoming persuaded by my argument. The difference is not in the goal but in the understanding of what this means, the beings involved, and their narrative.

The Sora Baptist avoidance of thinking about the fate of the dead is not inevitable. The same basic framework of Christian logic can lead to very diverse outcomes, according to local social and historical configurations. Writing about Western Europe, Peter Brown (2015) traces a shift in the link between redemption and money from the second to the seventh century AD. For the earlier theologians Tertullian (who lived around 160–240) and Cyprian (bishop of Carthage, 248–258), the trajectory of the individual soul was unimportant compared to the transformation of the universe, which was about to happen at any moment and which would make "the interval between death and the Resurrection of the dead seem short and empty of significance" (Brown 2015: 9). While animists ("pagans") of the time believed their souls would rise instantly to join the stars of the Milky Way, Christian souls hung around in an uncertain state waiting for something better (10–11). Tertullian and Cyprian gloried in the extraordinary, radiant souls of martyrs who had died for their faith, but in a way that "drain[ed] the color from average souls." However, by the time of Bishop Julian of Toledo, author in 688 of a handbook of futurology called the *Prognosticon*, the distance between death and resurrection had become longer, and even for ordinary people, "there was time for the trajectory of each soul to be charged with individual drama and interest. An entire history of the soul after death was spread out in all its richness" (14), since "each soul now had a story of its own. . . . Each was marked, for good or ill, by its own, irrevocable individuality, for which it had to give account in detail" (16). By this period people were asking what the living could do for the dead, and Brown answers: "Each side—the living and the dead—were believed somehow to need the other. The dead, in particular, needed the living . . . because [the living] also shared with the dead a fundamental incompleteness that was increasingly ascribed to sin" (17–18).

Paradoxically from the perspective of Sora intellectual history, the earlier view of Tertullian and Cyprian bears a resemblance to that of Sora Baptists today, while Julian's later view comes closer to Sora animism, but with one important difference: the incompleteness of the Sora animist dead lies in their unfinished social and emotional relationships, but the incompleteness of seventh-century European Christians lay in their sinfulness. This awareness of sin led in the opposite direction from the Sora Baptists, since it turned out there was actually something important the living had to do for the dead: redeem them from their sin by spending a lot of money—literally, ransom them. By the seventh century, this is how a key verse in Proverbs 13:8 ("The ransom of a person's life is his wealth") was interpreted. This led directly to the massive endowment of churches and monasteries as "powerhouses of prayer on behalf of the souls of the departed" (Brown 2015: 21), and ultimately, in "an age that glutted its imagination on the notion of a mystical transfer of treasure from earth to heaven" (197), to much of the high art of the Middle Ages.

In Soraland, the Baptist denial of a "history of the soul after death" enters subversively into an environment in which exactly this narrative history had a vivid and central function. For dead animists, dialogue makes each person's story emerge so as to become amenable to a specific redemption. But dead Baptists have no individual story. Only Jisu has a story, which must stand for everyone's. Jisu *is* his biography, and this story makes for the piteousness that is such a powerful element in Sora conversion visions. Animist stories of individual death are assimilated to generic scenarios such as Sun, Earth, or Leopard sonums, but Jisu's story is supergeneric. In animism everyone had their own little story, but now there is only one, huge story. This story too is a template, but it requires a greater leap for us to share it: unlike all the previous victims of Sun-Sonum or Leopard-Sonum, no Sora has personally experienced crucifixion or a crown of thorns. Some elements in Jisu's story may suggest a parallel with one's own, and this may be what triggers moments of pity for his suffering—perhaps a transformation of the logic by which pity previously brought animists to fall ill by sharing the symptoms of those they had lost.

Animist victims of suffering are redeemed by their own ancestors, who are empowered to do this because they have themselves been redeemed earlier in a similar way, in a great chain of redemption. The animist dead become agents of redemption only after a trajectory in which they turn from being a victim of, say, Leopard-Sonum to its agent, sending leopards to attack their descendants. By contrast, Jisu takes our suffering upon himself, and he is redeemed without transmitting his victimhood to us on the way. He is able to do this because in this dualistic cosmology Duang-sım, Bad Sonum, is available separately to carry the negativity that the animist dead also have to carry as part of themselves. Baptist thinking spreads negativity haphazardly around the entire semantic field of sonumhood, so that Bad Sonum is an awkward, tautological concept. As one of Miss Munro's helpers asked long ago, "Then what is a good sonum?" David Hayward acknowledges that the missionaries were unaware of the very specific ways in which aggression and love are distributed among sonum categories, according to a logic in which the dead are first violated by Experience sonums and then rescued by ancestor-sonums, who are often the same people.

It might seem as if the devil takes on the negative role of the Experience sonums, while Jisu occupies the redemptive role of the ancestors. But in animist cosmology, goodness and badness reside not in the *identity* or *essence* of beings but in the *modalities* of their being. The struggle to redeem each dead ancestor is based not on a dualistic rejection of some beings in favor of others, but on the gradual transformation of the modality of *any* being. In the shift to Christianity it is not only the agent of redemption that differs, but also the nature of the suffering which that redemption tackles. For Baptists, this suffering comes from being in a state of sin. For animists, suffering is the complex cost of your attachment to other humans—not the badness that lies *within* you but the badness that *happens* to you.

Looking back to a time when I avoided thinking seriously about Christianity, these theological parallels and differences were nonetheless prefigured in the psychological models I worked out around 1980 (see pages 124–25 above, and Vitebsky 1993: 238–47). Then, I saw Freud's "melancholia" as corresponding to Sora Experience sonums, and his "mourning" to the ancestor-sonums. Within this parallel, there was a contrast between Freud's either/or choice and the animist view of these as successive stages, whereby each dead person starts as a member of an Experience sonum and is gradually transformed into an ancestor.

If we now put this alongside Baptist eschatology, it is easy to see how Freud's "melancholia," being "pathological," might correspond in Christian dualism to the realm of the devil. But what of Freud's "mourning"? This is a response to a loss that, however distressing, is ultimately normal—a suffering that is existential. The texture of time in Freud's bereavement therapy is not nearly as elaborate as that of Sora animists. For them, the state of being dead is far from the undifferentiated *communitas* or antistructure suggested by Turner's notion of liminality (1969). It is a highly structured state because it is also the ground for transformation as a process—a consideration that invites a serious rethinking of Turner's model (Vitebsky 2015). Nonetheless, Freud's mourning still takes place within the mourner's own experience of time, and his model helps us to see how Baptist time is so different from animist time. Baptist postmortem time clusters around two opposed focal points. It is both immediate at the point of death, and indefinitely postponed in the expectation of an event that is utterly discontinuous with the present and takes place in a transcendent realm that lies beyond experience altogether. Between the day of the burial and this remote point in the future, the Baptist funeral omits most of the middle ground of living memory. It is exactly here, within the experience-near time span of a group of closely interlocking lives, that animists place their elaborate discursive procedures of dialogue and negotiation. The Baptist funeral is abrupt because the time that follows has nothing—no terminology, no structure, no process, no knowable experience. Even pastors disagree about when the dead reach Jisu, how long they spend waiting, and where. People come up with answers, but these are idiosyncratic and not followed through into ritual practice. One of many explanations I received was the following: "There are three skies. The first is where the sun, moon, and clouds are, the second is where the dead wait, the third is God's abode. The janggara soul goes to God, and the breath soul stays in this world like a butterfly."

Living Baptists, too, experience time differently. Apart from prayer when attacked by thugs or were-leopards, Baptist ritual acts are not usually responses to sudden events. Rather, they are scheduled regularly to maintain a time that is smooth, its flow marked by prescheduled dates with as few bumps as possible, even in the face of death. This seems related to a wider Baptist style of regulation. Besides faith and techniques of surveillance, control is upheld by the church's hierarchical structure, its measured and disciplined procedures, and a respectable style of dress and deportment.

But the price for this smoothness is uncontrol forever in quest of an opening, bursting through the surface in the form of backsliding: alcohol, fornication, excessive funeral laments, burying of used clothes, accelerated sorcery, demonic possession . . . Both animists and Baptists live with an invisible spiritual dimension behind everyday life. Where animist danger is located within the dynamic of social relations, Baptist danger is moral and cosmic.

Where animists have constant small emergencies of sonum attack, Baptist spiritual life is steadier, but this calmness is enjoyed against a distant, restless background of cataclysmic events such as crucifixion, acts of Satan, and the apocalypse. Apart perhaps from some little acts of Satan, the rest of these are not happening here and now but take place somewhere else in the past or the future, over huge time spans that cannot be directly experienced. It would be hard to imagine a more radical shift in the shape of time and in one's own place within it.

Unlike missionaries and pastors, I see Baptist theology not as more advanced or correct than animist theology, but rather as a currently more appropriate way of engaging with the same existential issues of mortality, love, and loss, in a modern national context where archaic forms of political humiliation are no longer tolerable and an intraverted system of symbolic compensation (marrying high-caste sonums in the Underworld) no longer satisfies. What changes with Christianization is not the goal of redemption but the idea of what we are redeemed from, the beings who bring it about, and the setting of all this within space and time. Baptists might claim that attaining everlasting life (*er-añiden a-mandreng-na*) is better than becoming a butterfly. But "everlasting" is not a meaningful concept in animist metaphysics, and *er-añid* is a word not of temporality but of stocktaking: it means that a resource like a pot of alin or a flashlight battery does not run out. Animist ancestors do not need to be everlasting: they eventually become butterflies because everything about them that matters to the living has been returned to the living. This is not just animism, but animistic humanism. With no active gods (and no separate impersonal domain of nature), humanity is all there is, and the humans are people we know. Life is not everlasting in a transcendent realm in the sky, but ever-renewing right here, in the voices and embraces of the flesh-and-blood shamans of Rajingtal, Ladde, Manengul, and Sogad.

. . . .

If love for a woman brought old Oransu to the Baptist church, it thrust Monosi away. Being less swashbuckling and more conscientious, Monosi was less able to brazen out the pastors' ban on polygyny. Throughout his years in disgrace he held firmly to his Baptist faith, reading the Bible assiduously first thing every morning, much of it passages that he had once helped to translate.

Even before he started attending rituals with me, Monosi had already been making his own far-reaching parallels between animist and biblical thinking. A radical liberal theologian pushing against a fundamentalist world partly of his own making, he reaches back across Damano's rupturism to a level

Figure 9.4 Monosi visiting his old church in Assam, 2015
He was the main founder in 1956, though the inscription is mistaken: Monosi was never a pastor. The church has grown from a modest hut to a grand edifice.

of universality that lies beyond religious difference. The hollow gourd that floated on the floodwaters and contained the twins who founded the Sora race corresponds to Noah's ark, Sun-Woman's python to Eve's serpent. Moses was a shaman because he did not see God's face in the burning bush but only heard his voice, just as we do with ancestors; Jisu was a shaman because he descended to the Underworld . . .

Monosi's travels with me have also made him more open to animist genres of impersonation. Already in 1979 I wondered what he was really doing when he started to ask direct questions of the dead, ostensibly to help me fill in gaps in my research data. Monosi's father had died many decades earlier and was beyond retrieval in any trance. But Monosi's love for the songs, words, and feelings of the rediscovered animist world merged with his love for his father and for his lineage-brother Mengalu—and increasingly for me, as the person he has come to rely on to record and preserve it all. When Mengalu died in 1994, Monosi felt that his people had lost a great repository of the old culture. "I'm sure it really was Mengalu who spoke to me the other day," he told me in 1998. "It wasn't just the shaman pretending. My soul was jolted (*je'e ñen sati'*) by its reality. As a Christian I couldn't go to his inquest or his stone-planting. If I hadn't talked to him later, I'd still feel angry about his sorcery." His eyes filled with tears, and he whispered, "I've still got his myths and chants in my ugar."

In 2008, after we had been listening to voices recorded back in 1977, he told me, "In that tape with Mengalu and Pasano singing as ancestor-men, they sang with my dead grandchild's face about me: 'Granddad, you're Christian, you don't talk to me you don't remember me, you didn't pour me rice you didn't pour me water. Now you've come with a Sahib and a tape recorder, but you wouldn't have come without him!' It really was like my grandchild, I cried a lot, I was very sad."

I believe that Monosi was weeping for the loss of an entire world, for his role as an agent of that loss, and for his conflicted faith as a devout Christian. Mengalu's songs had come to stand for so much that was precious, from Monosi's father to those unforgettable three nights in Manengul when Doloso so vividly incarnated the dead and Monosi met the love of his life, thereby putting that faith so severely to the test.

10

. . . .

YOUTH ECONOMICS

LIFE AFTER SONUMS

. . . .

In the 1970s my challenge was to understand the Sora's devotion to dialogues with the dead; since my return there in 1992 it has been to understand their rejection. I loved those dialogues and the people who engaged in them, so to me this change felt like a great loss. How can a new generation feel it as a great release? As one of the last of the old-timers who still talks to the dead through the last of the shamans, and openly drinks alin ("Granddad, that's not good!"), I must acknowledge that the emancipation that was just an agenda in Damano's liberation theology is now in full swing all around me. The missionaries understood so little about sonums and projected such an alien interpretation onto the Sora; and yet their vision triumphed. It cannot simply be that they imposed it; this was something the Sora were ready for. Doloso's Catholic daughter Ambadi, having rejected her father's shamanic profession, might well echo Prospero's daughter Miranda: "O brave new world, / That has such people in't!"

In 2013 I reached Ladde again for the first time since 1998. In the interval (on Wednesday, 19 December 2001, as Monosi recalled with his calendrical meticulousness) Dumburu, great shaman and feared sorcerer, had died on his remote clifftop above the village. I heard about it when I returned in 2005, with mixed feelings. In the 1970s Dumburu had been my easygoing host, my uneasy friend, and my cunning jailer. I had visited him several times in between, but I had largely left that frustrating year behind.

Others had had ambivalent feelings of a quite different sort. Dumburu's sons Arambo and Ronggia sent for Pastor Enusai and Deacon Buyajo. Monosi also went. He was keen to preserve Dumburu's ritual materials as cultural relics, but they insisted on consigning everything to the flames, proclaiming over each item, "This was used for Sun-Sonum, this for sorcery, this for . . ." The equipment included a sheaf of porcupine-quill darts, an amulet of bear's fur like the one Dumburu had tied on me twenty-five years earlier, and sixteen sonum-pots that exploded in the conflagration with bangs and screams of "Jiii! Juuuu!" This was no routine "banishing-rite" to lead a petty sonum out to the edge of the village. It was the irreversible destruction of a dangerous power that would otherwise seek an heir. Baby Saibori, the potential sorcerer whose birth I had witnessed, had died in infancy and had not been replaced. There was no inquest to discuss his death with Dumburu himself, but it was said that he had been murdered by his sons. I did not believe this literally but took this rumor as an acknowledgment of their symbolic parricide, expressed more brutally than Ambadi's repudiation of her father, Doloso.

Dumburu may have been feared, but nonetheless many Ladde people were tearful as we reminisced about him. A middle-aged man said, "You won't remember, but I used to stroke your legs and say you were like a bear." This was the little boy who had led me on the wild boar hunt! Dumburu's son Arambo was a Baptist catechist with oiled hair and a mustache, a person of many thoughts but few words, just as he had been when little. I returned again in 2015, and Arambo took me up to the huge slabs where we had spent part of his childhood together thirty-nine years earlier. The ancient laia creeper with trunks thicker than pythons had survived, and there was the rock with the beckoning kittung that had tried to recruit him.

The cliff I had climbed in the dark to raise the alarm about Jamani's afterbirth was hard to identify, but we found the stone outline of our little baby-hut. The stones formed a hot clearing on bare rock, surrounded by thin, spiny vegetation. This was not ringring a uyungen, the silence of the midday sun when everyone was busy somewhere else till the evening. It was a place that had become empty from lack of use. The Sora hills were rapidly being covered with cashew trees. The landscape may have looked more cultivated than when it was jungle, but it was less peopled because cashews needed almost no attention, and there was nothing much to do there. A generation earlier the hillsides were alive with tapping, cutting, drinking, gathering, cooking, traveling . . . Wherever I walked I would be hailed—"E Pirinooó!"—and look up to glimpse a woman on a slope half a mile away, a sickle in her hand, a basket on her head, and a cigar behind her ear: Wan ite, wan iyle? ("Where are you going, where have you been?") Or a man standing on the crown of an alin palm with a pot hanging from his elbow: Alin gale po? ("Have you drunk?") Now one can walk for hours on the mountain paths and meet almost nobody, while the last of those alin palms rise sere and untapped, dying from the effort of shedding seeds that cannot sprout in the caustic carpet of fallen cashew leaves. The Forestry Service has been transformed from random extortionists into useful suppliers of cashew saplings, and after a 150-year-long government campaign of suppression, shifting cultivation has finally come to rest.

Descending along the Ladde path, I gaze down on an expanding network of ribbon development that almost links Borei, Rajingtal, and Puttasing, and runs out toward Sogad. These villages along the road already have some light bulbs, and television will soon follow. Thirty or forty years earlier they were so separated by a belt of jungle that their ritual performances could play with their distinctive accents. Monosi's freestanding house in Ongara was a forerunner of a pattern in which people abandon the tightness of the village and spread out into a garden suburb. The reddish-brown mud wash of the old stone houses has been almost entirely replaced by cement-covered brick, and on the edge of Rajingtal and Sogad the government has built housing colonies for the children of my poorer friends, with rows of standard-issue houses fronting onto streets laid down in concrete slabs.

The cashew plantations are not luxuriant groves but an acknowledgment of how barren the jungle soil has become. The scorching juice of the wild cashew tree has long been used in antisorcery rituals, but its cultivated counterpart is a new introduction from the gritty sand dunes of the coast. The nuts are shelled somewhere in the plains and sold on, while the harsh residues are used to make brake linings and insecticides. In the Sora hills cashew trees have come to undermine the headmen and others who own paddy fields, by democratizing wealth. Previously, money accumulated from numerous small local people up a pyramid of exploitation to bigger people further away. But cashews can bring huge sums of money to almost anyone. By the 1980s local branches of the State Bank of India were already receiving millions of rupees in deposits, and during the 1990s these sums became enormous. Looking back to when we first met in the 1970s, Bala the bank manager says there is "a Heaven and Hell difference." These deposits are largely from young men who wear extraordinarily expensive dress, with fancy boots at thousands of rupees a pair, and Bala also adds "We don't know if these cashew trees are actually family property. And what the young boys will do with this money?"

The Forestry Service plants unirrigated hillsides with cashew trees and leases them parcel by parcel to Sora households that can demonstrate previous use of a plot in terms they understand (not by the distribution of ancestors in Earth-Sonum sites). In 2005 the annual tax was one rupee for every ten trees. In return cashews can yield up to 100,000 rupees per acre, and poor Sora have been able to roof their houses with tin after just one good season.

Cashews are the antithesis of the crops they replace. The mixed species of shifting cultivation ripen at different moments and diversify the risk of different pests and diseases. Though their yields are low, they offer flexibility and resilience, and can be used for either cash or subsistence. By contrast, cashew gives huge payments but is inedible to the growers. Also, like any monocrop, it is vulnerable not just to crop failure and disease but also to the vagaries of

Figure 10.1 Bala the helpful Oriya bank manager

the market. In 2007, cashews fetched 32 rupees a kilo in Sogad, or 34 if you carried them down to Gunupur; in 2009, they fetched 40 rupees, or 50 if you could wait for the market to rise later in the season; in 2012, they started at 100 rupees a kilo, but within days had slumped to 70.

The cashew boom has rendered the old paddy economy ambiguous. Until the 1980s most fights, murders, cheatings, and sorcery, if they did not concern women, concerned the tightly terraced, cooperatively irrigated paddy fields. From the headman Sidoro's gross abuse of his subjects to the duplicate stone-planting that men gave to their marongger cousins to keep open the possibility of one day inheriting them, these fields were the focus of acquisitive desire as well as the resting place of capital.

By inviting neglect, cashews have uncoupled wealth from hard work, from careful husbandry, and even from extortion. Paddy demands intensive labor, and with increased education there are fewer family members with the skill or willingness to cultivate (or the time, if they are employed elsewhere). In 1998, an average field might cost 30 rupees to plow overall and 50 rupees (or three maunds, 7.5 kilos, of rice) to level. By 2007, each workman cost 60 rupees each day for plowing and 80 for leveling (cash only by now). By 2009, these costs had nearly doubled, and in 2013 they had risen to 150 and 250 rupees respectively, while a plow buffalo cost 10,000 rupees an acre, and labor for planting out rice seedlings cost 15,000. For all the soil preparation, repair of steep stone terraces, manipulation of water flow, cooperation with neighbors, sowing, transplanting, and weeding, rice still fetched only a few rupees a kilo. Land in the hills is thus turning into a potential liability.

Yet the government still sees paddy fields as the key to long-term sustainable wealth. Land reform would have broken up Sidoro's empire of 60 acres to a mere 10–12, if the equal division among his five sons had not already split up his estate. The government's land settlement, like Christianity, makes the ancestors' relationship to land irrelevant. Plots undergo various arrangements of borrowing, mortgaging, sharecropping, sale, and inheritance as household fortunes fluctuate, and many of the dialogues I heard in the 1970s were concerned with adjudicating, reiterating, and memorizing these moves. People still know the detailed history of each plot, but now they do not use the dead to manage it. In November 2005 Monosi and Mengalu's son Pradipo went to the revenue officer in Gunupur to update their share of fields inherited over the years from their common ancestors. Their holdings were complicated: twenty-one separate plots in Sogad totaling 6.45 acres, and three plots in other villages totaling 0.94 acres. Some were the fields that had triggered the act of sorcery for which Mengalu was punished for the rest of his life. While all these plots had long since become subject to government paperwork, they had also been discussed in trances with their deceased former owners, and as a Christian, Monosi had retained his claim by contributing cash to their funerals in lieu of a sacrificial buffalo.

The small plots in such patchworks are often far apart, a strenuous walk while prodding buffalo and hoisting a plow on one's shoulder, and many changes of ownership are made to rationalize inconvenient holdings. These moves are beyond the ken of officials, and once upon a time they constituted very profitable knowledge for headmen and bariks. The register of rights measures each tiny plot throughout Soraland along with its "owners," their names recognizably filtered through the Pano accents of the bariks who controlled the surveyors' access to information. The register lists quantities but not locations, which are specified in specific title-deeds. In the late 1970s I made a study of some of my friends' plots. There was a general overall fit, but many discrepancies in detail, and some complete muddles. These may have been due to inaccuracies or untruths at the start, but also to subsequent changes as directed by the dead. The revenue officer's department could not have known, or cared, about any of this as long as somebody paid the annual land tax— plus an adequate stream of additional "charges." These charges discourage people from bringing their paperwork up to date: even in the enlightened postexploitation era of 2005, that afternoon in Gunupur cost Monosi— literate, Oriya-speaking former council chairman—a mysterious additional "fee" of 2,000 rupees.

Even without labor costs or competition from cashew, paddy fields are becoming less desirable for another reason. Yields have dropped, ironically since the introduction of high-yielding varieties. These require expensive, toxic chemicals that the growers cannot afford and that are said to provoke new illnesses, and they incur serious losses by rotting more quickly in storage. Most obviously, these varieties are less drought-resistant even while springs are drying out from deforestation, so that even early in the season one can now walk through paddy fields that have shriveled up or failed to flower. Soil and irrigation are easier lower down, and some people are selling up in the complicated ecosystems of Sogad or Rajingtal and buying larger, softer fields in the well-watered plains.

Soil, water, and people are all sliding downhill: from the high jungle clearings to the valley villages, and from the villages onward again down toward the lure of jobs, schooling, and the lifestyle of the towns, where government schemes revitalize unused badlands for new housing colonies. Monosi has given his old house in Ongara to a relative (who in an unusual act of fostering was breast-fed by Monosi's mother), and now lives with Likini in a cement house among new fruit trees in Manikpur, a pioneer settlement where the hill road flattens out toward Gunupur. His oldest daughter lives in Parlakimidi town, another daughter lives in a large plains village, and his son is a clerk in another town far away. Many of the proud highlanders of Manengul are his neighbors or have even settled beyond Gunupur in Domesara, among the alphabet worshippers who converted their headman to their cult. That headman's daughter married the son of the alphabet cult leader Orjuno, and the shaman Doloso's daughter Ambadi has settled there too in a move that would surely have infuriated her father. At first such people maintain their old house in the hills, and the family commutes between the two places, but gradually the new location takes over. This is where the main agricultural work is done, and also nearer to where their older children will go to schools and training colleges. The distaste for the dirt and clamor of the plains, so noticeable on visits there in the 1970s, has been displaced by a seductive magnetism.

Roads funnel more people onto fewer paths. The funnel effect of the Gunupur-to-Puttasing artery is reaching ever further uphill, draining people from the mountainside and drawing their thoughts away from its plants and animals. Paths lead to all sorts of places: baby-hut, drinking circle, bathing spot, secret love-nest, favorite tree, medicinal plants, commanding rock. By contrast, roads lead only to villages, which become a destination for riding rather than a starting point for walking. From Gunupur the bus now trundles up the mountain bends by Pattili and Rajingtal, through Puttasing and on up the wide valley to Sogad. Trekker jeeps stagger further, up the uneven tracks to Manengul and beyond, and soon even the road to Ladde will be finished. Similar roads penetrate the Sora hills from all starting points in the plains.

The dynamism of development leaves enclaves of refuge. I collect information on business and politics near the road, but relax clambering barefoot over high rocks with old-timers who still move around the hillsides for old-fashioned purposes. Remnants of the jungle are still worked for shifting cultivation by women, who are more inclined to accept its low-yield economy, and the steep stony shortcuts between bends in the road down to market are still well-trodden, as those who use them save on bus fares. However, their men increasingly stay in the villages and cruise up and down the road. Some use bank loans to drive trekkers and three-wheelers as taxis, others specialize in house construction as carpenters, masons, or purveyors of sand and cement from the town. The son of the shamans' wall-painter Dalimo is now the best house-builder in Sogad, raising numerous walls that will never bear his father's pictures.

Figure 10.2 New motorable road to Manengul, 2015

The descendants of my old friends obtain contracts through the block development officer to assemble men, women, and materials to build the roads, which continue to branch out to ever smaller and more remote villages. These are the same roads that convey cashews to market, so they are doubly profitable (though there are victims too: the strong, charismatic Ranatang supported the extension of the road from Sogad to Guddara and was beaten to death with an iron crowbar by a man who stood to lose some of his paddy field). For the contractors, they are the best business available. For the workers, breaking stones each day may be harder than harvesting cashews once a year, but in 2005 it paid 70–80 rupees a day; by 2013, under a national scheme said to guarantee 200 days of work a year to anyone and everyone, it paid 120 (like much of my data, these figures come from local perceptions rather than from official sources).

All of this money comes from the government as development and social welfare, and far surpasses the modest scale of the 1980s. Rice is distributed to everyone at rates far below the market price, and free to the poor; widows, the old, and the disabled receive pensions; and after their bank accounts, land titles, and motorcycles are verified to check their assets, subsidies of 52,000 rupees for building houses are given to families "Below Poverty Line."

Wages, pensions, and subsidies are paid not in cash, but directly into an account, which each person now has at the State Bank of India; the sons of the old bariks, even of the monstrous Jogi Ganta, are just petty traders, drivers, and laborers. Church and schooling have wiped out their linguistic monopoly, and this has allowed the State Bank to eliminate their economic stranglehold through dedicated officers who give and monitor low-interest loans (Bala's favorites are ladies' cooperatives, which have a 100 percent repayment record). During the recent international banking crisis, my Sora friends could not understand how the main exploiters of ordinary people in the West were banks themselves, with their "arrangement fees," "contingency fees," and bailouts (to say nothing of payday loan companies that exceed even Jogi's rates), but especially that they were faceless. They have no problem seeing these charges as I do, as bribes to get things done, but wonder, "How can you give bribes to something that isn't a person, to no one in particular?"

The impulse to embrace corruption has cheerfully adapted itself to new structures and pathways. The distribution of the greatly increased funds lies with the greatly strengthened *panchayats* (local councils), which also have the power to adjudicate people's eligibility for subsidies. The key positions are chairman and secretary. Their potential excesses are supposed to be controlled by a *gram sevak* (village worker), a liaison person who is generally a non-Sora from town. The compulsory routing of government handouts to personal State Bank accounts makes it more difficult to defraud individuals: as Bala puts it, "Diversion of funds should not be there." So though the new partnership of local knowledge with outsider contacts still echoes the old team of headman and barik, their target has shifted from multiple individuals to entire schemes. This gives corruption an additional economy of scale, but it also makes it less violent than in the past: a portion of your subsidy for rice or housing may never reach you, but it will not be beaten out of you after you receive it. One local chairman is said to have made a 50/50 agreement with an assistant engineer to get the same stretch of road approved three times, at 300,000 rupees a go. By the time the police got round to investigating, the engineer had been transferred and the chairman displayed innocent surprise. Another chairman was being profitably blackmailed by someone who had gotten hold of his secret accounts, but other villagers filed a police case anyway. In all such stories people flee across the bribescape, or are dismissed, arrested, and released in cases that drag on and come to nothing.

In the 1970s the Sora animist heartland had a freak, outdated isolation, and a freak, outdated level of abuse. When I saw how these hills were being drained, deforested, impoverished, and starved under a system of feudalism without responsibility, there seemed no way the curse of the bariks could ever be lifted. During my absence in the 1980s, with a freak speed that I shall never fully grasp, centuries of plunder were reversed, and the aura of boundless extortion was replaced by an aura of boundless subsidy. In the area around Serung, Christianity had long since taken over, but in my area it was the generation who were children in the 1970s, my little housemates in Rajingtal, who were born animists and grew up into the simultaneous advent of Christianity and subsidy. Those born from the 1980s onward can have little sense of what religion and economy were like before. Elders complain that young people have become scheming opportunists, but young Sora can now hold each other to account, and the scale of each family's victimhood has been drastically reduced. People still cheat each other but not in single grand acts to the point of destitution, and it is good for everyone that the government is making so much money available for so much embezzlement by so many people. This is true development. Channels and flows of funding are now very diverse, and any enterprising individual can have a go at tapping them: corruption too has been democratized.

In the 1970s, any time you had any money, even a modest remittance from a son working in Assam, the headmen and bariks would learn about it and take it away. Then they would watch you struggling to accumulate some more, then take it away again. The headmen would sink their spoils into gold necklaces and paddy fields, while the rest of the wealth would flow out of the area into villas for traders, officials, and police chiefs in the plains or be passed higher up into the stratosphere. Now much of the wealth that enters Sora country stays there, where it is transformed into smart clothing, cement houses, and motorcycles. The headmen have become insignificant, the bariks have been broken, and their toxic nexus with the police has been dissolved. The perpetual fear of Naxalite guerrillas not only encourages government subsidies but has also transformed the police station in Puttasing as the constables cower behind a barricade of sandbags and barbed wire, in fear of the same population they had previously terrorized. The lazy, complacent cruelty of the old days has been replaced by a grim military professionalism, and the government has started to recruit the sons of my friends, who suffer from a new concept of "unemployment," as paid home guards (auxiliary police).

The torrent of subsidies, in which wealth comes from outside more than it is generated from within, is surely not sustainable. It is hard to predict what will happen when there are no more roads to build and cashews have exhausted the soil, as they are said to do. Subsidy inflates consumption, which continues to outstrip inflated income; even if not at the old rates of interest, where borrowing a few cents could lead to enslavement for generations, or-dinary people are now in debt for hundreds of thousands of rupees. And if a valuable mineral is discovered under their land, the state will surely reverse its munificence and dispossess the Sora as ruthlessly as it is doing to the nearby Dongria Kond (Padel and Das 2010)—an industrial updating of feudal op-pression in which locals are no longer a resource yielding crops, taxes, and bribes, but just an obstruction.

Road building on the Chinese frontier seems to have ceased, and the economy of the Assam tea gardens has slumped. I toured Assam with Sora friends in 2015 and found whole communities of Sora who had settled there for generations, some having forgotten where they came from, but no lon-ger many short-term migrants. Now young Sora go to places their parents have hardly heard of: Mumbai for gem cutting, Gujarat for cloth printing, even Dubai. The biggest opportunities are in construction. In 2005 in Sogad I met Sagalo, whose baby Disamor I had helped to place in an orphanage in 1977 when his mother Panderi was killed by a Rattud-Sonum. I had not seen Disamor since. He was now working in the boom city of Hyderabad, and Sagalo wanted me to speak to him. We traveled down to Gunupur, a town with phone booths, and Sagalo read the numbers out to me laboriously from a scrap of paper. It was the first time I had spoken to a Sora on a cell phone, though they were appearing among young people even in hill villages with no electric points for recharging. Disamor did not seem surprised to speak to me for the first time in his life, and gave me directions: "From Secunderabad take the Kalakuya Main Road . . . statue . . . shop . . . the company's name . . ."

Hyderabad was 500 miles away, but this opportunity was too good to miss. I went immediately, and found Disamor in a white hut with a light-blue in-terior. It was clean and pleasant but completely bare, and home to several young Sora men who slept next to a heap of sand on the cement floor. The building sites of Hyderabad are not a specialized Tribal occupational niche like the Assam tea gardens. These lads had joined a generalized nationwide migrant labor force. There were few other Sora and no legitimate contacts with girls, so their main social contact was with Christians of any ethnicity or denomination. Disamor had failed tenth grade, a new concept of failure de-rived from the new concept of schooling, but he was economically successful. After loading metal onto trucks for five years, his pay had increased to 3,000 rupees a month, and he would soon be paid 5,000 a month for supervising eight men. His monthly expenses were just 1,000–1,500 rupees, and he sent

Figure 10.3 Cell phone: Paranto with grandson on his cement veranda, 2015

the rest home to his father, Sagalo, who had bought a paddy field down in Gunupur, where he was also building a house on land given by the Integrated Tribal Development Agency, "for when my grandchildren study in college."

How fortunes change! Sagalo had been a pauper subsisting on unirrigated millet-slopes, begging for occasional day labor on the paddy fields of others. But now he was also buying an additional field in Sogad from the son of the deceased old headman Sidoro, who had fallen short of cash. This transformation was made possible by his son Disamor, a modern young man able to think in terms of a future. Disamor knew I had been involved in rescuing him—indeed, the story has grown so that I am now absurdly credited with doing it single-handedly—but what else did he know about that terrible day twenty-eight years earlier? I had a recording in which every detail was recounted to a background of howling relatives, supposedly by his dead mother Panderi herself as she described her sensation of being eaten alive while she struggled to save him. The dead woman had passed on her name very quickly to her husband's next baby by her sister, so even without Christianization the memory of all this would have faded. Did I have a duty to revive it, or a duty not to? There was no precedent for this anywhere in Sora experience. Would it be a precious insight into his personal history, an archaic embarrassment, or a precipitator of emotional distress with no opportunity for resolution through dialogue? The inhibiting presence of the other youths in the hut made the decision for me, and the moment passed.

However, other reverberations of the past could not be hidden. Memories of sorcery can persist longer than memories of sonums, I think because they are not transformed and redeemed within a ritual structure. Sagalo was Mengalu's sister's son, and after Mengalu died he was repeatedly accused of receiving his uncle's sorcery powers. This was such an irony, since Mengalu's sorcery had earlier been directed at Sagalo, before bouncing off and killing Mando. To me Sagalo seemed completely un-sinister, but perhaps others feared that his poverty might conceal envy. To shake off the accusation he became an assiduous churchgoer, but this was not enough: Christians may dismiss sonums, but they are more terrified than ever of sorcery because the sonums' impotence leaves them nothing else to fear. In 2007 Sogad villagers threatened to burn Sagalo with gasoline, and he fled for a while to join his son in Hyderabad.

Disamor had risen from failure at school to become a master of paddy fields, but could rise no higher. All young people are literate, learning the Roman script for Sora in church and the Oriya script for Oriya in school. Those who take their education further look to *sakkiri*, a government job as a teacher

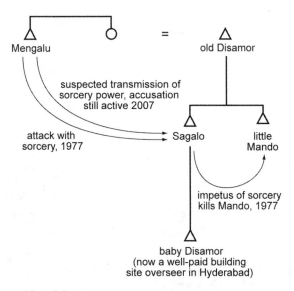

Diagram 10.1 Mengalu's sorcery transmission
Mengalu died in 1994, and it was expected that his sorcery sonums would seek out a new host. Despite having earlier been their target, Sagalo is now suspected.

or clerk, maybe helping on the family fields but otherwise crossing the basic Indian class divide between those who carry heavy loads in the sun and those who do not. The bodies of sakkiri people are softer and pudgier, less bashed and scratched, and after spending time with them it feels like a shock as well as a homecoming to return to the skinny little figures of the laboring Sora.

Monosi had no schooling, has never had a paid job, and has done no big-time trading. He has remained poor, and until recently unable to build a cement house. Yet he brought the ideal of education into the animist stronghold of Sogad. The first in that village to rise to salaried positions were his elder brother's sons Tisano and Elisai. Tisano has now retired as schoolmaster in Sogad, with one daughter married to a carpenter and another with an MA and a teacher husband. Monosi's daughter teaches in the school at Kerebba, while his son has an MA in "industrial relations and personnel management," and works in a government office.

Elisai works in a bank in Gunupur. His neat modern house stands incongruously on waste ground on the edge of the town, with an outdoor well and washing place behind a high compound wall with a wrought-iron gate. It serves as a base for Sogad people when visiting town, thereby ensuring a flow of up-to-date information both ways. From the flat roof one can watch the lights of the town at dusk to the sound of distant loudspeaker film music, a classic experience from the Indian mainstream that is still unavailable from the sloping roofs of the unelectrified hills.

Elisai has a well-trimmed mustache, with the fuller body and jowly face of a desk worker. While Tisano is lean and still plows the family fields in Sogad, Elisai and his wife do not join in the work or share in the harvest. The interior of the house has smooth cement surfaces and cement alcoves with ornaments and schoolbooks covered in newspaper. Here at the edge of town the houses stand apart among rocks and thorns, and the early morning lacks the animation of a village, with its leading out of cows and calling from house to house. Elisai gets ready for the office, and the children for a school that is entirely in Oriya even at primary level. The children can understand Sora (*ganludte*, "it enters their ears") but they cannot speak it. Elisai resembles my own grandfather in Wales, a small-town bank manager who spoke in English (with a strong Welsh accent) with the higher-ups and in Welsh with the farmers. In the transition to an assimilated middle class, my mother acquired an English accent and only a few Welsh words and catchphrases.

Elisai is not as comfortable speaking Sora as I am, though he still feels attuned to Sora mentality: "I can easily pass for Oriya, no accent," he told me. "But when Sora come to the bank, we know all their thoughts clearly (*kuddub ogandin galamtebe, pelid*). Some are embarrassed if they can't speak Sora, others don't care." This is more pragmatic than Bala's outsider's idealization of the honest Tribal falling from a primordial state of grace: "Earlier they were clean, obliging and didn't lie, they used to pay on time," he said recently. "Now they lie, we notice it in the bank."

This is not a new opinion. In 1933 one Indian official wrote, "The Savaras are losing their well known respect for veracity and trying to wriggle out of their legitimate obligations" to give unpaid labor and produce to local agents of the raja (quoted in Mojumdar 1998: 133 n. 25a). Another wrote in 1934 that they had "lost their spirit of compromise" (212). Legitimate! Compromise! My own information from the other side in the 1970s suggests that the old-time Sora managed to repay their bank loans by taking much worse loans from their bariks. Jogi's barik raj was part of a wider system in which everyone occupied a restricted niche in an ecology of ethnicity and caste. Each community in the bazaar was marked by distinctive forms of tattoos, earrings, and nose-rings, with skirts for Tribal women and different-colored saris to distinguish different Hindu castes. Now this is exactly what people mask through uniform mass-marketed trousers, shirts, saris chosen to taste, the ambiguously Hindu-Muslim *salwar-kameez*, and magazine-inspired jewelry, just as streets in

Figure 10.4 New Sora entrepreneur, Manengul 2015

town (Brahmin Street, Karan [Clerk] Street, Goldsmith Street) are named after castes that are no longer the only occupants.

In this ambience the Sora round faces and light skin are still recognizable, but less restricting. The conventional mystification of Tribals as honest because primitive is modified by the experience of seeing them carrying out professional roles like anyone else. A Sora elite is developing that thrives on this ethnic slippage while still benefiting from generous Tribal quotas for government posts. If the cashew traders roaring around on flashy motorcycles are hustlers who violate Bala's ideal, Sora government officers are still regarded as exceptionally clean. Sora men have served as revenue officer, as special officer and welfare officer in the Lanjia Sora Development Agency, and as district welfare officer. One holds a senior position in the Reserve Bank of India in the state capital Bhubaneswar, another married the daughter of a Telugu police chief and has been a district collector and secretary to a chief minister. Though these are Lanjia Sora from the hills and related to families in the Sogad area, they are all from other villages that are nearer to towns, and were exposed to education much earlier. Nonetheless they still lag behind other non-Lanjia groups of Sora in the plains who have many officers in the Orissa Administrative Service and even some in the national Indian Administrative Service. Those people are becoming assimilated into a regional and national elite in which class overrides ethnicity. They operate entirely in Oriya (and some Hindi), and within a generation their only Sora attribute may well be an exotic Tribal surname or a political career as a Tribal spokesperson.

The new wave of cosmopolitanism has brought its own wash of nongovernmental organizations (NGOs), with philanthropic titles or a crunch of acronyms, each with its own stationery, bank account, and pre-scripted appeal letter. I was standing on the road leading into Gunupur one day in 2005 when a large, sleek motorcycle squealed to a halt. The rider, slightly plump in black trousers and white shirt, wristwatch, and mustache, was Meru, a grandson of old Pastor Damano.

He gestured to a low cement building nearby with rows of well-watered red gladioli in a bare yard. "That's my school," he declared. "I teach children Sora." From a zippered briefcase he produced a document in English, which read: "Certificate of Registration of Societies Act XXI of 1860. Lanjia Soura Institute of Science and Technology [LIST] under Gunupur Block in the District of Rayagada is hereby registered . . ." LIST was an autonomous, nonpolitical, not-for-profit NGO dedicated to the "welfare of education, culture and socio-economic development of up-liftment for the values of both secular and socialist principles aimed at in our preamble of constitution." The objectives of the society included "to predicate social evils, practices like Sacrifices, Drinks, Gambling and various types of superstitions."

The members of the NGO were all Christian, but some had high Hindu names like Ananda (male) and Sunita (female). How did Meru himself acquire the name of a sacred mountain in the Himalayas?

"My original name was Theofil," he explained. "The teachers in school said it wasn't a proper name, so they changed it. They said, 'That's a Christian name, you're in a Hindu country.' "

The Indian state is constitutionally secular, but people in authority take mainstream Hindu forms and aesthetics for granted. Unknown to parents, teachers in residential schools regularly change children's animist or Christian names.

"Can you change it back?"

"No, when they do that it becomes your permanent legal name. They give all your papers and certificates in your school name."

Meru, ex-Theophil, showed me an Indian passport, a status symbol that had not yet been used for foreign travel, and asked me to invite him to England. "I have four professions," he explained, "LIST, social worker, local newspaper reporter, and I've just qualified as an advocate." He produced a certificate from the Orissa State Bar Council, written in English in imposing Gothic letters.

Here, sitting astride the ample padded saddle, was the essence of entrepreneurial Sora youth. His voice was smooth, making the up-and-down intonation of his older relatives sound overanimated. Meru was only thirty-one (as his passport certified). As with cashew traders and pastors, constant mobility was essential to keep his enterprise going, and the motorcycle was not just a symbol of modernity but also a vital life tool. Not for him the staid respectability of Elisai's government service in the bank, nor the power structure of his grandfather Damano's successors in the pastorate. He was an advocate, potentially an oppressive or emancipatory profession; I wondered what he would do with it. Someone photographed us on Meru's phone with our arms around each other, and I made a donation to his NGO.

School, school, school: whether run by government or NGO, schooling defines every child's life. Many schools are residential and far from home. The little boy who was commemorated in the 1977 karja hanged himself because he was unhappy there, but by now school has become the normal social setting of virtually all children.

Sometimes school replaces family to such an extent that it readily merges into the terminology of orphanhood. One such institution in Parlakimidi is run by Monosi's young relative James, the grandson of another pastor. There are seven girls and thirty-one boys, almost all Christian. Most are semiorphans, children who for some reason have no adult to look after them, though some are probably sent by relatives for the free education and boarding. The language is Sora, and the ambience is Christian, but James receives no church funding. The government provides some assistance, but most costs are covered by donations to his NGO, called Asuyum (Compassion).

Another orphanage on the other side of town is Oriya-speaking and orthodox Hindu. This school is supported by a Brahmin colleague of Bala's at the State Bank, called Anadhi. "All boys are Tribal," he told me in English. "We call them as *vanvasi* [jungle dwellers]." These children too are semiorphans, usually nominated by the local administration. Anadhi goes "from pillar to post" (as Bala puts it) to raise funds from Hindu temples and well-wishers. "We are fortunate that we are not orphans and our children are not orphans," he declared. "God has given us good health, sound mind, good family, and a job which leaves us free after five." With a true Hindu sentiment he added: "We must use our spare time in this life to beg for food for the boys in school, otherwise this time will be required in the next life to beg for our own food."

Both schools invite me to speak to the children in their own language. As well as attending formal assemblies, I try to meet them off the record too. They are being groomed for life in the Oriya town, but I feel that a big, unrecognized task is to help them use their own language without feeling ashamed, and develop it so that it will be able to keep up with their new future. Taking care to favor each religion equally, I have raised funds abroad for bicycles, flip-flops, and textbooks as requested. However, I was more keen to arrange for kindly, comforting monolingual elders to come into schools in the evening to chat to the children about their lives in town. The scheme has proved impossible to organize, and I am now working out other ways to support the language (see the epilogue below).

The vigorous survival of their language in the hills among those who do not go outside to residential school is an indication of their isolation. So was their lack of participation back in the landmark 1977 election. But even in Rajingtal and Sogad it was possible by 2000 to say of many people that they supported (or were clients of) a particular party. This area had mostly voted for the Congress Party since Rajiv Gandhi's development program of the 1980s and his charismatic appearance on the morning of his assassination in 1991. When Chief Minister Naveen Patnaik visited Rayagada around 2007, many people switched to his regional Biju Janata Dal Party. This was a shift of clientelism rather than of ideology, with some local coloring such as the funding of church halls and distribution of cell phones to pastors.

The Sarda Sora down in the multicaste region around Gunupur have long been involved in party politics. In elections for the state legislative assembly, their Bhagirati Gomango was elected from Gunupur almost continuously from 1955 to 1990 (while standing for various parties), and his successors too have been mostly Sarda Sora. In the 2014 Gunupur election, a disproportionate nine out of the eleven candidates had recognizably (Sarda) Sora names. The politicization of the Lanjia Sora, like their Christianization, started on the Parlakimidi side of the border. There, a man from Timlo called Gorsang, a relative of my friend Majji over in Sogad, stood variously as a Congress and a Bahujan Samaj Party candidate, won once and lost once, and regaled me with fascinating and amusing stories of alliances and betrayals. In 2004 James stood in a nearby constituency for the Bahujan Samaj Party; in 2009 he tried to get a ticket from Congress but failed, and then stood, unsuccessfully, as an Independent. "I've got an MA in political science, and was working as a clerk

Figure 10.5 James

in the Revenue Department in Ganjam when I gave up my job to run the orphanage. I saw lots of Hindu-Christian fighting and thought, 'We need a Sora
Member.' I knew the Christians would vote for me, and also the Hindu Sora."
Yet in this area both Christians and Sora are demographically insignificant.
Many recent MLAs have been Brahmins, and James lost to a man of the Paik
caste. He remains active, speaking at meetings and brokering conflicts and
alliances, in effect playing an updated version of Monosi's politically more
innocent role decades earlier as an all-round public wise man. At a recent
election for Monosi's once modest but now profitable old post of chairman of
the Sogad *panchayat*, Monosi's son stood, unsuccessfully, and one of the ten
candidates received 484 votes while another beat him by one vote, at 485. Then
it was suddenly claimed that the first candidate had received 486 votes after
all. Alerted by these unsubtle figures, the block development officer traveled
up the hill to supervise a recount.

If allegiances to political parties shift with charismatic leadership and the
voter's personal advantage, is religious allegiance so different? While the
animist person continues to evolve after death, the phrase "then he became
Christian" is made to sound like the final significant event in a person's exis-

tence. Yet Christianity too has become multiple and competitive. The Canadian Baptist missionaries did the hard work of translation and institution building, but now they are long gone. The Sora Bible and hymnbooks are there for the picking, making the 180,000 registered members of their self-funding association a tempting target for predator denominations moving in from the plains with more money and a less austere style of worship. Baptists are lured with food, lodging, and education grants by Pentecostals, Lutherans, East India, Orissa Baptist Evangelistic Crusade (OBEC), Buñangji (Brethren), Derna or Biswas (Faith, Trust), Seba Bharato (Serving India), Sanniara (Saturday, i.e., Seventh Day Adventists), Jisu Renukku (Assembly of Jesus), Compass, World Vision, Good News (whose American website says, "Connecting with primitive, savage and backward tribal people to bring social, spiritual and economic transformation into their lives"), and Agape or Prema (Love: "Jisu's love for John was like a soft yam with no stringy fibers").

Committed Baptists are resistant. "The Pentecostals shout Hallelujah over and over!" James complained. "We're very suspicious." I have heard Baptist men mutter that sacred word privately in their sleep or in a fervent whisper during predawn prayers, but never out loud. "It's alright to have God in your ugar," James agreed, "but crying out aloud is insincere (*jolda*), it's ostentatious (*ersantung*)."

A more serious battle for the soul goes on at the level of church leaders. Early pastors like Damano were rigid but incorruptible, and the late Pastor Pilipo was a truly beautiful person. But some others are involved in incidents of greed, sex, sorcery, and murder, which are unremarkable failings in the robust animist world but appear grotesque against new Christian values. Stories of pastors' vices resemble tales from Boccaccio's *Decameron*. Pastor Pilipo's brother, also a pastor but in sharp clothes and sunglasses, was already married when he took a second woman away from her husband. He then became a pastor in the OBEC, whose money he used to poach regular Baptists until the OBEC threw him out for further misdemeanors. Pilipo once asked me to reason with his brother, but as a non-Christian I felt unqualified. Another pastor inflated the fee of a few rupees for conducting a wedding. In 1998 he required 50–100 rupees each from bride and groom, and some pastors now charge ten times as much. This was not at all what David Hayward had intended when he negotiated with the government for pastors to be licensed for marriages.

In addition, pastors generally receive a substantial share of the harvest, which is danced to their house by their parishioners in a procession, and further large presentations are made to the deacons and catechists. All of these gifts and payments are personal and are separate from the 10 percent tithe that supports the church. It is an irony that the pastor of one parish is the successor to upright old Damano, the original prophet of emancipation from feudal servitude, yet is said to have demanded a second motorcycle (at 60,000 rupees) for his son and to get his house repaired free of charge by his parishioners. Even the police can no longer get away with demanding such corvée labor. Several other pastors are believed to practice sorcery; one is said to have hired assassins to kill his lover's husband by physical means, but the police exhumed the body, and the killers confessed after being subjected to a lie-detector test.

For a church with only thirty-one pastors, this seems a high scandal ratio. While headmen and bariks were appointed by outside forces, so their power and corruption were inexorable, pastors are appointed by their own congregation. Perhaps their grip is so tight because it is so insecure, as they can be criticized and sometimes even physically beaten. "Why do they not simply dismiss bad pastors?" I once asked Monosi.

"They can't beat us physically," he replied, "but with their tongue." Here was the power of the platform, blending God's judgment with social exclusion. Yet pastors can still lack courage. When Sagalo was being threatened with being burned alive, a pastor was asked to intervene, but he reportedly said, "No, I can't get involved, people would criticize me or beat me or bewitch me!"

The policing of doctrine cuts both ways. The pastors can sanction you in church, as they did with Monosi, but parishioners can threaten to join rival denominations. Moreover, evangelical Protestant groups have a tendency to split, and this risk is not confined to the Sora. Monosi experienced Miss Turnbull's and Miss McLean's questioning at his 1953 baptism as pushy and aggressive. No wonder: a published history of the mission reveals that they were flirting with a rival group ("All One in Christ") that aimed to take over the Baptists' building, and were both thrown out of the regular Baptist movement later that same year for going round the Sora congregation "denouncing their former co-workers." Miss Turnbull "held certain doctrinal views so rigidly that she was unable to enter into fellowship with her Canadian colleagues." She believed that all trust in medicine was "a betrayal of faith" and an "infiltration of modernism" (Knight and Knight 2009: 133–34). This view was seriously off message for a mission that combined the healing power of Jisu with scientific medicine to run the best hospital in the area.

Most rank-and-file Baptist youths know nothing of doctrinal nuances, and are generally uninterested in philosophical issues. Born into their religion, they were spared the spiritual agony of choice. The more enterprising aim for trading, government, and NGOs, but many are timid and inarticulate, unable to speak about their lives and ignorant even of the biblical character whose name they bear. To me, such youths seem like tentative persons, forming an underclass of lumpen Christians, a proletariat of unawareness, quite unlike the animists who would converse with their dead namesakes and participate in rituals with performative flair.

There are good pastors too, and their deaths put a special explanatory burden on the will of God. Pastor Apollo, who appreciated the voluptuous Song of Solomon when it was finally translated, encouraged dancing, and brought the oboe back from its exile among the funeral sonums, died very suddenly. He had just had a doctrinal disagreement with a less liberal colleague, so was it sorcery? "Or Rattud-Sonum?" mused Monosi, uneasy about the animist implications. "No," countered James, "he died of blood pressure." "Ah yes," Monosi agreed, gratefully picking up his medical idiom, "he'd been avoiding salt and sugar, but he must have eaten them this time, so he dropped dead."

Pastor Dulupet was another clean man, but rather than Apollo's sensuality he had something of Damano's sternness. He had snubbed Monosi after he eloped with Likini and was opposed to ecstatic Pentecostal tendencies. An old man dreamed of Pentecostally deviant Baptists pouring hot coals down the left side of Dulupet's face, and later he was indeed paralyzed on that side (by a stroke maybe, but some said *tungmadgijber ojoraile*, "the portent was fulfilled")—though in an important gesture of reconciliation, Dulupet waited for Monosi to visit his bedside before dying. Pilipo, the kindest of all pastors and generous to the last, gave up his seat for someone in a trekker and perched on the roof as it wound up a mountain road. When the vehicle fell into a gully, Pilipo, the most sin-free passenger, was the only one killed. Everyone lamented his death, but some also pointed out that he was returning from a trip where he had prayed together with a Christian group called Viswavani: was this God's punishment? So it seemed that Dulupet died for criticizing one rival sect while Pilipo died for fraternizing with another. In both cases, God must have "led them off" for a good reason. This was not so different from the ambivalence with which a sonum might take you, equally out of anger or love—except that neither God nor the dead man spoke to clarify those reasons.

Viswavani is a Christian movement from South India. In 2013 I visited the local branch, down in the plains near Parlakimidi. It was a very swish operation, with a huge, clean building in a huge, clean compound. Inside, very unusually, was a green carpet with a vacuum cleaner. All the well-dressed young men were Sora (women did the cooking and vacuuming), and they operated good computers. One man with fervent sparkling eyes explained, "My father was a Communist leader. Communism is alright, but it is of this world and leads to death. Buffalo blood is also of this world, but Jisu is of Heaven." He opened one of his well-ordered computer files called "Soura culture," and there on the screen was a film of Doloso and Rajani dancing at the karja in Manengul, which I had once lent on a DVD to a youth and which had been copied and found its way here, turned into heritage. I was digitally photographed and fed into the computer to join them. He gave me a pamphlet in English on the blood of Jisu. Its hysterical language was quite unlike the sober, orderly tone of Baptist leaflets, and a reminder that even a small sideways step to another Christian denomination may entail a huge transformation of behavior and emotion.

I then visited the headquarters of the original Sora Baptist Association at Bethany Bungalow, where I had not been for a long time. Their style of worship may have been sober, but this was no longer the modest pioneer shelter where I had met Damano and Monosi on my first day in Soraland thirty-eight years earlier. It had been completely reconstructed into a grand two-story statement with large meeting rooms and marble floors throughout, constructed like all Christian buildings by Sora themselves with voluntary labor. Even without the medieval Christian rationale of buying redemption for the dead, the church becomes a magnet for wealth. The Christian denominations are in competition, with Hindu temples and with each other. Austerity may be the ideal, but grandiosity is the temptation and the necessary advertisement.

Perhaps the most serious competitor to the Baptist Association is not the other Protestant sects nibbling round the edge of their congregation, but the Catholics. Catholic grandiosity is different. In contrast to the evangelical urgency of the others, the massive compound of the Catholic base down in Christnagar (Christ City) emanates the unhurried confidence of an institution that thinks in millennia. Father Joseph Moolan spoke Sora well and walked around the Sora villages, capturing them slowly but steadily as elaborately ornamented Catholic churches rose alongside the plainer Baptist ones. He vowed to stay in Soraland forever, and as an Indian citizen from Kerala he was able to do this until he died soon after our last meeting in 2013. By then, some Sora had been exposed to the Catholic concept of celibacy, a more thoroughgoing form of the sexual ambivalence of Pubic-Haired Sompa and her shaman successors, and one or two had become priests or nuns. Yet for the layperson, this is the church if you want to drink, have multiple wives, or commemorate the dead (albeit collectively and without trance) each November on All Saints' Day. When Monosi fell out of favor with the pastors, Father Joseph

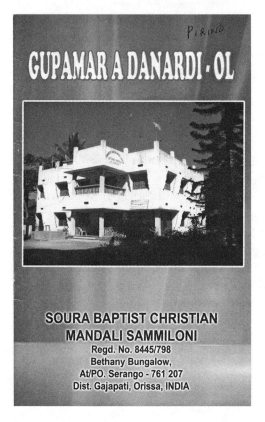

Figure 10.6 The rebuilt headquarters of the Sora Baptist Association *From the front cover of the Pastor's Handbook.*

made him an attractive offer, and of course Monosi would have been a great catch. He spent a month in Christnagar translating their hymns and praying with the Catholics every evening, and received alarmed letters from the pastors and even from Vancouver. Yet despite everything thrown at him from the platform over the years, he refused to abandon his Baptist faith ("This is where I began and this is where I'll stay").

· · · ·

Sonums pervaded every aspect of animist life, and dialogue was how one dealt with them. As I look back on the total world whose maintenance was the life's work of shamans like Ononti, Rijanti, and Doloso, and the surviving residue of that world as currently maintained by their final successors Lokami, Sompani, and Rajani, three functions stand out through all the pain of illness, the dancing, mimicking, weeping, and laughter. These are healing, the management of grief, and the management of inheritance. Each of these implies the other. They are inseparable, and it is through this inseparability that dialogues strove to resolve the tensions and ambiguities of my friends' lives.

The repertoire of the new post-sonum world cannot match this holism but provides uneven, piecemeal substitutes, revealing the unfinished nature of the Baptist or modernist project. The hospital medicine denounced by Miss Turnbull replaces rituals of acknowledgment and adds the power of prayer, but loses the link to human attachment. As for grief, the Baptists can almost be said to have abolished it. The dead are somehow with God and Jisu, but this idea lacks definition and leaves people almost in the same position as Western agnostics: we don't know, and we don't want to think about it.

Inheritance remains a practical issue whatever your cosmology. In the inseparability of these domains, shamans were not only theologians and psychotherapists but also probate lawyers. The church has nothing to say on inheritance, and written wills are still unknown, so now inheritance must be managed without any authority. Animist society was composed of patrilineages, and it was in the nature of this social structure that dialogues with the dead, however bitter and tangled, must always end in a consensus. In the absence of dialogues, the lineage too has lost its hold, and any case that cannot be resolved within the community becomes exposed, for the first time, to the law of the state.

Thus, Jamano and his shaman brother Uda continued to work their father's paddy fields jointly. After they died their sons prepared to divide their property. Jamano had three sons (Ranatang was the eldest); but Uda had been impotent, so Jamano had helpfully impregnated his wife for him. The resulting boy was always known as Uda's son. Should he take half the fields as Uda's only heir, or a quarter as one of Jamano's four sons? There was a dispute, within the traditional rules of patrilineal inheritance, but since everyone had become Christian there was no forum for arbitration. The argument raged around the lineage and around their wives. It was finally decided in favor of Uda's "son." Yet the voices of the dead owners themselves were missing. Others had to guess or assert their wishes for them, without the mirror of their confirmation.

Church, medicine, law, and development all push their own diverse agendas, and their lack of holism makes them overlap to undermine the old religion in unexpected ways. The masculist church constrains the freedom of women, yet it also abolishes the practices that sustained the patrilineage as the prime social unit. Having abolished the ancestor cult, along with the mnemonic techniques of the No-o-o chant, pastors are ineffectual genealogical gatekeepers. Since many young adults no longer know who their grandparents were, they cannot trace the links to the descendants of their grandparents' siblings, so that cousins often marry each other in ignorance or against the lingering knowledge of their elders.

What happens when a man dies with only a daughter? Among animists, his lineage-brothers sacrifice several buffalo, plant a stone, and claim his property. His daughter's husband's people also take away some of his ashes and bones for a duplicate funeral, thereby retaining the possibility of a claim on the dead man's property. Such claims can be resolved only through a series of dialogues with the dead man himself, staged by both parties, possibly using different shamans. How strong are the intimacy and affection between wife and husband, and between son-in-law and father-in-law, against the man's relationship with his own brothers? In effect, the principle of lineage inheritance is challenged in a tug-of-love.

But under a radical new national law of 2005, daughters now have an equal right of inheritance with sons. Furthermore, if a man dies with no sons but only daughters, they become his sole heirs. Jani of Sogad was an old animist in the headman lineage who somehow heard about this new law. He had a lot of land but no son, only an adored daughter. She had married a man from Sagalo's poor lineage, and Jani wanted to leave all his land to this daughter. He tested the reaction of his brothers, but they were outraged, since the land would subsequently pass to her sons in that other lineage: "You have the ancient name Jani from our ancestor. She can have your gold, she can have your grain, she can have your cash, but not your land, otherwise our lineage will be ruined!"

Jani died, and at his inquest the next day he revealed (or confirmed what people already suspected) that he had secretly been to the revenue officer and re-registered all his land in his daughter's name. At each stage of his funeral, the requisite dialogues took place. I was not there, but imagine they were even more heated than usual: Jani had used revenue officer's law to override ancestor's custom. It is hard to predict the effect of this law as it becomes known and fed into the mix of other disputes, but it can only take inheritance even further beyond the understanding of Sora ancestors, who know only Sora and speak through shamans who cannot read.

Sonumhood is not the only holistic domain that has fragmented. The metaphysics of sonums matched the political regime of headman and barik, and they have fallen together. Panchayat raj, the regime of village councils, arrived in the 1950s and 1960s, but its significance was limited until the 1980s because its budget was small and the system was easily captured by the bariks. It would require literacy and a consequent widening of opportunity for this

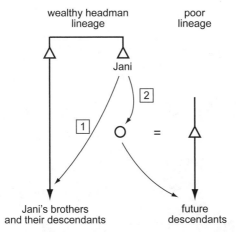

wealthy headman
lineage

poor
lineage

Jani

2

1

=

Jani's brothers
and their descendants

future
descendants

Diagram 10.2 Inheritance of Jani's land, after he died with no sons
*(1) Normative inheritance, favored by Jani's brothers. (2) Actual inheritance. By tradition
his daughter's male descendants might have had a claim through participation in Jani's
funeral as marongger cousins, but this would have gone nowhere against his numerous
and powerful lineage. Jani's recourse to the new national law has in effect actualized this
claim.*

structural transformation to take hold. The panchayat was not the only institution that undermined the headmen and bariks. The Baptist church was already
a more powerful machine, and sidelined them in every village where Christianity took over. In effect, the pastors are the headmen's immediate successors.
Like headmen, they are Sora, their families tend to intermarry along with the
assistant headmen (*dolbera*) to form an elite, and they accumulate wealth from
the community's own productivity rather than from outside subsidies.

Are pastors also successors of the shamans? Certainly, they offer a cosmology. Yet though they echo shamans by supporting healing through the mission
hospital, it is quite striking that they avoid the shamans' specialties of grief
and inheritance.

Sora animist culture was diffuse and uncentralized, matching the techniques of personal mediumship and small-group negotiation. There was
never an association of shamans, any more than of headmen. The fundamental unit of society was the patrilineage (*birinda*), which was the idiom and the
rationale for kinship, marriage, property, inheritance, drinking circles, *onsir*
work parties—and disputes, as I learned when I failed to support my lineage-
brothers over the man killed by a rolling log (pages 63–64). Though there were
headman lineages and others, richer and poorer, all lineages were equivalent

Figure 10.7 Building a Baptist church, 2005
Unpaid communal labor is now based on parish membership rather than kin reciprocity (onsir). Note the trousers and mustaches, on men whose fathers had loincloths and hairless upper lips.

structurally, corresponding to an egalitarian cultural style in which there was actually no deference to differences of status within the community. People married between lineages, which each cultivated their own ancestors and negotiated how far a married woman should be incorporated into the cult of each other's lineage as well as of their own. Your ancestors were the foundation of your identity, and your daily engagement with them was a constant fine-tuning of your existence.

By contrast the Baptists, the other Christian denominations, the social work NGOs, the political parties (and the neo-Hindu organizations to come in the next chapter) are each what the Sora call an *ompu*: an association, crowd, faction, gang, or clique. The social world of young Sora is now composed largely of these ompus. This new ompu-ism often uses a rhetoric of essence (caste, tribe, religion, perhaps not yet class) but is actually based on recruitment through patronage, clientelism, and the distribution of resources. Young people have a new arena of agency and opportunity, but must constantly scramble to find a position amid shifting units of solidarity, protection, and advantage. The multiplicity of forms and idioms is not a multiplicity of equivalence and complementarity, like multiple lineages, but of alternatives and rivalry.

These groups are supposedly based on shared "belief." But actually, membership in an ompu is fickle, as people switch between churches or parties for instrumental reasons—loyalty not necessarily rooted in ideological conviction. Faith is not what it was among those fervent early converts with their visions of Jisu's crown of thorns, and the Baptist church struggles to police its members' spiritual sincerity. Ultimately, religious apostates are not so different from voters floating between parties. Everyone must belong to ompus to live a modern life, and the more socially active you are, the more ompus you belong to or switch between. Panchayat raj, pastor raj, NGO raj, political parties, and democracy—all are subsumed inside a new style of governance and sociality, an all-encompassing ompu raj.

11

DANCING WITH ALPHABET WORSHIPPERS
ONCE AND FUTURE HINDUS?

Baptist conversion is threatened by more than fornicators, Pentecostals, and Catholics. The tone of the wider Indian world has also changed. During the 1990s a constant, unsleeping Hindu resentment grew into a major backlash against Christians. The "development" of the Tribal interior in the 1980s had concerned an obscure hinterland. But in 1991 the IMF pushed India into the large-scale economic liberalization where it remains to this day. Where previously the middle class had been a small world of modestly paid government servants ("officers") like my friends in the State Bank, suddenly there arose a powerful layer of privatized technocrats and thrusting entrepreneurs. Instead of simply becoming cosmopolitan, some of these also became right-wing Hindu nationalists, aiming to roll back the tide of Westernization and bring back the mythic golden age of Rama, hero of the ancient epic the *Ramayana* and avatar (incarnation) of the god Vishnu.

This was not the secular nationalism of the old anti-British Independence movement, but a militant, orthodox tendency that was against "backward" Hindu forms as well as the "foreign" religions of Islam and Christianity. In December 1992, only a few months after my first return to Soraland since the 1970s, a mosque, built by Muslim Mughal emperors over the god Rama's supposed birthplace in Ayodhya in northern India, was demolished by an angry Hindu crowd, and India entered a phase of religious hostility that has only partly abated.

Christian missionaries' approaches and successes since the nineteenth century have been mainly among the poorest Tribals and low castes, who have most to gain by slipping sideways out of the caste system. Only 2 percent of India's population are Christians, and the Sora Baptists are a tiny portion of these, linked to Vancouver by a tenuous thread. However, the question of whether pre-Christian Tribal culture is Hindu or something else goes far beyond scholarly debates and is highly politicized (see the online bibliographic essay). The total population recognized in the 2011 census as Tribal amounts to over 100 million, distributed over more that 600 ethnic names, and any of these could be regarded as vulnerable to Christian missionization. The term *adivasi*, literally "aboriginal inhabitants," is now seen by militant Hindu groups to make mainstream Hindu populations seem like newcomers on their own soil. Instead, they relabel the Tribals *vanvasi*, "jungle dwellers," identifying them rather with a backward ecological niche. The promotion of orthodox Hindu values among tribes is presented not as a conversion, but as "showing these people their true nature" as Hindus who became lost in the jungle and need to be brought back "into the fold." The genetic and linguistic connections of groups like the Sora with Southeast Asia are downplayed, as religion and national identity are combined: the soil of India is all Hindu, so how can anyone living there be non-Hindu unless they have been led astray by foreign proselytizers? Monosi, Paranto, and all my younger Sora friends have been perverted by unscrupulous missionaries, "rice Christians" bribed with handouts or even (implausibly) converted "by force."

During the 1990s, news reports were filled with newly prominent acronyms: VHP (Vishva Hindu Parishad, World Hindu Council), RSS (Rashtriya Swayamsevak Sangh, the paramilitary National Volunteer Organization), and BJP (Bharatiya Janata Party, Indian People's Party, which won the election and ruled the country from 1998 to 2004 and again from 2014). In Orissa these groups were intensely active in Tribal regions, and in some mixed Hindu-Christian areas there were serious clashes in 2008, with many Christian villages burned down.

The Lanjia heartland was already solidly Baptist, but other Sora areas were shifting to a brand of Hinduism that the Sora call Bisma (from Vishva, the first word of the VHP), which aimed to clean up local "superstitions" and replace them with the worship of Rama and Krishna.

In late 1998, I started going further afield to visit these neo-Hindu Sora communities. This was soon after the BJP took hold in Delhi and only weeks before an Australian missionary and his children were burned alive by rogue Hindu activists in a nearby Tribal area. With police permission I cycled with Monosi around the foothills and plains, passing houses plastered with rival calendar pictures of Jisu and the Hindu gods all equally garlanded with chains of orange marigolds. As a known animist sympathizer and a committed Baptist, respectively, we expected to be exposed to searching interrogation, and approached these potentially hostile communities with trepidation. Fortunately, Monosi had visited them in the past, not just as a Christian but also as a respected public figure. I too was known in many places by reputation, as someone who was definitely not a missionary.

In one large village hall in the Titinsing area, I disarmed our hosts by singing an invocation I had learned from Doloso. Though they were now devotees of Rama and Krishna, they were not hostile to the old religion and seemed to see me as a primitive unreformed Hindu. Speaking in Sora, they mentioned various gods and avatars, but had difficulty describing them or pronouncing their Oriya names. Like the Baptists, it seemed their religious style too was still under construction, and they were still looking to an authority that came from outside their own experience.

I asked: "How can you cure illness if you don't offer blood?"

"Illness doesn't come from sonums," a man called Mondo explained in a beautiful, measured voice. "No! Mosquitoes bite us, we get ill from their poison, we get insects inside our body. We get healed by medicine and prayer. The other is just our imagination." He adopted a tone of mock panic: "U gai, I've been brushed by a sonum!"

"Do you talk to the dead? Do you feed them?" I asked.

"No, we don't. After ten days we do a *dosa* ritual. We pray for the soul, we read from the *Gita*. We don't give them any rice, but we offer flowers, bananas, and coconuts, and a new cloth."

"But don't you feel sad?" Ever since Paranto's lament for his father, I had been pursuing this question everywhere I went.

"Yes sad, but the sonums who speak, are they really sonums—who knows? It's the shaman who does the voice. That's why I gave up going to them."

"I've heard you don't use a Brahmin priest?"

"No, that would be a huge expense, they demand so much cloth, so we do it all ourselves. I learned from a Sora called Pradhani Gomang, and he learned from some very high-status people." Pradhani was a very neo-Hindu name (though once when this same Pradhani was standing for election he asked a Baptist pastor to pray for his success). "I saw the book and I heard the reading: let's give up chicken blood pig blood, and I joined up . . . It's true we still do blood sacrifice for Durga, but not for Rama and Krishna. And I haven't eaten meat, fish, or eggs for twelve years."

He picked up his book and kissed it. I looked questioningly.

"It's in the *purana*, it's in the book," he confirmed. "There are great books: the *Rig Veda, Atharva Veda*, the *Gita*, the *Purana*, yogis, munis, rishis, Mahatma Gandhi, Gopabandu Das, Vivekananda." These names represented the cream of Hindu high culture. I had never heard a Sora talk like this. "When someone reads from a book, we listen and we learn."

"But you and the Christians both say your books are better?"

"No, it's not like that!" he retorted vehemently. "There's Hindu, there's Christian, Buddhist, Musulman, Jain—so many religions (*dharma*), but they're all one because God is all one. Look: rungkun is called chawlo in Oriya and rice in English but it's the same when you cook it!"

He proffered me his books and pamphlets. They were all in Oriya. "There's nothing in Sora yet," he apologized, "except for some hymns." This was how Miss Munro had begun too.

The hymns in Sora were in the familiar tune also used by the Christians, sometimes even with the same words, replacing Jisu with Rama or Krishna: "Krishna will return among us" (*Krishna dayirtai amang ba len*). Those in Oriya used quite different Oriya tunes and referred to events in the *Ramayana* and *Mahabharata* epics:

Ari Ramo, Krishna Kittung,	Hari Rama, Krishna God,
garber na ñen amdanga.	Hear my prayer.
Amen jinglin garbertenai,	I pray in supplication,
erbangsa ñen sabnaja.	Remove my badness.
Ayé Ramo, Krishna Kittung,	Ayé Rama, Krishna God,
tulab lingen pargaraban	As with the spotted deer in the forest
kanalkal ñeni ñangle.	I too am in difficulty.
Amen Kittung drabdrable,	You, God, protected me,
a garber nan amdangle.	You heard my prayer.
Ayé Ramo, Krishna Kittung,	Ayé Rama, Krishna God,
dusasono Durupati	When Durupati's sari was unwound
a burdij bɪn susule	She began to become naked,
sindrin tiyle amen Kittung	But you, God, gave her a cloth
a do'ongen dangdrable,	And protected her,
Ayé Ramo Krishna Kittung.	Ayé God Rama Krishna.
Ayé Ramo, Krishna Kittung,	Ayé Rama, Krishna God,
eran raja aduai	That wicked king—
amen Kittung dangdrable.	You, God, blocked him.
eran raja aduain mar	That wicked king,
amen Kittung kapnidle,	You, God, killed him,
Ramo Krishna Kittung.	God Rama, Krishna!
Ayé Ramo Krishna Kittung	Ayé Rama, Krishna God,
nami ayam ñeni jenang	Now, as for me,
kanalkal ñen sabnaja	Remove my troubles,
Kittung kanalkal ñen sabnaja	God, remove my troubles,
dijne mang nam garbertenai,	I pray so much to you,

esuyung tung amdanga,	Hear me, compassionate God,
Ayé Ramo Krishna Kittung.	Ayé Rama, Krishna God.

It was not only the tune that was completely different; so was the verbal format. Animist invocations use highly allusive syntax, often with no main verbs and without specifying the purpose of the song. By contrast, this was clearly a prayer. It was structured to make an analogy between the present situation and a sacred past and also between the supplicant now and the characters then: hear me, do things for me now, just as you did remarkable things before. Just as Rama was deliberately distracted by a beautiful deer and thereby allowed a wicked demon-king to abduct his wife Sita, so I too have troubles; just as you killed that king and saved her, so now help me.

"The Sora old-timers called their own ancestors," I said, "but where do Rama and Krishna come from?"

"Long ago," he explained, "when the earth and sky were made, the Sora worshipped Krishna and Jagannath [Juggernaut]. But they didn't know Oriya, they didn't know writing. They were scared of the Oriyas and fled into the forest. There we forgot about our god and just worshipped our parents and grandparents and thought they were making us ill. We didn't know about God at all." Mondo was reproducing the orthodox Brahmin narrative that the Sora are really Hindus who lost contact. The advantages of rejoining civilization were clear: "Now Brahmins invite us into their houses and they also eat our food. They tell us, 'You used to be unwashed and untoothbrushed (*ertangjina*), you ate cows and pigs. But now we can mix with you.'"

The Oriya Brahmins themselves tell a colorful story about how their ancestor found Jagannath being worshipped in the jungle by a Sora priest, seduced the priest's daughter, and stole him. Jagannath is now installed in a massive temple at Puri, where he has become the most important god in all of Orissa and is regarded as another incarnation of Vishnu, like Rama and Krishna. Entry to the temple is strictly forbidden to non-Hindus, including Christian Sora.

This fits a common pattern in central India, in which mainstream Hindu gods are said to have local Tribal origins (Sinha 1962). In the 1970s, most Sora did not seem to know or care about this story, and I heard it only from educated Oriyas. By the 1990s, there was widespread resentment that their god had been stolen—and by those same Brahmins who now tried to charge them to perform funerals. Mondo's people had cut the Brahmins out of the funeral. Would they now start to reclaim their god? Earlier that year (1998), I was told, a large crowd of Hindus had come to the foot of the Sora mountains pulling a

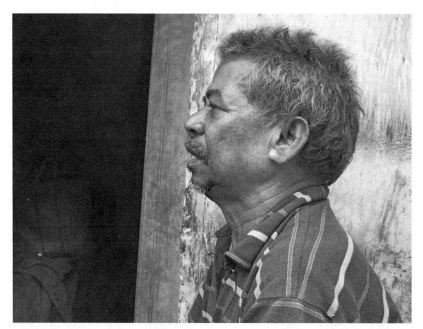

Figure 11.1 Pettua, Timlo 1998

statue of Jagannath on a *ratha* (chariot). The ratha could not go further uphill, so they stopped at the edge of the plain and shouted through loudspeakers:

"Who eats cows?"

"Christians!"

"Who taught them?"

"White people (*sahib*)! Kill those who kill cows!"

While police kept the groups apart, a Christian Sora from Timlo responded, "That's our god you've got on that chariot, you stole him from us. For a long time we've said nothing and just worshipped our ancestors and rocks. We used to be very low-status (*oseng*). You kept us out of your temple, so we welcomed the sahib missionaries. You had no sympathy for us then, so why do you suddenly want us to join you? Whoever wants to, let them, but why chase and kill the others? Mahatma Gandhi said all religions are equally good." When the demonstrators threatened to come back with 40,000 supporters, the Christian retorted, "You'll perish in the hills because you only know how to move in the plains."

Timlo was one of the few villages in the Lanjia Sora area to have some Bisma Hindus. Earlier that same year, 1998, a cross erected there by Baptists had been uprooted and thrown down a cliff. In October I went there to find Pettua, an old man related to my friends in Sogad who was said to be a moderate Bisma Hindu. I also wanted to ask about his brother Gorsang the politician, who I heard had performed a theatrical tableau at their mother's funeral in which he had acted out the dead woman's part.

Pettua wore a dhoti and had a lined, friendly, round face. He dismissed the cross incident as the work of outside agitators, echoing the view of such incidents I was given by police chiefs and other officials. "My family were animist before," he reminisced, "then my father went Christian. He worked in the Assam tea plantations in the 1930s. He noticed the British bosses didn't go for sacrifices when they were ill. They went to the hospital—and they prayed on Sundays. So he thought, 'Why shouldn't I do that?' He was the one who converted Damano. Damano's wife was very ill, and Damano was crazy with anxiety. My father took them to church, and she got better."

This was a revelation. Through Damano's later liberation theology, Pettua's father had indirectly changed Sora history. "But now you're Bisma Hindu?" I asked.

"My father didn't stay Baptist. He wanted to drink and smoke. And they threw him out because he had various wives, so he gave up the church." Pettua himself currently had three Sora wives, and we were being served tea by his fourth wife, who, most unusually, was Paik. "My father was somewhere in between Christian and animist. I was the one who became Hindu. There's a Paik called Ranahati. He was the local Member for the Congress Party. He wasn't like other Paik, he was friendly with Sora, he would eat with them and sleep in their houses. He told us, 'Don't sacrifice buffalo, goats, chickens, and don't believe in Jisu.' He led us into the Bisma Hindus, he told us, 'Rama and Krishna are not just for Brahmins but for everyone, even low people.'"

Here was a missionary of a different sort but with a similar message of equality, though Ranahati might claim that he was not an outsider, since they were all equally Hindus and citizens of India. Through his party affiliation, he was also an actor in the idiom of the national democratic state. It is easy to change political parties, and in the early twenty-first century Ranahati himself switched from the secular Congress to the Hindu-nationalist BJP. But how can you suddenly change your religion? Here was a Hindu version of my Baptist quandary.

"Do the Bisma Hindus talk to their dead?"

"No, we commemorate them, but we don't go into trance, and we don't sacrifice any animals. We call on Rama and Krishna instead. Three days after the death we cook rice and lime leaves just like Kshatriyas and Brahmins, then ten days later at the cremation-ground we do a ritual called *dosa*, like a stone-planting but without a stone." This was just what Mondo had described. "We don't dance or drum but we draw a sacred diagram and lay out bananas, coconuts, incense, candles. We sprinkle everything with water and burn coconut-fumes to ward off ghosts. A year later we do something like a karja. We bring the dead person into the house, give them new clothes, and feed them rice."

"Do you feel sad?"

"When they've just died we lament," he replied, "but not the following year—there's just a meal."

What about causality? "If you don't talk to the dead, how do you ask, 'Which sonum took you?' "

"No, we don't ask which sonum—it's just an illness (*rugam*)." Pettua could just as well have been a Baptist, except that he did not mention the will of God.

"Do you mean sonums are not involved?"

Pettua corrected himself. "We may say, 'Which sonum took you?' But they don't answer!" he laughed. Here was another version of the gap in causality opened up by the absence of dialogue. As if reading my thought, he said, "But we do blame sorcerers a lot. Christian or Hindu, we all believe a lot in sorcery." Again, like the Baptists, I thought. In a universe that runs on human intention, if the dead are not responsible for bad happenings it must be the living. ("Though I don't believe in it," he added hastily.)

"No Brahmin priests?" I asked.

"We do it all ourselves. A printed text (*purana*) tells us what to do. A man who knows speaks from his thoughts, but paper is greater (*bogad galam maran a ogandin bate berte, bɪndo a ola muda*)."

"Is this in Sora?"

"In Oriya. Sora speech doesn't fit (*Soran a geramgamen a'tame*)." Both schooling and Hindu texts are available almost entirely in Oriya. This combination draws young people toward this religion, and also undermines the further development of the Sora language.

The pantomime enacted by his brother Gorsang after their mother's death: was that in Sora?

"Yes, in Sora," he replied. "That's just something we made up in our family. My brother learned to read Oriya in school and the teacher liked him. Even though he was a Brahmin he would eat my brother's cooking. When our mother died my brother said, 'I'm going to Brahminize myself (*bambratenai*)' and went off to Puri for a month. He came back smeared with sandalwood paste and with his head shaved!" Pettua laughed uproariously. "We were very confused (*gege*)!"

"He didn't trance?"

"No, he just pretended (*opjong*) to be her. He became a very old woman and picked up a bundle of firewood. [Pettua put on a quavery voice] 'Don't beat me! My work here is finished,' he said. 'I'm going to join my ancestors!'"

What did this mime mean? In Sogad, the baby-naming ritual is full of pantomime, and Mengalu had made me dance the abduction of a bride. Yet that had been just an add-on to a detailed dialogue with the baby's ancestors. Was Gorsang's mime meant to serve as a gesture of farewell because dialogue was not available? Later I went to Titinsing to ask Gorsang himself. "Shamans are frauds," he said bluntly. "I was just mocking them." Gorsang was a politician, and once when he was standing for election, Ranahati the Paik at first supported him and then betrayed him by switching allegiance. In response, Gorsang pretended (*opjong* again) to take poison and jump down a well, as a ruse to evoke sympathy among voters. He was laughing at his own manipulative political *opjong*-ing, but was serious about his devotion to his mother, and wished he could really talk to her. As a Bisma Hindu he could not do this, but the admission was suggestive. I was beginning to see dialogues with the dead as just the most verbally elaborate form of a range of possible impersonations and projections.

Two years later I walked into Pettua's house again. He had become frail and was suffering from diabetes. "I was wondering where you'd got to," he said graciously in his old man's voice. "God brought you to me again." (Which God? I wondered.) Later, people on his veranda started talking about the origin of the name Sora: "It's because we hid (*so*) in trees (*aṟa*); it's because we once hid an elephant (*ṟaa*); it's because we wiped our bottoms with leaves like white people instead of using water so we smelled (*so'o*) . . ."

"No no," said Pettua. "It's because Rama was served by Sabari." He then retold an episode from the *Ramayana*, which he had seen in the cinema. One day during his fourteen years' exile in the jungle with his wife Sita, Rama was hungry. He picked a wild mango, but an old woman came out of the forest. This was Sabari. She told him the mango was sour and offered him a delicious sweet mango instead. To prove that it was not poisoned, she took the first bite herself before handing it to him. Sita said, "Issí! You're a raja and you take her leftovers!" But Rama said, "Because she had love (*tımyım*) for me, it's as pure as a temple offering (*prasad*)."

Outsiders often pronounce Sora "Sabara" or "Savara," and Sabari is now widely believed to have been Sora. The episode with Sabari is not the Sora's only supposed role. With the long tails (Lanjia) of their men's loincloths, the hill Sora are also called Arsid (understood as "Monkey") Sora. Rama's entire

Figure 11.2 A gigantic statue of Hanuman under construction, 2015
On National Highway 5 near Srikakulam.

story hinges on his loyal companion, a strongman monkey-god called Hanuman. The cult of Hanuman fits well with the gymnastics and muscular Hinduism of the militant RSS, and since the 1990s cities and main roads across India have been increasingly adorned with Hanuman temples and 300-foot-high concrete statues of the bright pink monkey-god with a humanoid face and a massive war-mace resting on his shoulder. "When Sita was abducted by the demon Ravana, Rama looked for her, but at first he didn't go himself," Pettua confirmed, "he sent Hanuman to look. Hanuman means a monkey. Who is that monkey? The Sora! When a shaman trances, she becomes like a monkey. And shamans don't eat monkeys because that would be cannibalism. Now a lot of Sora are saying, they're always worshipping a monkey, but none of them have a monkey's power, only Sora have that."

So this was to be the Sora's distinctive role in the new Hindu revival: Hanuman himself was a Sora! Without a Sora helper Rama could not do anything for himself: he needed the jungle knowledge of Sabari to teach him how to eat fruit, and the monkey strength of Hanuman to find his abducted wife. In the Sora quest for recognition, this interpretation is becoming widespread even among Christians: "All Sora should know this," Monosi fulminated. "It should be put in a book for as long as the sun lasts the moon lasts!"

Back in the 1970s, the fanciful etymologies of the name Sora were just-so stories. Now the Sora's primitive jungle origin feels like a state to be emerged from, as these turn into developmental etymologies of potential advancement. There is a race to place the Sora in mainstream Hindu cosmology. However, any high-caste agenda to give them a humble role is turning out to be more complex. Sabari was more than Rama's servant, and Hanuman was more than his sidekick. And then there is Jagannath. "When we started going Christian," Pettua explained, "Ranahati the Paik said, 'No, you have your own god, Jagannath!' He took a Sora called Pradhani Gomang and made him a priest (purohito)." The genealogy of the local movement was starting to emerge: Pradhani was the same man who had taught Mondo in Titinsing. Jagannath points in quite another direction from Hanuman or Sabari, who offer the Sora only a subordinate role. As he moves from distant metropolitan temple to local politics, Jagannath makes the Sora into the source of the patron god of Orissa and also offers them a new, better-informed reason to feel aggrieved.

Pettua was a friend, but among strangers it was not always easy to avoid being mistaken for a missionary. By 2005 the Congress Party had wrested back control of the central government in Delhi, and in the Tribal areas of Orissa religious tensions were still high when I set out with Monosi to climb a sacred Hindu mountain called Mahendragiri, which rises 5,000 feet above the territory of the Jurai Sora.

This was far out of our area. "It's dangerous country," Monosi warned. "Those Jurai put things into your food. If you don't hold onto your balls with your other hand while you're eating, they'll disappear." Yet in this region where white people are never seen, and where I had declined the offer of an escort from highly placed Hindus in town, the danger would turn out to be not from ethnic sorcery but from religious politics.

We stayed with a contact on the Baptist side of a mixed village called Mondalsai, then went out to the Hindu side to find a Bisma priest who was named after the god Jagannath. He was young, in a saffron robe and with a round, smiling Sora face. This was auspicious, unlike the journey there, when we unwisely stopped by the roadside to buy supplies, and our vehicle was blocked by an aggressive Paik activist in a dhoti, and with red paste on his forehead, who seemed convinced we were missionaries.

We were accompanied on the long climb by Jagannath and several Hindus and Baptists from his village. The path took us under huge, luxuriant forest trees of species that I had not seen in our area since the 1970s, and some others I had only read about in botany books. The Forestry Service forbade all cultivation, and it was eerily silent, with no axe thuds and no women whooping and calling to us from high rocks. There were marks of pilgrims scraping medicinal bark from trees and creepers, and one of our companions harvested several of the twenty-nine rare ingredients for his herbal remedies against snakebite and HIV.

The forest thinned out before the summit, which was capped by an astonishing, unfinished ancient temple made of massive blocks of dressed stone. It was hard to imagine how these could possibly have been brought up here, but mythology supplied the answer. "This was built by Bhima," Jagannath explained. Bhima was another hero of phenomenal strength in the *Mahabharata*. "He piled up all these huge dressed stone blocks in one night, but when the cock crowed, he left them half-built." The entrance to the chamber was so tight that it was frightening for a large European to squeeze in sideways. Inside there was a small lingam with a few broken clay lamps and coconut shells. While the others chatted and joked, Jagannath offered bananas and made a brief prayer.

We descended by another route, and found functioning temples to Yudhishtira and Kunti, other characters in the *Ramayana*. A group of Oriya holy men and Sora cooks were reproducing Rama's forest hermitage as a pilgrims' guesthouse. "Rama's group spent four years of his exile right here," they explained. "It was from the Sora that they learned how to use bows and arrows and axes. And it was here that Sabari gave Rama the mango."

So the Sora had a place in the Hindu national project, because it now turned out that these events happened right here! Bethlehem and Galilee could not compete with this. (I later asked Pettua, "Why, out of the whole of India, would Rama come just here?" "Just as you did," he laughed.) A swami added, in Oriya, "Mahendragiri is the axis of the world. This mountain holds the balance between the percentage of land and sea throughout the world, not just India. It was because they quarried granite here that an earthquake and tsunami happened in Indonesia." Compared with this, the Sora animist cosmology of personal ancestors seemed rather modest.

They invited us to eat and stay the night, but my Christian companions feared we would be poisoned, so we returned to Mondalsai in the dark. This sounded another ominous note, but still I felt safe with Jagannath. The next day, in front of the marigold-strewn shrine in his backyard, I recorded his lengthy prayers, and he answered my questions. He was surprised that my animists did not know about Vishnu's ten avatars, but also amazed at their elaborate three-year funerals.

At one point we also encountered a group of Jurai Sora led by Paik, including the man who had blocked our car. They shouted, "Why are you leading Jagannath into Christianity?" Jagannath defended us and explained, "They say I'm selling out our religion to you. Yesterday on the mountain they wouldn't normally have talked to you, but they wanted to check you out. But tomorrow in the temple, I'm the preacher, and you can also speak."

The next day was Sunday, when many Hindu temples held their main services in direct competition with the church. The layout and procedures were remarkably similar to those of the Baptist service: the same table and plastic flowers on the platform, the same harmonium and two-ended muringga drum, and the same smooth, well-finished cement floor where men sat on one side and women with their heads covered in saris on the other. It made me realize how Indian the Baptist format really is. Who was copying whom? The icons of gods on the wall predated similar pictures of Jisu, but some of the hymns had obviously substituted Rama or Krishna for the Jisu of a Christian original. As in Titinsing these were sung to the non-sonum tune adapted by the Baptists from animist work songs, suggesting that this tune flows equally through all religions as a marker of Sora identity. When hymns were sung in Oriya the tunes were quite different, confirming a tight unity between Sora tunes and the Sora language.

A well-groomed preacher in a gleaming white dhoti, like a pastor, addressed everyone as brothers and sisters as a pastor would. Youths stood to read haltingly from a verse (sloka), which was then explained by Jagannath or the visiting preacher, both of whom also gave very long sermons. Yet even if the formats were similar, if Krishna fitted in the songs with the same rhythm as Jisu, if the moral teaching was similar (avoid sin . . . if a man's work is good he'll meet God), the theology behind all this was very different: God is in water, in the earth, God has multiple incarnations. There was also a difference in the devotion itself. A woman sitting on the floor started to heave and undulate ecstatically while having an erotic vision of Krishna. This would surely not have been tolerated in a Baptist service, but here no one was bothered, and her vigorous trance was allowed to run for many minutes till she subsided, all passion spent.

When Jagannath called me up to make a speech, I avoided mentioning religious differences at all, but spoke in admiration of the Sora language and about the need to preserve it—and develop it. In the applause that followed, a woman fell at my feet, and I was sprinkled with rice grains and marigold petals while all the women ululated. But there was trouble outside. A group of men had gathered outside the temple, claiming that white people were a polluted race who eat cows and that we had really come to pay Jagannath to mislead his congregation into Christianity. It seemed wise to leave immediately.

Figure 11.3 Jagannath preaching in his neo-Hindu temple
The dhoti and microphone could easily be in a church, except for some items on the altar.

I had better luck in Sarda Sora country. In 2009 I was staying with Lokami, the child I had known in the 1970s, who was now the funeral shaman of Rajingtal. It was the February full moon, when I always miss the throb of the great karja festival, even at home in England. Yet now there had been no karja for several years, in Rajingtal or anywhere else.

Suddenly Soimani appeared, my friend from those same early months in Soraland, having bussed up from Gunupur with a scrap of paper written in Sora: "Respected brother Pirino, come immediately to Kujendri as they are doing a karja tomorrow. Very many greetings, your brother Monosi."

Kujendri was far away in Sarda territory, a fascinating area in the plains beyond Gunupur near the printing press of the mysterious alphabet worshippers. Without hesitation, Lokami said, "Let's go!" and left the household chores to her amiable husband. We hailed a young man from Sogad as he passed in his black-and-yellow three-wheeler. A friend of Lokami's, who had been combing her hair on the veranda, also jumped in. We would be away for two nights.

We slept on the cement floor of a smart house in Kujendri where Monosi's son had once lodged when studying, and awoke to find our Sarda Sora hostess in a sari doing early morning prayers above our heads in front of calendar pictures of Hindu gods. Adults spoke Sora to us but Oriya among themselves; the children putting on their blue school uniforms knew no Sora at all.

When we reached the main house (*muda-sing*), where the karja was being held, the single room was packed so tight that we could not even see in through the doorway, and could slip in only one at a time as others left. Inside, a lamp was burning, and women were sitting along one wall, each awaiting her dead relative with a bundle of clothes. Three ancestor-women surrounded a female shaman in trance, all standing. One ancestor-woman brandished a bow, arrow, and archaic axe. There were no young people, and few men.

Male and female sonums came mixed up together. Each new sonum as it entered the shaman's body drank aba from a plastic cup, while the dead person's clothes were draped over the shaman to represent an identification between them, and an orchestra of flute and percussion drowned out the words I would have liked to hear. Each sonum spoke only briefly, not to the mourner who handed up the clothes from her sitting position but to the ancestor-women who leaned toward the shaman. Wedged in their standing position above the crowd, the shaman and the ancestor-women danced together. As the sonum departed, the dancing and the orchestra stopped, the client left, and another woman flowed into the house to join the queue. Outside, another orchestra with very loud drums circulated continually round the village, surging back and forth past the house and away into the distance. A man in the corner was recording everything with some serious equipment: it seemed someone already regarded this old women's ritual as cultural heritage.

Lokami watched intently. This was a variant of what she did, but throughout our visit she never once let slip that she was a shaman herself. The dead showed the same attachment for their material possessions, but the attachment between persons seemed attenuated. There was no dialogue, and the sitting client could not hear what was sung or said over her head. Did this mean that these people felt more or less grief, were more or less susceptible to illness from the dead? Did the ancestor-women stand in for the mourners as they danced with the possessed shaman in a kind of communion that substituted for dialogue? Why were the mourners not dancing with them?

There was too much noise to ask questions. Lokami just observed and turned to me to make jokes. Later we followed a procession of women with new pots to collect water from a stagnant pool, where the shaman sang cooling frog songs similar to Lokami's own. Other actions, like the breaking of an egg in the middle of an astrological diagram, were completely unfamiliar. We were told that goats were now sacrificed, since the government had supposedly banned the sacrifice of buffalo, and that buffalo meat used to be buried in the fields to feed the crops. This was fascinating information, since we were on the edge of the territory of the Kond tribe once famous for planting the meat from human sacrifices for this purpose. Lokami was less surprised, though she looked skeptical when we were told that the memorial stones in a *ganuar* started small and then grew larger over time. When the procession reached the cremation-ground the drumming grew louder, and the crowd was swelled by dozens of shouting young men who danced riotously on a year's worth of ash, kicking up a huge pall of dust and flinging charred human bones all over each other and the spluttering women. I enjoyed dancing with them, but Lokami kept far away.

But where were the alphabet worshippers? They called themselves Marirenji, meaning the Pure, Alert, or Clear-Sighted Ones, and would have had nothing to do with this ash revelry and bloodshed. They consume no meat or alcohol, and after a cremation they sweep the ash into a river, leaving the site of the pyre with no material residue from the polluting event.

Intrigued by their conversion of the Manengul headman in the 1970s, I had visited their headquarters in 1998. This was down in the plains in Domesara, in the territory of the Sarda Sora near where we were today. There, a young priest called Orjuno had explained how a Sarda Sora called Mallia had received a dream showing him where to find a special Sora script magically inscribed on a mountaintop (like Moses, as my Christian friends observe). In this script, each animist sonum had turned into the letter that began that sonum's name. People thought he was crazy, but "his standard of thinking was so high" that he remained without food on that mountain for twenty-one days. His daughter married a man called Manggai, who propagated the script and turned it into a cult. While Mallia was cremated normally, Manggai was buried squatting upright "like a coconut," so that he would resprout; a bamboo tube stuck out of the grave to carry the script around the land in the fumes from the decomposition of his brain. Mallia's dream occurred on 18 June 1936, and the inscription on his son-in-law Manggai's grave, in this new script, read, "Born 16/6/16, Died 19/7/80."

I had not understood much of Orjuno's explanations. This evening, eleven years later, I was glad to find him in the house where the Pure People were

Figure 11.4 The long night of the alphabet worshippers
The women on the left brandish bundles of peacock feathers; the man on the right, bending, holds a bow and arrow. On the wall behind, the letters of the script are contained within a diagram of the syllable "om."

holding their own karja. Perhaps it would help if I could see what they actually did. The floor was covered with smoking incense and vegetarian offerings of coconuts, flowers, and bananas. Everyone constantly drank tea in scalding plastic cups. Outside on the veranda two groups of dancers, men and women together wearing saffron garments and white turbans, swaying forward at the waist and brandishing bows and arrows, advanced toward each other and retreated to a hypnotic, clattering drum rhythm, while beneath them a man played an accordion and sang the same song over and over in a *bhakti*-like devotional style. The cheerful low-level ecstasy diffused among all present contrasted with both the intense devotion in Mondalsai, where it was concentrated in a few people only occasionally, and the restrained seriousness of a Baptist event, where nobody is supposed to act ecstatically at all.

I was dressed up in saffron, given an axe, and made to dance all night. I had never seen the basic simple Sora step lead to such variations in effect. The choreography kept shifting, and the dancers broke off to act out elaborate mythological and comical scenes. "Great god!" *Mapuru!* one dancer exclaimed amid laughter as he fell at my feet. This was an eye-opener: it was a Sora-speaking world, but with its dhotis and saris, big drums, and sweeping dance gestures, it looked more like the Tribals from Bastar or Jharkhand than the Sora I knew.

I decided to enjoy myself and leave questions till tomorrow. It was just as well. Orjuno's explanation was complicated, and given in a dialect that even Monosi and Lokami found hard to follow. He sang the song again in his high tenor, with the infectious swing that had made it so danceable the previous night. The entire song is a mnemonic for a sequence of alphabetical signs. Though these signs are new, they resemble other Indian scripts in their order and in being syllabic—that is, representing a consonant with a vowel built in (preferably "a" where a suitable word is available): sa, ta, ba, cha, da, ga, etc. The significant sounds are underlined:

almadaiba buñang
sonumlen sompengen

permodaiba buñang
bornalenji

gaze far, brother
our sonums

gaze deep, brother
have become letters

sundangsımen gamle
tangorsımen gamle
babusımen gamle
chondisımen gamle
dangkisımen gamle
gadasımen gamle

lemlebeji aying
jenglebe
lemlebeji aying
jenglebeji
lemlebeji aying
jinglebeji

House-post-Sonum
Path-Sonum
Bureaucrat-Sonum
Boundary-Sonum
Pot-Sonum
Forest-Sonum

we have greeted, little sister
we have acknowledged
we have greeted, little sister
we have acknowledged
we have greeted, little sister
we have acknowledged

almadaiba buñang
sonumlen sompengen

permodaiba buñang
bornalenji

gaze far, brother
our sonums

gaze deep, brother
have become letters

mundarasım gamle
angalsım gamle

lemlebeji aying
jinglebeji

283

labosım gamle	lemlebeji aying
naasımen gamle	jinglebeji
barosım gamle	lemlebeji aying
pattasım gamle	jinglebeji

Shrine-Sonum [?]	we have greeted, little sister
Garden-Sonum	we have acknowledged
Earth-Sonum	we have greeted, little sister
Name-Sonum	we have acknowledged
Baro-Tree Sonum	we have greeted, little sister
Fish-Sonum [?]	we have acknowledged

almadaiba buñang	permodaiba buñang
sonumlen sompengen	bornalenji

gaze far, brother	gaze deep, brother
our sonums	have become letters

yuyubojen gamle	lemlebeji aying
ranggisımen gamle	jinglebeji
harosım gamle	lemlebeji aying
kittungsım gamle	jinglebeji
jenanglosım gamle	lemlebeji aying
ñanajolsım gamle	jinglebeji

Grandmother-Smallpox-Sonum	we have greeted, little sister
Wind-Sonum	we have acknowledged
Haro-Sonum [?]	we have greeted, little sister
Kittung-Sonum	we have acknowledged
Kittung-Shrine-Sonum	we have greeted, little sister
Flowing-River-Sonum	we have acknowledged

almadaiba buñang	permodaiba buñang
sonumlen sompengen	bornalenji

gaze far, brother	gaze deep, brother
our sonums	have become letters

And finally, as in the sequence of any Indian script, the vowels (underlined):

anggaisım gamle	lemlebeji aying
ıldasım gamle	jinglebeji
idaisım gamle	lemlebeji aying

ụyungsɪm gamle	jinglebeji
ọnalsɪm gamle	lemlebeji aying
[ọ]irsɪm gamle	jinglebeji
almadaiba buñang	permodaiba buñang
sonumlen sompengen	bornalenji

Moon-Sonum	we have greeted, little sister
ɪlda-Sonum	we have acknowledged
ancestor-sonum	we have greeted, little sister
Sun-Sonum	we have acknowledged
Mortar-Sonum	we have greeted, little sister
Winnowing-Fan-Sonum	we have acknowledged [representing the "schwa" sound]
gaze far, brother	gaze deep, brother
our sonums	have become letters

Not only was the dialect very different, but so were many of the sonums. Sun, Moon, Earth, Kittung: these at least seemed familiar. Others were features of the immediate environment, but with a different significance: for the Lanjia Sora "Garden," "Boundary," and "Forest" would not have been sonums at all. Others corresponded more closely, but the rationale was different: for the Lanjia the "Path" is where Rattud-Sonums attack travelers, whereas here it was revered because "the Health Department tells us to go far out of the village to excrete." But the essential message of the song was clear: our sonums have become letters.

"Sonums are all around us in the world, and in our bodies," explained Orjuno in an intense voice. "Their forms (ɪl-*na*, "becomings," also meaning "avatars") come to us, and when we remember those forms we do the karja."

Here was the fetishization of writing taken to an extreme: not as a means to the divine, but as an end in itself because it *is* the divine.

"How do these sonums cause illness and death?" I wondered.

"They don't," he replied fervently. "Why would they harm us?"

Lokami and I exchanged glances. The whole point of sonums is that they cause death. That is how death happens. "Then how do we die?" I asked.

"It's like when our battery runs out," he explained. "It's just our time."

"Then where do we go after we die?"

"We merge with the sonum which starts with the initial of our name. So if your name's Lokami you'll go to Labo-Sonum (Earth), if it's Monosi you'll go to Mundara-Sonum (Wayside Shrine). If it's Pirino you'll go to Patta-Sonum (Fish)."

Figure 11.5 Script of the alphabet worshippers

Here in Sarda Sora country, Orjuno was confronting us with an entirely new theory of experience. Our Lanjia Sora sonums combined kinship and motive to precipitate an encounter; their actions became known through symptoms and were countered through dialogue. But Orjuno had turned life and death into a predetermined alphabet game. No wonder there was no need to hold dialogues with the dead: there was nothing to find out or negotiate, since there was nothing you could change!

286

"Once everyone believes this, then there will be no more fighting, debt, or robbery." So this was a Hindu reform movement, with a utopian subtext of social liberation. Perhaps not so different from Damano's Baptist movement, beneath the difference in religion?

"And it's important to teach this alphabet to our children: sa ta ba cha da ga . . . ," Orjuno went on. "Otherwise the Sora language will be lost."

This raised more immediate problems. All Sora children everywhere were now saturated in Oriya schooling (or Telugu across the border in Andhra Pradesh), and our hosts' children yesterday knew no Sora at all. I thought of the fluent, quick-witted wordplay of the adults in last night's performance: was all this about to collapse into a beleaguered pidgin and evaporate?

How might this script serve the language? There were political as well as technical issues. The Roman (English) script introduced with the Bible was unknown here, but among the Lanjia Sora it was used by anyone who needed to write, even animists scraping their name with an arrowhead on their bamboo flute or sending back money orders from Assam. Now it is considered tainted with Christianity, and the governments of Orissa and Andhra Pradesh encourage the use of the mutually illegible Oriya and Telugu scripts, respectively. Christians insist that these scripts do not fit their language well, and see this as an attempt to cut them off from the Bible, as well as from the possibility of learning English. Sora on different sides of the border would be unable to communicate on paper at all without the Roman script as an intermediary.

Now here is yet another script, based on the same syllabic principle as Oriya and Telugu, but thought to be entirely Sora. Some elements in the government now want to introduce Manggai's script into Sora schooling, thereby introducing a fourth competitor. Yet the litheness of the alphabet worshippers' language play lies in oral performance. There are only a few texts written in the script, and these date back to Manggai himself. In 2011 I went back to Orjuno and asked him to read these aloud. The language was stilted, and even he could pronounce them only slowly, admitting that only a few hundred people could read the script at all. Since their texts are a limited homemade corpus locked up in almost unknown symbols, one could only worship this script as a mystery rather than use it as a tool for everyday purposes: literacy without literature.

Even though the Lanjia Sora all use the Roman script, the Sarda Sora elite support Manggai's. I went with Monosi to visit Bijoy Gomango, a lawyer and chairman of the local Congress Party youth wing, at his home in Gunupur. Not only was he the nephew of an established Sarda politician; he was also the grandson of the Mallia to whom Manggai's script was revealed. He spoke to Monosi in Oriya and to me in English. He insisted that the script was better fitted than the Roman script to the sounds of Sora, but did not seem to follow much when Monosi and I spoke to each other in Sora. I had noticed before that the strongest supporters of the script were often people who did not know the language, including Oriya officials.

Though a Hindu, Bijoy moved comfortably among Christians. "They needn't accept the Pure People's religion, which is completely Hindu-oriented," he argued, "but they should definitely accept the script." Later he added, "It's a pity the script originated in my family but my wife and children can't read it." I suspected that neither could he, since he did not know the language well. Here was a further obstacle to the formation of a Manggai-reading elite: anyone educated will be educated out of the script, even faster than they are educated out of the Sora language. As one young Christian remarked, "The officials support Manggai's script, but they wouldn't let me use it to sign my name, or to address a letter!"

In the 1990s I had thought that the Bible was the strongest written guarantor of the language's survival. However, Christianity can be conveyed in any language, and with the pastors' increasing use of the Oriya Bible as a status symbol the church is now beginning to join schools in creating a death zone for the Sora language. Similarly, though their personal prayers and some of their hymns may still be in Sora, the Bismas look to a wider background literature, which is entirely in Oriya.

The alphabet worshippers are the only people whose commitment to the language is built into their religion. They keep sonums at the core but silence their voice, remove their power to harm (or, cyclically, to give), and modernize them by making them into literacy itself. Yet despite the saffron and coconuts that link it to the Hindu mainstream, Manggai's script is hard to propagate. The price of creating such a narrowly Sora movement is isolation and stagnation.

Monosi sees the old Sora worldview as "culture" (Oriya: *sanskruti*), which leads him into the paradox of trying to encourage young people to "preserve" something he himself does not actually believe. Lokami sees it as reality. Although she was fascinated to see another kind of Sora, with similar rituals, she was appalled at the Sarda way of wallowing in charred human bones and did not think much of their shaman's feeble trance. She also found fault in ways I could not have predicted. "How ridiculous to say they plant small stones in the *ganuar* and they grow," she laughed. "Stones just don't grow like that!"

Above all, she ridiculed the alphabet worshippers' theory of death. For several hours as we rattled homeward through the night air over the potholed plains, wedged tightly together in the back of the little three-wheeler, one of us would say, "Issí, he died! Which sonum took him—was it the sun was it the moon?" Another would reply, "No, his battery ran out!" and we would all shriek with laughter. Occasionally I would add "bloop bloop!" representing the way I would talk after death if I joined a Fish-Sonum. For days after we got home to Rajingtal we would address my flashlight or voice recorder, asking it solicitously, "Issí, has your battery run out?"

· · · ·

That was in 2009. From the 1970s to the 1990s, I thought of dialogues with the dead as the defining essence of Sora religion, culture, and identity. Was I wrong? Since then I have seen new Christian and Hindu forms closing in on the last of the Sora shamans like Lokami, squeezed between two expansionist superpower religions that leave no room for the nonaligned. Do these movements spell the end of Sora religion, or are they *new* Sora religions? Should I acknowledge a whole range of Sora movements—dialects of theology, or theolects—that have yet to be studied?

It is no accident that Manggai was elaborating his Hindu system in the 1940s around the same time as Damano was working out his Christian liberation theology. Both were reaching out to a wider world that was passing from feudalism and colonialism into nationalist modernity. Though I did not want to understand this at the time, the Sora world I inhabited in the late 1970s was already obsolete. The outsiders who were previously kept at arm's length had to be engaged in new ways. Especially since Rajiv Gandhi's development thrust in the 1980s, the point has been not simply to fend them off (or co-opt them by marrying them in the Underworld), but to find ways of joining them.

Animist culture ventriloquizes these outsiders. From shamans' high-caste husbands to the lowest Gansi blacksmith-sorcerers (Vitebsky 1993: 170–71, 268), they are all introjected and theatricalized. Apart from a few snatches of mock-Oriya or Telugu, they speak only the language of the monolingual shamans who manipulate their simulacra. They are controlled in the form of sonums because this cannot be done with their real-life counterparts. This is a thin version of what is done with the Sora's own dead. These are one's own people, but even here, talking with them is an attempt to impose control from a position of vulnerability. Within this closed, introverted universe, dialogues with the dead can also be understood as an extended, multivoiced monologue, since all the participants come from within the same collective self.

In this community of victimhood, dialogues are not only about mortality, but also about coping with weakness. Each of the new movements offers its own solution, ranging along a spectrum from rejection to reform. Baptists seek a way of being Sora with no reference to sonums at all, either as causes of events or as ancestors. While Hindu visions accommodate the coexistence of alternative forms and a sliding scale of orthodoxy, Baptists simply take Jisu's message as superseding other religions. This is rupturism as a core ideology, now maybe even to the point of abandoning the language that the missionaries spent so much effort translating, as the pastors start reading from the Oriya Bible instead. Apart from the chance location of the mission bungalow, this impulse toward rupture may explain why Baptist beliefs took root in the Lanjia Sora mountains, where extreme isolation had allowed extreme oppression.

Though early colonial sources and modern Oriya stereotypes agree in portraying the Lanjia hills as the wildest, fiercest, most inscrutable Sora area, no other Sora religion has ever been studied in depth, so that it is difficult to know whether the cult of ancestors was more intense here or whether this is just where it persisted longest. Apart from eccentric details like sprouting stones and the astrological diagram, the karja festival of the Sarda Sora in Kujendri seemed very familiar to Lokami, right down to the invocations and melodies. Their style of possession by spirits, but with less speech or none, resembles "village Hinduism" among lower castes, including non-Christianized Pano.

This religion has no political ambitions or futurist discourse. Whatever may become different over the years is not heralded as change because change as such is not the point. By contrast, Bisma Hinduism is a highly politicized, almost prophetic movement. As with Christianity, its impulse comes from outside the community, bringing a complex blend of attraction and inducement. But becoming a Bisma Hindu does not involve the Baptist shock of repudiation or bring the same pressure to abandon one's parents. In its direct link with national forms of militant fundamentalism it represents not rupture, not continuity, but reform through a turn toward greater orthodoxy. A modernist social and political agenda is presented as a restoration of a purer ancient time; the Sora are to be retrieved from their jungly state and led via classical texts to a higher cultural level. The old-time shaman's Kshatriya helpers already pointed to an emulation of status; but rather than being resigned, accommodating, or ironic, this new Hindu form can be angry and violent. Through talk of Rama and Sabari, Bhima and Hanuman, it draws the Sora into a national mythology and localizes that mythology in their territory through narratives of their own participation. Yet like the Canadian missionaries, the Bisma advocates cannot control what local people will do with the impulse they provide. Nationally the Bisma (Vishva Hindu Parishad) movement is driven by Brahmins, but locally it is promoted most vigorously by Kshatriya Paik, and among the Sora it emerges with an anti-Brahminical tone. Meanwhile, local interpretations of the gods Hanuman and Jagannath are already veering off in unpredictable directions.

If Bisma Hinduism emphasizes purification to join the mainstream through orthodoxy, the alphabet worshippers go even further by taking the word "Pure" as their name. In contrast to the more aggressive, anti-Western tone of the Bisma movement, their revitalization program is gently utopian (there will be no more crime). Perhaps this explains why they could more comfortably draw me into their ritual activities. In 2015 an alphabet missionary gave me a leaflet in English that explained the cult in a more concise and focused way than anything Orjuno had told me. The god Jagannath transferred his favors from the ancient Sora to the Brahmin Vidyapati, who had stolen him and taken him out of the jungle. This much is a mainstream Oriya story, but what follows seems unique to this cult. In response the Sora switched to a ritual style based on blood and liquor (that is, sank back into primitivism); Mallia's dream in 1936 marked the return of the god to the Sora, but in the new form of Akshara Brahma, which means both "Imperishable Brahma" and "Alphabet Brahma."

This is Sora revivalism with a high Sanskritic tone. As expounded in commentaries on the Sanskrit word *akshara* in section 8 of the Bhagavad Gita, it applies both to the eternal, immutable god Brahma and to the syllabic symbols of writing as the fundamental elements of sound, speech, and truth, and especially to the syllable *om* (*aum*). The leaflet does not elaborate this point, but combines typical Indian language of social reform ("persuaded to give up the use of country liquor and animal slaughtering . . . it helped their economic uplift") with the tribulations of the missionary ("Travelling village to village [Manggai] tried to create a consciousness among the people. But the Soura people who were living in the darkness did not accept it easily"), even borrowing Christian terminology ("Those baptised by him tried to lead a disciplined life . . . He creates such a new pulsation among the Soura of Gunpur [sic] region that his fellowmen thought as if he was an angel, who saved a declining primitive society"). I did not hear any talk of Akshara Brahma from Orjuno and his companions, and have not yet found out how they bridged the gap from high Hindu philosophy to the sonums of their Sora alphabet (Orjuno has recently died, and I am trying to locate his successor). Sonums do not feature in the Bhagavad Gita, but they remain at the heart of this movement: reform comes not from discarding them, but from sanitizing them.

However, the main thrust of all these new Sora religions is clear. Apart from the old ladies of Kujendri (whose religion is not new), these are all discourses of awakening and joining the mainstream. They reinforce the impact of schools, roads, and jobs by drawing the Sora more directly into the nation-building and political parties of the Indian state. For Christians, animists were always ignorant; for Hindu reformists they have *become* ignorant by losing contact with the gods (although this is double-edged: maybe it was those Brahmins who made them ignorant by stealing their god and leaving them behind in the jungle). Compared to the ancestor-laden animist landscape, all of these universes are virtual. But while biblical Israel and missionary Vancouver remain completely outside Sora experience, the epic of Rama is becoming less distant as it starts to take root in Sora geography.

This broadening of the field is accompanied by a change in the ontology of the beings who serve as the focus of religious energy. For animists, the entire cosmos is ancestorized. In this combination of immanence and humanism, even the Sun and the Earth are knowable mainly through words spoken by dead Sora relatives whom they have absorbed. Religion is an unending and unendable dialogue that centers round the needs, motives, and feelings that swirl back and forth between all the interlocutors.

None of the other Sora religions holds dialogues with the dead, so none has this intimate family drama. Instead they have devotion. In every one of the new religions there is a shift of attention from ancestors to gods, from a more immanent to a more transcendent metaphysics. All use the word *kittung* for their gods and bring this concept back from a remote figure in animist creation myths to the heart of their faith. These religious styles also have political implications. It is hard to claim the loyalty of people focused only on their ancestors, but easier for the state or any other ompu if it speaks on behalf of a transcendent universal figure like Jisu or Rama. It is as if we are witnessing a local "axial age" at the moment of its formation.

Jisu, Rama, Krishna, and Jagannath are objects of prayer, a format almost unknown to animists. This format is not dialogic, since any response is not made explicit or vocalized directly. The implication, most militant among Baptists, is that ordinary human ancestors are not enough for a proper theology. Nor are dialogues with the dead. Such dialogues are not devotional, because ancestors are not gods or even gurus. The animist Sora had a cult of ancestors, but they did not worship them. If kittungs as creators contained a resonance of monotheism, this too was without the worship. The shift to currently active gods introduces a new respect and distance toward such beings, which is justified by a dignity that comes from a lack of neediness in their relationship with us. This dignity matches a reformist tendency throughout India, which is now linked to a rising middle class. Baptists replace messy sacrificial animals with the symbolic blood of Jisu, itself further sanitized via wine into fruit juice; orthodox Hindus replace blood sacrifice with coconuts, fruit, and flowers.

In contrast to all other Sora, my animist friends put an extraordinary emphasis on dialogical exchange. They are the ones who most fully cross the line leading from symbolism (fruit juice) or make-believe play-acting (*opjong*) to the full suspension of disbelief. Their verbal articulateness allows them to act and feel as if they believe their performances literally. Should I now adjust my vision and see their sonums as part of a cosmology with certain potentials, onto which a practice of dialogue has been projected, perhaps as the ultimate development of the grammatical necessity of quoting other people's direct speech? Or put differently: should dialogue be seen not as the essence of Sora culture but as an extraordinary efflorescence that takes off from this cosmology but is not necessitated by it?

How might the answer affect our understanding of redemption as a release from suffering? Theology addresses the mystery of life and death, and psychoanalysis the drama of love and jealousy, but all of this is also set in history, and we have seen a close parallel between spiritual and political dimensions of redemption. The culture that I witnessed in the 1970s matched an archaic metaphysics with an archaic system of domination. Sora dialogues with the dead are ultimately defensive in relation to everyone, from the most distant officials to one's own dead relatives; they are structured to deflect attack at the time or, where it cannot be prevented in advance, to transform victimhood after the event. Fawcett's description of the Sora contains a hint that dialogues were already going on then in a similar way, along with prodigious buffalo massacres (1888: 250, 257). Maybe those dialogues were themselves once a new religious form, a response to earlier intimidating feudal violence. The parallel to a Freudian interpretation would then be not simply as an insight into attachment but also as a product of a particular historical moment—a new understanding that emerged in its time and is now fading in its time. Christianity (John 3:3) and Hinduism (through the term *dvija*) both talk of a spiritual rebirth that makes one "twice-born" (Carstairs 1958). Animist Sora religion was based on a carefully paced forgetting of ancestors; with conversion to the Baptist faith this pacing has accelerated, so that these ancestors now become twice-forgotten.

INTERLUDE

. . . .

GOVERNMENT KITSCH AND THE
OLD PROPHET'S NEW MESSAGE

. . . .

If some memorial stones get vandalized in religious wars, others simply die of neglect. In 2005, in a long-Christianized village, I found the remains of a grove of megaliths. They had retracted so deep into the soft soil between the snaking roots of a jackfruit tree that only the tips of some stones were still showing: I counted twenty-eight. An upright stone has no features but leaves the evocation of the deceased person to the creativity of the dialogue that takes place around it. What could a future archaeologist retrieve from these silent stones, once fed with alin and blood as they were embraced amid drumming and weeping?

While the profundities of Sora culture are repressed, it can be hollowed out and its surface rendered banal. Missionaries and government agree on one thing at least: "culture" is picturesque and should be "preserved." Wall-paintings were once dictated by sonums in dreams to give shamans the power to descend to the Underworld; they represented everything that church and school teach young people not to know. They have now been placed at the center of a residential college of Tribal painting called Ideetal in Bhubaneswar, where the children of real shamans are brought out of Soraland and trained to produce "Sora" cloth paintings for sale in government handicraft shops and to paint frescoes on walls of schools throughout Orissa. A government brochure explains that the Department of Scheduled Caste and Scheduled Tribe Development "has extended all sort of helping hands for the upliftment of the heritage art form to preserve, propagate and to bring income generation . . . to fine tune their traditional form into the modern concept, making it used [sic] friendly. . . . After the visit to different sites [of great Hindu temples], many changes are seen in their work of art to which we pin high hopes." The photos of the children include Ranatang's daughter and Lokami's son, both Christians whose mothers are shamans. The rebranding of spiritual imagery as "art" mirrors what has happened to religious iconography in the West.

In a similar fashion, the distinctive dancing and the swinging tails of the Lanjia Sora loincloths serve as shorthand for authentic Tribals, as they are

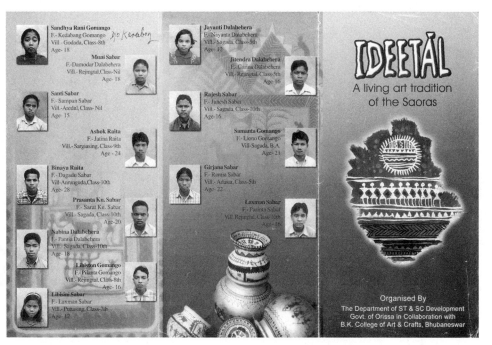

Wall-painting brochure

summoned to perform at local public meetings and at Republic Day parades in New Delhi. The wild dancing that leads the victim of an Experience sonum into the company of his ancestors is now reproduced for politicians' command performances. The women's breasts are covered, and the men reveal no dimpled buttocks. When Monosi as Tribal Leader met Prime Minister Rajiv Gandhi in Delhi, he wore the traditional Sora costume, which in reality he had renounced in his teens. The bells, red turban, and egret-feather headdress were authentic funeral dancewear. However, his bare chest was covered with a banian, his loincloth was enveloped by a white sheet, and in one photo his bare legs ended in absurd long socks and clumpy shoes.

The old headman Sidoro appeared to Monosi in a dream and said that the memorial stones of their lineage, the largest and most imposing cluster in Soraland, should be preserved. Suddenly for Monosi it was not enough just to leave them alone—they should be made into a monument. "Why don't we set the stones in a cement platform, and put up an inscription with the names of all the ancestors you've collected?" he asked me, and even "Why don't we use your photos to make statues?" As always, he found a biblical parallel, this time in the pillar on Rachel's grave in Genesis 35:20, and added, "We could

Monosi meets Prime Minister Rajiv Gandhi, Delhi 1980s
To the left, representatives of other tribes wait their turn.

have a Jubilee every year when we read out the names and do prayers." This would update the No-o-o chant into a new format of public announcement (no doubt with loudspeakers).

We did not get round to doing this, but the mood was shifting. By the early 2000s, the militant phase of youthful contempt for the ways of the old-timers was softening. The Baptists were emerging from their Cultural Revolution, and the surviving clusters of memorial stones felt less vulnerable to demolition.

In 2003, Monosi's first wife, Onai, died ("on 20 October"). Her *ugar* had shriveled up from chewing tobacco, and she still came to him in dreams dressed in rags, not having found a resting place either with Jisu or with her ancestors. For all their problems together, Monosi remembered her generous role in the wooing of Likini and felt compassion for her.

But suddenly he was no longer a bigamist, and the young pastors were finally pleased to welcome back their wise elder, the only surviving pioneer of their Bible translation. He had been banned for twenty-seven years from taking communion or speaking in church. Likini was baptized ("on 15 March 2004"), a fully legitimate wife at last, and was given an easy examination by

Likini in a hotel garden, Visakhapatnam 2008

Deacon Buyajo of Abada. She has remained beautiful but has become very small, the huge, round tattoos on her cheeks made startling by their modern rarity.

"I went around various churches," Monosi told me, naming them at length, "and especially to Pastor Pilipo, to ask forgiveness: 'Yes, I had two wives but now the first one's died and I'll be coming to church with my second wife. Please accept us in.' So they did forgive me. I asked Likini, and she said, 'I need to be baptized,' so the pastor and the deacon examined her:

'Why have you come?'

'I now understand about Jisu, and how he died. My husband took me as a second wife, so I wasn't registered, I wasn't baptized, but now I believe Jisu really is God's son and he gave his blood on the cross.'

'Do you truly believe, jadi ná?'

'Yes, I believe.'

'Have you given up alin and aba?'

'Yes, long ago.'

Then they conferred, and baptized her. Since her baptism, I go to communion and eat Jisu's flesh and drink his blood."

It must have been complicated for Likini to know that she was at the root of Monosi's apologies and loss of status, at the same time as being the object of his deepest love. I remembered how she had said she was a sinful woman, and now felt she was referring not just to her youthful affairs, but also to her entire happy marriage.

Another time Monosi told me, "There was a big meeting in Limaliguda, lots of brothers came: 'He's been forgiven, he's come back inside!' Twenty congregations invited me to visit: 'He translated the Bible, he composed hymns, he was the founding secretary of our Association . . .' A lot of young people had heard my name but never seen me."

He started making long, passionate speeches from the platform. "The government will test you to check you're real Sora, otherwise they'll classify you as Pano. And the Pano are very cunning, they speak Sora and they'll impersonate you to take over your Tribal land titles. How will you prove to the officials you're Sora if you don't know who your ancestors are?" (Surely officials knew less than the Pano did about Sora custom, but I did not like to point this out.)

Monosi was speaking directly against the ancestor-neglect in the rupture of conversion, and against the whole tradition, which stretched back to Damano and Miss Munro, about walking in darkness. "Our ancestors were very wise, it's just that they hadn't heard about Jisu." He was cleansing the concept of ancestor from its contamination by the concept of sonum, as perhaps nobody had ever done before. He had long thought that animist Sora were like the pre-Christian animal-sacrificing Jews. If we study their ancestors, why not our own? "Whatever stories there are in the Bible, our grandparents had something similar." Sometimes he used me as an object lesson: "He came all this way, he learned our language, he wrote everything down just like the Bible, he respects our grandparents . . . His father's Jewish, he's one of the original people from the Old Testament, that's why he's not a Christian!"

Monosi even sang sonum invocations from the platform, but these were carefully framed within his speech as examples of the old people's wisdom, given the limited knowledge available to them. The young audience seemed quite receptive. We went to some very remote churches like Tondrong where there were no pastors, just naive young catechists who were overpowered by his performative charisma. His mission now paralleled his evangelizing in the 1960s, when he was forcibly chased out of these same villages, though the message was partially reversed. Monosi was a prophet by temperament, and this was an agenda he had developed through his relationship with me. Where his teacher Damano had grown narrower with age, Monosi (by 2005 already aged about seventy-five) was growing ever more liberal.

Perhaps the times are with him. The photo of Monosi meeting the prime minister fits the Delhi elite's fantasy about Tribals, picturesque in their distinct costumes but somehow contributing to national unity. More closely reflective of the Sora's own interests is the way the DVD of Doloso and Rajani dancing at the Manengul karja now appears on hundreds of young people's cell phones. Even if they are alienated from the original context, this is something they are willing to recontextualize into their current identity.

Once in 2009, as we were discussing neglect of dead parents, Monosi broke down, saying, "I used to be like that, but now I miss my father and mother very much—what can I do for them?" (*wañen yangñen boiboi sintatai—aninji a dong ian lımai?*) "Truly," he added, "I want to make them a cement shrine, with that photo you took of my mother." When I invited him to England the following year and introduced him to my own elderly mother, he wept again. "I learned about Sora custom through you," he told me. "I saw everything, but I didn't properly understand its meaning (*kudduben gijlai, do a geramgamen sa'kailoge ergalam*). I remember the first time you asked Mel Otis, 'Where are the Sora rituals?' and he said, 'Oh I don't know.' In those days I was very hostile to sonums (*kun adnang ñen sonumenji apsele boiboi asanggeman*). It was that peacock song that changed me."

· ·

12

SIX REMARKABLE WOMEN
AND THEIR DESTINIES

· ·

Manikpur, in the Plains near Gunupur, December 2005

Present: six female shamans, five living and one dead
From Rajingtal: Gallanti, Taranti, and Lokami, and their newly deceased teacher
  Ononti
From Manengul: Rajani
From Sogad: Sompani

By 2005, I had been away since 1998 and had not seen any Sora for seven years. That December I was not able to stay in the hills for administrative reasons, and so made my base with Monosi and Likini in their house on the edge of the plains in Manikpur. It was in this raw new colony of Christian settlers, a place devoid of sonums and old memories, that I experienced an uplifting, redemptive event, which was without precedent and can surely never be repeated.

Three of the villages where I had spent years of my youth had turned out to be almost the only places where shamans survived to offer an alternative to the abrupt Christian funeral. I sent messengers to five shamans inviting them to come down to Manikpur.

All five women came down the mountains to meet me. From Rajingtal came Gallanti, Taranti, and Lokami, successors of my first and most enigmatic shaman, Ononti, who had only just died that June. Gallanti and Taranti were lineage-sisters who had sung some of the first songs I ever tried to transcribe, while Lokami was the child-egg I had saved in a dream in 1976. From Sogad came Uda's successor Sompani, whose initiatory torture by snakes and centipedes I had witnessed in 1994; and from Manengul came Rajani, long-suffering successor of the overbearing Doloso, whose death in 2002 I had missed. For two days, in an enchanting atmosphere of intimate companionship, away from jealous husbands and censorious Christian children, these women chatted, giggled, and wept, held hands and leaned affectionately against each other. Though other men occasionally peeped around the door, Monosi and I were the only men present throughout.

Rajingtal was the nearest of the three villages, but Lokami and Taranti

Figure 12.1 Gallanti, 2005

had been summoned to dance in costume for a politician in the distant town of Koraput. So the first to arrive was Gallanti. She was barefoot, dressed in her best cream-colored woven skirt (*gatungkaben*) and a freshly bought brilliant white blouse, with heavy silver jewelry. Apart from her covered breasts, she was an apparition straight out of the 1970s. A proud, upright figure with white hair, she had grown tiny like a sparrow, and cataracts blurred her alert brown eyes. She called me Pede, my early Sora nickname used only in Rajingtal.

As we squatted in the shade of Monosi's veranda, squinting against the dazzling sunlight beyond, he pursued his long-running comparison between the python in the stream near Sogad and the snake in the Garden of Eden: how was the python's ritual sung in Rajingtal? Gallanti swung effortlessly into a long recital, and over the next few hours moved without a pause through a catalogue of rituals, songs, and myths: Peacock-Feather-Bundle-Sonum (Gal-bed-sım), Monosi's other favorite since hearing my old recording of Taranti;

Wine-Offering-Sonum (Pang-sal-sım), who makes girls sick by proposing marriage to them; Grandfather-Man (Jojo-mar), who was killed in a landslide and became a leopard; and Rattud-Sonum (Rattud-sım), who seizes travelers on the path. Often she would sing a passage, then revert to speaking a section, ending with the word *gamtebe*, "we say," before singing once more, like someone alternating between running and walking.

Gallanti's outpouring was strong and enthusiastic, but I occasionally sensed some anxiety. Were the Rajingtal sonums dangerous to her down here? Or was it the opposite problem, of singing powerful songs so openly in a Christian village? She sometimes used the past tense, *gamlebe*, "we used to say," so maybe she had given up?

Aha! "My children went Christian and forced me to stop. My son wouldn't even thatch my house because I dealt with sonums." This was the Baptist catechist whose baby Subijito I saw being named in Rajingtal (pages 211–14). "So I said to Lokami, 'I'm getting old, my hands are feeble my legs are feeble, my sons have become Christian, you do it all!' I even washed my wall-painting over with fresh mud."

Yet her sonums would not give up so easily. "My children in the Underworld refused to let me go, they made me ill they drove me crazy. Five years after giving up I was very sick. So now I've started again. With my ıldas I got better. A few months ago I redid my wall-painting and started doing trances again. Now I don't get ill any more."

All her songs so far were from the repertoire of minor shamans, rituals of acknowledgment and healing. Yet Gallanti had graduated to the funeral tradition to fill the gap after Ononti gave up, and now she started to sing tunes from the stone-planting and karja. Here were the very words that I had labored to understand thirty years ago with almost no grounding in anything, hunched next to Ononti with my gritty microphones and failing cassette recorders, straining my ears against the throbbing of drums, the blaring of oboes, and the howling of mourners. Here was the very first chant I ever took to Monosi, which at that time baffled him as much as me: *Dangdonging Kansid!* "Don't block my way, Kond!"

At one point Gallanti stopped. "I'd be afraid to sing this up in Rajingtal," she murmured. It seemed the difference between the two kinds of place served as a firewall. Uphill was subject to her comprehension and techniques, but also to sonum dangers; down here in the plains it was alien, but thereby safer for singing powerful songs without the protection of context and ritual procedure.

During another pause, I showed Gallanti a photo of Ononti in 1976 (fig.

1.1, p. 6). A dead person's distinctive speech habits could be preserved through dialogue, but the Sora had no way of fixing the memory of their physical appearance. Even dialogues conjured up the person only as they were at the end, so earlier stages of a person's life could never be recalled. Ononti had ended frail and wizened, and Gallanti had forgotten what she looked like before. Ononti herself had been unable to recognize any photo at all, but Gallanti was clearly able to read her commanding face and firm, upright body. She gazed at the photo adoringly, murmuring "Lovely (langgi)!" and tucking it into the top of her blouse. "Don't tell Lokami," she added, "or she'll want it!" I wished I had brought more copies.

As I recorded her every word, free of any distracting orchestra, this was Gallanti's moment of importance before the arrival of Lokami. "Ononti gave up after Maianti died. She told me, 'The ıldas say I smell, I'm polluted. So you do it, you're our lineage, you belong.' Lokami started doing funeral trances long after me—I was the one who trained her." Looking back now, after observing several tiffs between them, I sense mixed emotions in this remark. Despite their intimacy, Gallanti was claiming some acknowledgment to compensate for her children's harassment, her estrangement from her ıldas, and her younger pupil's preeminence.

"Let Ononti tell you everything herself," Gallanti said with a smile. "I'll bring her to you tonight!" I had missed my last chance to talk to Ononti while she was alive, but a sonum could not be summoned without a ritual occasion. I took her offer as an affectionate joke, since there was surely no way this could actually happen.

Rajani arrived in the afternoon, after eight hours walking down from Manengul. She too was preoccupied with her old teacher, but her memory of him was very different. "Doloso snubbed me (dong ñen kile) because of my affair," she said. "He said the sex made me unclean, he wanted me to devote myself to being a shaman. But you remember how I married my lover."

I also remembered how Doloso forced her into a botched abortion during her first pregnancy, leaving her infertile (kampungen yagale, "her womb was scorched"). Doloso, the most vivid, the most compelling shaman of them all. But also a controlling bully.

"I sat in trance beside him, but didn't feel comfortable," she continued. "There was his daughter Ambadi sitting between us. I wanted to give up for the sake of my husband, but my father encouraged me to keep at it. It was only after Ambadi refused to follow Doloso that he started to encourage me. And he encourages me specially now that he's dead!"

An encouragement that must be double-edged, I thought. "What's happened with Ambadi?" I asked, remembering Ambadi's own nonchalant dismissal of her father's mysteries.

"Ambadi never tranced properly, she was only pretending all along," Rajani replied. "She never actually spoke during her trances." She added with a sting, "She's not really sorry her father's dead! She said 'I won't get a husband in the upper world.' That's why she gave up. She's specially not sorry now that she *has* got a husband! Her brother and his children were more sorry, they gave a sword and fine cloths at his stone-planting, she just gave one cloth and not even an animal."

Of course! Ambadi had become a serious Catholic to get away from her father, whereas her brother's conversion had been casual. Monosi turned to me. "Ambadi told me she'd felt him shuffling behind her *ñadip ñadap* along the path, and turned round to say, 'Stop following me, you're dead!'" In death as in life, Doloso was not easy to evade.

"He's coming after you too," Rajani said to me. "'Pirino talked to me in the old days, so why isn't he talking to me now? I'm going to go and catch him!'" It felt uncanny to be the target of a threat from the next world, though this was what animists experienced all the time. It was also strange to hear a quotation of a quotation, from the medium whose soul had been absent from her body when those words were spoken through her mouth. If an encounter with the dead Ononti would be obscure, what would it would be like to face the sharp and demanding Doloso?

Like a host who invites people from different parts of his life to the same party, I was concerned that Gallanti would now feel left out of this torrent of Manengul talk, which was fueled by Monosi's interest in every nuance of his in-laws' village. But Gallanti was reinforced in the evening by the arrival of Lokami and Taranti from Rajingtal. They had been dropped off from the Koraput dance by truck, with no chance to sleep, and had walked fifteen miles back downhill to join us.

There was an immediate sense of Lokami taking charge. She had grown slightly plump, still with unusual wavy hair, and burst into her familiar toothy laugh: *E dadi!* (Hey uncle!) She did not raise my hand to her forehead in the usual gesture of greeting, but clutched me in a long embrace.

E amonsel! I felt privileged that I could call this remarkable woman my niece. Taranti too was laughing, her sparkling eyes offset by her three nose-rings, enormous wooden earplugs, and the huge tattooed circles on her cheeks.

Other women from neighboring houses came in and out, including Soimani, the girl from my first years in Rajingtal, now married and emigrated down to Manikpur. There were too many people for Monosi's modest house, so he moved everyone to the bigger, modern house of his brother-in-law Sap-lud (Torn Ear), who was away. We unrolled mats to cushion ourselves from the cold cement floor, so unlike the warm, yielding cow-dung floors in old houses. In the past the mats would have been woven out of rushes by hered-itary Sora mat-weavers, but now they were from the bazaar and woven from strips of plastic.

Out of sight of religious puritans, the topless photos from the 1970s that I had brought as presents felt like dangerous contraband. Here was the in-triguing moment when Gallanti had been given her baby to breast-feed while in trance—the same baby Labaiño who had grown into a church official and pressured her to give up. Here were Taranti and Gallanti performing the har-vest festival together (fig. 1.6, p. 23), with the very young Taranti singing the peacock song. The peacock flew only around the old villages in the mountain-ous heartland, and the song did not mention Manikpur. In a magical moment, she sang the song again in a voice that was huskier now, but as touching as ever. This was the first time that Monosi had ever seen her performing the song that had so captivated him on tape and changed the course of his life.

Taranti too had given up practicing, torn like Gallanti between the demands of her living family and of her abandoned sonums. She was under pressure not only from Baptist children but also from a husband who was jealous of her other husband in the Underworld. The strain had driven her mad: "After I gave up, the sonums made me do crazy and shameful things. I had a compulsion to strip off all my ornaments and hide them under a rock. I dressed in rags and went begging; one moment I couldn't eat, and then I'd be insatiable and slurp up everything, *sabap sabap sabap!* I would sing with no idea what I was singing. I tried to bite a Pano trader. Once I was breast-feeding my baby, and saw a dog doing the same with a puppy. The puppy was so lovely, I looked and looked at that dog, deep inside I felt a craving (*ati arangting*): my soul was trembling my soul was wobbling—shall I, shan't I? I so longed to suckle at that dog's breast although it was unclean, I was ready to abandon my baby!"

Taranti had no safe space to practice like Gallanti's poorly thatched, leak-ing little hut. "If only I had a house where I could keep a wall-painting and hang up a sonum-pot! I think of asking someone to build me a little house, but then my soul sinks and I give up. It would be alright in an old mud house, but we live in a new cement one."

Like the house we were in now. How would the archaic Ononti have man-aged here? I had focused my original research on her all those years ago, she had embodied my quest, and she had remained the most enigmatic of all. I retrieved the photo of Ononti from Gallanti, and showed it to the others.

I had never understood my strange encounter with Ononti in 1994, when she told me she had parted from her sonums. Now that she had died, would her pupils give me the key to her mystery? "Is it true (jadi po)," I asked, "her ıldas rejected her her ıldas divorced her?"

Gallanti, Taranti, and Lokami all started answering at once. At first I thought they were saying that yes, her sonums had blinded her to the Underworld path. But gradually I realized they were saying that she had used medicine to make herself invisible to her own ıldas—to blind them to her (paditsumadle). As often in relations with sonums, it was hard to tell who was taking the initiative. Clearly Ononti had lost heart. "She gave up trancing when Maianti died," Lokami explained. "Where can I sit, she said." Ononti was broken by the loss: they had worked closely together and tranced side by side. "She never did another ritual," added Gallanti, "she would sit at home and never attend, even if it was happening right next to her house. She never even came to a stone-planting or karja. When she saw Lokami doing those big funeral rituals, she was ashamed she was afraid (garojle batongle), she wouldn't come near. 'How come they've sent her into trance?' she said. 'The ıldas have come back, but not to me!' "

In an extraordinary open mood of laughter and joking the four women worked their way through a huge repertoire of songs associated with preparations for the karja: the peacock-hunting song, the journey from village to village to obtain newly woven mats, a soul-flight traversing the habitations of ılda sonums from one mountaintop to another, the pot-filling (gındapır) song about frogs and cool water, the song for pounding rice into flour, and the one about the origin of cremation-ash.

Though Taranti had given up, she was joining in the singing of tunes and words, which surely she had not uttered for many years. Sometimes the three Rajingtal women and Rajani sang together, blending the versions of their two villages. Lokami took the lead in singing the first element in each couplet just ahead of the others, which allowed them to join confidently in the predictable second element. This was exactly how I had sung under Mengalu in Sogad. Rajani sometimes had difficulty keeping up with a missing final half-beat as the distinctive Rajingtal style jumped quickly into the start of each new stanza.

It was getting dark outside. Someone lit a lamp as Rajani sang an invocation to her ıldas. Gallanti looked anxious: "Don't mention their names, or we'll go into trance!" Surely it was safe as long as they kept their knees drawn up and did not straighten their legs out along the floor? And in any case, there was no alin to feed to the sonums. Gallanti pretended to trance, while Soimani mimicked her part as patient. The acting out (opjong) was astonishingly realistic—except for an added aura of play. While Soimani poured out the rapid monologue of a patient ("It hurts here, and here, and here!"), the other shamans whooped with laughter (E *mangdong!* "Hey, don't laugh!" she protested through her own giggling). Later, I saw Rajani leaning back onto Soimani, who held her arms round her shoulder as they whispered affectionately head to head. I was sure there had never before been a situation like this in which to play or compare traditions, and the mood would be unthinkable among Christians. A Baptist man looking through the door commented, "I haven't heard this since I was a child. It wouldn't have touched my soul (*je'en gatarre*) if I'd just read about it." My newly coined phrase "Christians die mute" was greeted with peals of laughter. I felt that this little house with its cement floor and harsh tin roof had brought together some of the most admirable and enchanting women in the world.

Long after midnight, we fell asleep where we had flopped on the hard floor, still with no word from the fifth shaman, Sompani. The next morning she arrived from Sogad, her distinctive ears sticking out from her oiled, swept-back hair. She had been delayed by a seasonal ritual (*lajab*) to infuse ancestral soul-force into the ripening rice. The others were still in a buoyant mood from the previous night, but Sompani as a newcomer seemed hesitant, almost surly as she challenged me: "Why didn't you come to my ritual?" ("How could I know, they didn't tell me.")

Sompani livened up when I gave her the photo of herself swooning backward into the arms of an old woman on that tense night of her failed initiation seven years earlier, sweat and tears flowing indistinguishably down her cheek and onto her breast (fig. 7.4, p. 187). "That was the very moment when I died!" she exclaimed. "The sonums had been driving me crazy, I'd been running wild for months, I crawled along the ground, I felt dizzy I felt drunk, I was blind, I couldn't recognize anyone."

I asked about the poisonous snakes and centipedes in her song. "They put those in your way the first time," she answered. "They were testing me. Now I don't get frightened. Really, it's as if I died at that moment! I used to work as an ancestor-woman. But the ildas said, 'Rijanti has died Uda has died, and now Sindai sits for trances all alone—you have to sit with her.' I held Sindai's hand on the path to the Underworld, and Rijanti came up from down below and led me on downwards."

Later she said, "The sonums also led me on a journey round the mountaintops of Badong, Madia, Samanti . . ." Each mountain site is linked to a particular succession of shamans and tradition of performance. Samanti is the most sacred site in the Sogad tradition. After Sompani's initiation I had gone

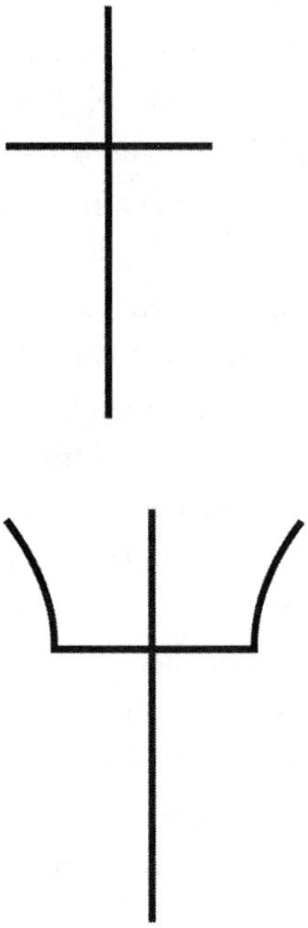

Diagram 12.1 Cross and trident, from the cliff at Samanti

there in 1998, two days' bus ride away. It was a shock. The massive cliff, hundreds of feet high, lay in an area of Hindu-Christian conflict, and the whole area was plastered with religious graffiti. White-painted crosses on the rock faces above one village were opposed across the valley by lingams and symbols of the god Jagannath; boulders along the road were sprinkled with holy swastikas and "om" signs, reinforced by messages urging people to attend rallies. The sheer, supposedly inaccessible rock face of Samanti itself was dominated by a huge painted trident. This had started as a cross with a long stem that appeared overnight, marking a triumph for Christian nocturnal climbers—until a few weeks later when rival rock-climbers had added two outer prongs, turning it into the sign of the Hindu god Shiva. The gesture would have been witty if the mood had not been so ugly.

The modest rice-flour paintings inside Sompani's house in Guddara could not compete with this aggressive image blitz. I did not have the heart to tell her what I had seen at Samanti, where she traveled regularly in dreams and trances but had never been in the flesh. I was glad I had gone without her, as the site had been transformed into a battleground between world religions that took no account of local homegrown shamans.

Figure 12.2 Hindu graffiti near Samanti cliff
Symbols include Shiva's lingam, the "om" sign, the auspicious swastika of the sun, and the face of the god Jagannath.

By the afternoon all five women were sitting in a row against the wall of the darkened house, wrapped in cloths so white they glowed almost mauve: the three Rajingtal women together, with Lokami in a commanding position at the center, then Rajani to the right, and finally Sompani at the end. Such a gathering would never have been possible when the entire system was in full flow, since shamans from different villages did not work together and would rarely witness each other's trance.

They sang one invocation after another, uttering powerful words in a hub-bub of joking and play-acting as they explored variations between their songs and traditions. Gallanti did a funeral lament with compellingly authentic sobs, her face downcast and intonation perfect—then laughed as she paused to clear her throat. What was Gallanti feeling as she did this, and how would she weep if she was genuinely bereaved? It was Gallanti who sometimes expressed anxiety when others called on the actual names of sonums, and perhaps she was partly mourning her half-severed relations with her ılda family down below. Her performance was utterly realistic except for the absence of tears, and renewed my puzzle about how even genuine mourners can readily switch their lamentation on and off. It was pretense, but not deception. Rather, it was theater, every bit as accomplished as the emotional manipulations of Doloso, but with a kinder heart.

Shamans and laypeople sometimes do a pastiche of a ritual, either for a laugh or to demonstrate a verse, but this *opjong* was lengthy and realistic in a way I had not seen before. In this unprecedented situation, I was no longer sure of the boundaries between play-acting and reality, or of the threshold of safety. Nor perhaps were my friends. Sompani stretched out her legs and started to sing me the invocation from the lajab I had missed the previous day. After a few minutes she suddenly keeled over sideways and toppled unconscious to the floor. She had *opjong*-ed herself into a real trance.

For an instant the others seemed shocked, almost as if she had done something indecent. Then they crowded round to prop her up while Lokami directed them in unclenching her fingers and bending her elbows and knees. Sompani's ılda announced his arrival in a loud, unyielding song that was met by a simultaneous monologue from Lokami: "Our brother has come from far away . . . he traveled round our country long ago . . . he studied our shamans' words . . . 'tell me, show me,' he would say . . ." She added forcefully, "Don't be angry!"

Rajani was squatting close, facing Sompani with a sad-looking frown on her old, wise face. Taranti was a little further away, smiling with her lips pursed out in a way she had not done when she was a young girl, but as so many Sora women do as they grow older. Gallanti was silent and thoughtful throughout, while Lokami continued to talk about me in a forceful voice above the ılda's signature tune.

Monosi was impatient to meet Sompani's teacher Uda, who was also his own lineage-brother: "Tell him to come! The sahib wants to talk to him!"

"He knew him long ago," added Lokami. I had often spoken with the Sora dead, but only as a sideshow in another family's drama. This was the first time that I had been the main focus.

The ılda left Sompani's body. Lokami filled the silence with chat and laughter until Sompani's hands began to twitch up and down on her knees. Uda was coming. His high-pitched, whiny voice was unmistakable as he echoed Sompani's complaint: Why didn't you come to yesterday's lajab? He acknowledged that I had given a buffalo at the funeral of his brother Jakuben, but why not at his funeral?

My defense was well practiced: "Yes but . . ." (*u'u do* . . .), a standard opening when being criticized by the dead. "I was far away, I didn't hear I didn't know . . ."

Lokami chimed in dismissively: "He was busy." She started a long lament, even though she had hardly known Uda, with no tears at all and perfectly formed verse couplets: "You've gone and left us you've gone and departed, we won't see the features of your face we won't see the lines of your face . . ."

The mood became more distressing after Uda left and was succeeded by Ranatang. Here was the tall handsome man with muscular stomach whom I had seen at my very first weekly market, a tower of strength who met a sad death when he was beaten for supporting the extension of the road to Guddara. He sang no lament, but just wept, with real tears. Monosi too was crying and moved across to address him in a strangled voice. He no longer held back from doing this with any relative or important upholder of tradition, and was convinced each time that he was talking to the real person.

Ranatang departed. Sompani twitched and emerged from her trance very slowly, rubbing her eyes with the heel of her hand and looking round a little sheepishly. Lokami stood up, stretched, and moved back to sit among the Rajingtal women, leaving Sompani once again at the edge of the five.

I had not thought it was possible to trance without fasting in advance and feeding the dead with drinks of alin, but these women had taken this Christian cement house and turned it into a setting for trance even without these essentials. I was deeply implicated, for inviting them here and throwing them together with our shared histories—and for my identification with their beleaguered religion. The encounter made me reflect on friendship and illness. I had hung out with Uda and transcribed his rituals, but we had not been extremely close. I could brush off his complaints, but the closer the relationship the more stinging the reproaches, the more binding the demands, and the more they are translated into bodily sickness. Yet though I had been subjected to divinations and healing rituals, I had never fully believed that my illnesses were caused by a dead person; and when I had faced the sonums of some of my dearest friends, I had never completely let go of my researcher's curiosity.

The chatting and joking resumed, and picked up pace again. This time, it was easier to see that Rajani was also starting to work herself into a trance. She was no longer simply comparing notes, but competing. I recognized the familiar phrases of the Manengul tradition as she reached the brink of trance by calling on Pubic-Haired Sompa and the man from Gailung with swollen testicles (hoots of laughter from the Rajingtal women: "a'dibe, we don't list those ones!").

There was only one sonum I should expect, and I braced myself for an encounter with Doloso. Rajani's face and personality were so unlike Doloso's, yet it was uncanny to watch her bring his manner perfectly to life: grudging, domineering, perfectionist. His arrival too was addressed to me: "Why weren't you there by my side when I died? Why didn't you send a buffalo from England for my stone-planting? Don't you care enough about me?" And lastly, "Make sure Rajani puts my lamp back in my house every time she finishes a ritual—I still haven't given it to her!"

This was the special lamp that Doloso had grandiosely commissioned from a caste of brass-workers in town, instead of from the humble Sora potters in Allangda. When he got it, I remember hearing, he went into a wild, frantic trance. I was fascinated by Rajani's performance of Doloso's presence, and also by the split in how she did this. When in trance, she acted as a conduit for his psychologically realistic bullying of her own self, but when "outside" she was open about her resentment. "He resprouted through me, but he still won't pass on his lamp!" she exclaimed indignantly. "He blocked me and pushed me aside, he said, 'Your voice is no good.' He said, 'I bought the lamp, my daughter should inherit it!' After I do a ritual he demands a payment in grain and tells me to put the lamp back in his house. He does it in my dreams, and also in trance when he speaks though my mouth."

It would be hard to imagine a more literal internalization of Doloso's continuing control. When Rajani defied his strictures on her marriage above ground, she paid a heavy price with her scorched womb. Below ground, she married his ılda son, so he is both her teacher and her father-in-law. This is usual: Taranti and Lokami both married Gallanti's ılda sons. Yet here the resentment was striking. "He makes his wife keep the wall-painting in the house! After you die you should get your sonum-pots smashed and your wall-painting washed over!" This seemed a clear case of an attachment originating from the dead, linked to Doloso's refusal to accept the loss of Ambadi as his successor and her rejection of his entire world. And yet . . . was Rajani not somehow also caught up in a collusion of victimhood?

The mood became lighter again and less resentful as Gallanti and Lokami started the Rajingtal version of the song that closes the karja: *Dayirai dayirai kuṭṭorinal ban.* "Come back come back up to the hollow mortar." This was one of the first songs I had ever noticed in Ononti's repertoire during my early, uncomprehending visit in February 1975. Every performer—pyre-lighter, drummers, ancestor-women, and finally the shaman herself—had to be retrieved from the realm of death and brought back to the living, and later in Sogad I myself had been one of the ancestor-men subjected to the song while my return was sealed by drawing a protective sword along my arms and legs.

After this closing song Lokami and Gallanti moved on to the opening invocation, like a musician who casually plays the last movement of a piece, then goes back to the beginning of the whole work for a more serious engagement.

Gallanti's promise to call up Ononti might not be a joke after all. As they sat down to trance, backs to the wall, legs outstretched across the cement floor and singing in unison, I felt the pull of the familiar tune, like the opening lines of a great drama one has studied over and over again:

Teetering at the edge	dizzy at the brink
Don't glance back	don't vacillate . . .

I was puzzled to see Taranti sitting alongside them, the three of them wedged together waist to waist. Having finally renounced her sonums, could she be planning to take part? Taranti drew her knees up to her chest, as if unsure of making the leap, but finally she straightened them out and joined their rhythmic chanting. Their voices tailed off, fainter and fainter, until Lokami and Gallanti entered trance in perfect synchrony as their souls slipped through the floor and continued downward into the earth. Their bodies had locked rigid. Lokami's trance was so deep that it took three people to bend each of her knees and elbows.

I was left on my own to unclench Taranti, but her trance had somehow gone wrong. She kept her legs out for a moment, then withdrew them. Tears were streaming down her cheeks, and she was whimpering wordlessly, at one point sobbing so convulsively I feared she might choke. Gallanti and Lokami continued plunging down to the Underworld without her. They left Taranti uttering a passionate monologue: "Why couldn't I do it . . . I was terrified on the path, I came back I woke up . . . I gave up twelve years ago I've forgotten . . ."

"It's alright, never mind (*atsun*)," Rajani and Monosi soothed her as she sat wretched and silent beside her companions' vacated bodies.

The two shamans were now in full trance, each channeling separate ıldas who babbled, no longer in unison, as they listed other ıldas and ancient shamans of the Rajingtal tradition. Lokami's ılda confirmed that he would bring Ononti. He warned that she now drank only tea and coconut water (not a problem, since there was no alin in this Baptist area). "How come a Sahib has come, a Paik, a high-caste person (*raji*)?" They assured him that I was a Sora.

There was a long silence, broken by low chatter and laughter. Then a voice spoke through Gallanti's mouth: "Maianti! I've come to accompany my aunt. Who's the Sahib?"

Ononti was already speaking through Lokami's mouth. She knew who I was: "E Pirino E Pede, you came to my house, you heard my songs you heard my myths, you knew my soul (*puradan*) my heart (*je'e*) my face!"

"I've come to greet you (*olongben asen*)," I said. "Which sonum took you, what ate you what drank you (*iten jumamte iten gaamte*)?"

In the background Taranti started to gasp out couplets improvised to the lamentation tune: "E sister, E dead one, E mother, E friend, E woman!" It was if she was lamenting her own state through a lament for Ononti.

The hubbub of uncoordinated voices grew louder, with several simultaneous torrents of words from all the dead and living women. In death as in life, it was hard to get clear explanations from Ononti. She did not answer my question, but continued, "You listened to my songs, you gave me a cloth, we visited those villages together . . ." She spent a long time repeating how she had given up and her younger sisters were now doing her shaman's work. Her speech did not contain the information I sought, nor any hint of complaint or self-pity, but projected two main messages: friendship with me, and legitimation of Lokami as her successor. I suspect that the occasion also served to give voice to Lokami's own agenda, and that all that evening's trances allowed the shamans to express particular messages to me, to each other, and to themselves.

After Ononti departed, Lokami and Gallanti sang a unison song to an Earth-Sonum tune, dwelling on the imagery of cool water and green plants. "That's Ononti's Earth-Sonum husband singing," Rajani whispered to me. This seemed to me unusual, and indeed it was the beginning of an unusual answer.

Lokami and Gallanti came out of trance and rinsed their mouths with weak tea, an insipid substitute for alin. They launched into the post-trance song for cooked sacrificial meat even though we were not about to eat, then the song for breaking their fast, even though they had not fasted. They were setting Ononti's five-minute appearance within a full ritual framework, and the whole event lasted more than an hour.

With the ending of the trance the tone of chatter became less intense, interspersed with Lokami's characteristic giggle.

"How did Ononti die?" I asked.

"She took several days to die. She fell unconscious," said Lokami, "then she woke up and wept. 'What's happened to you what's happened to you?' I cried. 'A boy and a girl from the Underworld hugged me,' she said, 'you gave birth to us, they told me. They've grown up since I stopped trancing. Your outer-world (*bayira*) body is unclean your living body stinks, it's better to die. But don't go to any other sonums, stay with us, they told me.'"

Lokami gave me the outcome of her own performance, from which "she" had been absent: "I didn't hear I didn't see, but at the inquest she spoke through my mouth and said, 'Earth-Sonum took me.'"

"She said, 'That Earth-Sonum has cared for me looked after me (*mona-ingten kujiingten*) since I was a child,'" confirmed Taranti. "Those were the last words she spoke while she was alive." The words she used for "looking after" could refer ambiguously to both childhood nurturing and sexual embrace. I remembered all the talk in Sogad about male oboists like my friend Sundanto, with their puffed-out cheeks, who are raped to death (*gamelo*) by female Earth-Sonums. Ononti's above-ground husband in Sogad could not compete with all this, especially once she had lost the living children who might have consolidated that marriage.

"That Earth-Sonum was her real lover," confirmed Gallanti. "It's where her family used to cultivate. All their grain, turmeric, alin, came from that Earth. 'He washed the pollution (*juta*) off my body, he rubbed me with turmeric he rubbed me with oil, he didn't leave me outside, he led me straight into his multistory cement house,' she said."

I did not fully understand. A shaman is usually taken after death by her ildas. Ononti had become high-caste like them, but in an unusual way. She seemed to have undergone a particularly intense apotheosis, in an extreme idiom of Hindu purity: "Her Earth-Sonum husband said, 'Why did you leave me?' 'No, I haven't left you!' He told her, 'Don't drink alin don't drink aba!' So she drank only tea, like a high-caste person (*raji*). After her death they offered her alin but she flung it to the floor, so they cut down a coconut and gave her the juice to drink. They offered her a knee-length woven Sora skirt (*gatungkaben*), but she snatched it and threw it away (*tampidle sidete*). 'No, my Earth-husband will be angry,' she said. 'Bring a sari and tie it so it hangs right down to the floor (*arandana*)!'"

My time in Soraland was stamped from the very first days with the mystery of Ononti, and my interpretative triumph in the 1970s had been to understand what shamans like her were doing for their clients. But however much time I spent with Ononti or any other shaman, their own experience and fulfillments remained obscure. Even now, thirty years later and after her death, I could still work out the inscrutable Ononti not by talking to her directly, but only through the commentary of her pupils. Perhaps my command of the language has never been subtle enough. Ononti was an exceptionally archaic and idiosyncratic person: the center of a clique of strong, independent women, unable to recognize a photograph, intimidated in town and refusing to eat the food there, childless and never engaging with modernity, and unable rather than unwilling to explain her own words. Like the old lady in Peter Metcalf's Borneo fieldwork (2002), Ononti teased her researcher with obscurity till death and beyond. Lokami was much easier, and not only because she had called me uncle since she was a child. Her laughter is free, her gaze on the outside world is open, and her comments on rituals as we traveled together in Sarda country were lively and penetrating. I plan to go carefully over these recordings again, and hope this will equip me to ask Lokami all over again in more detail.

Just like any layperson's, Ononti's life-story was now becoming completed through postmortem dialogue with an entourage of supporters. Her destination was special, and I think this represented a special form of redemption. She had overcome the loss to her tradition of Maianti, Gallanti, and Taranti and transferred her skills to Lokami as a robust, reliable successor; and by finally joining her Earth-Sonum she had consummated a spiritual and erotic union that had beckoned to her since she was a child. This was a story of resolution and transcendence on a scale beyond the usual death of a shaman—and at a moment when the entire tradition was dangerously close to extinction.

Throughout the night, while the women comforted her, Taranti sometimes sang snatches of an incantation, sometimes wept wordlessly, sometimes crooned the verses of a lament. Outside in the cool before dawn, the first cocks began to crow, and we heard the sounds of water being fetched and firewood being axed. A Christian youth in trousers and shirt passed the house playing on a one-stringed gourd and singing an early-morning song that had survived conversion because it did not refer to sonums and used the melody that had also been adapted for Baptist hymns:

andreng soi dele	*andreng soi yirai*
kandrumdal yungen	*sanodal yungen*
andreng soi ele	*solo da maren*
andreng soi gule	*simtir da maren*
It's already happened	it's already come
The kandrum-leaf sun	the turmeric-leaf sun
The abandoned-clearing peacock	has already cried
The dew-drenched peacock	has already screamed

As if heeding his words, the five shamans stood up and stretched. It was almost first light, and the sharp stones were damp and cold underfoot as they set out in single file, all with dead straight backs, to wash at the well. I was reminded of a Christian hymn I had learned at school:

And in the dawn those angel faces smile
Which I have loved long since but lost awhile.

Figure 12.3 Taranti (*left*) the morning after her failed trance, with Lokami
They are drinking weak tea from metal cups.

Lokami seems to fear nothing, but I remembered Gallanti's anxiety ("Supposing we fall ill") and took the hint. When the women returned from washing I promised to buy five goats (expensive but pure) and to sacrifice one to the ilda husband of each of my dear friends. Not one of us suffered afterward, but the wife of the Baptist owner of the house we had borrowed was later beaten up in a dream by a Christian angel, much to Lokami's amusement.

After breakfast the five shamans sat in the shade of the veranda in a row, just as they had done indoors during the night. Taranti's eyes were clear and her husky voice was steady as she gave me the rawest insight I have ever heard into the pain of losing one's sonums: "When my sisters did their harvest ritual I didn't go I was afraid, I avoided their mouths their voices. When sonums turned up, my tears fell. But what can I do? How could I abandon them? It's not their fault, it's mine. They've cared for me since I was a child. My ilda husband says, 'Come,' but I'm ashamed because I've neglected him. I've got a baby girl down there, in a dream at harvesttime I picked her up I cradled her in my arms. They showed her to me before but now they don't any more because I've given up, they don't even tell me her name."

"You started along the path this time," Lokami said gently. "You might have gone into trance."

"Yes, I might have. I was astonished: 'Am I really starting to trance?' It was so sudden, after such a long time." Taranti turned to me: "This has never happened to me before, it's because of our conversation." She continued, "The sisters I'd abandoned long ago, the grandmothers whose path I'd seen, they led me along, they didn't scold me. 'Come back to us,' they said, 'it was beautiful with us,' they said. But I said no, I was afraid I was ashamed, I'd abandoned my ıldas, how could I go down that path again? My mouth seized up my teeth seized up. I even forgot my sonum grandmother's name—how could I call on her? I just wept."

"If you blub if you snivel, your words come out weak your words come out garbled," advised Gallanti. "You must say out loud all the things you did together, you must list all the things you miss." It was true. When Taranti disciplined her inarticulate feelings into a formal song, it did seem to ease her pain.

Taranti's problem was not quite the same as Gallanti's, who had a Baptist catechist as a son. "My children are Christian," said Taranti, "but they're not the ones—it's mostly my husband who blocks me. 'Don't go doing rituals, you're living among your in-laws,' he says. 'How can you utter their names in trance, it's not decent, their men will pick you up from the floor (runjangtamji), they'll unclench your legs and arms, they'll hug you and embrace you when you're in trance, they'll touch you in the joking and horseplay.'" But then she added, "He says, 'You're promiscuous because of your shaman activities,' but really he says that because he has sex with other women." This was not so much the new problem of Christian pressure as the old problem of a female shaman with a jealous earthly husband—and one with double standards. I could not imagine why someone married to Taranti would possibly want anybody else.

Taranti's torment was the culmination of a series of recent dreams. "After Ononti died I saw her down in the Underworld with Maianti, saying, 'Stitch some plates with us out of laia leaves.'" Laia is the special leaf used for funeral feasts, and this was a clearly coded instruction to revive her shamanic practice and extend it from healing rituals. "'I don't know how, I only know the healing path,' I said. 'Come with us on the funeral road,' they said. 'No, I've never been, only the path for healings—go away,' I said.

"I also had other dreams. An old woman from Sogad said, 'You're at fault.' Then my uncle (mamang) fondled my back and pulled off my skirt. I was very frightened to tell my husband about this. Then there were monkeys clawing and pinching my back. 'Help me!' I called to Gallanti. But she just gave a little inner laugh (kerjoi'loge mangle). Then I saw five policemen leading someone they'd arrested. 'It's you, you're guilty,' they said. 'We're going to judge you!'

'Alright, you can judge me, but I don't know the words,' I said. My mouth seized up my teeth seized up. 'Just use your own words,' they said."

These dreams seem to contain a consistent message. The policemen and the old woman say that Taranti is failing to do something she should do. The dead shamans Ononti and Maianti make this failure explicit: she should resume her work as a shaman and even expand her repertoire from healing to the funeral tradition. Dead shamans are like any other dead person: they are reluctant to let go of the living, and they still try to direct their lives from beyond the pyre.

Just as the ancestor-men supposedly list every lineage ancestor who is still active, so shamans invoke all their predecessors, in some funeral traditions going right back to Pubic-Haired Sompa. Whereas laypeople rely on shamans to embody and envoice their many predecessors, shamans do this for themselves. Rather than calling up a client's relatives over various branches of their lineage, shamans concentrate their continuity into the thinnest thread of teachers and successors. Each link is consolidated by marriage and childbirth in the Underworld and sustained through trances, dreams, wall-paintings, and consecrated pots. Yet the thread is fragile, like the guttering flame of the shaman's lamp with its homemade wick. The process of initiation is painful, and a shaman's personality may be very different from that of her teacher. Rajani's resentment at Doloso's unceasing bullying, even while she channels it against herself, makes the handover in Manengul seem insecure and tormented compared to the healthy tone of Lokami's relationship with her teacher Ononti.

Neither of Ononti's other pupils has managed to achieve Lokami's fulfillment. Gallanti is blocked by her Baptist son and lives uneasily as a half shaman, half-tending her scrappy wall-painting and sonum-pots in a tumbledown thatched hut. Taranti is blocked by a jealous animist husband who allows her no ritual space in their modern cement house. I suspect that the policemen in her dream could be domesticated into ilda sonums, if only her husband would allow this. In 2009 I appealed to him to be flexible. He was charming but adamant. Meanwhile, Taranti fluctuates between good health and high fevers in which she says she is ready to die and join her other husband down below.

The confident Lokami went successfully through the steps that for Taranti were blocked, graduating from healing shaman to funeral shaman. Her husband is soft and supportive, and her grown-up sons, although Catholic, are proud of her work, telling her, "Don't cut off your soul." One of them went to the Ideetal school, where he was taught "Tribal handicraft" by government teachers who could have had no inkling of what he knew from home as they sent him to the Punjab to cover the wall of a huge new building with his "folk-art."

"Yes, I went through all that," Lokami said later as we were discussing Taranti's period of madness. "It was after Maianti died and I'd had children. Gallanti's children were pressing her to give up. Then the ildas chose me, they led me to Gallanti's harvest ritual (abdur): 'You two sit together—not just for the healing path but also for the funeral road!' Gallanti taught me, she's my father's sister (awang) and I married her ilda son in the Underworld. Maianti also taught me from the Underworld: 'Because I've lost my seat I'll make you trance!' She was the one who made me run crazy."

Compared to any layperson's relationship with their own ancestors, a shaman experiences an exceptionally complex, multiple personhood in which the most fulfilling parts of her life may be when she is incarnating others, both the ancestors of her clients and her own ildas. Lokami is probably the last great Lanjia Sora shaman there will ever be, and we both know it. Every myth, every line she utters in her light, laughing manner is a treasure that I rush to record even as its context fades away in front of my eyes.

Lokami's clientele is diminishing, but she is still sought after and has frequent opportunities to trance. Taranti no longer has powerful and passionate sonum others as part-authors of her own complex self. I think this is what she misses, and what makes her living husband so jealous. That moment of failure must have revealed so much to her: she had not simply lost a skill but had become a different kind of person; a failing virtuoso in an obsolete form of projection and introjection, she was suffering not only from trance deprivation, but also from a simplified personhood; and these changes had become irreversible.

The shaman's vocation combines a piquant blend of terror and seductive allurement, in which fear is overcome to reach a bliss that seems almost erotic. "Come back to us, everything was beautiful, the path was beautiful," Taranti was urged. Yet this is the same path of leaps and precipices that so terrified Sompani with its snakes and centipedes. This beauty seems to be tinged with a sexuality, which never quite comes into focus. The founding myth of Pubic-Haired Sompa is about brother-sister incest, and shamans incestuously marry a category of cross-cousins in the Underworld whom one should not marry above ground. Female shamans are polyandrous, with one husband above ground and one below (a reversal of the polygyny that is available to men above ground); and some, like Ononti, abandon their living husband and find their entire fulfillment in the Underworld.

On one level Underworld marriage is a political relationship with a powerful ally; but it is also an intimate personal relationship in a Tribal society where most partnerships are made for love. Marriages in the Underworld seem more like high-caste arranged matches, and shamans' answers always become vague when I press them about the actual experience of marriage and family life in the Underworld. "I don't know what my ilda husband looks like, I don't actually see him when I go there," they say, "it's too dark."

The ildas are known mainly through their words, when they speak either aloud through the shaman or to her alone in dreams. I had noticed that shamans always said they had been informed by their ilda husbands that they had given birth in the Underworld, and were told the names and number of their children, but they never mentioned the experience of childbirth itself. So I recently asked Lokami, "Do you actually feel yourself giving birth in the Underworld?"

"No, we don't actually feel it," she answered. "We're just told about it."

There was something missing here about physical sensation. "Can you feel yourself breast-feeding?" I asked.

"No, we don't know when it's happening. And then our ildas tell us how fast our children are growing up."

It is not that bodily sensations are not experienced in the Underworld at all. Journeys down cliffs and along threads are described in terrifying sensory detail. But the more intimate the sensation, the harder it seems to be to experience it vividly. If intense sensual contacts are felt at all, they are fleeting and easily lost. Taranti's feeling of actually holding her baby is unusual and only serves to intensify her pain now that she is deprived of this joy.

What about the sexual act itself? This must be a crucial aspect of the shaman's experience, which I could not have tackled with Ononti.

"No," said Lokami, "we know it happens, but we don't actually feel it." I wondered whether this was because of embarrassment, since the ilda is a cross-cousin and a high-caste Hindu, both categories of person with whom a sexual relationship should be unthinkable. But even if there is a thrill of transgression, this seems to be only part of something much bigger. Faintness of light in that perpetually predawn "cock-crow land misty land" (*tartarim desa mormorin desa*), faintness of the sight of one's husband there, faintness of bodily senses, all the while against an insistence on exquisite beauty: sensual and spiritual fulfillment in the Underworld surpasses anything above ground,

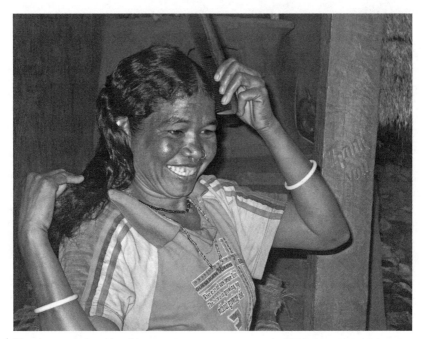

Figure 12.4 Lokami laughing, 2013

but it cannot be grasped and held. The narrative becomes hazy just at the point where I am pressing for clarity: the enchantment is always beyond capture, and the longing can never be assuaged.

"I've had four children above ground," Lokami told me, "but when I became a funeral shaman the sonums took my fourth. They said the baby's poo and wee would smell. I shan't have any more. I still bleed every month, but I don't get pregnant."

"Weren't you angry when your child died?" I asked, remembering Oransu's sharp reaction to his wife's death, and other similar reactive conversions.

But Lokami's response was quite different: "To tread the path to the Underworld I had to give something up—it's like a sacrificial substitute (*apanadu*). Otherwise who will sit for the dead who will call them? Isn't this what you saved me for when I was little?"

This was the first time that Lokami had mentioned my dream of the snake and the egg since that morning thirty years earlier. I had never forgotten it, but had not realized how significant it had been for her too.

EPILOGUE

· ·

SPIRITUAL ECOSYSTEMS AND
LOSS OF THEO-DIVERSITY

· ·

People like Ononti will never exist again. However, such people did exist, and they were my friends. It has been a privilege to share in that world that has now gone. It is also a responsibility, but of what sort? What duty do I owe the Sora, past, present, and future?

In 2013 I found a lone French traveler, who had somehow managed to reach the area, sitting on Jani of Rajingtal's cement veranda. He was disappointed. "The houses look like everywhere else," he complained. "And they're not wearing costumes." He soon left, not knowing that Jani is the person who keeps the village's supply of costumes in a tin trunk in his cement house for whenever a politician needs a "Tribal" dance ensemble.

That visitor was like a swimmer without a snorkel, unable to gaze beneath the opaque reflective surface of the sea at formations in the depths. The past was different not only in the spectacle of clothing and houses, but more profoundly in mentality, emotions, and relationships. But these are not completely separate. Anyone without a brick-and-cement house now counts officially as "homeless" and qualifies for the 52,000-rupee subsidy to build one. The consequence is a building frenzy and the mass destruction of all remaining traditional Sora houses. In 2009 I lay on the floor beside Lokami and her husband in the unique, characterful house they had built long ago with an *onsir* work party, drifting off to sleep at eight o'clock as the embers of the dying fire glowed on the dark red mud coating of her stone wall and lit up her faded white ilda painting while she recounted the myth of the brother and sister who survived the primal flood by floating in a gourd and went on to populate the world. A mere four years later a new brick house had risen on the site and was filled till midnight with neighbors sitting in a row on a wooden bed and laughing at a Hindi comedy on television, while a fluorescent light-tube illuminated a green pastel wash on the cement walls.

Anthropologists' data are partly given by our relationships, as are our interpretations, and another anthropologist might have produced a very different account. We are our own scientific instrument, with which we measure the world. The Sora would have been there even without me, yet I did arrive at a particular moment in the life span of each person I met, and their networks of relationships expanded to include me. I am Lokami's uncle (*dadi*, father's younger brother), and in relation to current cohorts of young Sora adults, I have aged over 40 years from *ubbang* (little brother, especially of that youth who thought he was 100) to *jojo* (grandfather or ancestor). Everything from the 1970s—those first months shadowing Ononti in Rajingtal, the isolation on Dumburu's clifftop in Ladde, and finally my relief at being included among the ancestor-men in Sogad—feels like a baseline, an original ethnographic present against which to gauge my experience of change. Some later chapters have been hard to write because I was struggling to understand the Baptists and to accept the change, but the early chapters, set in the 1970s, were hard for a different reason. I felt that I did understand those animists, but the emotional intensity of that early fieldwork tinged this experience with a magic, and this magic combined with the irrevocable pastness of the experience to give it a mythic aura.

The very nature of pastness can change, and I have lived through a transition from myth to history. I still believe in my interpretation of the theology and psychology of dialogues with the dead. But even though I was aware of the Sora's political situation, it took decades of change for me to make the link between this and their religion. Sora animists narrated past events either as myths (*kata*) that happened "long ago" (*purban*), as true secondhand stories (*juana*), or as events witnessed at first hand (*gijlai, amdanglai*, "I saw," "I heard"). They had no terminology of historicity as such, and gave their experience little if any "historical" interpretation. Whereas Christian discourse is sharp with terms of temporal change (*kadab*, "give up," *abyir-je*, "turn back your heart/soul," i.e., repent, or *banda-je*, "change your heart," i.e., convert), animists see customs and institutions as falling into abeyance by "fading" (*masuna*). Thus Taranti experienced the historical transition from animism to Christianity as a loss of access to her sonums, and Likini conceptualized her own historically momentous "heart-change" in terms of the familiar routine of a woman moving from one house to another on marriage.

One consequence of studying conversion after the event is that the sources themselves may already emphasize or exaggerate the element of rupture. How much would we fail to understand about Sora animism if our only sources were missionaries and pastors, or that Brahmin teacher (pages 15–16) watching the dance during my first visit, each repelled by their own imaginings of Sora primitivism?

In his account of Catholic conversion in the Philippines from the sixteenth to the eighteenth century, Vicente Rafael (1993) describes some Christian understandings that he sees as great innovations. Rafael's contextualization is careful, and the historical Philippines are not modern Soraland. Yet some of his remarks make one want to hear directly from the religion being supplanted: Christianity provided "a discourse that claimed to offer a way of domesticating death" (Rafael 1993: 194), and a "means of transcending death by conceiving loss itself from the perspective of an afterlife" (193); while a "highly formulaic" prayer "fills the listeners' minds with a catalogue of names that block other chains of associations," and "these prayers substitute for the threat of loss the monotonous comfort of names" (205–6).

This sounds very familiar, but not as part of Christianity. Ononti too "domesticated" death by bringing her clients' dead right back into domestic space during the annual karja and other house-entering rites; then, shifting those same dead people into a different mode, she too "transcended" death by naming their new babies. She too operated the entire system from "the perspective of an afterlife," as the dead described their grievances and satisfactions in their own words. Similarly, when I joined Mengalu's ancestor-men in their No-o-o chant, we too "block[ed] other chains of associations" with a "monotonous comfort of names."

Andrew Shryock (2013), commenting on Marshall Sahlins's book *What Kinship Is and Is Not* (2013), writes that Sahlins's mutuality of being "seems to gloss over all the conflict, abuse, abandonment, exploitation, and outright hatred that suffuse kinship ties." For Sahlins, the mutuality of kin "is experienced in their *joint* being. They live and die together, feel joy and misery together, *as one*" (2013: 272–73; italics in the original).

Shryock is pressing Sahlins to broaden his vision of intimate kinship relations beyond an idealized "amity" and to acknowledge the coexistence of affection and aggression. Sora dialogues with the dead go straight to the heart of this ambivalence, and accommodate both Sahlins's ideal and Shryock's criticism at the same time. "Feeling misery together as one" is exactly what happens, as love, anger, and pain are linked through a specific process of transgenerational transmission. Where Rafael points to a supposedly new Christian "shock of recognizing in another's death the possibility of one's own" (1993: 202), and Freud saw bereavement as a *psychological* trigger for melancholia, animist Sora went further by seeing the death of another as the *literal, mechanical* cause of one's own death. The move to Baptist beliefs has transformed this entire universe of causality and mutuality. Despite its total-

izing rhetoric, this transformation is still uneven, and the Sora Baptist movement seems like a religion still in the process of becoming—as that earlier
animist universe must have been, too, over millennia before I observed it.

Each time I return, I catch up with gossip: who has died, eloped, or been
cheated. But the stories after that first thirteen-year gap in 1992 were not
simply repetitions of old stories about the succession of generations, which in
animist cosmology were a narrative device of timelessness. Rather, they were
about the coming of roads, schools, and salaries. This was an opening for a
new way of being to make sense, and Christianity was there to provide that
way. The Sora people, the social and genetic descendants of my old friends,
continue to exist, but they have become quite different persons, relating to
each other (and to me) in a quite different way. If they knew enough English
to read my first book, *Dialogues with the Dead*, they might have difficulty understanding their ancestors and sympathizing with them, or even believing my
account, as when I sometimes shock young Baptists by using earthy language
that they cannot accept I learned from their own parents.

Is rupture a solution, or a new problem? In assessing the balance between
loss and liberation, how can I dispute a new generation's choice? What right
do I have to speak for the memory of these people's parents? I have photos,
tapes, and the stories of hundreds of lives, all annotated, indexed, and cross-
referenced. My archives contain narratives, intonations, laughter, irony, and
sobs, even songs that are no longer remembered by those who uttered them.
At the time this material had no other reason to be recorded than my own
need, but it is now developing an unforeseen need of its own. Earlier, Ononti
feared that her vocation and her sonums might be at an end, but she died
knowing that her tradition would be continued—for a while—by the bold
and confident Lokami.

The 1980s and 1990s were a rush in the flow of Sora history, and now
there is a lull on the Baptist front because the sonums have been decisively
defeated. On the way, that transitional period gave rise to some contradictory
emotional eddies, and in this hyperverbal culture I witnessed some revealing
moments of inarticulateness when people were literally lost for words. These
moments arose under new emotion scenarios, which were not matched by
currently available formats of expression. The people who experienced them
were caught by surprise, and for the moment no existing form of expressivity
could work.

Here, we can identify three kinds of scenario. Paranto's frustrated longing
to talk to his father reveals feelings that *can no longer* be articulated. On the
other hand, I have argued that the abruptness and hesitance of the Baptists'

farewell to their dead reveal that they have not worked out a comfortable procedure for pacing their forgetting. Here there are feelings that *cannot yet* be articulated. Finally, Taranti's sobbing as she realizes that she is no longer capable of entering trance expresses feelings that *may never be* articulated. This moment of history may pass without a corresponding expressive format ever coming into being: unlike the old clusters of memorial stones, which at least leave the archaeologist with a puzzle, this scenario will disappear without a trace.

Paranto and Taranti were formed by the old techniques of dialogue. Their ambiguous transitional scenarios of loss and expressiveness are unlikely to recur as the next generation settles down into a postconversion spiritual (if not political) lull. Taranti has no outlet for her mourning for the sundered relationship with her family in the Underworld. Today, more than ten years after that failed trance, she stays close to Lokami and talks gently and humorously about her life, but she has no framework for developing her story in wider terms. Paranto, too, has not found a way through his distress. Whenever we are together he reminisces about his father, and I try to talk him out of his melancholy, but I sense he wants something from me that I cannot give him. One day they or their descendants may use my notes to reconstruct something of where they came from, and this will be at least some reparation for their tears at those extraordinary moments.

Someone who continues to evolve is Monosi, the subtle visionary who suffers from the tension of a progressive prophet who also feels a nostalgia—not only behind his time but also ahead of it, as he has been all his life. While other Baptists rush headlong to a new world, it is as if he is mourning a disappearing way of life on behalf of his entire society. He turns this impulse into projects—his rousing speeches, an album of photos and texts we put together, our plans for a future dictionary. Monosi had been an informant for missionaries and linguists long before I met him. So he was open in advance to the possibility of friendship with me, even if not at first to my agenda. An anthropologist may not be so different from a missionary after all, since we both draw out personal narratives that go beyond those that people are used to articulating, show them new perspectives, and change their lives. Monosi's youthful vision of a Christian future has accelerated beyond his control and rendered his past irretrievable. His nostalgia is for a way of life that as a reformist he has done so much to abolish. Having worked in his youth for this new social order, he uses his community's anthropologist to help him salvage and reconstruct that past. In sharing his nostalgia, and even feeding it, my 1975 baseline is caught up with his in a shared mythicization. Indeed, I may stimulate the revival or development of further myths that reach back beyond my arrival to his childhood.

Monosi expects me to create something monumental out of my decades of note-taking and tape-recording. He has come to feel that whatever it is I have been pursuing all these years is not just a way of being and doing, but something that can be packaged and transmitted. He now calls this "culture" (using the newly known Oriya word *sanskruti*) and is concerned to archive all possible information about the old ways, in order to provide documentation for future generations who are only just becoming interested. "All our kittungs, all our myths, all our rituals—don't let them be lost! You're the person who has gone deepest," he says through sobs. In an extraordinary blend of contradictory religious purposes, he says, "Truly, God sent you to preserve our ancestors' customs!" It seems theological salvation is not incompatible with salvage ethnography.

Monosi dreams that monkeys are chasing him ever upward until he is flying. Monkeys are considered long-lived because white-haired, and often feature in the dreams of old people approaching death. But Monosi experiences these dreams with elation. He alternates between robustness and frailty, and for more than a decade I have been providing the medication that keeps him alive. Young people cannot utter the names of their elders, but only refer to them in kinship terms. So when James phoned in 2007 on his new cell phone to say, "My grandfather (*jojo*) is dying," I took the next plane to India. I arrived to find Monosi healthy: James had been talking about Monosi's brother. But it was a reminder that we had to do more, and also that we had to train younger people to continue this work after us.

But how? There was nothing to read in Sora except the Bible and Christian leaflets, timetables, and wedding invitations. Around 2000, even before Monosi's rehabilitation in the church, young Baptists were becoming less contemptuous of their pre-Christian forebears, and started to ask me for photos of their parents: "He died when I was a child, I don't know what he looked like . . ." "Have you got a picture of my mother . . . ?" I saw this as an opportunity and decided to compile an album of photos from the 1970s. But I would write very long captions. If young Sora wanted to know about the people in the photos, they would have to read accounts of their lives, descriptions of their rituals, and transcriptions of their songs.

With help from our friend Bala in the State Bank we obtained a birth certificate and the necessary police clearance so that Monosi could acquire a passport, and spent the summer of 2010 in Cambridge going through my archive.

কেন্দ্রীয় সমিতি
সদৌ অসম চাওৱা সমাজ
CENTRAL OFFICE
ALL ASSAM SAWRA SAMAJ
[এটি অৰাজনৈতিক সামাজিক সাংস্কৃতিক সংগঠন]
(A NON POLITICAL SOCIO - CULTURAL ORGANISATION)
স্থাপিত - ৩-১১-৭৯ ESTD. 3-11-79

Ref No. A.A.S|১০|09   Date. 10|12|09

To,

    MR. MONISHI RAIKA
    Manikpur

Sub : Tour of All Assam Sawra Samaj People to Orissa and Andhra Pradesh.

Respected Sir,

In combination of Hindu and Cristian brothers and sisters All Assam Sawra Samaj (A Non-political Socio-cultural Organization) which was established on 3rd November, 1979 wishes you 'A very coming New Year 2010".

It would not require to explain briefly that before 150 years ago our Sora Community people left their own motherland, Ganjam, Gajapati, Koraput, Raigoda etc living places and are now an inhabitant of Assam for a long period of time. With this 150 years being an inhabitant of Assam the Sora people are aside of their own Sora Language, Culture, Traditional, system, Entertainment programme like dances, Songs etc. Therefore, now it has become very important for us to go to Orissa and Andhra Pradesh inorder to collect the proper bio-data which are related to our own Language, culture, Traditional System, entertainment programme. So, by regarding this matter we have selected a 15 members delegate for fifteen days to this tour from in 10th Feb to 25th Feb 2010. In this tour we would like to visit the Sora peoples   (i) Culture Museum (ii) The Holy Places (iii) The Historical Places (iv) To visit ST/ SC/ Horizan Research and Training centre of Govt. of Orissa. (v) To meet some important persons of Sora Community for discussion. (vi) To organized seminar and Meeting among our own community inorder to collect our musical instruments, dresses, ornaments etc.

So, we request you to think us as your own brothers and kindly arranged all the requirements that will be necessary for us for the tour like Meeting some important person's, officers, Fooding, lodging etc.

By getting this letter we aspect to get a kind reply from you.

Thanking You,

With regards

sd/-   (signature)
(Dinanath Sawra)   (Jayanta Sawra)
President   All Assam   Gen. Secretary
                Central Committee
AII Assam Sawra Samaj Central Committee

Note: Tour start from Assam on 10th Feb 2010 and Back from Orissa on 22nd Feb 2010

Letter from Assam

Leaders of the migrant Sora community in Assam plan an official visit to the motherland. A similar letter was addressed to the author but did not reach him.

We spent the next summer in Visakhapatnam formatting and correcting the text, and produced a volume (Vitebsky and Raika 2011) entitled:

JUJUNJI DO YUYUNJI A BANUDDIN
SORA JATTIN A SANSKRUTI
Sora beran batte
ABOI TENUB

Kambolan idolleji do sapjaleji
Pirino Saibo do Monosi Raika

THE WISDOM OF OUR GRANDFATHERS AND GRANDMOTHERS
THE CULTURE OF THE SORA PEOPLE
in Sora
PART 1

Piers Vitebsky and Monosi Raika

Pomolleji idolmaranji / Printed by the authors
Visampatana, Agosto 2011 / Visakhapatnam, August 2011

This was the first book ever written in Sora about themselves rather than about ancient priests of a different race on another continent. We distributed a hundred copies to selected recipients, and ever since then groups of young people have sat on verandas throughout Soraland reading it aloud. We have calculated that if we had the funding the demand could soak up another 50,000 copies. The government's head of linguistic policy would like to see this work adapted into other scripts for use in schools, though no other script has yet been adapted to take Sora to this level. Our next goal is to revive an unfinished dictionary begun by American linguists in the 1960s (Donegan and Stampe 2004, itself including material supplied by both of us forty years ago), to blend in our own data and train young Sora to collect field material and input it coherently so as to build up a multilayered lexicon, digitally and on paper, which will be owned by Sora themselves as well as used by comparative linguists. This will require money and energy, and also the training of the young people who are urging us to do this before we become too old to give them this legacy.

By the 1990s there was a growing awareness of the worldwide threat of the extinction of plants, animals, and ecosystems. The United Nations Convention on Biological Diversity (United Nations 1992) was closely followed by the International Union for Conservation of Nature's Red List of Threatened Species (www.iucnredlist.org), which established a grading of endangerment

Monosi explains our book of old photos and texts to a young audience, Guddara
2015

(Moseley 2012: 2). This approach was soon extended to the idea of endangered languages (UNESCO 2010). Though languages are not simple entities, and their boundaries are debatable, linguists reckon that there are only 6,000 languages surviving in the world today, and that half of these are endangered (Evans 2009; Moseley 2012). The greatest threat to a minority language worldwide is schooling in a dominant language. Whatever the benefits of residential schools, they are also a notorious medium of alienation, separating children not only from their parents but also from their cultural and linguistic milieu. However many people speak a language now, if it is not spoken by the children and carried forward into their adult life it can become extinct in a generation. Sora may be reaching this point.

At stake are not only languages themselves but "entire worldviews, religious beliefs, creation myths, observations about life, technologies for how to domesticate animals and cultivate plants, histories of migration and settlement . . ." (Harrison 2007: 159). Daniel Nettle and Suzanne Romaine (2000: publisher's blurb) argue that "the extinction of languages is part of the larger picture of near-total collapse of the worldwide ecosystem . . . and that the causes of language death, like that of ecological destruction, lie at the intersection of ecology and politics." My research points to a further endangerment, that of untold thousands of religions that have formed most of human history (Rappaport 1999) for hundreds of thousands of years. Almost all of these religions (themselves worldviews in flux rather than static or bounded entities) have been unwritten and undocumented, and as they disappear they leave little trace. The analogy with endangered species is not complete, and that with languages is closer, since religions can rapidly transform themselves, split, amalgamate, and make compromises in ways that species cannot. But my experience with the Sora suggests that each religious form may be tightly adapted to local social and historical situations, which are like ecological niches. Until the missionary hospital, this was a society totally without medication. In earlier times there may have been more healing plants than I saw, but these were probably worn rather than ingested. The Sora lived and reproduced themselves in a situation of extreme survival, in which a high mortality rate reflected a process of extreme natural selection and extreme antibody production, experienced culturally as an extreme level of sonum activity. By the 1970s, the government was following the missionaries in providing medicine locally, but there were many obstacles to its availability, not least embezzlement by medical personnel (and there was also one large scandal in the mission hospital), and I still had to watch helplessly as people of all ages dropped dead around me. Yet the Sora did not have a concept of a lack of medical facilities; rather, their attention was focused on a different understanding of survival and flourishing, based on familial relationships. Today the person has become more individual and less relational, and this has combined with the greater availability of medicine to narrow the chains of reasoning about misfortune.

If we compare Sora animist religion to the Baptist movement, Catholicism, orthodox Hinduisms, psychoanalysis, political and economic ideologies, even other animisms and indigenous religions around the world, in every case it stands out as distinctive. All the same, making animistic inferences about the world is one of the most basic human intuitions, perhaps the primal root from which all subsequent religions (and science?) have emerged in recent millennia as the so-called world religions have supplanted their own ancestral origins in a theological parricide. In Soraland today, the reduction of sonum diversity to one God goes hand in hand with the reduction of the botanical diversity of shifting cultivation to cashew plantations, just as on the global scale there is a parallel between economies based on single commodities like plantations or mines, the single financial market and globalized banking sys-

SAVARAS.

Early photo of Sora

From Thurston 1909, facing p. 315. Apparently photographed in the plains, but no caption or information. The clothing resembles that in the photos in Fawcett 1888, which are more interesting but too poor to reproduce. I saw (and wore) identical clothing in the 1970s, though everyone's expressions were livelier. No such sight can be seen anywhere today.

tem, and religious fundamentalisms—a parallel between monocropping and monotheism as a non-pluralist, totalizing approach to the world.

This parallel makes it more pressing than ever to explore the largely unknown diversity of human religious thinking, most of it physically and philosophically difficult to access, ignored by theologians, and left to the small, dedicated, but theologically untrained profession of anthropology. At moments, Sora thought parallels psychoanalytic attachment theory, and this parallel seemed sufficient at the time to round off my first book, *Dialogues with the Dead*. However, I now see that Sora animism is not simply a restatement of this psychological insight in another idiom, but spins off into quite other notions of logic, time, relationality, and purpose. Diversity of forms is essential for flexibility and survival in every domain. The Sora language can perhaps be saved—so long as it can be updated and developed for contemporary use. It is harder to save endangered gods and spirits, and the extinction of Sora animism will be one more step in a global loss of theo-diversity. In the twenty-first century, when space exploration may well present us with extraterrestrial religions, we shall need a broader, more pluralistic repertoire of responses than ever before. Animistic traditions constitute an archive of possibilities, a spiritual and intellectual gene bank to fall back on as we become trapped inside the world's few dominant religions and ideologies of the moment.

· · · ·

Ñen Monosi Pirinon apsele kan a kanenken sabjalai, ardingan a sarangan bate karjan a takudle adnang (I, Monosi composed this song for Piers, to the tune of the return from the Underworld at the end of the karja):

ganugudadam Pirino kakung la	*tanımyımdam Pirino buñang la*
Baratto a desa ban dayirai dayirai	*Indian a desa ban dayirai dayirai*
Indian a desa Orissa lingan	*Indian a desa a tangnod lingan*
Rayadaga a jila lingan la	*Gajapati a jila lingan la*
Gunupur a maneng a palli lingan	*Parlakimidi a palli lingan*
Puttasing tana lingan la	*Serung tana lingan la*
respected brother Pirino	dear brother Pirino
come back come back to Bharat	come back come back to India
in India's Orissa	in India's space
in Rayagada district, la	in Gajapati district, la
in Gunupur borough	in Parlakimidi borough
in Puttasing police station zone, la	in Serung police station zone, la

kani a barun a maneng lingan la
kani a Sora si'ing banji la
kani a Sora birindanji amang
arukkunaba kakung yirai la

kani a tulab onsing lingan la
kani a Sora gorjang banji la
kani a Sora idaienji amang
amandanaba kakung yirai la

in the direction of this hill, la
to these Sora houses, la
among these Sora lineages
come let's gather, brother, la

in this forest baby-hut, la
to these Sora villages, la
among these Sora ancestors
come let's assemble, brother, la

amen arusing yiraien den la
juju kataber a idoleten
Inggland desa nam maggad dongamte
gugudam desanam satung dongamte

amen arusing iylaien den la
yuyu juaber a idoleten
London desa nam mangsar dongamte
suradam desanam madai dongamte

after you've come home, la
you who wrote our grandfathers'
    myths
don't delay in your country England
don't disappear in your great country

after you've gone home, la
you who wrote our grandmothers'
    legends
don't linger in your country London
don't vanish in your fine country

omdale maiñ yirai buñang la
urungle maiñ la yirai buñang la
kukuren juri nam maiñ ate

sɪddale maiñ yirai buñang la
tongtongle maiñ la yirai buñang la
dumulen juri nam maiñ ate

come, brother, whether leaving her, la

come, brother, whether leading her, la

your kukur-dove partner

come, brother, whether
    abandoning her, la

come, brother, whether escorting
    her, la

your turtle-dove partner

· · · ·

Just as this book was going to press my seemingly indestructible friend Monosi, too frail to endure dialysis, finally succumbed to his years of low red blood cell production and failing kidneys. His son Joyanto (offspring of his marriage to Likini, who survives him) buried him between his parents in his old village of Ongara. I intend to continue to work with younger Sora to fulfil Monosi's dream—and their request—of preparing the texts we worked on together for publication and creating a Sora dictionary in a format that will be useful for Sora speakers as well as for linguists.

··································

ACKNOWLEDGMENTS

··································

My deep indebtedness to innumerable Sora stands out on every page, and it would be impossible to name them all here. The remarkable and farsighted Monosi has now joined the many people I knew forty years ago who have since died. Others are still alive and remain my close companions today, especially Paranto, the son of my first Sora friend, Inama; and Lokami and the other shamanesses in chapter 12. Each of these has made a complicated journey through the historical transition that this book explores, and they have allowed me to follow their personal and social lives through that journey. However, none of them is in a position to understand what a book of this sort really is.

It is a wonder of human generosity that thousands of people could welcome a lone stranger from far away to eat and sleep in the midst of their families. I came to understand how their lives were rooted in kinship, and this has helped me to reflect on my own family life. I am grateful to my late parents, Bernard and Phyllis, for giving me an enchanting, musical childhood and supporting me to enter a profession that they did not fully understand; to my children, Patrick and Catherine, who taught me what it is to be a parent in a way I had not fully grasped when I first watched the Sora's concern about their babies' vulnerability; and to my wife, Sally, *kukuren juri ñen dumulen juri ñen* (my kukur-dove partner my turtle-dove partner), for her openness to other ways of life, her insights from psychotherapy, and her patience in looking after our children during my many absences.

I have benefited for the rest of my career from early training in how to analyze texts in other languages by the late Johnny Usher, a meticulous and inspired London schoolteacher of Greek and Latin. In subsequently becoming an anthropologist, I have been fortunate in my association with many fine practitioners. I remain particularly grateful to Roberte Hamayon, Olivier Herrenschmidt, Caroline Humphrey, Ron Inden, Alan Macfarlane, and Marilyn Strathern for believing in me during those first years in the 1970s. My 1982 PhD thesis was published as a monograph called *Dialogues with the Dead* (1993). Much of that book was taken up with a detailed account of two exemplary rituals from 1979, Jamano's funeral and Rondang's healing trance, which reappear in chapter 4 of the present book with less microanalysis but more attention to their historical and political implications. In an otherwise positive review (1995) of that first book, Gananath Obeyesekere urged me to stand further outside the Sora's inner world, and also asked why young Sora were turning away from their parents' religion if it was as fulfilling as I had claimed. This was a reminder that any interpretation is never final. Nor is any field-work. In the 1990s (while employed by the University of Cambridge to study indigenous people in the Siberian Arctic) I started to go back to the Sora in my spare time, and was overwhelmed by the changes that were taking place. This book is the story of those changes. It is a story that had to be told anyway, but it is also a response to Obeyesekere's challenge.

The fascination of the animist Sora culture can never be exhausted, and it would have been tempting to continue simply lecturing and writing about the old days. I am grateful for some invitations that pushed me to face this huge transformation head-on: the Marett Memorial Lecture at Oxford University in 2000, and the Royal Anthropological Institute's Henry Myers Lecture at the conference of the European Association of Social Anthropologists in 2006 (Vitebsky 2008); a 2006 conference organized in Oslo by Signe Howell and the late Aud Talle on long-term fieldwork (Vitebsky 2012); and presentations at the retirement conferences of Stephan Feuchtwang in 2011 and Caroline Humphrey in 2012.

A lifetime of research depends on many funders. Among others, I am es-pecially grateful to Girton College, Cambridge, for a research fellowship long ago, and most recently to the British Academy small research grants scheme and to budgets associated with my current professorships at the Arctic univer-sities of Tromsø in Norway and Yakutsk in Siberia.

I should like to thank the following people for taking the time to read part or all of the present manuscript, each with their own very different per-spective: Peter Berger, Uday Chandra, John Dunn, Stephan Feuchtwang, Tim Jenkins, Bruce Kapferer, Bengt Karlsson, Julius Lipner, Joel Robbins, James Scott, Marilyn Strathern, Nandini Sundar, Anna Tsing, Peter van der Veer, and especially Anastasia Piliavsky for a line-by-line critique of several chapters. This is a nonstandard ethnography, and the encouragement of these schol-ars gave me reassurance to pursue it to completion. I have learned from their comments and have followed some of their suggestions, if not all. Any short-comings that remain are entirely my responsibility.

Outside the world of anthropology, I especially appreciate the openness of the retired Canadian Baptist missionaries David and Ruby Hayward, who, while aware of the radical differences between us, invited me to stay in their home in Vancouver. David Stampe and Patricia Donegan have been ever keen to discuss the nuances of Sora and Austroasiatic linguistics. In India I have received numerous acts of kindness over forty years from all sorts of people, friends and strangers, ranging from government officers to tea-shop workers. I am especially grateful to Direndra Prasad Pattanayak and Bhupinder Singh for important support in the early days, and to Bala Patnaik for continuing essential help at the local level.

Thanks too to my editors at Chicago, David Brent and Priya Nelson, for their enthusiastic support, to Jane Brooks, Frances Brown, Niamh O'Mahony, and Marian Rogers for proofreading, to Ian Bolton and Adrian Newman for formatting photos, and to Phil Stickler for redrawing my handwritten maps and diagrams. I am also grateful to the Scott Polar Research Institute in the University of Cambridge for providing me with a secure academic base over the past thirty years; and to Girton College and to Erhan and Semra's Turkish beach hut for a quiet hideout during periods of intensive writing.

GLOSSARY OF ETHNIC GROUPS AND COMMUNITIES

animist
: Someone who perceives a spiritual power or presence in the landscape or environment (see the online bibliographic essay). Not a formal identity.

Baptist
: A kind of Christian who emphasizes baptism with water to wash away sin.

Brahmin
: Traditionally, Hindu ritual specialists, though now engaged in a range of (often elite) occupations and generally encountered by Sora as teachers and government officials. Conventionally considered the highest, most ritually pure caste.

Canadian
: White Baptist missionaries from a distant country called Canada (*Kanada-desa*).

caste
: A hereditary grouping (*jati*) of Hindu society, traditionally often linked to a specific occupation. An English term, not used by Sora.

Catholic
: Christians who are less strict than Baptists; their missionaries and priests are usually Indians from Kerala.

Hindu
: A follower of India's majority religion, which has many different styles and cults. Animist Sora may call themselves "Hindu" in opposition to "Christian."

jati
: General Indian term for caste, tribe, race, community, or species; also used in Sora.

Jew
: The biblical *jati* from a distant country where Jisu lived long ago. Sora are generally not aware that Jews still exist today.

Komati
: A Telugu-speaking caste of traders and merchants.

Kond
: A neighboring tribe who practice either animism or Christianity and speak a Dravidian language; until recently, often thought of by Sora as human sacrificers and were-leopards.

Kshatriya
: India's warrior-aristocracy, in this area today generally involved in military, police, administrative, and clerical occupations. Also includes rajas (kings). Historically, Sora have had more (often negative) contact with Kshatriyas than with Brahmins. Not a term used by Sora.

Oriya

> The majority people of the state of Orissa (now Odisha), comprising many different castes and speaking Oriya (Odia), a language of the Aryan (Indo-European) family.

Paik

> An Oriya Kshatriya caste who were in royal military service and are still prominent enforcers in this area.

Pano

> Also called Pan, Dom, or Domb. One of the lowest castes in eastern India, now Christianized, who live in an antagonistic relationship with the Sora by trading and moneylending.

Sora

> Also sometimes spelled Saora, Soura, Sabara, Savara, etc. A tribe who speak an Austroasiatic language of the South Munda group, and who are divided into several subgroups, like Sarda Sora and Jurai Sora. This book concerns the Lanjia Sora, the most isolated, animistic group.

Telugu

> The majority people of the state of Andhra Pradesh, comprising many different castes and speaking Telugu, a Dravidian language.

Tribe/Tribal

> Numerous supposedly aboriginal (*adivasi*) peoples, many of them, including the Sora, marginal and living in remote areas (see the online bibliographic essay).

REFERENCES

Anderson, Gregory, and David Harrison. 2008. "Sora." In *The Munda Languages*, edited by Gregory Anderson, 299–380. London: Routledge.

Babb, Lawrence A. 1975. *The Divine Hierarchy: Popular Hinduism in Central India*. New York: Columbia University Press.

Bailey, F. G. 1960. *Tribe, Caste, and Nation*. Manchester: Manchester University Press.

Barua, Ankur. 2014. "Interreligious Dialogue, Comparative Theology, and the Alterity of Hindu Thought." *Studies in World Christianity* 20 (3): 215–37.

Bates, Crispin, and Alpa Shah, eds. 2014. *Savage Attack: Tribal Insurgency in India*. New Delhi: Social Science Press.

Benjamin, Geoffrey. 1967. "Temiar Religion." PhD diss., University of Cambridge.

Berger, Peter. 2015. *Feeding, Sharing, and Devouring: Ritual and Society in Highland Orissa, India*. Berlin: de Gruyter.

Biligiri, Hemmige Shriniwasarangachar. 1965. "The Sora Verb: A Restricted Study." *Lingua* 15: 231–50.

Boal, Barbara M. 1982. *The Konds: Human Sacrifice and Religious Change*. Warminster: Aris & Phillips.

Bowlby, John. 1980. *Attachment and Loss: Loss, Sadness, and Depression*. London: Hogarth Press.

Brightman, Marc, Vanessa Elisa Grotti, and Olga Ulturgasheva. 2014. *Animism in Rainforest and Tundra: Personhood, Animals, Plants, and Things in Contemporary Amazonia and Siberia*. Oxford: Berghahn Books.

Brown, Peter. 1995. *Authority and the Sacred: Aspects of the Christianisation of the Roman World*. Cambridge: Cambridge University Press.

———. 2015. *The Ransom of the Soul: Afterlife and Wealth in Early Western Christianity*. Cambridge, MA: Harvard University Press.

Burke, Peter. 1978. *Popular Culture in Early Modern Europe*. London: Temple Smith.

Campbell, John. 1864. *A Personal Narrative of Thirteen Years Service amongst the Wild Tribes of Khondistan for the Suppression of Human Sacrifice*. London: Hurst and Blackett.

Cannell, Fenella, ed. 2006. *The Anthropology of Christianity*. Durham, NC: Duke University Press.

Carmichael, David Freemantle. 1869. *A Manual of the District of Vizagapatam, in the Presidency of Madras*. Madras: Asylum Press.

Carrin, Marine. 1986. *La fleur et l'os: Symbolisme et rituel chez les Santal*. Cahiers de l'Homme 26. Paris: EHESS.

———. 2008. "Santal Religious Discourse and the Assertion of Adivasi Identity." In *Contemporary Society: Identity, Intervention, and Ideology in Tribal India and Beyond*, edited by Deepak Kumar Behera and Georg Pfeffer, 7: 23–37. Delhi: Concept Publishing.

———. 2014. "The Santal as an Intellectual." In *The Politics of Ethnicity in India, Nepal, and China*, edited by Marine Carrin, Pralay Kanungo, and Gérard Toffin, 77–99. Delhi: Primus Books.

Carrin Tambs-Lyche, Marine. 2007. "The Impact of Cultural Diversity and Globalization in Developing a Santal Peer Culture in Middle India." EMIGRA Working Papers 46. Accessed 29 July 2015. www.emigra.org.es.

Carstairs, G. Morris. 1958. *The Twice-Born: A Study of a Community of High-Caste Hindus.* Bloomington: Indiana University Press.

Chandra, Uday. 2015. "Towards Adivasi Studies: New Perspectives on 'Tribal' Margins of Modern India." *Studies in History* 31 (1): 122–27.

Chua, Liana. 2012. *The Christianity of Culture: Conversion, Ethnic Citizenship, and the Matter of Religion in Malaysian Borneo.* New York: Palgrave Macmillan.

Comaroff, John L., and Jean Comaroff. 1991. *Of Revelation and Revolution: Christianity, Colonialism, and Consciousness in South Africa.* 2nd ed. Vol. 1. Chicago: University of Chicago Press.

———. 1997. *Of Revelation and Revolution: The Dialectics of Modernity on a South African Frontier.* 2nd ed. Vol. 2. Chicago: University of Chicago Press.

Condominas, Georges. 1965. *L'exotique est quotidien: Sar Luk, Viet-Nam central.* Paris: Plon.

———. 1994. *We Have Eaten the Forest: The Story of a Montagnard Village in the Central Highlands of Vietnam.* New York: Kodansha International.

Connerton, Paul. 2009. *How Modernity Forgets.* Cambridge: Cambridge University Press.

Crapanzano, Vincent. 1980. *Tuhami, Portrait of a Moroccan.* Chicago: University of Chicago Press.

Descola, Philippe. 2013. *Beyond Nature and Culture.* Translated by Janet Lloyd. Chicago: University of Chicago Press.

Detienne, Marcel. 2008. *Comparing the Incomparable.* Translated by Janet Lloyd. Stanford, CA: Stanford University Press.

Donegan, Patricia, and David Stampe. 2004. [Untitled Sora-English dictionary.] http://www.ling.hawaii.edu/austroasiatic/AA/Munda/Dictionaries/Sora.

Dumont, Louis. 1962. "Correspondence: 'Tribe' and 'Caste' in India." *Contributions to Indian Sociology* 6: 120–22.

———. 1980. *Homo Hierarchicus: The Caste System and Its Implications.* Translated by M. Sainsbury, Louis Dumont, and B. Gulati. Chicago: University of Chicago Press.

Dumont, Louis, and David Pocock. 1959. "Possession and Priesthood." *Contributions to Indian Sociology* 3: 55–74.

Dunn, John Mountfort. 1979. *Western Political Theory in the Face of the Future.* Cambridge: Cambridge University Press.

Eliade, Mircea. 1964. *Shamanism: Archaic Techniques of Ecstasy.* Translated by W. R. Trask. New York: Pantheon.

Elwin, Verrier. 1945. "Saora Fituris." *Man in India* 25 (4): 254–57.

———. 1947. *The Muria and Their Ghotul.* Bombay: Oxford University Press.

———. 1955. *The Religion of an Indian Tribe.* Bombay: Oxford University Press.

————. 1964. *The Tribal World of Verrier Elwin: An Autobiography.* Bombay: Oxford University Press.

Eschmann, Anncharlott, Hermann Kulke, and Gaya Charan Tripathi. 1978. *The Cult of Jagannath and the Regional Tradition of Orissa.* Delhi: Manohar.

Evans, Nicholas. 2009. *Dying Words: Endangered Languages and What They Have to Tell Us.* Oxford: Wiley-Blackwell.

Favret-Saada, Jeanne. 1980. *Deadly Words: Witchcraft in the Bocage.* Cambridge: Cambridge University Press.

Fawcett, Frederick. 1888. "On the Saoras (or Savaras), an Aboriginal Hill People of the Eastern Ghats of the Madras Presidency." *Journal of the Anthropological Society of Bombay* 1: 206–72.

Fenichel, Otto. 1946. *The Psychoanalytic Theory of Neurosis.* London: Routledge & Kegan Paul.

Francis, W. 1907. *Vizagapatam District Gazetteer.* Madras: Government Press.

Frazer, Sir James George. 2000. *The Golden Bough: A Study in Magic and Religion.* Pt. 5, *Spirits of the Corn and of the Wild.* London: Macmillan.

Freud, Anna. 1936. *The Ego and the Mechanisms of Defence.* London: Hogarth Press.

Freud, Sigmund. 1957 [1917]. "Mourning and Melancholia." In *The Standard Edition of the Complete Psychological Works of Sigmund Freud,* translated by James Strachey, 14: 239–58. London: Hogarth Press.

Friend-Pereira, J. E. 1904. "Totemism among the Khonds." *Journal of the Asiatic Society of Bombay,* vol. 73, pt. 3, no. 3: 39–56.

Fuller, Christopher. 2004. *The Camphor Flame: Popular Hinduism and Society in India.* Revised and expanded edition. Princeton, NJ: Princeton University Press.

Gadgil, Madhav, and Ramachandra Guha. 1993. *This Fissured Land: An Ecological History of India.* Delhi: Oxford University Press.

Gardner, Peter M. 1982. "Ascribed Austerity: A Tribal Path to Purity." *Man,* n.s., 17 (3): 462–69.

Gell, Alfred. 1997. "Exalting the King and Obstructing the State: A Political Interpretation of Royal Ritual in Bastar District, Central India." *Journal of the Royal Anthropological Institute,* 433–50.

Gell, Simeran. 1992. *The Ghotul in Muria Society.* Chur, Switzerland: Harwood Academic Publishers.

Ghurye, Govind Sadashiv. 1943. *The Aborigines—"So-Called"—and Their Future.* Poona: Gokhale Institute of Politics and Economics.

Guha, Ramachandra. 1999. *Savaging the Civilized: Verrier Elwin, His Tribals, and India.* Delhi: Oxford University Press.

Hamayon, Roberte. 1990. *La chasse à l'âme: Esquisse d'une théorie du chamanisme sibérien.* Nanterre: Société d'Ethnologie.

Hardenberg, Roland Josef. 2005. "Children of the Earth Goddess: Society, Marriage and Sacrifice in the Highlands of Orissa." Unpublished habilitation (postdoctoral thesis), Westphalian Wilhelms University, Münster.

Harrison, K. David. 2007. *When Languages Die: The Extinction of the World's Languages and the Erosion of Human Knowledge*. Oxford: Oxford University Press.

Harvey, Graham, ed. 2013. *Handbook of Contemporary Animism*. Durham, UK: Acumen Publishing.

———. 2014. *Animism: Respecting the Living World*. New York: Columbia University Press.

Hefner, Robert W., ed. 1993. *Conversion to Christianity: Historical and Anthropological Perspectives on a Great Transformation*. Berkeley: University of California Press.

Herrenschmidt, Olivier. 1989. *Les meilleurs dieux sont hindous*. Paris: L'Âge d'Homme.

Heusch, Luc de. 1981. "Possession and Shamanism." In *Why Marry Her? Society and Symbolic Structures*, translated by Janet Lloyd, 151–64. Cambridge: Cambridge University Press.

Horton, Robin. 1971. "African Conversion." *Africa* 41: 85–108.

———. 1975a. "On the Rationality of Conversion (Part 1)." *Africa* 45: 219–35.

———. 1975b. "On the Rationality of Conversion (Part 2)." *Africa* 45: 373–99.

Howell, Signe. 1984. *Society and Cosmos: Chewong of Peninsular Malaysia*. Singapore: Oxford University Press.

Jenner, Philip N., Laurence C. Thompson, and Stanley Starosta, eds. 1976. *Austroasiatic Studies (Proceedings of the First International Congress of Austroasiatic Linguistics)*. 2 vols. Oceanic Linguistics, Special Publication 13. Honolulu: University Press of Hawaii.

Jha, Jagdish Chandra. 1996. *Aspects of Indentured Inland Emigration to North-East India, 1859–1918*. Delhi: South Asia Books.

Joshi, Vibha. 2013. *A Matter of Belief: Christian Conversion and Healing in North-East India*. Oxford: Berghahn Books.

Kapferer, Bruce. 1997. *The Feast of the Sorcerer: Practices of Consciousness and Power*. Chicago: University of Chicago Press.

Kar, Ramendra Kumar. 1981. *The Savaras of Mancotta: A Study on the Effects of Tea Industry on the Tribal Life*. Delhi: Cosmo Publications.

Karlsson, Bengt G., and Tanka B. Subba, eds. 2006. *Indigeneity in India*. With an afterword by Dipesh Chakrabarty. London: Routledge.

Keane, Webb. 2007. *Christian Moderns: Freedom and Fetish in the Mission Encounter*. Berkeley: University of California Press.

Knight, Kenneth, and Shirley Knight. 2009. *The Seed Holds the Tree: A Story of India and the Kingdom of God*. N.p.: Lulu.

Kulke, Hermann, and Burkhard Schnepel, eds. 2001. *Jagannath Revisited: Studying Society, Religion, and the State in Orissa*. Delhi: Manohar.

Laird, M. A. 1972. *Missionaries and Education in Bengal, 1793–1837*. Oxford: Oxford University Press.

Laugrand, Frédéric B., and Jarich G. Oosten. 2010. *Inuit Shamanism and Christianity: Transitions and Transformations in the Twentieth Century*. Montreal and Kingston: McGill-Queen's University Press.

Lienhardt, Godfrey. 1961. *Divinity and Experience: The Religion of the Dinka*. Oxford: Clarendon Press.

Lindbeck, George A. 1984. *The Nature of Doctrine: Religion and Theology in a Postliberal Age.* London: SPCK.

Lindquist, Galina. 2005. *Conjuring Hope: Healing and Magic in Contemporary Russia.* Oxford: Berghahn Books.

Lucian of Samosata. 2nd century AD. *Bion Prasis* [Greek title] or *Vitarum Auctio* [Latin title] [Sale of Lives / Belief Systems]. Greek original, various editions and translations.

Mageo, Jeannette, and Alan Howard, eds. 1996. *Spirits in Culture, History, and Mind.* New York: Routledge.

Malamoud, Charles, ed. 1995. *La dette.* Vol. 4. Collection Purushartha. Paris: EHESS.

Martin, David. 1993. *Tongues of Fire: The Explosion of Protestantism in Latin America.* New York: Wiley-Blackwell.

Masuzawa, Tomoko. 2005. *The Invention of World Religions: Or, How European Universalism Was Preserved in the Language of Pluralism.* Chicago: University of Chicago Press.

Merkur, Daniel. 1992. *Becoming Half Hidden: Shamanism and Initiation among the Inuit.* New York: Routledge.

Metcalf, Peter. 2002. *They Lie, We Lie: Getting On with Anthropology.* London and New York: Routledge.

Meyer, Birgit. 1999. *Translating the Devil: Religion and Modernity among the Ewe in Ghana.* London: University Press for the International African Institute.

Middleton, Townsend. 2015. *The Demands of Recognition: State Anthropology and Ethnopolitics in Darjeeling.* Stanford, CA: Stanford University Press.

Mojumdar, Kanchanmoy. 1998. *Changing Tribal Life in British Orissa.* Delhi: Kaveri Books.

Moseley, Christopher. 2012. "The UNESCO Atlas of the World's Languages in Danger: Context and Process." World Oral Literature Project, Occasional Paper 5.

Nettle, Daniel, and Suzanne Romaine. 2000. *Vanishing Voices: The Extinction of the World's Languages.* Oxford: Oxford University Press.

Obeyesekere, Gananath. 1981. *Medusa's Hair: An Essay on Personal Symbols and Religious Experience.* Chicago: University of Chicago Press.

———. 1995. Review of Vitebsky 1993. *Journal of the Royal Anthropological Institute* 1 (2): 458–59.

Orchard, M. L., and K. S. McLaurin. [1924.] *The Enterprise: The Jubilee Story of the Canadian Baptist Mission in India, 1874–1924.* Toronto: Canadian Baptist Foreign Mission Board.

Padel, Felix. 1995. *The Sacrifice of Human Being: British Rule and the Konds of Orissa.* Oxford: Oxford University Press.

Padel, Felix, and Samarendra Das. 2010. *Out of This Earth: East India Adivasis and the Aluminium Cartel.* Delhi: Orient Blackswan.

Pati, Rabindra Nath, and Jagannath Dash. 2002. *Tribal and Indigenous People of India: Problems and Prospects.* Delhi: APH Publishing Corporation.

Petit, Christian. 1974. "La culture matérielle des Saora." PhD diss., Université de Paris.

Pfeffer, Georg. 2001. "A Ritual of Revival among the Gadaba of Koraput." In *Jagannath Revisited: Studying Society, Religion, and the State in Orissa*, edited by Hermann Kulke and Burkhard Schnepel, 99–123. Delhi: Manohar.

Piliavsky, Anastasia, ed. 2014. *Patronage as Politics in South Asia*. Delhi: Cambridge University Press.

———. 2015. "Patronage and Community in a Society of Thieves." *Contributions to Indian Sociology* 49 (2): 135–61.

Pinnow, Heinz-Jürgen. 1959. *Versuch einer historischen Lautlehre der Kharia-Sprache*. Wiesbaden: Otto Harrassowitz.

Prasad, Archana. 2003. *Against Ecological Romanticism: Verrier Elwin and the Making of an Anti-Modern Tribal Identity*. Delhi: Three Essays Collective.

Rafael, Vicente L. 1993. *Contracting Colonialism: Translation and Christian Conversion in Tagalog Society under Early Spanish Rule*. Durham, NC: Duke University Press.

Ramamurti, G. V. 1931. *Manual of the So:ra: or Savara Language*. Madras: Government Press.

———. 1933. *English-So:ra: Dictionary*. Madras: Government Press.

———. 1938. *So:ra:-English Dictionary*. Madras: Government Press.

Rappaport, Roy A. 1999. *Ritual and Religion in the Making of Humanity*. Cambridge: Cambridge University Press.

Robbins, Joel. 2004. *Becoming Sinners: Christianity and Moral Torment in a Papua New Guinea Society*. Berkeley: University of California Press.

———. 2007. "Continuity Thinking and the Problem of Christian Culture: Belief, Time, and the Anthropology of Christianity." *Current Anthropology* 48 (1): 5–38.

Robbins, Joel, Bambi Schieffelin, and Aparecida Vilaça. 2014. "Evangelical Conversion and the Transformation of the Self in Amazonia and Melanesia: Christianity and the Revival of Anthropological Comparison." *Comparative Studies in Society and History* 56 (3): 559–90.

Robinson, Rowena, and Sathianathan Clarke. 2007. *Religious Conversion in India: Modes, Motivations, and Meanings*. Oxford: Oxford University Press.

Rousseleau, Raphaël. 2004. "Vers une ethnohistoire des relations 'tribus'-royaumes en Inde centrale: Les institutions politico-rituelles des Joria Poraja (Orissa)." PhD diss., Paris: EHESS.

Rycroft, Daniel J., and Sangeeta Dasgupta, eds. 2011. *The Politics of Belonging in India: Becoming Adivasi*. Abingdon and New York: Routledge.

Sahlins, Marshall. 2013. *What Kinship Is and Is Not*. Chicago: University of Chicago Press.

———. 2014. "On the Ontological Scheme of *Beyond Nature and Culture*." *Hau: Journal of Ethnographic Theory* 4 (1): 281–90.

Sarkar, Sumit. 2002. *Beyond Nationalist Frames: Postmodernism, Hindu Fundamentalism, History*. Delhi: Permanent Black.

Schieffelin, Bambi. 2002. "Marking Time: The Dichotomizing Discourse of Multiple Temporalities." *Current Anthropology* 43 (Supplement): S5–S17.

Schmidt, Wilhelm. 1955. *Der Ursprung der Gottesidee*. 12 vols. Münster: Aschendorff.

Schnepel, Burkhard. 2002. *The Jungle Kings: Ethnohistorical Aspects of Politics and Ritual in Orissa*. Delhi: Manohar.

Scott, James C. 2009. *The Art of Not Being Governed: An Anarchist History of Upland Southeast Asia*. New Haven, CT: Yale University Press.

Seligman, Adam B., Robert B. Weller, Michael J. Puett, and Bennett Simon. 2008. *Ritual and Its Consequences: An Essay on the Limits of Sincerity.* New York: Oxford University Press.

Shah, Alpa. 2010. *In the Shadows of the State: Indigenous Politics, Environmentalism, and Insurgency in Jharkhand, India.* Durham, NC: Duke University Press.

Shah, Alpa, and Sara Shneiderman, eds. 2013. "Toward an Anthropology of Affirmative Action." Special section of *Focaal: Journal of Global and Historical Anthropology*, 3–93.

Shryock, Andrew. 2013. "It's This, Not That: How Marshall Sahlins Solves Kinship [Comment on Sahlins 2013]." *Hau: Journal of Ethnographic Theory* 3 (2): 271–79.

Singh, Bhupinder. 1984. *The Saora Highlander: Leadership and Development.* Bombay: Somaiya Publications.

Singh, Kumar Suresh. 1985. *Tribal Society in India: An Anthropo-Historical Perspective.* New Delhi: Manohar.

Sinha, Surajit. 1962. "State Formation and Rajput Myth in Tribal Central India." *Man in India* 42: 35–80.

Sitapati, G. V. 1938. "The Soras and Their Country." *Journal of the Andhra Historical Research Society* 12: 57–76, 157–68, 189–207.

———. 1940. "The Soras and Their Country." *Journal of the Andhra Historical Research Society* 13: 113–36.

———. 1943. "The Soras and Their Country." *Journal of the Andhra Historical Research Society* 14: 1–16.

Slater, T. E. 1882. *The Philosophy of Missions: A Present-Day Plea.* London: James Clarke and Co.

Stampe, David L., ed. 1965. "Recent Work in Munda Linguistics I." *International Journal of American Linguistics* 31 (4): 332–41.

———, ed. 1966. "Recent Work in Munda Linguistics II." *International Journal of American Linguistics* 32 (1): 74–80.

Starosta, Stanley. 1967. "Sora Syntax: A Generative Approach to a Munda Language." PhD diss., University of Wisconsin.

Sternberg, Leo (Lev Shternberg). 1925. "Divine Election in Primitive Religion." In *Congrès International des Américanistes, Compte-Rendu de la XXI Session,* Pt. 2 [1924]. 472–512. Göteborg: Göteborg Museum.

Sundar, Nandini. 2007. *Subalterns and Sovereigns: An Anthropological History of Bastar, 1854–2006.* Delhi: Oxford University Press.

———. 2016. *The Burning Forest: India's War in Bastar.* Delhi: Juggernaut.

Thurston, E. 1909. "Savaras." In *Castes and Tribes of Southern India,* 6: 304–47. Madras: Government Press.

Turner, Victor W. 1967. "Aspects of Saora Ritual and Shamanism: An Approach to the Data of Ritual." In *The Craft of Social Anthropology,* edited by A. L. Epstein, 181–204. London: Tavistock Publications.

———. 1969. *The Ritual Process: Structure and Anti-Structure.* Chicago: Aldine Publishing.

Tuzin, Donald. 1997. *The Cassowary's Revenge: The Life and Death of Masculinity in a New Guinea Society.* Chicago: University of Chicago Press.

UNESCO. 2010. *Atlas of the World's Languages in Danger*. Edited by Christopher Moseley. 3rd ed. Paris: UNESCO Publications Office.

United Nations. 1992. "Convention on Biological Diversity." United Nations, Treaty Series. Rio de Janeiro: United Nations.

Valeri, Valerio. 1985. *Kingship and Sacrifice: Ritual and Society in Ancient Hawai'i*. Chicago: University of Chicago Press.

van der Veer, Peter, ed. 1996. *Conversion to Modernities: The Globalization of Christianity*. London: Routledge.

Vilaça, Aparecida. 2016. *Praying and Preying: Christianity in Indigenous Amazonia*. Oakland, CA: University of California Press.

Vitebsky, Piers. 1978a. "Political Relations among the Sora of India, Paper I: Internal Relations." Unpublished typescript.

———. 1978b. "Political Relations among the Sora, Paper II: External Relations." Unpublished typescript.

———. 1978c. "Sora 'Tag-Words': A Preliminary Sketch of Their Use as Metaphor in the Grammatically Parallel Verse Forms of Ritual." Paper presented at the Second Congress of Austroasiatic Linguistics, Mysore.

———. 1984. *Policy Dilemmas for Unirrigated Agriculture in Southeastern Sri Lanka: A Social Anthropologist's Report on Shifting and Semi-Permanent Cultivation in an Area of Moneragala District*. Cambridge: University of Cambridge Centre of South Asian Studies.

———. 1992. "Shifting Cultivation Comes to Rest: Changing Values of Land and the Person in an Area of Moneragala District." In *Agrarian Change in Sri Lanka*, edited by James Brow and Joseph Weeramunda, 155–87. Delhi: Sage.

———. 1993. *Dialogues with the Dead: The Discussion of Mortality among the Sora of Eastern India*. Cambridge: Cambridge University Press and Delhi: Foundation Books.

———. 1995. *The Shaman: Trance, Ecstasy, and Healing; Voyages of the Soul from the Amazon to the Arctic*. London: Duncan Baird. Reprinted as *Shamanism* (Norman: University of Oklahoma Press, 2001).

———. 2005. *The Reindeer People: Living with Animals and Spirits in Siberia*. Boston: Houghton Mifflin; London: HarperCollins.

———. 2008. "Loving and Forgetting: Moments of Inarticulacy in Tribal India." Henry Myers Lecture for 2006. *Journal of the Royal Anthropological Institute* 14: 243–61.

———. 2012. "Repeated Returns and Special Friends: From Mythic Encounter to Shared History." In *Returns to the Field: Multitemporal Research and Contemporary Anthropology*, edited by Signe Howell and Aud Talle, 180–202. Bloomington: Indiana University Press.

———. 2015. "Structures and Processes of Liminality: The Shape of Mourning among the Sora of Tribal India." In *Ultimate Ambiguities: Investigating Death and Liminality*, edited by Peter Berger and Justin Kroesen, 36–55. Oxford and New York: Berghahn Books.

Vitebsky, Piers, and Monosi Raika. 2011. *Jujunji do Yuyunji a Banuddin: Sora Jattin a Sanskruti, Sora Beran batte, Aboi Tanub* (The Wisdom of Our Grandfathers and Grandmothers: The Culture of the Sora People, in Sora, Part I). Visakhapatnam: Privately printed.

Viveiros de Castro, Eduardo. 1992. *From the Enemy's Point of View: Humanity and Divinity in an Amazonian Society*. Chicago: University of Chicago Press.

Volkan, Vamik D. 1981. *Linking Objects and Linking Phenomena: A Study of the Forms, Symptoms, Metapsychology, and Therapy of Complicated Mourning*. New York: International Universities Press.

Whitehead, Henry. 1921. *The Village Gods of South India*. Calcutta: Association Press (YMCA).

Willerslev, Rane. 2007. *Soul Hunters: Hunting, Animism, and Personhood among the Siberian Yukaghirs*. Berkeley: University of California Press.

Winnicott, D. W. 1980. "Transitional Objects and Transitional Phenomena." In *Playing and Reality*, 1–30. Harmondsworth: Penguin Books.

Zide, Arlene R. K., and Norman H. Zide. 1973. "Semantic Reconstructions in Proto-Munda Cultural Vocabulary, Part 1." *Indian Linguistics* 34: 1–24.

———. 1976. "Semantic Reconstructions in Proto-Munda Cultural Vocabulary, Part 2." In *Austroasiatic Studies (Proceedings of the First International Congress of Austroasiatic Linguistics)*, edited by P. N. Jenner, L. C. Thomson, and S. Starosta, 1295–1334. Oceanic Linguistics, Special Publication 13. Honolulu: University of Hawaii Press.

Zide, Norman H., ed. 1966. *Studies in Comparative Austroasiatic Linguistics*. The Hague: Mouton.

———. 1999. "Three Munda Scripts." *Linguistics of the Tibeto-Burman Area* 22 (2): 199–232.

INDEX

Page numbers in italics refer to maps, diagrams, and figures. Page numbers preceded by the letter B refer to the online bibliographic essay, available at http://www.press.uchicago.edu/sites/Vitebsky.